SEAPOWER STATES

SEAPOWER STATES

MARITIME CULTURE, CONTINENTAL EMPIRES AND THE CONFLICT THAT MADE THE MODERN WORLD

ANDREW LAMBERT

YALE UNIVERSITY PRESS
NEW HAVEN AND LONDON

For information about this and other Yale University Press publications, please contact:
U.S. Office: sales.press@yale.edu   yalebooks.com
Europe Office: sales@yaleup.co.uk   yalebooks.co.uk

Set in Minion Pro by IDSUK (DataConnection) Ltd
Printed in Great Britain by Gomer Press Ltd, Llandysul, Ceredigion, Wales

Library of Congress Control Number: 2018953243

A catalogue record for this book is available from the British Library.

10 9 8 7 6 5 4 3 2 1

The State is a work of Art.

Jakob Burckhardt

For my Mother

CONTENTS

ILLUSTRATIONS AND MAPS

Plates

1   Late Minoan wall painting depicting a fleet coming into harbour, Santorini, 1550. akg-images / jh-Lightbox_Ltd. / John Hios.
2   Marble bust of Pericles bearing the inscription 'Pericles, son of Xanthippus, Athenian', Roman copy after a Greek original, *c.* 430 BC.
3   The replica trireme *Olympias* under sail, Poros, August 1988. Photograph by Paul Lipke. Courtesy of the Trireme Trust Archive at Wolfson College, Cambridge.
4   Reconstruction drawing of Carthage, Carthage National Museum. Damian Entwistle.
5   *The Battle of Lepanto, 7 October 1571*. National Maritime Museum, Greenwich, London. Caird Fund.
6   *Andrea Doria* by William Henry Furse, 1466–1560. National Maritime Museum, Greenwich, London, Greenwich Hospital Collection.
7   *Amsterdam, Dam Square with the Town Hall and the Nieuwe Kerk* by Jan van der Heyden, 1667.

Pictures in the text

Maps

ACKNOWLEDGEMENTS

As any manuscript heads for publication authors return to the beginning, to reflect on the debt they owe to others, fellow scholars, students, family and friends, delightfully loose categories reflecting the reality that the first and last are often one and the same. Furthermore, as a historian I am acutely conscious of my debt to those who have gone before, a debt we honour by reflecting on works written long go, for very different audiences. The ideas and arguments of these authors run through this book, they are the building blocks for what follows. I cannot thank them in person, and only hope they would not be too offended by what I have made of their work.

Many friends and colleagues in the academic world have shared in the debate, offered fresh material and sage advice. I cannot thank them enough, and any attempt to be comprehensive would be foolhardy. First on the list is my old friend John Ferris, who has entertained more iterations of this thesis than anyone else. He provided sound advice, clear judgement and honest criticism, as did Beatrice Heuser, another friend of many years, and Richard Harding; all three have shared their expertise in fields that range far wider than the historical, and recognised the rhyme in the text. My colleague Alan

James, with whom it has been a pleasure to share the naval history curriculum at King's College London, read the manuscript and discussed the many things that separate France and England with his delightfully wry detachment. His support, and that of the War Studies Department, is greatly appreciated. Maria Fusaro, Larrie Ferreiro and Gijs Rommelse read draft chapters that crashed into their fields of expertise, corrected my errors and provided excellent advice. Michael Tapper and Catherine Scheybeler read the whole thing, and despite instructions to the contrary Catherine proofread the penultimate draft, picking up more keying infelicities and errors than even the author had expected. Many more friends and colleagues have helped turn the initial premise into a coherent argument, directly or otherwise, and I can only hope they will not be too disappointed by the result.

Thanks are also due to Paul Kennedy, who encouraged me to pursue my interests forty years ago, the late Bryan Ranft, who taught me far more than I realised at the time, Sir Lawrence Freedman, for allowing me to work in the best department in which to write such a book, and his successors who have retained the unique multidisciplinary ethos. Many of my colleagues in War Studies have supported the project, with words, ideas, time and the unique camaraderie of the place, none more so than Alessio Patalano, a student of seapower identity in East Asia and elsewhere, and Marcus Faulkner and Carlos Alfaro Zaforteza, who spoke up for alternative continental models of naval power.

This book is built on the scholarship of others, books, articles and other outputs: the one quotation from an archival source was borrowed from another project, because it expressed the argument so perfectly. Today such research is greatly aided by access to online resources, books, journals and data that still seem magical to someone who began work in the era of the card index, pencil and typewriter. Modern scholarship has fewer barriers, but this cornucopia challenges us in different ways. Setting boundaries has become the big issue, and in a book that is intended to generate debate I chose brevity and concision. I am only too well aware of the obvious limitations imposed by that choice, but without it the project would have outlasted the author, the timelines of the REF (Research Excellence Framework, next due in 2021), and the patience of readers.

Once again Julian Loose has overseen the process of the book, from commissioning to completion, with the able assistance of the team at Yale's

London office, and Richard Mason, who has removed the inevitable authorial obscurities with great skill. Despite the best efforts of friends and colleagues imperfections will remain, and for those I alone am responsible.

My family has been with me throughout the project. Their support has been unwavering, and essential. Words cannot express how much that means, and why it mattered so much.

Andrew Lambert

Kew, 5 April 2018

In 1851 an English intellectual grappled with the great question that has preoccupied mankind since the dawn of civilisation, the future of the political unit in which they live:

> Since first the dominion of men was asserted over the ocean, three thrones, of mark beyond all others, have been set upon its sands: the thrones of Tyre, Venice, and England. Of the First of these great powers only the memory remains; of the Second the ruin; the Third which inherits their greatness, if it forget their example, may be led through prouder eminence to less pitied destruction.[1]

John Ruskin understood that Britain was unusual, a great sea empire, not a continental power, and that it was also the only such state in the contemporary world. As the self-appointed champion of J. M. W. Turner, the artist who elevated the imagery of the sea from the prosaic to the sublime in his pursuit of a British seapower identity, Ruskin had followed his hero to Venice. There, beside the Grand Canal, he discovered the tools he needed to

HMS *Hood*, the 1919–41 iconic vessel of the last seapower

grapple with past, present and future. At one level *The Stones of Venice* was a history of Venetian architecture, a record of fading splendour, captured with photographic precision.[2] Yet it was so much more. Ultimately the question remained, as Turner had shown, one of culture.[3] Ruskin read Venetian maritime culture through the very fabric of the old city. In a book driven by a growing concern for the future of Britain, he made architecture the ultimate expression of Venetian seapower, a record of 'the warning which seems to me to be uttered by every one of the fast-gaining waves, that beat like passing bells, against the Stones of Venice ... derived from the faithful study of history'.[4] The tragic beauty of the image, the elegance of Ruskin's phrasing and the deceptive simplicity of the message confronted a nation, glorying in the year of the Great Exhibition, with the reality of decline.

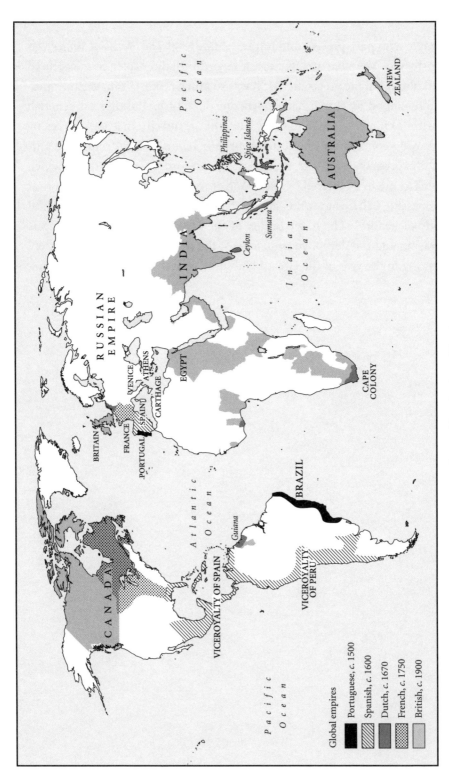

The World in the Age of Empire

Global empires

Portuguese, *c.* 1500
Spanish, *c.* 1600
Dutch, *c.* 1670
French, *c.* 1750
British, *c.* 1900

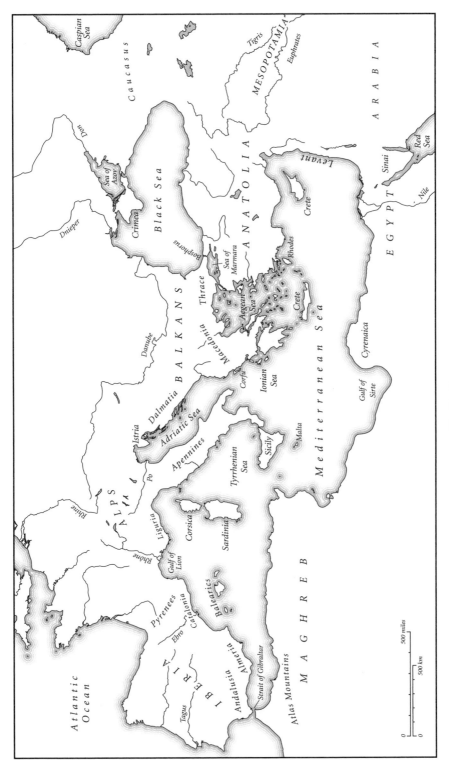

The Mediterranean

Seapower as Culture

John Ruskin traced the doom of Venice, as a seapower, to the replacement of the native Gothic architecture, a suitably maritime compound of Roman, Byzantine, Arabic and Italian influences, with an imported mainland Palladian Baroque. The choice reflected deeper, cultural, currents that led the city-state to focus on other roles, after the loss of the sea empire. He identified themes that recur in all the great seapowers: inclusive politics, the central place of commerce in civic life, and opposition to universal monarchies, hegemonic powers intent on conquest and dominion. These hegemonic threats came from Ottoman Turkey, Habsburg Spain and the Roman Church, threats that still resonated with British audiences. Above all seapowers fought for trade. The British had recently levered open the Chinese Empire with amphibious power, much as the Venetians used the Fourth Crusade to create their seapower empire. Whatever their private religious views Venetian leaders carefully 'calculated' the economic advantage the state could secure by breaking their faith, because 'the heart of Venice was in her wars, not in her worship'.[1] In a text aimed at his own age Ruskin observed that Venetian decline, which began with the demise of the aristocracy, was hastened by the loss of private faith.

Hannibal Barca: Carthaginian statesman of seapower

Two years earlier the concept of a seapower state had, somewhat belatedly, entered the English lexicon. It did so in the fifth volume of George Grote's monumental *History of Greece*, a text that appeared just as Britain began a naval arms race with the French Second Republic. Grote did not think it necessary to link British and Athenian seapower: none of his contemporaries would have missed the message. His book contained the earliest uses of seapower and thalassocracy cited by the *Oxford English Dictionary*, terms that Grote took directly from ancient authors. He used them to connect contemporary British concerns with an exemplary Athenian state, echoing Herodotus' observation that the Athenians consciously made themselves 'a maritime power'.[2]

A decade later the Swiss historian Jacob Burckhardt developed Ruskin's method, building a magisterial analysis of states, culture and power in the Renaissance around the thesis 'The state as a work of art'.[3] Burckhardt used the concept of a constructed identity to analyse the states of early modern Italy. Both men recognised the critical role of choice in the evolution of the state, while identities were fluid, not fixed. Ruskin, immersed in the seapower-suffused culture of Victorian Britain, chose to focus on Venice, while Burckhardt, a native of Basel, looked to Florence.

In 1890 the American naval officer Captain Alfred Thayer Mahan produced a more prosaic attempt to categorise the constituents of seapower in his epochal text *The Influence of Sea Power upon History 1660–1783*, published in 1890.[4] Unlike Ruskin, and Burckhardt, Mahan did not engage with the soul of seapower, only the strategic surface. He split the Greek word into a phrase – 'sea power' – because he could not turn to Venice, or Britain, in his search for a sea power precursor for his native country. They were too small, too weak and above all too maritime to inform the identity of an emerging continental superpower. Instead Mahan looked to the naval might of Republican Rome, a continental military empire, bent on hemispheric dominion. The classical model he advanced was not the rise of Carthaginian seapower, but its annihilation by Roman military might. Similarly his modern example was not the rise of Britain but the failure of Continental France to achieve the naval hegemony it needed to crush its feeble seapower opponents and become a new Roman Empire, under Bourbon, Republican or Imperial rule. Mahan wanted his countrymen to understand the root causes of French failure lay in poor strategic choices, not a continental identity, because he realised that they would succeed to the Roman mantle, not the British.

While Mahan may be a better guide for students of strategy, Ruskin's approach to seapower was at once more sophisticated, and more significant. His eloquent lines open a massive work examining the interwoven histories of Venetian architecture and oceanic empire. Ruskin did not address the issue of seapower as a choice; he treated it as a quality organic to the era of Venetian greatness. The choice had been made long before. He assumed that it had been so for Tyre and he knew it had been the case for Victorian Britain.[5] Ruskin bound Britain into a seapower chain that connected London through Venice to the richest city of the Old Testament.[6] The purpose of this thalassocratic succession was obvious: Victorian Britain was obsessed by the prospect of decline, the creeping concern of a great power fearful it had reached the zenith of glory. It was also a society shaped by classical learning: educated men like Ruskin knew Thucydides' Peloponnesian War, a text he considered to be 'the central tragedy of all the world', and George Grote's great history.[7] Amidst the exuberant pomp of rapid technological progress and global dominion Ruskin was searching for the soul of the state. He feared for his country, fears that would drive his pen for the rest of his life, returning again and again to Venice, culture and destiny.

The Stones of Venice inspired the erection of countless Venetian Gothic buildings across the British Empire, building the concept of precursor seapowers into the intellectual core of Britishness. There it lay, until awakened by the direct argument and ponderous prose of the American Captain, who suddenly found himself famous for telling the British something they had known for at least three hundred years.[8]

Both Ruskin and Mahan had been right to trace seapower back to ancient history. The intellectual achievements of classical Greece remain the foundation for any enquiry into the meaning of seapower as strategy, culture, identity or empire. Athenian debates have informed the subject ever since – not because the Athenians invented ships, seafaring, navies or oceanic empires – but because they analysed and recorded the ideas that these phenomena prompted, along with the history in which they were shaped, debated their meaning in a relatively open society, and created the first seapower great power. They understood that seapower culture lay at the heart of Athenian politics, economic development, art and identity.

Above all they realised that becoming a seapower was altogether more complex than acquiring a navy.

At this point it will be useful to establish the difference between seapower as a constructed national identity and sea power as the strategy of naval power. Mahan split seapower, derived from the Greek *thalassokratia*, into a phrase to increase the impact of his thesis.[9] In the process he changed its meaning. Hitherto a seapower had been a state that chose to emphasise the sea, to secure the economic and strategic advantages of sea control to act as a great power, through a consciously constructed seapower culture and identity. Seapowers were maritime imperial great powers, dependent on the control of ocean communications for cohesion, commerce and control. Mahan's new phrase was restricted to the strategic use of the sea by any state with enough men, money and harbours to build a navy, a list that included more continental hegemons than cultural seapowers. This was necessary because Mahan's object was to persuade contemporary Americans to acquire an expensive battlefleet navy, and the United States had not been a sea state since the 1820s. In 1890 there was only one seapower great power, but Mahan concentrated on the failure of France, a continental military power, to defeat Britain, through poor strategic and political choices, rather than Britain's rise from a small offshore kingdom of limited economic and human resource to a seapower world empire. He was advising his countrymen to avoid the mistakes made by France, not to emulate Britain. Mahan's America was too big, and too continental, to become a seapower. He urged the need for a sea control battlefleet, to secure the United States' place in the world, rather than the US's normative naval strategy of commerce raiding and coast defence, a strategy that had consistently failed to deter or defeat Britain. This shaped the structure of his book, and explained why Mahan ended it in 1782, when the French battlefleet had secured American Independence. When the Comte de Grasse's ships isolated the British army at Yorktown and forced it to surrender in 1781, the British government accepted the inevitable. Mahan wanted his fellow Americans to grasp the existential impact of a well-handled battlefleet. He measured the impact of sea power on land, not at sea. Once America had adopted the battlefleet model of naval power, Mahan shifted focus. In subsequent books he emphasised how potent naval might have been in the rise of Britain, and reminded his fellow countrymen that Horatio Nelson was the exemplary naval leader.

Mahan recognised that Britain became dominant at sea by defeating Bourbon France, after the 'Glorious Revolution' of 1688 had introduced the political and fiscal tools necessary to create a seapower state: inclusive government, centralised finance and politically negotiated revenue-raising methods, sustained investment in naval assets and infrastructure, according strategic primacy to the navy, and privileging oceanic commerce. These were conscious choices, deliberately echoing the construction of other seapower great powers. Britain, like Athens, Carthage, Venice and the Dutch Republic, became a seapower by actively constructing a cultural identity focused on the sea. This process was driven by political choice, as the men in power used state funds to build sea control navies and the bases they required, ensuring ships and structures conveyed the core message of seapower, through naval and terrestrial architecture, carefully chosen names and religious affiliations. They built maritime temples, which served as prominent seamarks and navigation beacons, and embellished their public spaces with the art of seapower – creating distinctive cultural forms to express their divergent agenda. This consciously crafted identity spread beyond political elites and interested parties: it flowed into popular culture, pottery, coins, graffiti, books, printed images and by the 1930s cinema. That many of these outputs were sponsored, endorsed or otherwise sustained by the state emphasises the national significance of the project. This culture attracted support from those whose livelihoods were wrapped up in the ocean, or favoured progressive politics, before flowing out into the wider community. Furthermore it was actively disseminated. Coins had carried seapower messages across the trading world from ancient Tyre to imperial Britain, using images of ships, deities and power to express ownership of the oceans. Because seapower states were essentially oligarchic, these choices reflected a debate, and the opinions of the majority. All seapower states contained a vocal opposition, one that pressed the obvious priorities of land, army and agriculture. This opposition, often aristocratic and socially elitist, was a critical part of the political discourse that kept the seapower state in being. One such aristocrat, Thucydides, was a significant critic of the political consequences of seapower, even as he explained its strategic impact. The choice to be a seapower only lasted as long as the political nation was prepared to sustain it. The grisly fate of Johan de Witt in 1672 highlighted how quickly such constructed identities could be overthrown. Having shaped and directed a distinctive seapower republic for two decades, de Witt was literally torn to pieces on the streets of The Hague by those who wanted a return to an older tradition of princely rule. Examining how such identities were created in five states, for no two were identical, even if they shared many core elements, and why the attempt failed in a sixth, demonstrates that the process had to be politically driven, economically attractive and strategically effective.

That seapower states employed sea power strategy has tended to conflate the meaning of the word and the phrase, but this problem is easily addressed. In the contemporary world Russia, China and the United States all possess sea power, a strategic option that can be exercised by any state with a coast, money and manpower, but these continental military super-powers are not seapowers. The sea is at best a marginal factor in their identities.

This book examines the nature and consequences of seapower culture and identity through a collective analysis of the five seapower great powers, Athens, Carthage, Venice, the Dutch Republic and Britain. This group can be distinguished from terrestrial peers such as Russia, sea states such as ancient Rhodes and early modern Genoa, and maritime empires such as those of Spain and Portugal. All five created seapower identities, exploiting the ideas and experiences of precursors, intellectual debts that were openly acknowledged. As a group they did more to advance trade, knowledge and political inclusion than their landed peers: they shaped the global economy and the liberal values that define the contemporary Western world.[10]

Most catalogues of seapower states are longer than the one used in this book, attributing undue significance to the possession of powerful navies or overseas empires.[11] While continental great powers from Persia to the People's Republic of China created both, their acquisition did not change the underlying culture of the state which has been, in almost all cases, terrestrial and military, excluding merchants and financiers from political power. In general terms these states were too large and powerful to profit from a sea identity. Seapower identity was a confession of relative weakness, seeking an asymmetric advantage through a different approach to the world. Adding navies and colonies to an existing great power, as was the case with Imperial Germany between 1890 and 1914, did not change the underlying strategic and cultural realities that compelled it to sustain a massive army and policies dominated by the European continent. This continental logic drove the agendas of ancient Mesopotamian kingdoms, the Roman Republic, Ottoman Turkey, Imperial Spain, Bourbon and Napoleonic France, and the twentieth-century continental hegemons Germany and the Soviet Union. It ensured Peter the Great's naval revolution would fail, and that contemporary superpowers are terrestrial empires.

Today Mahanian sea power belongs to the West, a consortium of liberal, democratic commercial states that trade globally, and act collectively to secure oceanic trade against pirates, conflict and instability. While the United States provides strategic sea power, seapower identity is shared among a group of second- and third-rank powers, from Britain and Denmark to Japan and Singapore. These states are disproportionately engaged with global trade, unusually dependent on imported resources, and culturally attuned to maritime activity. The sea is central to their national culture, economic life and security. Seapower identity remains a question of national engagement with the sea, a definition reserved for states that are inherently, and even existentially, vulnerable to the loss of control over sea communications. As the concept includes mythology, emotion and values it is not capable of accurate calculation.[12] The cultural legacy of seapower has long been wrapped up in the collective identity of Western liberal trading nations, including the United States of America. It is contested by regimes and ideologies that fear change, inclusive politics and free markets. It remains a key analytical resource for students of the past, present and future.

The central argument of this book is that Mahan's phrase 'sea power', which describes the strategic options open to states possessing navies, shifts the meaning of the original Greek word from identity to strategy, weakening our ability to understand seapower as culture. For the ancient Greeks a seapower was a state dominated by the sea, not one with a large navy. Herodotus and Thucydides used *thalassokratia* to describe cultural seapowers. Persia, which had a far greater navy than all the Greek states combined, remained a land power. Sparta used naval force to defeat Athens in the Peloponnesian War, but it never became a seapower. Athens was one, however, and the deeper cultural implications of that identity explain both the causes of the conflict with Sparta and why Sparta and Persia became allies and used their victory to force Athens to become a normal continental state. The disruptive, destabilising nature of seapower culture, combining levelling populist politics with maritime commerce, imperial expansion and endless curiosity, horrified many commentators. Plato's aversion was obvious, as was that of Confucius, and if Thucydides' anxieties were more subtly expressed, they were equally clear. These responses emphasised a clash of cultures that stretched across politics, economics, society and war, one that divided seapower states from continental powers.

Seapower states are not powerful; they focus on the sea because they are weak, choosing an asymmetric emphasis to survive and prosper. Furthermore seapower identity is wholly artificial. As the cultural boundaries of any political organisation are set by families, tribes, faith, land and possession, a maritime identity is at once unusual and unnatural. It is not a consequence of geography, or circumstance. The creation of seapower identities has been deliberate, and is normally a conscious response to weakness and vulnerability. While seapower identity may enable states to become great powers, it is not a choice that existing great powers make, even if the sea is important to their national life. France acquired many navies and several overseas empires, but they never achieved the status or priority of European expansion and continental armies.

Although some small polities have become sea states almost by default, impelled by location, population and economic life, there was always an element of conscious choice in such identities. However, the strategic and political consequence of such states remained limited. Ancient sea states, small, weak trading polities, used coastal locations and seafaring skills to avoid or ameliorate absorption into continental hegemonic empires. While the Minoans, with the advantage of an insular base, were able to achieve a mythic *thalassokratia*, Phoenician sea states relied on political skill and timely concession. Sea states were most effective when operating in the watery spaces between large continental powers: they became irrelevant in eras of universal monarchy or negligible inter-state trade.

The synergy between inclusive politics and seapower is critical. Progressive political ideologies, spread by sea as part of the trading network, have always been a primary weapon in the arsenal of seapower. Such ideas appealed to commercial actors who moved by sea and recognised the need to challenge rigid autocratic systems. Athens spread democracy to build an empire, to the consternation of Sparta and Persia. Having chosen a seapower identity the Athenians were quick to invent quasi-mythic Minoan seapower precursors, to avoid the stigma of being novel. The ideas that shaped these states were essentially consistent. Both Athens and Carthage drew heavily on Phoenician precursors, while those that followed reflected on the Athenian debates and the terrible fate that befell Carthage.

Athens became a seapower because it faced destruction at the hands of a Persian universal monarchy. This, and this alone, propelled Themistocles' transformation of Athens in the 480s, which reconfigured the state as a seapower, unified by politics and culture, capable of creating a purpose-built navy and ultimately acquiring a sea empire to sustain the fiscal burden. This decision was only possible because Athens had already undergone a democratic revolution, releasing the city's hitherto latent power through collaborative decision-making, and the rewards of external action. The consequences were electrifying: the population expanded rapidly, which made Athens ever more dependent on the distant wheat fields of the Black Sea, and therefore increasingly vulnerable to naval blockade. Having literally voted to be different the Athenian choice led inexorably to an ever more distinctive identity within the Greek world, one that prompted profound questions about the process and the direction of change.

When an Athenian amphibious force annihilated a large Persian fleet at the Eurymedon river in 466 bc the demonstration of skill, aggression and above all the ambition to spread their democracy alarmed the Spartans, while attempts to liberate Egypt persuaded the Great King to support Sparta, the status quo power in Greece. Ultimately Spartan armies, Persian gold and Athenian arrogance destroyed the seapower state. In victory the two continental powers dismantled Athenian democracy, destroyed the fleet, and demolished the walls that made the city an artificial island and enhanced seapower identity. The divergent threat posed by seapower ensured Rome annihilated the Carthaginian seapower state, because it was a fundamentally different, profoundly threatening cultural alternative. Although Carthage had not been a military power for half a century, the Romans had read Plato: they knew the real threat was cultural.

Given the disproportionate strategic weight of land and sea states in these contests – sea states lacked population, territory and mass armies – the fear they have inspired among larger and more powerful continental rivals requires explanation. The answer lies in the cultural dimension. Seapowers depended on inclusive political systems, primarily oligarchic republics, progressive systems that challenged the monarchical autocracies and socially elite oligarchies of their continental contemporaries. This inclusive model was essential; only by mobilising the full range of human and fiscal resources, through political inclusion, could small weak states hope to compete with larger and militarily more powerful rivals. This political reality alarmed imperial states that measured their strength in military might, occupied land and servile populations. For such states inclusive politics, be they oligarchic republics or democracies, were terrifying harbingers of chaos and change. The ideal solution for continental powers was a universal monarchy: one ruler, one state, one culture and one, centralised, command economy.

Seapower states resisted such imperial hegemons, because the alternative was abject submission to military power, the destruction of their economic interests and their identity: harbours and minds closed to the exchange of goods and ideas. The high cost of sustained naval power, the primary strategic instrument of the seapower state, ensured public policy was shaped to serve the interests of capital and commerce, which funded the fleet, and depended on its protection. These concerns obliged seapower statesmen to build coalitions to oppose hegemonic states and universal empires, and their command economies. Once their security had been assured seapower states shifted the economic burden of naval power onto overseas commercial empires, taxing trade to fund their fleets.

Seapower identity had significant limits. Weak mainland states that chose to be seapowers remained prisoners of geography, still vulnerable to military might. Island states had different options. The sea would be the key to security, trade and empire. Ancient Crete exploited long-distance maritime trading networks, and possessed a potent seapower culture, represented by commerce, docks, oared vessels and endless supplies of brain-function-enhancing oily fish.[13] Ancient seapowers instinctively looked for an insular location, hence the Athenian lament that their city was not only on the Attic mainland, but also some distance from the sea. To reverse this reality Themistocles built the 'Long Walls', connecting Athens to Piraeus – the consequent Spartan alarm demonstrated that his purpose was understood across the Greek world. While seapowers have privileged islands this book avoids crude geographical determinism. Only one of the seapower great powers was really an island, post-1707 Britain. The remainder, including Venice, depended on the resources of adjacent continental territory to achieve that status. Similarly Imperial Japan, 1867–1945, did not become a seapower, despite being an island and acquiring a powerful navy. Japan was a military power focused on continental conquest: the navy secured military communications with Korea, Manchuria and China.

Critically the construction of a seapower state was, as Jacob Burckhardt observed, a work of art best understood through the lens of national culture. As states moved out to sea their art, ideas and literature took on an increasing burden of maritime images, words, concepts and values – heavily impacted by constant contact with other seapowers, contemporary and historical. Yet negative mirror-imaging was an even more potent mechanism in the formation of identity than emulation. Seapowers did not face an existential threat from similar states. Such a significant change of state identity was more likely to be a response to the existential threat posed by the ambition of continental hegemons. For the Dutch Republic those hegemons were Habsburg Spain and then Louis XIV's France. As a constructed identity seapower required constant refreshment and repetition: states that failed to remind themselves of their sea identity, for any reason, slowly but surely lost it. The identity could be lost in a generation or two, along with the necessary skills. Modern Britain stands on the cusp of such a failure: for most Britons the sea is little more than a leisure opportunity. Yet the naval might of continental powers is far less durable. The endless cycle of Russian naval activity – generation, zenith, destruction and reconstruction, perhaps the only truly circular pattern in world history – demonstrates that anything which has not been rendered central to the national identity will be sacrificed in adversity. While the sea does not trouble most Russians, Vladimir Putin's decision to seize the Crimea in 2014 demonstrated how deeply the heroic defence of the fortified naval base at Sevastopol in two major wars had been embedded in their souls.

While seapowers were politically inclusive, outward looking and dynamic, they were also weak. Weakness obliged them to wage limited wars, seek allies and negotiate settlements; they were unable to do any more. The sea, unlike the land, cannot be subject to permanent control or absolute rule. Great land powers frequently resorted to unlimited, existential wars, none more so than Rome, because they could. Seapowers could be defeated if they lost command of the sea, land powers had to be defeated on the battlefield, and by the occupation of core territory.

Modern discussions of the origins and nature of seapower have been restricted to a narrow, circular framework of utilitarian ideas about strategy, which interpret classic texts in the light of modern practice.[14] The obvious example, Mahan's claim that he discovered the primary role of sea power in history in the pages of Theodor Mommsen's *History of Rome*, highlights the dangers of an enclosed mental world. Mommsen (1817–1903) lived through the era of German unification, and served in the Prussian and later German parliaments between 1863 and 1884 as a spokesman for German nationalism. Mommsen's vehement anglophobia may have coloured his hatred of Carthage. He publicly advocated the use of violence to extend German power, and suppressed a draft history of Imperial Rome, because it could be read as a critique of Wilhelmine ambitions for a universal monarchy. His history of the Roman Republic was published in the 1850s, heavily coloured by his advocacy of German unification. He accepted the Roman version of the Second Punic War without question, not least the central premise that Rome had been forced to defend itself against an aggressive, treaty-breaking Carthage, led by Hannibal, a cunning, treacherous barbarian. There were obvious parallels to be drawn with Napoleon, and Napoleon III.

Modern scholarship has overturned Mommsen's caricatures, and refuted the strategic conundrum that inspired Mahan.[15] Mahan, a late nineteenth-century American strategist, happily repeated the judgements of the German historian, because both were primarily concerned with the expansive imperial agendas of their own countries. Both were continental states that built navies to project military power across the ocean, which gave their analysis of sea power a peculiarly militarised quality.[16] Neither state was a seapower. Mommsen and Mahan missed the rich debate about the nature of the seapower state that engaged Plato, Aristotle and Aristophanes, as well as Thucydides and Xenophon. Furthermore they were wrong.

Mommsen's famous contention that Hannibal decided to invade Italy by way of Gaul because Carthage lacked the naval power to project a large army across the central Mediterranean was wholly erroneous. Mahan used it as the foundation for a system of thought that equated sea power with naval might, rather than cultural choice. Mommsen treated Carthage as a symmetrical imperial rival of Rome. In reality Carthage was far weaker than Rome, and Hannibal's aims had been to create a coalition that could contain Rome within the regional system; he had no expectation of over-throwing the mighty Republic, nor did he plan to destroy it. He marched through Gaul to recruit troops and allies, and could not move his army by sea because Carthage lacked naval bases on the Italian coast: acquiring them was a major aim of the Italian campaign.

While the Romans destroyed the record of Carthaginian seapower, the Greek debates survived from the Hellenistic world through Rome and Byzantium to Venice, where movable-type printing made seapower a universal possession of the Renaissance. Ancient Greece was the fount of seapower wisdom for sixteenth-century England, accessed by university-educated Greek scholars like Lord Burleigh, Francis Walsingham, John Dee and Richard Hakluyt, all of whom owned the Greek edition of Thucydides, produced by the Venetian humanist scholar and publisher Aldus Manutius.[17] Dee used it to promulgate the first vision of a thalassocratic 'British Empire', melding the legal, territorial and economic interests of the state with an oceanic identity.[18] He set the intellectual parameters of English seapower, inspiring others to steal his books and develop his ideas. The Tudors propelled seapower into English culture and strategy as they moved away from a restrictive European system dominated by the Holy Roman Empire and the Papacy. They linked the growing economic power of the City of London with a national identity in which the Armada became England's Salamis, an event that vindicated the claims and contentions of previous decades. At every stage in this process ideas shifted form and focus, to suit an evolving reality, while retaining their unimpeachable ancient authority.

This fluidity makes it essential to take a long perspective, to distinguish original ideas from later glosses. Typically Victorian responses to ancient Crete were shaped by contemporary assumptions about the British Empire, rather than archaeological insights into a quasi-mythic past. The archaeologist Arthur Evans awarded King Minos a peaceful Victorian seapower empire long before he had mastered the evidence.[19] While the Englishman recognised a seapower, archaeologists from continental states brought very different assumptions to the evidence. Many of Evans's claims have been sustained by modern research.

Ultimately this book is about the ability of states to change their culture, from land to sea and back again, driven by political choice, not geographic inevitability, and the impact that the choice to become a seapower has had on the handful that became great powers. It emphasises the fundamental difference between Mahan's sea power, a strategic tool that could be deployed by continental powers, and the cultural reality of being a seapower state.

Acquiring a professional military navy was an obvious option for continental military powers that had to deal with seapower states. However, the object of such military navies, from Persia to the Soviet Union, was to destroy seapower, not acquire it. Rome became the universal monarchy of the Mediterranean world by annihilating seapower and imposing a Roman monoculture that crushed all alternatives: this, as the Carthaginians had learnt, was the 'desert' they created when they imposed peace.

Roman actions reflected a profound fear of alternative cultural models. They were alarmed by the political inclusion and cultural dynamism of seapowers, not their strategic power. Rome destroyed seapower culture, not strategic sea power. Culture rather than power drove Roman anxieties about Carthage and the persecution of Hannibal. After the battle of Zama, which ended the Second Punic War, Rome had no reason to fear Hannibal's military genius; Scipio had defeated him in battle, and Rome possessed far better armies. They drove him out of Carthage because he was mobilising the people to rebuild the state along populist inclusive lines, very different from those favoured by the land-owning oligarchs who dominated the Roman Senate. Those fears persisted until Hannibal's death.

Pericles and Thucydides established the intimate connection between seapower and limited war. As commercial capitalist states, seapowers had stronger financial resources than agrarian land powers, enabling them to outlast the enemy, as long as they were secure from an unlimited counter-stroke on islands, or behind impregnable walls. The exhaustion of the enemy, leading to a compromise peace, was the seapower alternative to 'decisive battle', the single knock-out blow that exercised the minds of continental military thinkers. In the 'Funeral Speech', Pericles effectively reversed the logic of Greek warfare, replacing the short, sharp land battles fought between armoured infantry that had settled Greek disputes for centuries with a maritime strategy of amphibious power projection, economic war and endurance. It was not without reason that Pericles was referred to as the son of Xanthippus, the Athenian commander who used an amphibious strike force to destroy the remnants of the Persian fleet at Eurymedon, open

14

the Dardanelles for grain supplies, and secure Athenian hegemony in the Aegean.[20]

Seapowers relied on limited war and maritime strategy because, as Julian Corbett demonstrated in 1911, these were the only choices that would enable them to operate as great powers. They acquired asymmetric advantage by focusing on the sea, but had to accept the limits consequent on that choice. Corbett's elegant exposition bears repeating, because it emphasises that the strategy of a seapower is maritime, relying on the combined operation of navy and army. He might have been thinking about the Athenians at Sphacteria, as well as the British at Quebec in 1759:

> Since men live upon the land and not upon the sea, great issues between nations at war have always been decided – except in the rarest cases – either by what your army can do against your enemies' territory and national life, or else by the fear of what the fleet makes it possible for your army to do.[21]

Seapowers that attempted to wield the weapon of continental might, mass military mobilisation – the Dutch Republic between 1689 and 1713, and Britain from 1916 to 1918 – were destroyed by the effort, even if they 'won' the war. Only continental powers use navies to advance total-war strategies of annihilation or unconditional surrender. This strategic model, employed by Rome, was Mahan's legacy to the United States. Rome possessed strategic sea power, but neither Rome nor the United Sates were seapowers. Contrasting the unique, contingent decisions that shaped the construction of seapower states with the creation of a powerful naval state in Petrine Russia, a process driven by a dynastic autocrat bent on continental military hegemony, emphasises the difference between the two concepts.

Seapowers, as knowledgeable states, were profoundly conscious of precedent. They knew that what they were doing had been done before, expressing that reality as part of the historical process that shaped their identities. Furthermore their enemies were equally adept at exploiting the past. Seapower became enmeshed in a profound clash of cultures, where ideas and arguments from precursor states were used to explain, justify, condemn and annihilate. While no two seapower states were identical, what they shared was far more important than any differences. They form a group, distinct from other states. These patterns, and the transmission of ideas across time, make this collective assessment coherent and compelling. Nor is the argument closed: key elements of seapower identity remain central to the Western progressive collective, as points of connection and difference.

The significance of seapower as culture is best understood across the long term – the synergy between seapowers enhances the insights that can be derived from individual examples. Furthermore the intellectual transmission of seapower culture, in many forms, through successive seapowers, is a prime example of history in the service of society. Seapowers depend on maritime activity, and employ versions of Mahan's sea power as their strategy of choice. However, that strategy can also be used by major continental states, without significant cultural transformation.

In the past century old eurocentric maritime histories have been complemented by and integrated with growing understanding of other regions, from the Red Sea and the Indian Ocean to East Asia and Polynesia. These histories have highlighted states with strong maritime identities, the use of sea power strategies, and striking developments in maritime technology.[22] The decision to restrict the focus of this book to the European experience reflects my intention that it be read as the collective study of a coherent, interrelated group of seapower states, states that were acutely and overtly conscious of the intellectual heritage left by their precursors. By 1900 this experience was shared across the globe: the navies of China, Japan and the United States were all essentially European. Every state examined in this book, including Tsarist Russia, used the European past as a precedent, building the case for becoming or remaining a seapower on what had gone before. The best proof of this contention is that ancient Athens, the first seapower great power, invented the thalassocracy of Minoan Crete to avoid the stigma of having been the first such state and to obscure a profound debt to the Phoenicians, and every subsequent seapower built on that legacy. This is the history of an idea, and its transmission across time.

CHAPTER 1

Creating Seapower Identity

Seapower evolved at the margins of early civilisation, not in the centre. Marginal coastal communities responded to limited terrestrial opportunities by developing Mediterranean trade networks that supplied vital resources – timber, copper and tin – to the great land empires of Egypt, Anatolia and Mesopotamia. After 1000 BC Phoenician and Greek sea cities pushed the original Levantine trade system into the Aegean, the Adriatic and the Tyrrhenian Sea, and through the western Mediterranean to Gadir (Cadiz), beyond the Pillars of Hercules, in pursuit of metal ores. When these maritime actors protected and controlled the sea routes that connected resources and markets, they laid the foundation for sea power strategy, the control of maritime communications and seapower identity. The vulnerability of maritime trade to rival states and pirates prompted the creation of constabulary forces, while the long-term costs of the necessary ships, sailors and infrastructure, obliged sea states to develop more inclusive forms of government, forms that gave merchants, traders and shipowners a share of political power, in exchange for services or financial contributions. The political structures of these sea states moved from absolute rule through

A Phoenician war galley on an Assyrian wall relief

constitutional monarchy to republican oligarchy. Large or medium-sized states that consciously chose this socio-economic-strategic model became seapowers, states that put the sea at the centre of their identity, in contrast to continental powers, which deployed fleets for terrestrial strategic objects. Sea states and cities developed distinctive cultures dominated by seafaring and commerce.

In the absence of significant sea trade, controlling maritime communications had little strategic value. Failure to comprehend this central reality has caused much misunderstanding for those who try to create direct parallels between the strategies of sea and land power. The two concepts are fundamentally different in origin, purpose and method. Land powers could secure victory through 'decisive' battle and the occupation of core territory, sea power was restricted to limited outcomes, achieved by economic exhaustion. Sea power strategy focused on controlling the sea for security and economic advantage, not the empty glory of naval battle. The seapower states that used it operated at the watery margins between great land powers in eras of balance and stability.

The synergy between land empires and sea states reflected the geography and culture of Egypt and Mesopotamia. The 'cradles of civilisation' were constrained regions, river based, hemmed in by desert and mountains, their political heartlands distant from the ocean. Domestic stability and territorial conquest defined political success. Their geography fuelled a sense of exceptionalism and superiority, based on territory and manpower that discouraged enquiry and exploration.[1] Sea states responded to their supply of limited agricultural land by exploiting the sea for fishing and commerce. Seafaring and the spirit of enquiry were commonly paired characteristics, while land-bound minds were restricted to pedestrian prospects and military solutions.

The existence of something approaching a balance of power on land created the political space in which sea states could operate. While large land empires were in competition they valued sea trade, and had more important concerns than small seafaring states. By contrast the hegemonic universal empires of Assyria, Babylon and Persia annihilated Levantine seapower as a political and cultural force, creating the opportunity for Athens and Carthage, states beyond the immediate reach of Mesopotamian military power, to develop into true seapowers. The collision between the seapowers and expansionist continental military states, fearful of their dynamism and difference, would define the political development of the ancient world. In a series of cultural clashes that ran from the Greek defeat of the Persians at Salamis in 480 BC to the annihilation of Carthage by a Roman army under Scipio Africanus in 146 BC seapower strategies of limited war – coalition building, economic exhaustion and negotiated settlement – challenged the continental alternative of unlimited war, mass armies, decisive battle, territorial occupation and absolute destruction. In the process the intellectual origins of seapower were established, and the first seapower empires were destroyed.

Seapower was a direct consequence of evolving Mediterranean trade patterns. In the third and fourth millennia Levantine trade in oil, wine and timber developed to meet demand from Mesopotamia and Egypt, not that of relatively limited local populations. The need to protect this trade against rival economic actors, states or pirates, prompted a militarisation of maritime activity – using ships as fighting platforms or amphibious transports for overseas raids like the Trojan War.

The first strategic commodity to be traded was timber. Both Egypt and Mesopotamia needed large, strong timbers for shipbuilding and temple projects, timbers that indigenous tree species could not supply. Not only did they import timber, but they fought for control of the cedar and resinous forests in the Lebanese mountains. The first maritime trade routes carried Lebanese timber south to Egypt, or north to the port of Byblos and then over the mountains to Mesopotamia. Economic need breached the cultural isolationism of these static riverine societies. The expansion of long-distance sea trade to include strategic metals began the process of creating Mediterranean civilisation, a cultural space defined by the sea.[2]

Although the sea was marginal to the great river-based civilisations, their reliance on imported resources generated maritime trade. By 2500 BC the Egyptians were importing oil from Syria, along with cedar, pitch and other shipbuilding and construction materials. Although the ships were financed by Egypt, and resembled the river craft used to transport building materials along the Nile, they were probably built and crewed in the Levant. By 1800 BC there is pictorial evidence of Levantine mariners landing goods at Thebes from very similar ships. However much they contributed to this development, the Egyptians displayed little curiosity about the outside world. They left most external trade in foreign hands and, despite creating major port infrastructures on the Nile, did not build a coastal harbour, and allowed the first Suez Canal to fall into disuse. Egypt attracted trade, but did not generate an indigenous seafaring/commercial class, relying instead on Cretan, Phoenician and Greek merchants. It remained a barter economy until the Persian conquest in 525 BC. Parallels with Imperial China, another vast riverine empire, are hard to avoid. Egypt was a mandarin state, driven by tradition, continuity, priestly power and self-satisfaction. Defeats prompted xenophobia, rather than reflection.[3] It is significant that Egyptian maritime activity peaked under non-native dynasties.[4] Theban priestly elites hated the sea, opposing plans to move the capital to the Nile Delta, to avoid interacting with foreign traders and foreign ideas.[5] By contrast maritime communities consciously chose to become outward looking, a choice reflected in all aspects of their culture, from politics to warfare.

Between 2800 and 1300 BC the growing interconnectedness of Bronze Age Mediterranean trade created the opportunity for seapower. Around 2000 BC sailing ships replaced oared 'canoe'-style craft, marking a shift from local luxury trades to bulk traffic. The new ships displaced up to 500 tons, and they began to appear in written records from the thirteenth century BC. Their importance can be judged from the world's oldest known shipwreck. The fourteenth-century BC Uluburun vessel, discovered off the south-western coast of Turkey, carried six tons of copper ingots and one ton of tin, enough metal, once smelted into bronze, to equip a small army.[6]

Ancient states consumed metals in large quantities, as weapons, high-profile celebrations of power and wealth, or stockpiles for future use. Sea trade serviced a demand created by the strikingly uneven distribution of key metals across the Mediterranean.[7] In northern Europe metals were relatively evenly spread, generally within reach of land transport, but in the Mediterranean areas of high agricultural productivity and population, including Mesopotamia and Egypt, lacked both high-grade timber and vital metals. The main source of copper was insular Cyprus.[8] Initially tin, almost entirely absent from the Mediterranean, arrived from Central Asia through Mesopotamia, with Ugarit (Ras Sharma) as a key centre of exchange. Later sources included Bohemia, Brittany and Cornwall, while small supplies in Iberia, Tuscany and Sardinia attracted Levantine traders west to the Adriatic, the Tyrrhenian Sea and ultimately the Atlantic, connecting with the overland routes that brought metals into the Mediterranean. Not only were these trade routes critical to ancient power, but they also had profound strategic implications. The lure of metals and timber pulled successive Mesopotamian empires to the Mediterranean coast, and created Levantine maritime contractor states. Those contractors forged ever larger trade networks to secure fresh supplies of ore. When Phoenician and Greek traders and settlers entered the Tyrrhenian Sea, the centre of the tin trade from northern Europe, they collided with the Etruscans, another culture shaped by metalwork. The contest to control maritime commerce became violent, with the first recorded naval battle occurring off Sardinia.[9] 'Despite the obvious dangers, sea transport so far surpassed land communications in ease as to make of the Mediterranean a milieu of interlocking routes onto which coastlands and harbours faced.'[10] This enduring reality created an alternative perception dominated by sea routes and navigational techniques that began reducing the ocean to a wide river.

The dramatic increase in trade, connection and exchange did not meet with universal approval. Sea trade provided the vector for ideas of progress, change and empowerment, a divergent cultural model that challenged the stasis of contemporary land powers: philosophers and rulers alike feared the 'Corrupting Sea', which threatened civil order and political stability.[11] Although sent out to trade, ships carried men, ideas and images as well as goods. These non-elite travellers connected the regions and empires of the eastern Mediterranean and Mesopotamia, across seas that were generally open to all. The diffusion of sea-based cultures was largely restricted to port cities and their immediate hinterlands. The freedom of intellectual connectivity by sea transformed the message and excluded the elite. Every aspect of life took on a different meaning for sea cultures: while the priest-kings of Mesopotamia and Egypt studied the heavens for astrological portents, sailors stared upwards to develop the 'haven-finding art' of navigation and placed it at the centre of their worldview. The process worked both ways: the Greeks acquired sculptural art from Egypt, only to infuse the static gods of the Nile with the life and vigour of an altogether more humanist culture. The Egyptians brought ship designs from the Nile to Phoenicia, where they were translated into sea-going form. We know that these cultural exchanges informed the evolution of Greek seafaring; the same exchanges were perfectly capable of carrying rich cargoes of ideas in both directions.

Across most of the ancient world the sea remained a threat rather than an opportunity. Peregrine Horden and Nicholas Purcell conclude that, for all the centrality of maritime trade to the ancient Mediterranean, 'it was a commonplace among Greek and Roman writers that the effects of this communication by sea were profoundly damaging to good social order'.[12] While the anxiety of kings, priests and static cultures was predictable, even the Greeks believed there had been a 'golden age' before ships and trade, without cash or corrupting seafaring. They considered land and agriculture morally superior to seafaring. Rome transmitted these ideas to early Christians, who feared the 'corrupting' influence of a greater knowledge of the sea. The artificial moral distinction between trade, fishing and agriculture that this implied ignored the reality that Mediterranean peoples had always exploited both land and sea for food.

Both the Theseus cycle, complete with Minotaur and Jason and the Argonauts, reflect the darker side of the story.[13] The metal trades were a source of conflict, while their economic impact changed the balance of power within states, reducing the political weight of landed wealth, handing power to new men. The profits of the metal trade made seapower a serious cultural model. Although iron was more widely available than copper and tin, its very ubiquity encouraged the use of ever more metal, and more shipping.

The carriage of heavy metal ores and ingots must have refined ship design, providing opportunities for other less bulky trades, such as deck cargo, and an opening for specialist contractors. Minoan Crete and the Phoenician and Greek cities provided the connectivity that propelled the Bronze Age economy, spreading ideas and means of exchange. The Phoenicians created an alphabetic written language to simplify trade, and the Greeks adapted it for similar purposes. Egyptian pictograms and Mesopotamian cuneiform never escaped a ceremonial world of priest-kings, doomed to destruction by international trade. The complex idiomatic characters used by East Asian languages were equally ill-suited to international exchange. Coins, another consequence of sea trade, also developed in sea cities, as a means of exchange and symbols of maritime identity.

Despite cultural reservations the sea became central to the imagined world of the ancient Mediterranean because sea transport was far easier, and cheaper than that by land. Sea routes shaped the region as 'a milieu of interlocking routes onto which coastlands and harbours faced'.[14] The system combined economic exchange with cultural cross-fertilisation long before the sea had acquired any strategic significance.

By the mid-sixteenth century BC the Hittite, Egyptian and Mesopotamian empires, vast, consuming societies, were importing timber and metals from regions far beyond their control. The sea economy revealed by the Uluburun wreck linked the Levant with the Tyrrhenian Sea, creating the preconditions for the development of culturally distinctive sea states and the exercise of seapower strategy. The volume and value of trade made the sea an attractive source of revenue. Sailing ships needed secure harbours, pushing the development of port cities, where increased populations provided seafaring manpower for commercial and constabulary functions.[15]

Trade enabled strategically located sea cities and states, primarily the Phoenicians, to become rich, spreading people, customs and beliefs, and reshaping regional identities, notably that of Greek coastal settlements. However, the transformation from port to sea state and potentially seapower required a degree of stability and security against continental threats that the Levantine coastal cities could not hope to achieve. Internal stability was essential to encourage investment and maintain the political and cultural changes that sustained maritime commerce. Although much Bronze Age trade centred on palaces, maritime societies were noticeably more inclusive than landed contemporaries, often involving women and non-royals. In these trade-based polities political power was shared. Free-standing sea states run by 'consortia of sea-trading families accumulated a degree of wealth belied by their diminutive size'.[16] Archives from Ugarit (Ras Sharma) reveal a merchant class with real political power and a thriving maritime culture, without a hint of naval power. Ugarit prospered as the commercial link between Mesopotamia and the Mediterranean. However, such cities were at the mercy of larger terrestrial states.

By contrast insular Crete operated as a sea state, free from threats of conquest or demands for tribute. After 2200 BC, when much of the eastern Mediterranean had been disrupted, Crete underwent dramatic social change, culminating in the first palace system around 1950 BC. The development of sailing ships transformed Crete from an isolated economic backwater to the strategically secure hub for long-haul commerce. The port at Kommos, on the south coast, ideally placed for prevailing wind systems, enabled Cretan traders to access the Levant, Cyprus, the Aegean and Italian waters. Crete became an entrepôt for 'exclusive maritime networks', including colonies of settlement in the Cyclades, the classic source of wealth, acquiring rock-cut quays to facilitate shipping operations. Crete imported wheat, the staple food, in exchange for woollens, wine, oil and timber.

Crete became a major maritime power, with extensive shipping and trade links across the region but, as Fernand Braudel observed, it was not a 'naval' power, in the modern sense. There were no rival navies to combat, and Crete did not seek continental political power.[17] His Mahanian analysis missed the larger point. The Minoans did not have to fight for sea power: they acquired effective control of the sea for economic and strategic purposes without opposition. Consequently they had no need for naval power. Similarly while Thucydides would use Minoan thalassocracy as a precedent for Athenian seapower, the seapower of his day was very different in form and function. Minoan 'thalassocracy', a network of trading posts, was typical of sea states: small and weak, but agile and economically effective. Far from competing with the great land empires the Cretans depended on them for their prosperity.

Sailing ships, insularity and expanding trade created the conditions for seapower on Crete. It is probable the Minoans had a navy, to combat pirates – the classic seapower mission – suppress rival traders, secure colonies and extract revenue. Down to 1200 BC the profits of trade with Egypt and Phoenicia sustained a vibrant palace culture. Contemporary wall paintings at Akrotiri show distinctive warships and trading vessels.[18] Growing demand for resources encouraged sea traders to cut out middlemen, outflank land routes, increase speed of travel and reduce the cost of goods, creating a competitive advantage. The new sea routes pushed the development of navigational knowledge, while the struggle to control them would create naval warfare, sea power strategy and seapower states.

Between 1950 BC and 1700 BC large regional centres were built in eastern Crete. Although destroyed by an earthquake in 1700 BC, these centres were quickly rebuilt. A second wave of destruction, this time by fire, was followed by the reconstruction of a single major site at Knossos, which remained in use down to 1050 BC. These palace complexes combined political and religious functions with trade, manufacture and storage. Crete bore the imprint of commercial/cultural networks that stretched from Mesopotamia and Egypt via Syria to the Aegean. Cretan palace culture was heavily influenced by older, landed societies. Ideas and artefacts were part of the return cargo.

The success of Crete and Ugarit demonstrated that, although the great land powers could control territory, they could not control the sea or the maritime cities that delivered key resources.[19] Sea states bartered trade and tribute for relative independence. However, everything depended on benign trading conditions. Cretan trade with the Hyksos kingdom of Egypt, based in the Nile Delta at Avaris, the commercial mega-city of the era, proved short-lived. Nilotic Egyptian elites at Thebes destroyed the Hyksos, their capital and the connection with Mediterranean trade, shifting power back to the centre of the country, and restoring old inward-looking cultural models. The economic impact of these changes may explain why Cretan society ceased to be sea-based around 1500 BC, when mainland agendas from Mycenean Greece became dominant. Continental Ugarit was destroyed at this time.

Minoan thalassocracy rose and fell in an open trading network that linked the major powers and rewarded middlemen.[20] This network was sea-based and ship-driven: it affected maritime Crete and Phoenicia far more than the great landlocked river empires at the eastern and southern edges of the system. Thalassocracy could survive earthquakes and tidal waves; it collapsed when the regional trade system collapsed. Without trade seapower became irrelevant.

The Cretan legacy endured among the Greeks, a folk memory of an older seafaring culture, referenced in the Homeric stories and through a language that used Cretan words such as *thalassa*, along with the names of wheat, olives, vines and figs. Greek intellectuals tapped into these memories when they created the next seapower. By the fourteenth century BC the eastern Mediterranean connected the three great empires of the Bronze Age, Egypt, Mesopotamia and the Anatolian Hittites. All three relied on Levantine and Minoan cities for trade, in cedar, ships, local manufactures, tin, Cypriot copper and imported luxuries, including the Afghan lapis lazuli, beloved of Egyptian artists. This synergy of trade and manufacture reflected the pull of Egyptian wealth. Coastal cities flourished by supplying the needs of great land-locked, land-centric powers. The Levantine cities may have recognised the dominion of Hittite or Egyptian rulers, the spheres of influence divided north–south, but they remained relatively independent actors in a multi-polar world.[21]

This system collapsed between 1300 and 800 BC. Major population movements destroyed the Hittite Empire, badly damaged Egypt and prompted a spectacular collapse of elite society across the region. However, maritime trade continued, and many Levantine trading centres survived. Copper-rich Cyprus was devastated, but quickly recovered to become the centre of sea trade for the next three hundred years: 'aggressive mercantile entrepreneurship' allied to 'growing prowess in the realm of open ocean navigation' brought Cypriot goods to Sardinia in the thirteenth century, where they were exchanged for Sardinian metals.[22]

Trade continued because mariners developed the ability to exploit winds and currents and the movement of heavenly bodies, and recorded experience to avoid dangerous landfalls, including the myriad risks of human interaction that they involved, from taxation to enslavement. Sea routes reduced the cost of trade, empowering waves of anti-monopolistic traders around the Mediterranean. Cyprus lay at the centre of these operations. With copper to trade the Cypriots pioneered routes to the west. The new trade system succeeded because it was more flexible than the older palace system, emphasising the importance of open political structures for economic development.

This invasive mix of trade and culture alarmed landed societies. In a characteristic example of the enduring continental aversion for all things maritime the Egyptians demonised invading 'Sea Peoples' as enemies of civilisation, a metaphor that appealed to those who felt more 'civilised'. Identifying the 'Sea Peoples' as a specific ethnic group reflected the inability of static societies to understand those who made their living by the sea and the desire of modern scholars to find a suitably apocalyptic end for the Bronze Age. Many people were moving by sea at this time; they did not share culture or ethnicity, only maritime economic ambitions, ranging from robbery to settlement. They overwhelmed the restrictive palatial economic model of sea trade and the static societies in which it operated. The focal point of the process can be inferred from the striking resemblance between Cypriot bronze gods and the 'Sea Peoples' portrayed on temple walls by anxious Egyptian priests. The Egyptians were deeply troubled by stateless travellers, with no obvious home, or ruler, who were hard to tax and brought with them dangerous ideas about sharing political power. It was easy to blame 'Sea Peoples' for destroying civilisation when most cultures viewed the sea as a source of danger and corruption. Egyptian writings, which exhibit striking parallels with priestly accounts of Viking activity, may have shaped Plato's argument. The same anxieties have endured down to the modern era in some parts of the world, notably China and Russia.[23]

Terrestrial cities and states, hidebound by static, monolithic political and social systems, lost their purpose when they lost control of the metal supply. New traders prospered because they pursued profit, not land or symbols of power, and developed political structures that enabled them to work together for a common economic purpose. The spread of iron-smelting techniques, largely by ship, also helped end palatial trade monopolies. Having escaped royal control by taking to the sea and working together, maritime peoples overwhelmed the old stasis, resorting to violence where necessary.

A new type of state developed on the Levantine coast, on Cyprus and Crete, combining trader kings with merchant adventurers, integrating local production and sea commerce. These sea states, most little more than tiny 'cities', became fabulously wealthy. The Phoenician ports, which seem to have been closely linked to the sea peoples, were typical: 'a patchwork of widely scattered merchant communities. Maritime trade, not territory, defined their sphere.'[24] Distinct Phoenician communities existed from around 1500 BC until the Macedonian conquest Hellenised the region. These cities recovered quickly from the economic downturn associated with the weakness and economic stagnation of Egypt and the collapse of the Hittite Empire around 1140 BC. When the Aegean palace-based economies collapsed, they were replaced by new political organisations that mirrored the successful Phoenician sea states.

Phoenicia, in Fernand Braudel's determinist argument, 'became a sea power by force of circumstance'. Emerging on a long coastal strip, dotted with useful ports both nautical and increasingly man-made, rarely more than 7 miles wide, much of it backed by forested mountains and steep valleys, Phoenician cities had little chance of becoming major land powers. Instead they remained independent of each other, and increasingly maritime. Tyre, the city that John Ruskin read about in his Bible, was an island, with a natural harbour, later supplemented by a second man-made refuge, and a fresh water spring. This ideal seapower site was secure as long as it had control of the sea and could import food.[25]

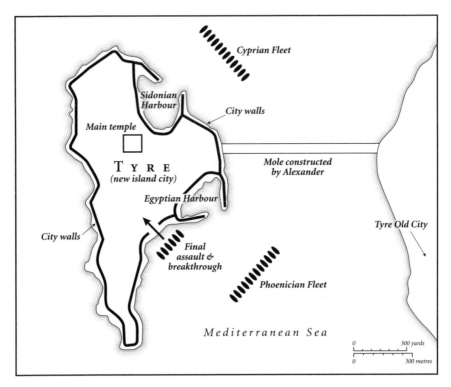

Cyprian Fleet

Sidonian
Harbour

City walls

Main temple

T Y R E
(new island city)

Mole constructed
by Alexander

Egyptian Harbour

Tyre Old City

City walls

Final
assault &
breakthrough

Phoenician Fleet

Mediterranean Sea

0   300 yards

0   300 metres

The Siege of Tyre

The Phoenician cities emerged as key trading centres linking east and west in the twelfth century BC. When Egypt recovered and began to trade, Tyre, the most southerly major city, became the most important. It pioneered long-distance trades to the Aegean and to east Africa via Israel and the Red Sea. Closely attuned to the ebb and flow of regional power, Tyre was quick to break with Israel when Egypt recovered and sacked Jerusalem. Tyrian self-interest was paramount and, as a sea-trading nation, the Tyrians had an excellent intelligence network to inform their judgement.[26]

While they made maximum use of any land they had, developing advanced agricultural methods, the Phoenicians fed themselves by trade and industry. The manufacturing sector provided cargo and exchange for outbound ships. Tyrian dyes and dyed cloth were renowned across the ancient world, as were their works in metal, ivory, gemstones, pottery and glass. The Tyrians pioneered open-ocean navigation by night, an achievement that even the landlocked Israelites thought worthy of recording.[27]

Explosive economic development increased political ambition. Around 1000 BC the Phoenician cities, especially Tyre, 'began to adopt a more hegemonic, sometimes territorial attitude towards geographies of trade, by which political actions abroad became more overtly dictated by economic logic' than had been the case in earlier trading states. These prototype seapower empires used islands and ports as trading posts and way stations, controlling sea lanes and trade, not territory. Phoenician settlements on Cyprus, at Gadir (Cadiz) in southern Spain and in Sardinia supplied metals, while Carthage was established in the eighth century BC as a refreshment station halfway to Gadir, where silver and tin were obtained in massive quantities.[28] It is no coincidence that later seapower empires used the same island locations.[29]

Phoenician seapower faltered when the widespread use of iron ended the monopolistic advantages of bronze traders, and, around 1000 BC, Assyrian armies arrived on the Levantine coast seeking tribute and control. Egypt responded: a new Libyan dynasty moved the capital of Egypt back to Tanis in the Nile Delta in the tenth century BC, emphasising the sea-conquering god Seth, and hiring mercenary troops from the Aegean. Both superpowers, Assyria and Egypt, depended on Levantine and Greek shipping.[30]

In the ninth century BC the Phoenicians annexed Cyprus, to control the copper trade and Cypriot routes into the Tyrrhenian Sea, the source of northern European tin. Cyprus also traded with Greece. Waves of warriors, traders and craftsmen settled in distant regions to access metal and trade.[31] Their baggage included distinctive seapower cultures, which used ships as icons, employed languages of commerce and engaged in pluralistic politics. The attractions of seapower became obvious in the seventh century BC, when Assyria conquered the Levant and Egypt, creating a universal monarchy. A consuming state with a massive army Assyria compelled Tyre to submit by conquering Egypt, the last regional balance for the Mesopotamian imperialists. This obliged the Phoenician cities to become Assyrian clients, harnessed to a war machine that demanded ever larger tribute payments, while exploiting their skills to create fleets and supply war materials.[32] Phoenician cities expanded international trade and domestic manufacturing to satisfy those tribute demands, while the dominion of militarised land empires, wars, sieges and rising tribute payments encouraged the Tyrian settlement at Carthage to become a distinct state.

Phoenician colonisation in the west began around 800 BC at Gadir on the Atlantic coast of Spain, beyond the Pillars of Hercules. An island some 6 miles from the main local port of Tartessos (Huelva), Gadir positioned the Phoenicians at a discrete distance, avoiding any suggestion of territorial ambition, and was easily defensible.[33] It became the focus of metal exports from the Rio Tinto region as well as the Atlantic tin trade. The choice of an island with a good harbour revealed the settlers' maritime focus. The Phoenicians exchanged finished goods and luxuries such as wine and sophisticated pottery for local ore and metals. Cyprus, Crete and Laconia were early trading partners, for copper and iron, which may account for Homer's numerous Phoenician seafaring references. Sardinia and Sicily were also linked to the system. Phoenician colonising activity had a relatively light touch: they wanted trade, not territory.

Phoenician commercial ties to the Gadir region seem to have faltered after the Babylonian sack of Tyre in 573 BC, but they would be revived by the Carthaginians in the third century BC. Other Phoenician settlements across the western Mediterranean also fell into Carthaginian hands, including Ibiza and the coastal towns in Sardinia, Sicily and the far west, such as outposts on the Portuguese and Moroccan Atlantic coasts.[34] These outposts valued and preserved nautical and commercial knowledge, but the remorseless destruction of both Tyre and Carthage, the perishable nature of their written records, and a lack of interest in the 'losers' of history means that little evidence has survived. Separated from the mother city by great distances Phoenician colonies quickly developed distinctive economic and political ideas.

Both Phoenician and Greek sea states proved to be dynamic colonisers. They sought insular or isolated locations, to access metals, farmland or strategic bases for shipping: such bases helped define spheres of influence and support warships that controlled sea communications.[35] Cultural ties between colonies and founding cities were strong. By the end of the seventh century BC trade between Phoenicians and Greeks had broken down. Conflict over trade and resources may have been a consequence of the general crisis in the late sixth-century BC Phoenician world, which Barry Cunliffe has linked to the end of the Bronze Age, when societies based on control of bronze were replaced by those controlling agricultural surpluses. The causes may have included the wide availability of iron and a significant population increase,[36] developments that enabled the great land powers to wage war on a far larger scale.

The Greek challenge obliged the Phoenicians to work with regional allies. In 600 BC Phocean Greeks set up a colony at Massilia (Marseille) in the Etruscan economic zone, ousting them from the trans-Alpine market, and controlling much of the coast to the west. Sixty years later more Phoceans, fleeing the Persian occupation of their homeland, took over the international trading centre of Alalia (modern-day Aleria), which challenged both Etruscan and Carthaginian interests, and led to a major naval battle off Sardinia around 535 BC. This battle may have prompted the expulsion of Massilian traders from Gadir around 540 BC. Eventually the Phoenician sphere included north Africa, western Sicily, southern Sardinia and the sea area west to Gadir, while the Greeks dominated the Aegean, the Adriatic and southern Italy: the Tyrrhenian Sea was divided.[37] Sea power strategy controlled access to key markets, demarcating 'spheres of influence', as seapowers fought to maintain exclusive spheres of interest, defined by trade not territory.

Carthaginian sea power denied Greek traders access to the rich mineral deposits on the Atlantic coast of southern Spain. The 'Pillars of Hercules' were the end of the world for Greeks, because Carthaginian warships at Gadir blocked access to the seas beyond.[38] This strategic use of naval strength suggests that by the sixth or perhaps fifth century BC the Carthaginians had developed a seapower concept similar to that advanced by Themistocles in the 480s. While Phoenician ideas influenced all aspects of Greek maritime culture, their approach to seapower remained essentially maritime/economic; those of the Greeks always contained a strong military element. Warrior culture, largely absent among the Phoenicians, made Greek politics combative, fractured and arrogant. Militarised arrogance would be Greece's major contribution to the development of seapower, encouraging them to fight for trade and for independence.

As sea states with limited populations the Phoenician cities were effective in limited wars of economic endurance, using sea communications, money and alliances, but they proved utterly incapable in meeting the massed military might of Egypt, Assyria, Babylon, Persia and ultimately Macedon. Phoenician towns, cities and trading posts were strikingly similar:

With few exceptions, they were compact, geographically defined settlements situated on or near the coast in navigable, easily defensible positions. Offshore islets, peninsulas, and headlands formed favoured locations. As trading establishments, nearly all were located near sheltered anchorages – in natural bays or harbours, lagoons, or riverine estuaries.[39]

These seapower settlements were dominated by the business district, marketplaces, warehouses and harbours. Industrial processes, including foul-smelling dye works, were set apart from the more prosperous residential areas. These cities began with a natural harbour, while larger sites such as Tyre and Sidon acquired a second man-made harbour of advanced design, built with cut masonry or carved out of solid rock. These harbours included naval bases, defended by narrow, walled entrances, within impressive city defences, while warships and naval bases controlled trade routes.

Between 1000 and 800 BC Phoenician 'mercantile, maritime, middleman societies' became wealthy by taxing private trade. However, their collective identity was constructed by others; even the term 'Phoenician' was a Greek invention. Their fragile papyrus records largely perished, leaving their history in the less than generous hands of Greek competitors, Israelite neighbours and a Roman state deeply traumatised by the Punic Wars.[40] The resulting loss of evidence obscured the role of the Phoenicians in creating seapower, leaving little record of their priority and prowess.

Fortunately Phoenician coins, critical cultural artefacts, reveal something of their self-image. Widely used from the fifth century BC, coins offered a convenient way of paying for goods abroad, and were a vehicle for displays of strategic and cultural power. Many featured war galleys; those of Sidon link the sea and the city, placing a war galley before the city walls. The hippocampus, or sea horse, stressed the links between land and sea, while Tyrian coinage combining the Athenian owl with an Egyptian flail and crook reflected a culture moving from an old connection to something new: using standard Greek coin weights facilitated commerce.[41]

The critical connection between dynamic sea trade and inclusive political development cannot be overstated. The political structure of the Phoenician cities reflected commercial/maritime agendas. Their kings may have held the political initiative, and some religious significance, but they shared power with the mercantile elite through a Council of Elders and a People's Assembly. Enfranchising commercial wealth tied policy to economic interests, ensured the king did not forget the overriding importance of the sea, and offered a voice to those who owned the ships that made Phoenician cities significant. The people of these small cities needed to be political realists: they spent much of their existence as subjects, direct or indirect, of great powers, securing economic interests by timely concessions, support or tribute.

As voyages became longer, merchants needed capital to cover the period between investment and income. Banking emerged, along with a financial 'City' linking trade with investment. The dramatic growth of maritime trade can be measured through the development of efficient port infrastructure. Before 1500 BC quays enabled sailing ships to dock alongside, rather than rely on lighters for cargo handling. As trading volumes increased, smaller ports such as Byblos were overtaken by larger multi-harbour sites such as Sidon and Tyre. By 1000 BC the Levant and the eastern Mediterranean possessed many purpose-built docks, to handle bulk trades in ores, metals, timber and stone. Artificial harbours were created and canals dug to carry goods between them and into markets.[42] Clearly the economic returns justified the exercise. In a region with low tidal ranges simple facilities allowed loading and unloading at all times. The Tyrians created an artificial six-hectare northern basin, linked by canal to a natural harbour south of the island, and the main market areas.

Insularity helped Tyre become the grandest city of the era, fabulously wealthy on the proceeds of a dynamic expansive trade linking Arabia to Spain. The obvious synergy between insularity, identity and seapower was captured in the writings of the Israelites, who could only look on in wonder at the prosperity of their neighbours. The densely packed high-rise city replaced defensive walls with sea marks and a suitable new deity, Melquart, god of cyclic fertility, the sea and overseas ventures. His temple became the navigation beacon for the sea traders who funded the project. Twin pillars of gold and emerald, the talk of the Mediterranean, were echoed in the Temple of Melquart at Gadir, while the Temple at Tartessos contained bronze replicas.[43] Those twin pillars live on as the 'Pillars of Hercules', named for the Greek version of Melquart. The use of religious structures for such prosaic trade-related functions emphasised the centrality of the sea in Phoenician culture. These developments reflected the relative freedom of the region from external great powers, a freedom that enabled Tyre to absorb Sidon and trade with Israel for foodstuffs, in order to concentrate on cash crops. While this 'maritime imperial' model would be destroyed when military great powers returned to the region, it was 'a foretaste of a strategy that Mediterranean sea cities would later take to far more ambitious levels'.[44] The parallels between Tyrian policy choices and those of later seapowers reflect enduring economic and strategic realities.

The instrument of Phoenician seapower was the bireme, a compact, sturdy vessel ideally suited to carry cargo or combat other oared craft. By contrast Phoenician armies were unimportant, outside the defence of cities. Most troops were allied or mercenary, while a small native 'Sacred Battalion' provided ceremonial functions and internal security. These cities had no answer to the mass armies and siege engines of the Mesopotamian imperialists. This weakness exposed the fatal flaw of Phoenician pretensions to greatness. It was an indication of just how far Carthage had escaped the Phoenician model that it tried to become a great power. The destruction of Carthage demonstrated the vital lesson: seapowers can only defeat continental hegemons as part of a coalition.

Between 800 and 500 BC the Mediterranean became a single economic system. A colder, wetter period in the eighth century BC increased agricultural output, sparking a population boom, possibly doubling that of the Aegean. The subsequent fall in food production propelled moves into overseas markets, making sea routes and colonies increasingly important for import-dependant populations, and may have prompted an increase in Greek mercenary service.

Insularity proved to be of little value to Tyre when the Assyrians took control of the Levantine coast in the eighth century. The city astutely submitted on terms. Assyrian demand for tribute silver drove the expansion of Tyrian trade across the Mediterranean, moving goods, people and ideas over long distances. Nor was trade restricted to the Mediterranean: northern European products and metal ores were traded for Mediterranean goods that reached as far as England.[45] Much of this trade revolved around Sardinia, a focal point for the emergence of strategic sea power. The Phoenicians actively sought new markets, often exploiting diplomatic links. Trade and expanding cities linked the Iron Age Mediterranean, creating the preconditions for Roman dominion.[46]

Phoenician sea states prospered in periods of relative regional balance, preserving their independence by playing off two or more larger powers against each other. This favourable situation ended when the universalising military-bureaucratic Assyrian state conquered the Levant in the mid-eighth century. Tyre survived, but other Phoenician cities were conquered. Egypt, the other great power, was conquered a century later, removing the last vestiges of regional balance. The Assyrians celebrated their success on the walls of bombastic palace complexes, where Levantine cities and ships jostled alongside other enslaved peoples in the art of subjugation. Under Assyrian dominion trade declined and conquered lands were ruled by alien governors, while the forced relocation of peoples, increasing tribute demands and the 'intensification and reordering of regional economies', created a 'command economy', the normal model for continental imperial states.[47] In multi-polar state systems traders could limit their exposure to taxes or destruction. As Frederic Lane observed, 'A king who destroyed his merchants, lessened his power to compete with other kings'. The economic opportunities generated by multi-state systems enabled more wealth to remain with individuals, who tended to use it to innovate.[48] Universal monarchs had no such discipline.

Assyria demanded ever more metals, and pushed local economies to specialise in cloth, dyestuffs, ivories and other luxuries to service the imperial agenda. Tyre paid a tribute of 4,500 kilos of gold in 730 BC, which may explain the dramatic growth of long-distance trade and the Tyrian revolt of 701. Many Tyrians followed their king into exile on Cyprus. Other cities that revolted were refounded as Assyrian possessions: Sidon was renamed and became a useful economic tool to control Tyre, now stripped of its territorial hinterland.[49] Yet Assyrian military might was restricted to *terra firma*. King Sennacherib installed a wall relief at Nineveh showing the Tyrian fleet fleeing from his armies in 702, but he remained powerless to follow them.[50]

The Tyrian revolt created an economic opening for Greek traders, whose cities remained beyond the reach of Mesopotamian great powers. Greek emulation of the Phoenicians combined admiration with distrust. The impact of Phoenician food and wine culture and their written language on Greece implies close contact and conscious borrowing. From Iberia to Attica there is ample evidence that Phoenician culture and identity were widely emulated, indeed the history of seapower is one of endless, intelligent emulation. The expansion of seapower states by colonisation increased the reach and weight of these ideas. Strategically placed islands and estuaries, occupied to control trade routes, were among the first places to abandon royal systems of government as people acquired local identities. Here the middling sort, fearing competition from foreign traders, were quick to denigrate and stereotype the 'other'. The Phoenician reputation for sharp practice and greed was a Greek construct.[51] Such ideas circulated quickly in expanding commercial towns, the centres that shaped emerging civilisations in the seventh and sixth centuries BC. Sea trade civilised states by compelling them to settle core values and sustain them through law. As societies became stable, and shared political power across the populace, their military forces evolved from chaos to order, from warriors and sea raiders to citizen armies and standing navies, serving the interests of the state, not elite rulers.

In the Levant the destruction of the Assyrian Empire was followed by the short-lived Babylonian imperium. Babylon swallowed its precursor, crushed the Phoenician cities, sacked and depopulated Jerusalem in 587 BC, and took Tyre after a thirteen-year siege in 572. The last Tyrian king died in captivity. Sidon, which bent before the storm, survived and became the leading city of the coast – a position it retained long after this wave of conquerors had ebbed. Babylonian absolutism, oppressive resource extraction and the destruction of alternative cultural models, including sea-based republican oligarchies, was typical of a universal monarchy. Phoenicia lost its age-old maritime ascendancy to the continental ambition and unthinking brutality of Mesopotamian imperialists who devastated sea trade in pursuit of centralised authority. Cyprian Broodbank has observed: 'for certain highly continental, alluvium focused empires, the threat of disorder from the maritime realm outweighed its economic allure and benefits'.[52] Yet Babylon could not suppress maritime activity; it continued to operate, profiting other maritime powers.

With the Mediterranean on the cusp of dramatic economic expansion the Phoenicians, who had done so much to create the maritime economy, were no longer in a position to share the profits. Phoenician trade fell increasingly to 'free' Greeks and Carthaginians, who had significant economic advantages over their long-time rivals. When Persia conquered Babylon in 539 BC, Sidon remained the leading Phoenician trading city, and naval headquarters. Persia left the coastal trading cities no option but compliance, tribute and service: the penalties for revolt were death, destruction and higher taxes. By contrast Lydian kings in Asia Minor prospered by encouraging commerce and levying sustainable tribute.[53] The wisdom of Croesus emphasised the difference between sea states and continental military empires.

Tyre and later Carthage prospered as quasi-independent economic maritime actors in a multi-polar age, using alliances, money and diplomacy to avoid heavy blows from more powerful states. Even the emergence of military superpowers was not a disaster, so long as there were at least two, who could cancel each other out, leaving space at the margins for sea power operators. But they could not compete with hegemonic superpowers. When Alexander the Great destroyed Tyre, and Rome annihilated Carthage, they were deliberately crushing the very idea of seapower.

Mesopotamian universal monarchy annihilated Phoenician sea states that depended on a balance of power, and prompted the creation of true seapowers. These emerged in rapidly expanding cities, centres of regional economic life, as the balance of advantage shifted towards larger ports and trading communities that could provide protection for commerce and fund maritime infrastructure, docks and harbours, to facilitate trade. That these cities were also building large temples, which served as navigational beacons, using the same tools, techniques and raw materials, suggests a critical synergy between economic and cultural concerns. Both were funded by taxes, or by prosperous citizens performing liturgies. Carthage, the greatest city in the Mediterranean at this time, grew rapidly on the proceeds of trade, as did cities in central Italy and the Aegean.

These changes were connected to a shift in the political structure of sea cities that began around 650 BC in Carthage. This process privileged merchants, while enhancing the political role of the middling order in the Greek maritime world. Now, the rulers of sea cities, kings, tyrants or oligarchs, needed the consent of the ruled. Unlike contemporary continental military powers Carthage was ruled by a Senate and two annually elected magistrates, or suffetes, drawn from the elite.[54] The magistrates 'derived their power from a combination of land, ships and trade, given sanction by ties to the priesthood'. To reinforce the new state the priests served a new god: Baal Hammon replaced the royal Tyrian deity Melquart.[55]

In 566 BC Athens established the Panathenaica as an inclusive state religious festival, combining costly ceremonials with the large-scale distribution of meat, a luxury for most Athenians. This may have been a conscious echo of Phoenician developments or a similar synergy of sea state politics, alphabetic writing, commerce and banking. Critically these ideas, as Plato observed, had been spread by maritime commerce. Sea states became oligarchies and even democracies to fund and protect maritime trade. When Athenian oligarchs brought the lower orders into mass participatory democracy, to restrain other oligarchs, they created a concept of civic life that emphasised debate, power sharing and progress. Solon made elite responsibility a civic duty, although the levelling process was slow.

The new political leaders secured the consent of the extended body politic through displays of public munificence and magnificence – cultural activity that engaged with ideas and methods from beyond the local region. Polycrates of Samos hired Mesopotamian scientists and astronomers, built a library and constructed a war fleet, complete with shipsheds, to bolster his legitimacy.[56] Later Greek authors concluded that he had made Samos a seapower. Both Greeks and Phoenicians erected gigantic temples and monumental statuary, based on Egyptian models, to demonstrate power and identity.

These developments reflected the rapid extension of seaborne commerce; falling transport costs created a pan-Mediterranean market, focusing trade into ever larger regional centres. By the late sixth century BC the Aegean was a major trade generator, 'the new Levant, a cluster of independent, dynamic, maritime trading centres as the interface between a colossal, centralised world of continental consumers in the east and an expanding mosaic of resources and markets, at all other points of the compass'.[57] When the Assyrians conquered the Levant, Carthage began to evolve into a separate, although still culturally connected state. The process was completed by the Babylonian conquest, which fatally damaged the Phoenician trading system. Profiting from an exodus of Phoenician traders and seafarers, Carthage closed the western seas to control Iberian trade. These ambitions, evidenced in the Roman-Carthaginian Treaties, were realised through specialised naval forces and state-controlled ports. Carthage chose to be a seapower when it chose to be independent.

The devastation of Phoenicia also created the opportunity for Greek seafarers to exploit the knowledge and methods of their stricken precursors. This process can be traced in Athenian literature, where the sea came to occupy a central role, one that led some authors to challenge the place of sweaty oarsmen and trade in civic life. After Salamis the Athenians selected Sidonian galleys as their ceremonial victory offerings, a tribute to the superior seafaring skills of the Phoenicians and their critical role in the creation of seapower culture. Ultimately Greek communities would fight for the independence that enabled them to prosper – this was the freedom that they valued. The ideas they fought for and many of the tools they used, from triremes to a written language, bore the imprint of the older civilisation. Athenian seapower had deep roots in an older culture.

Trade networks BC became more efficient and city-states increasingly self-aware. The old trade free-for-all, mixing commerce with random violence, was 'replaced by more discrete spheres of influence'; Greeks and Carthaginians marked out and policed exclusive sea areas. As trade expanded and ships became larger, power shifted from city to city: Corinth and Aegina, early leaders in Greek commerce, gave way to Athens, which had better harbours, ideally placed for eastern trade networks, and significant silver deposits. For practical reasons trade was taxed when it came ashore, at ports and markets, making large trading cities uncommonly wealthy, especially those that operated as entrepôts. Athens created the status of resident alien to accommodate the influx of wealthy merchants while recognising the importance of national identity. Most cities preferred a detached port, to isolate the civic populace from the destabilisation and cultural variety of the trading centre. The ports of Rome, Ostia and Portas were conveniently distant from the city walls.

In the mid-fifth century BC competition for exclusive control of trade routes and economic zones led to specialist warships, triremes and expensive standing navies. The cost of naval power in the trireme era obliged sea states to develop new resources. Hitherto privately owned multipurpose penteconters – vessels with two banks of oars, using up to fifty oarsmen – had been perfectly adequate for trade and warfare. They were eclipsed by the trireme, a specialised warship delivering a powerful blow with the ram, and reinforced by an upper deck carrying hoplite infantry for combat and amphibious operations. With three stepped, interlocked, banks of rowers, pulling 170 oars, triremes were configured for combat, settled by ramming and disabling enemy ships. Sea control could be secured by a fleet of triremes, relying on seafaring skill, not soldiers. Herman Wallinga attributed this breakthrough to Sidon and Carthage, around 540 BC, following their defeat by Phocean Greeks in the Tyrrhenian Sea. The costly new design forced states to build their own fleets, rather than rely on privately owned craft, and concentrated naval power in 'a few exceptionally rich cities'.[58] To protect their investment massive shipshed complexes were erected, enabling triremes to be brought ashore to dry out and refit. This startling escalation in defence spending was justified by the economic benefits of seapower: merchants gravitated towards cities that offered the best balance between protection, taxation and political participation. Outlying areas were gradually integrated into the new Mediterranean world, as supply centres, markets and colonies. By 500 BC the Mediterranean was effectively integrated, sharing trade, with a common means of exchange – and increasingly standardised methods of making war. The cultural exchange that propelled this synergy was commerce-led. Dynamic cities and states looked to the sea for prosperity; they needed naval power to secure the necessary control, and became sea states in the process.

As the scale of naval warfare escalated, the strategic capabilities of sea states, small port cities or islands, were overwhelmed by seapowers, larger, more populous states that consciously chose the sea. While Athens may have acquired the intellectual model of a sea state from the Phoenicians and the nearby island of Aegina, it would be silver, booming exports and control of grain supplies from the Black Sea that enabled it to become a seapower.

Carthage, the other ancient seapower, 'faced resolutely seaward, largely ignoring the land mass at its back, with its presence in north Africa accidental to the maritime logic of its location'.[59] It had little impact on local communities until the seventh and sixth centuries BC when the enslavement of the home cities of Tyre and Sidon turned Carthage into a free-standing trade hub; expanding demand for food obliged the city to extend its terrestrial footprint. Carthage developed the Phoenician seapower model in a more benign environment. Initially it obtained timber and food from Sardinia and Sicily, developing local resources with advanced Phoenician agricultural methods. Local peoples were assimilated. Critically, Carthage controlled access to highly profitable Spanish metals, and it would fight for those trade routes.

Located at a distance from any other great power, Carthage had little need for armies, and nothing in its Phoenician origins equipped it to meet the continental military savagery of hoplite battle. Limited terrestrial security costs helped Carthage become the largest Mediterranean city, following the Babylonian conquest of Phoenicia and Egypt, shifting the economic centre of the sea westward. By the fifth century BC Carthage had become 'a huge city-state, powerful at sea, where it deployed slave-propelled galleys to extract tribute from distant ports (themselves intensifying extraction from their hinterlands), but whose later explicit terrestrial militarism, much of it dependent on mercenary armies, was in part a subsequent response to aggression by others, in the first instance heavily armed, probing Greeks'.[60] The Carthaginian economy was monetarised in the fifth century, primarily to pay mercenary armies deployed against Greek Sicily.

As the Mediterranean became a closed political system the struggle for resources intensified and the most powerful states sought empire, using naval power to escalate the level of violence.[61] While many states built impressive navies, few were seapowers. Fifth-century BC Athens built an empire on a rich vein of silver, a population boom and a warrior culture that turned citizens into socially prestigious hoplites. After the democratic reforms of 508–507 BC these assets were harnessed by elite leaders, exploiting the political weight of the middling sort. The growth of political participation was mirrored in other areas of civic life, in the arts, theatre and commerce.

Persia, the first superpower, placed peninsular Greece in a similar position to the Phoenician cities in the Assyrian period, 'if with more immediately surrounding sea room for manoeuvre'. Persia ruled a population greater than that of the entire Mediterranean basin, and controlled almost one-quarter of the Mediterranean coast, Cyprus, Anatolia, the Levant and Egypt. It directed vassal fleets, including the first triremes, that dwarfed the Greek and Carthaginian fleets, and appeared bent on exceeding the territorial limits of previous Mesopotamian empires. Levantine and Ionian satellites profited from trade that brought Attic pottery and Argive purple cloth to distant Susa, and in return they provided Persian naval power. These cities were tributary naval subcontractors. Persia was not a seapower, having no sense of the sea, or any strategic vision beyond military 'power projection'.[62]

Trade-focused Athens incurred the wrath of Darius the Great by supporting the Ionian Greek revolt against Persian rule. The revolt was crushed by a massive Persian/Phoenician fleet at Lade in 494 BC, leaving mainland Greece exposed. A mere fourteen years later, Greek resolve, tactical insight and warrior ethos smashed the Persian fleet at Salamis, reversing the tide of universal monarchy, and heralding the dawn of seapower as a fundamental cultural and strategic factor.

Seapower, a distinctive socio-political response to unique circumstances, emerged in the eastern Mediterranean between 2000 and 500 BC. Sea cities evolved to service the resource demands of great land-locked powers: Egypt, Anatolia and above all Mesopotamia. Sailing ships moved timber and metals over increasing distances. Insular Tyre, the ultimate sea city, relied on the sea for security and wealth. By 1000 BC these networks were expanding westward, to Sicily, Sardinia and the Atlantic coast, to obtain scarce metals. These trades made the sea worth controlling, and they facilitated cultural exchange between traders and suppliers. Trade required a degree of security from predation, by rival states or pirates, which became core missions for sea states, and a key point of distinction between them and land states. Merchants transformed the Mediterranean, operating from cities on or near the coast, dominated by artificial harbour structures and marketplaces. Sea empires were created to control and tax trade, in order to fund maritime security.[63] Making the sea a controlled space and legislating for exclusive state control turned predators into pirates, and dealing with this threat gave sea states internal political legitimacy. Specialist, standing navies were funded by reconstructing the state as a tax-raising, increasingly inclusive polity. The constabulary force that dealt with pirates could be expanded to deny vital sea routes to rival states. The instrument of that transformation was the trireme, the defining motif of ancient seapower. By contrast, autocratic continental empires generally ignored the economic problem of piracy, using naval power to suppress seapower states and project their military might.

While many cities and states were active at sea, dominion over the ocean was of limited strategic significance until control of the sea could be sustained. The great powers of the Bronze Age, continental land empires operating on the same land mass, settled their differences at key terrestrial communication hubs. Sea power could not be a serious strategic choice until important states were separated by significant bodies of water and navies were capable of controlling them, stopping economic activity and the movement of armies by sea. Consequently seapower identities were only suitable for small, weak states that could secure an asymmetric advantage by focusing on the sea.

The politics of sea states evolved as trade expanded. Bronze Age palace cultures were replaced by less formal structures, dominated by elite groups having 'strong mercantile interests'.[64] Trade escaped the control of cities and states, which had to compete for a share of the taxes of an unruly offshore world. Sea culture impacted land powers, the hitherto static continental Egyptians shifting their capital north into the Nile Delta on several occasions. When Alexander the Great established a new coastal capital he emphasised Egypt's belated integration into the wider Mediterranean world. Shifting the capital back to riverine Cairo after the Arab conquest marked another significant cultural shift – from Mediterranean to Middle Eastern state. Dynamic maritime cultures prompted alphabetic writing, and reduced the regional languages to Greek, Punic, Aramaic and Latin.

Sea power became a serious strategic force in the fifth century BC, as Carthage and Athens built seapower empires, 'superbly adapted to, and successfully exploitative of, the Mediterranean's attributes and rhythms'.[65] Both harnessed specific combinations of internal and external opportunity, while their popular government and wealth prompted a fatal combination of fear and envy in land powers. Ultimately the sequence of conflicts that stretched from Salamis in 480 to the annihilation of Carthage in 146 BC transformed the Mediterranean into a single political and economic unit, linked by sea trade, but controlled by Roman Continental Imperialism, which swept aside all rivals – by sea as well as land.

Sea-based cultures and forms of representative government overcame the opposition of larger, more populous river-based theocracies, with their unchanging cycles of flood and harvest, because they offered hope, and above all progress – both intellectual and material. People made new lives in port cities. The Greeks came to dominate the cultural dimension, transmitting their dynamic, inclusive thinking through an alphabetic language, sea trade and success in war, shaping the great western powers, Rome and Carthage. The key lay in the creation of civic political authority, and a shared 'Greek' resistance to the imposition of a Persian monoculture. At its beating heart seapower was a response to the challenge of expanding maritime trade systems in a precarious world, one that existed at the whim of vast, static continental/military cultures.

The battle of Salamis transformed seapower into a political force. In a narrow channel, separating an island from the mainland, close by the ports and cities of trade, a fractious group of city-states, riven by diffuse political structures and deep-rooted rivalries, pooled their resources to defend an idea. They were heavily outnumbered, and their leaders, the Athenians, had already seen their city reduced to ruins. They were saved by a shared sense of Greek identity, largely built outside the peninsula, where men from many cities took part in shared maritime enterprises. To meet an existential threat to this imagined homeland the Greeks were prepared, if only temporarily, to pool their efforts against a common enemy. That temporaneity was a consequence of sea culture, with its emphasis on individuals, competition and variety. Ironically, the fighting method that gave the Greeks an edge, once the triremes had smashed into one another, namely armoured hoplite infantry, was a product of their endemic fratricidal struggles. The same methods gave the Syracusan Greeks a notable victory over the Carthaginians at Himera, on the very same day as the battle of Salamis, if Herodotus is to be believed. These triumphs were the culmination of the many processes that created the Mediterranean.

It was appropriate that seapower struck the decisive blow against Persian ambition. Little wonder that the Greeks felt obliged to provide it with a pre-history and open a debate about its meaning that has resonated down to the present. The seapower state that evolved in the classical Mediterranean would be a model for other sea empires: the last of them, Britain, applied the ideas that had ruled the Aegean to a world empire.

CHAPTER 2

Constructing a Seapower
ATHENS, DEMOCRACY AND EMPIRE

Modern concepts of seapower, as identity and strategy, were constructed after the battle of Salamis in 480 BC. Recent events were read back into dim and mythic pasts, providing precedents for something that was, in reality, both novel and unique. While Athens consciously chose to become a seapower, developing a distinctive cultural identity, the process was informed by pre-existing ideas and examples. In the Greek world dynamic change needed the validation of past precedent, often reimagined or even invented. Mythology occupied a central place in the construction of seapower. New versions of the past were repeated until they became integral to Athenian culture, reflected in art, literature, science and statecraft.

The intellectual history of seapower began with a relatively short list of Greek literary sources that applied the Athenian model retrospectively, obscuring the early development of maritime hegemony, in theory and practice, behind ideas and approaches from their own era. Fifth century BC Greeks did not invent navies or naval warfare.[1] The sea was important in the Bronze Age, leaving a legacy of folk memories, including Minoan thalassocracy and

An allegory of Salamis by the nineteenth-century German artist Wilhelm von Kaulbach

The Athenian Empire

Agamemnon's Trojan expedition, memories that retained their power for more than a thousand years after the fall of Knossos.

Greek naval power had been relatively insignificant before the Persian War. Although some Greek states possessed significant commercial fleets, developed through long-distance trade, they could not compete with the Phoenician war fleets deployed by Mesopotamian and Egyptian rulers. Greek state 'navies' consisted of privately owned two-banked penteconters, ideal for trade, piracy or war, moving fighting men and high-value cargoes. Such activity made relatively limited demands on the host society. Seafarers and seafaring were marginal to the culture of most Greek cities. Relatively late to embrace seapower, the Greeks borrowed extensively from the Phoenician pioneers.[2]

The Greeks became the pioneers of seapower theory because their literary tradition transmitted seapower concepts to later ages. Ideas, opinions and events that they recorded influenced every subsequent discussion. Victory at Salamis prompted the literary construction of a distinct seapower concept and the necessary myths to ensure it did not appear unduly novel in land-based societies that venerated precedent, real or imagined. While Herodotus and Thucydides recognised the Phoenician contribution they needed Greek precursors, quietly transforming Themistocles' revolutionary seapower argument into the culmination of an evolving Greek thalassocratic concept.[3]

It is revealing that they provided different explanations for this process. As the historian of Greek relations with barbarians, Herodotus dismissed Minos as mere legend, focusing on Polycrates of Samos: 'the first Greek known to us who planned to have the mastery of the sea [thalassokratia] ... who entertained every hope to rule Ionia and islands'.[4] In this passage Herodotus was the first, but certainly not the last, to conflate the possession of a large navy with being a seapower. In reality Samos was far too small to entertain such ambitions, and Polycrates was a naval contractor to Saite Egypt, a continental power that could not generate the timber needed to build large ships, let alone a cultural model that empowered the ocean. The Egyptian kings hired Polycrates when their Lydian allies and Phoenician naval agents fell under Persian rule. When Persia conquered Egypt in 525 BC Samian naval might withered, and the Persians executed Polycrates in 517.[5]

Thucydides, equally anxious to construct lists of prior thalassocratic states, developed the legendary Minos to debate the profits and penalties of seapower. His Minoan seapower created order and stability, important elements of progress, suppressing the random violence and theft of pirates. Athens inherited the task of policing the seas because it did not want to share the economic benefits of seapower with others.[6] The continuation of this constabulary work during the Peloponnesian War emphasised the critical part it played in legitimising seapower.[7] According to Thucydides, Minos created a navy to maintain order, control trade routes and acquire hegemony over other cities. Many Greek cities willingly accepted 'enslavement' in return for a share of the commercial profit, highlighting the moral failings of empire and subject peoples. The same flaws, he implied, lay at the heart of the Athenian Empire. He did not name the cities enslaved by Minos, but his audience knew Minoan domination was central to the Athenian foundation myth, the Theseus cycle. The price of enslavement had been blood sacrifice, Athenian youths slaughtered and eaten by the Minotaur. Thucydides used this cruel precursor to question the moral basis of seapower; Athenian resentment of Minoan imperialism had been echoed in Greek resentment of Athenian imperialism. The monster, he implied, would always be slain.

Athens had transformed the Delian League into a sea empire, by the ruthless application of force, and Thucydides wished his audience to reflect 'on the long-term consequences of the forceful exploitation of other states, rather than to build approval for Athens' empire'. Minoan rule had been an improvement on the chaotic world of pirates, but it was fuelled by avarice, and came to ruin after the Trojan War, a grand piratical raid organised by Agamemnon, who was Minos' successor as the Aegean thalassocrat. Thucydides preferred the order and stability of cultured city-states to such rampant ambition. As long as they were free Sparta and Athens were bulwarks of this world. Freedom from alien rule was the greatest gift; it had been the key issue in the Persian War, and he lamented that Athenian ambition had allowed the Persians to re-enter the Greek world.[8] Thucydides' account of the Trojan War was an exemplary precursor of the Sicilian expedition. In both cases greed and ambition, fuelled by power and wealth, led to catastrophe.

Herodotus' treatment of Polycrates stressed the link between sea power and specialist warships. Thucydides understood that the significance of seapower changed when states realised it was worth fighting for, which he dated to the seventh century BC, when Phocean Greek traders fought the Phoenicians and Etruscans for access to Spanish and Sardinian metals.[9] While the battles were small they pushed the development of warships from mobile fighting platforms for infantry to specialist single-purpose craft that expressed the user's seafaring skills. The first naval battles involved pente-conters. Defeated by the Phoceans, the Phoenicians and the Carthaginians developed the first specialist warship, the trireme.

The trireme rendered older approaches to naval power, battles settled by close-range missile fire and infantry combat, obsolete. However, it was significantly more expensive to build and operate than any previous ship, and useless for commercial purposes. No longer able to rely on mobilising privately owned vessels, states were obliged to build their own warships. Trireme crews needed constant practice to master the complex rowing system, followed by squadron manoeuvres to be effective in battle. Trireme navies required new harbours, shipsheds for maintenance, large stocks of shipbuilding timber and other supplies, along with effective administration. In sum, just as navies became capable of implementing a sea power strategy their operating costs rose exponentially.[10] Persia could mobilise the neces-sary funds, but smaller states could only compete through fundamental cultural transformation, remodelling the state to sustain trireme fleets.

The trireme made sea power a viable strategic alternative to land power, especially for medium-sized states, as long as they were insular or suffi-ciently distant from Persian military might. However, it was costly: trireme fleets required a money economy and new revenue streams. Persia bought this naval power from contractors, but Athens had to rebuild the state to generate the necessary resources – in the process it became a seapower.

The Phoenician cities pioneered the trireme to secure the trade of the western Mediterranean, but they remained naval contractors to the Levantine great powers, paying part of their annual tribute in professional services. The trireme was first adopted on a significant scale by Egypt, which funded the Samian fleet. By 530 BC a combined Egyptian and Samian fleet threatened Persian interests, prompting Cambyses to invade and conquer Egypt 'and the sea' in 525, using a Phoenician fleet.[11] Persia acquired 300 triremes and new bases, strategic instruments it needed to attempt a universal monarchy. The running costs of the fleet, even in peacetime, consumed much of the empire's revenue. Cambyses' response, increasing taxes, sparked widespread revolts across the empire.[12] The element of choice was critical: the Persian navy existed to project military power beyond the Levantine coast, to Egypt, Ionia, Greece, Italy and even Carthage. It did not reflect defensive needs, a shift to a seapower identity, or a change in Persian culture.

Persian ambitions were not satisfied by the conquest of Egypt. In 517 BC a Persian fleet seized Samos, which had not operated a fleet since the conquest of Egypt, and a reconnaissance mission travelled west to Sicily, to assess the naval powers at outer reaches of the Greek world. Another fleet, based in Ionia, was used to coerce Greek cities. In 500 BC it forced Naxos to cease economic competition with Ionian cities under Persian control.

Although the mainland Greek states remained outside the Persian Empire, the conquest of Egypt meant their days of independence were numbered. Persian power and wealth could overwhelm any competitor. When the Ionian Greeks revolted against Persian rule in 500 BC, 300 locally based Persian triremes fell into rebel hands, along with enough timber to build another 53. Persia soon dispatched a Phoenician fleet into the Aegean. Despite losing a major naval battle they were back in Ionian waters by 494 with over 600 triremes, winning a comprehensive victory at Lade by a combination of overwhelming might, superior skill and bribery. The example was intended to terrify smaller states into submission.

Instead the defeat at Lade prompted Athens to build a trireme navy, a costly process that transformed it into a seapower. Hitherto sea states had been marginal players, small cities or islands, caught between the millstones of continental great powers. Athens was different: it was larger, wealthier, proudly independent and above all democratic. Athenian seapower was only possible in the wake of the democratisation of domestic politics engineered by Cleisthenes in 508–507 BC. Themistocles exploited the political, social and cultural consequences of democracy to create Athenian seapower in the 480s, the second fundamental transformation of the Athenian state within a generation.

Little wonder that the novelty and cost of seapower generated a heated political debate between an oligarchic elite and a populist demos. For Herodotus seapower as democracy, strategy and culture made Athens 'greater than ever': 'the new freedom from tyranny released reserves of power and confidence which enabled her to achieve successes that would have been unthinkable only a generation before'. The Athenians became the bravest of the Greeks, because they were fighting for themselves.[13] Long before Athens became a seapower, democracy made it powerful and alarmed the Spartans. Athenian freedom and progress challenged their static worldview; the Spartans feared that 'if the people of Attica were free, they would be likely to be as powerful as themselves' and no longer acknowledge Spartan leadership. To retain their dominance the Spartans proposed restoring the Athenian tyrants, by force. Although Corinthian objections blocked the Spartan plan, Persia shared these concerns, telling the Athenians that if they wanted peace they must restore the tyrants. Athenian democracy and progress challenged Spartan dominance of Greece, and its ability to control the helots, along with Persian control of Ionia. Critically, Spartan fears pre-dated the creation of an Athenian trireme navy. Herodotus demonstrated Athenian cultural difference with a theatrical reference. When a play dealing with the fall of Miletus to Persian troops reduced the Athenian audience to tears, the dramatist was fined a thousand drachma, 'for recalling to them their own misfortunes', and banned from putting on any further productions.[14]

Having supported the Ionian rebels, and helped destroy the Persian regional capital at Sardis, Athens faced annihilation at the hands of a vengeful Great King. In 490 BC, 600 triremes transported 20,000 of King Darius' troops to Greece. As the Greeks lacked a significant trireme force the Persian ships operated as transports, rowing only one bank of oars.[15] After defeating the Persians on the beach at Marathon the Athenian General Miltiades recognised that the enduring threat required a naval response. Themistocles persuaded the Athenian demos to use a dramatic increase in silver output from the mines at Laurium in 483 to build another hundred triremes, adding to the original century, and pay for sustained crew training. The initial 100 Athenian triremes had been built after Lade to prevent Aegina, which owned around 99 triremes, from becoming a Persian invasion base.[16]

Athens consciously rebuilt itself as a seapower to sustain a large fleet of purpose-built warships for control of the seas. Themistocles recognised that Persia posed an existential threat to Athens, and all of Greece. Persia had the military and naval power to overwhelm the annoying, independent states of

Greece, reducing them to tribute-paying satrapies. He used that danger to persuade his fellow citizens to transform newly democratic Athens into a seapower, and deepen the democratic grip on power. This radical double reconstruction shifted political power from the landed elite to the urban demos, increased state revenues, bound the elite into state service and laid the foundations of seapower imperialism.[17] These processes were profoundly controversial, and remain critical to our understanding of seapower as culture. Having created a trireme navy the extraordinary costs compelled Athens to become a seapower empire.

Undaunted by defeat at Marathon, Darius planned another, larger, operation, only to be distracted by an uprising in Egypt. On assuming the throne in 486 BC, Xerxes, initially uninterested, was persuaded to act by his cousin Mardonius and the Pisistratidae, exiled Athenian tyrants. Herodotus had Xerxes declare: 'we shall extend the Persian territory as far as God's heaven reaches', and 'bring all mankind under our yoke, alike those who are guilty and those who are innocent of doing us wrong'. This blasphemous outburst neatly foreshadowed Themistocles' attribution of victory at Salamis to the gods, envious that one man should claim to rule over Europe and Asia.[18] He viewed Xerxes' defeat as divine punishment for overweening ambition.

The Persian invasion plan may have been prompted by the very public passage of Themistocles' naval bill in 483. Shortly afterwards Xerxes ordered a strategic canal to be dug at Mount Athos, and in 480 decided to eliminate any naval power that could threaten Persian coastal possessions. This last point is critical. The Ionian revolt, and Greek interference in the Persian Empire, fuelled by democratic ideas and aggressive commerce, challenged the Persian political and economic model. Xerxes mobilised 1,200 triremes, 'by far the largest battlefleet ever assembled in antiquity, certainly in combination with the land forces', including large reserves, vital when operating at a distance from Levantine bases. The Great King assumed that all Greek cities, including those on Sicily and Corfu, might become involved. Having assembled a monstrous fleet, Xerxes considered exploiting it to maximum advantage, following up the anticipated conquest of Greece by striking west, to deter other states, and perhaps reduce the outlying Phoenician city of Carthage to subservience.[19] Such imperial extension would be consistent with the ambitions of previous Mesopotamian rulers.

The Persian invasion depended on the fleet to support and sustain a massive army. Despite losing many ships in storms as they rounded Cape Artemesium, and the delay at Thermopylae, the Persian army pushed on, seizing and burning Athens. The populace fled to offshore islands. Xerxes' strategy of systematically reducing the Greek states to vassalage collapsed at the battle of Salamis in 480 BC. It is probable that Persian warships, once again being used as transports, were not fully manned. A trireme could be rowed effectively with only one bank of oars, sixty men, but it could not generate maximum power. By contrast the Greek ships had full complements of oarsmen and extra infantry. This was why Themistocles chose to fight in a bottleneck: a battlespace that minimised the importance of maritime skill, and emphasised superior muscle power and armoured infantry. Herodotus attributed victory to the Greeks holding their line, whereas the Persian squadrons did not.[20] This should be instantly recognisable as a description of hoplite combat.

On the day of battle, Athens remained a state in transition; it owned 200 triremes but could only crew half of them. The rest were loaned to allies. These manpower shortages compelled the statesmen of Athenian seapower, beginning with Themistocles, to create an empire to fund the fleet.[21] Their rationale was simple: victory at Salamis, and at Platea in the following year, could not secure the freedom of Greece. To resist the Persian threat Greece needed unity and allies; Athens sought those allies in Ionia and Egypt.

In Thucydides' carefully chosen words Salamis became the defining moment of cultural transformation. Themistocles' revolutionary concept reinvented the staid, landed City of Athens, a city that considered Marathon the acme of glory, as the imperial metropolis of a unique sea empire. In Thomas Hobbes's translation the Athenians abandoned their city, 'went a shipboard and became seamen'.[22] This was not a tactical choice: it marked a change of culture. The credit and the blame belonged to Themistocles.

However, the glory days of Athenian naval superiority lay in the future, and required further fundamental change. It required a generation of professional training to create the battle-winning tactical sophistication of the Second Peloponnesian War (431–404 BC). In 480 BC the Athenians acknowledged the Sidonians, who had the honour of carrying Xerxes in their flagship, as the masters of trireme warfare. After Salamis three Sidonian triremes were laid up as trophies, reflecting Athenian pride that they had triumphed over the victors of Lade, their sea power precursors.[23] The Athenian victory statue erected at the pan-Greek cult centre at Delphi held the beak of a trireme; it was paid for from the spoils of battle. Yet Salamis was the precursor of Athenian naval greatness, not the proof. The navy would only mature when Athens possessed an empire to fund it.

The return of a reduced but still powerful Persian army to Attica in the spring of 479 BC exposed fundamental divisions within the Greek alliance. The Spartans, more concerned to fortify the Corinthian isthmus than aid their Attic allies, delayed the dispatch of their army until the Athenians pointed out that no walls could secure the Peloponnesus against a Persian army conveyed by Athenian ships. Having learnt the value of sea power, the Persian general Mardonius invited the Athenians to join the Great King, and help conquer the rest of Greece. The Persian offer prompted belated Spartan action, although in a bitter exchange that foreshadowed future conflict Spartan envoys blamed the Persian War on Athenian ambition 'to extend your empire'.[24] In a passage of startling ferocity Herodotus demanded that his audience acknowledge the dark side of the new democracy: when an Athenian councillor suggested accepting the Persian terms he was stoned to death by fellow councillors; his family shared his fate, at the hands of the wives and children of his killers.

Having demonstrated Athenian resolve Herodotus followed the land campaign to victory at Platea before turning back to the sea. In the spring the Greek fleet, predominantly Athenian, but under Spartan command, sailed to attack the Persian fleet off the island of Samos, encouraged by reports that the Ionians would rebel. Forewarned, or short of money, the Persians dismissed the Phoenician contingent; the rest, manned by Ionian Greeks, fled to Cape Mycale. Here the ships were pulled ashore, surrounded by a hastily built stockade, and guarded by a sizable army. Undeterred by the show of resistance, and aided by Ionian rebels, the Greeks landed, formed up and, led by the Athenians, stormed the stockade. Having plundered the camp they incinerated the Persian fleet. Victory prompted more Ionian cities to rebel, reopening the fundamental clash of cultures that would spark the next war. The Spartans wanted to resettle Ionian rebels in mainland Greece; the Athenians preferred an Ionian empire. With Greece secure the Spartans went home, leaving the Athenian Xanthippus in command.

Having liberated the Ionian Islands the fleet sailed north, to the Hellespont. Finding Xerxes' famous bridge of boats had been scattered by wind and wave, the Greeks besieged and captured Sestos, the European end of the bridge, dedicating the mooring cables, the keys to Europe, at the Athenian temple. Having expelled the barbarians from Europe, Xanthippus left a grim warning for other would-be conquerors, providing a dramatic finale to Herodotus' cyclical history of the rise and fall of Persian imperium.

At the fall of Sestos the Greeks captured the Satrap Artacytes, a man they believed guilty of murder, theft and defiling sacred ground. Despite the offer of suitable bribes Xanthippus showed no mercy: 'having nailed him to a board, they left him hanging thereupon. As for the son of Artacytes, him they stoned to death before his eyes.' Not only did Artacytes have Greek blood on his hands, but his grandfather had encouraged Cyrus to begin Persia's unholy wars of empire, making the punishment righteous, fitting and appropriate.[25] The crucifixion of Artacytes, an act of unprecedented savagery, conveyed a powerful message. Xerxes should have remained quietly in Asia, while his failure had been foreshadowed by the defeat and death of Cyrus and Cambyses in the vainglorious pursuit of universal monarchy.[26] The Athenian victory restored balance, the central aim of any seapower.

Having expelled Persian power from Europe the scene necessarily shifted to the politics of Greece: the Second Peloponnesian War was raging when Herodotus completed his book around 430 BC. While Athens and Sparta struggled for hegemony in the Greek world, his audience looked to the Persian War for heroes and examples.[27] Deliberately projecting historical events into the present Herodotus made Athenian resolve and determination at once essential to Greek victory in 480 and 479 BC, and 'a threat to Greek freedom and the cause of unavoidable conflict and suffering'. He laced this theme through the text, using the plot device of ironic foreshadowing, inviting readers and listeners to link past and present. Thucydides has Pericles quote Herodotus in the 'Funeral Oration' of 430 BC, emphasising thematic continuity between the two authors, and the contemporary familiarity of Herodotus' text.[28] The impact of Herodotus' critique of Athenian imperialism on Thucydides has rarely been acknowledged.

Fascinated by variety, expressed through culture, Herodotus' text was an extended exercise comparing and contrasting different cultures, the rise of Imperial Persia, which threatened to impose an alien monoculture on the

Greek world, providing the narrative thread. He foreshadowed the next existential clash of cultures, constantly contrasting the Spartans, who lacked ambition and foresight and were content simply to expel the barbarians, with the expansive, dynamic Athenians. Thucydides developed the argument that cultural divergence caused the Peloponnesian Wars.[29] Sparta had little to fear from sea power strategy, it was effectively self-sufficient, and dominated the military balance. The Spartans feared Athens' seapower culture of radical democracy, imperialism and expansion – agendas that culminated in the construction of the 'Long Walls' that made Athens a strategic island in the Attic countryside, and a bastion of imperial grandeur – far more than it feared her triremes. As Athens moved from democratic state to seapower the radical combination of naval might and democratic politics threatened the existing balance of power in Greece, challenging Persian imperialism and Spartan authority. The symbols of the Athenian empire were the trireme and Athenian grandeur.

Furthermore the character of Athenian seapower was closely linked to that of Themistocles, a man of genius and resolve, but widely considered ruthless, cunning, deceptive and greedy. Herodotus suggested Themistocles' trickery had made the rest of Greece suspicious of the Athenians before Salamis in 480 BC. Yet Themistocles alone understood that the Persian army and fleet formed a single strategic unit, one that could be defeated at sea. He chose the battlefield at Salamis, and lured the Persians to their defeat, only to be denied any credit for the victory. His agenda was obvious: his first thought after Salamis was to force other Greek cities to contribute to the cost of the Athenian fleet, besieging the nearby island of Andros as an example.[30] To fund the Athenian fleet, vital for both Athenian and Greek security, Athens needed a larger economic base, an empire. Thucydides emphasised how Themistocles' deception and guile made Athens equal to Sparta: the 'sudden growth of Athenian seapower and the daring which the Athenians had shown in the war against the Persians alarmed the Spartans and other Greeks'. While Thucydides saw Themistocles as an Athenian patriot, opponents cited his supposed 'treachery' to discredit democracy and seapower, rendering the alleged flaws of an individual as generic failings of culture and identity. Herodotus acquitted him of doing his country any harm, while Thucydides used his clashes with the Spartans, imagined and real, as the foundation of later Athenian policy.[31]

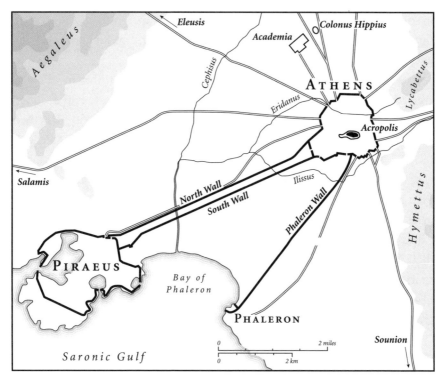

Ancient Athens

Themistocles' 'Long Walls' were begun before the Persian War: linking the city to the Piraeus harbour they enabled Athens to adopt a sea power strategy. By transforming Athens into a strategic island the walls shifted the focus of the city from land to sea, protecting the urban demos, while leaving aristocratic landed estates unprotected. Thucydides had Themistocles argue 'that if the Athenians became a sea-faring people they would have every advantage in adding to their power. Indeed it was he who first ventured to tell the Athenians that their future was on the sea. Thus he at once began to join in laying the foundations of their empire.'[32]

Thucydides' brief discussion of the period between the Persian and Second Peloponnesian wars emphasised Athenian imperial aggression, including the war in Egypt, as a struggle for control and resources. The creation of the Delian League, and the conversion of the League into an Athenian Empire of tribute payments, enforced by amphibious power, was followed by the crushing victory over a Persian fleet at the Eurymedon river in southern Asia Minor around 466 BC. In this campaign the triremes were fitted with additional deck space for infantry. Athens no longer feared any naval rivals, so it could focus on projecting its power.[33]

Athens had only accepted leadership of an Aegean/Ionian alliance, created following the victory at Mycale in 479 BC, after Sparta had declined the honour. The Delian League traded independence for security, Athenian protection enabling Ionian cities and islands to remain outside the Persian Empire. The League was essential to fund Athenian security, and Athens was the dominant member. Athenian seapower was far more expensive than the military might of Sparta: men were cheap, fleets were not. Athens used the League as a tax base, combining revenue from commerce and land. Cities that revolted were conquered, stripped of ships and city walls, lost their vote at League meetings and forced to pay. In many cases revolts were sparked by oligarchic leaders who preferred Persian rule or Spartan hegemony. Little wonder that Athens preferred its satellites to adopt democratic government.[34] Democracy became a strategic weapon.

Initially the alliance was sustained by the ongoing war with Persia. Victory at the Eurymedon river was celebrated by setting up a red-figure shield showing Athena 'holding the decorative prow of a Phoenician ship'. The League quickly became a tribute system. Athens used the cash to maintain and above all drill the fleet, creating a tactically dominant professional naval force. In effect Athens disarmed its allies, reducing them to subjects: 'the foundation of Athens' power was her fleet. The Delian League, composed almost entirely of islands and coastal cities could be controlled only by a powerful fleet.' As the number of League members that owned warships fell, Athens acquired absolute dominion at sea. Sea power controlled the exports and imports of League members, which could be stopped without the need for land operations, while Athenian expertise in siege warfare enabled it to conquer recalcitrant cities. By 460 BC only three islands, Chios, Lesbos and Samos, provided ships; the rest paid in cash. A decade later Athens began installing garrisons in League cities, a trend that increased when war broke out in 431 BC.[35]

The legitimacy of the League was built on security, against foreign threats and piracy. Not only did League forces occupy the pirate island of Skyros, but Athens continued to provide anti-piracy patrols during the Second Peloponnesian War. It was cheaper to conciliate than conquer, so the tribute levied from the islands fell when the League Treasury was moved to Athens, and used to transform the city into an imperial capital.[36] Athens took the opinions of islands more seriously than that of mainland communities, because island bases were the strategic keys to the Aegean and the Hellespont, the core of the Athenian Empire. Losing control of the islands would transform the Aegean from economic highway to battlefield, and the cost of restoring Athenian control would be high. Conquering Samos cost 1,200 talents. The League's massive monetary reserves, held on the Acropolis, enabled Athens to fund a sea-control strategy based on trireme fleets and siege warfare. League revenues enabled Athens to act as a great power.[37] Such long-term funding has always been critical to sea power strategy. After the Persian War, Athens dropped the level of League tribute to 'moderate' levels, but the outbreak of war with Sparta in 431 BC prompted forced collections of additional cash and trade controls, using the fleet to coerce erstwhile allies. Straining the resources of subject communities led to revolts.[38]

Relations between Athens and Sparta broke down after the Thasian Revolt of 465 BC and the replacement of Athens' pro-Spartan aristocratic leadership by radical democrats who took their lead from Themistocles.[39] Although ostracised and resident in Asia Minor, the founding father of the seapower state remained a major influence, hoping for a return to power. His reputation became a battleground on which rival political ideologues marked out their positions. The contemporary significance of Themistocles' ideas explains his prominence in the texts of Herodotus and Thucydides.

The election of Themistocles' associate Ephialtes, and Pericles, to command Athenian forces after the victory at Eurymedon, ensured further democratisation. When the Athenian Assembly discussed sending aid to suppress the helot revolt at Ithone, Ephialtes publicly stated that Sparta was a 'natural enemy'. Although the aristocrat Cimon won the subsequent vote, taking troops to aid Sparta, Ephialtes exploited Cimon's absence to push through further democratic reforms, and ostracised him in 461 BC. Fearing their allies would bring 'some revolutionary policy' into the conflict zone, the Spartans sent Cimon and his Athenian army home with ill-mannered haste. This insult ended the alliance of the Persian War, and accelerated the evolution of the Delian League into an Athenian Empire.[40]

The empire combined hard power with legal controls: Athenian law courts became the court of appeal, friendly to democrats, steadily encroaching on the higher jurisdiction of the Delian League. Athenian law upheld continuity and stability, key requirements for effective economic exploitation. It legitimised the obligation of allies, later subjects, to pay their dues, provided a public forum in which these obligations could be justified, and sanctioned the use of force. Ultimately, Athenian law subverted the independence of their allies as effectively as the shift from ship and soldier service to cash payment.[41] The law worked hand in hand with naval power to sustain an empire that could only be maintained with the resources of the allies, later subjects.

Although the initial object of the new navy had been achieved at Salamis and Mycale, the Athenians, unlike the Spartans, could not simply go home. To secure their city against Persian attacks they needed to mobilise much of maritime Greece and vital shipbuilding resources from outside Greece. Ropes and sails came from Egypt, timber and pitch from Macedon. Resource dependency and economic necessity forced Athens to engage with the wider world, increasing the temptation of imperialism.[42]

The astronomical cost of running a large trireme fleet meant few states attempted to join the front rank of naval powers. Few could afford the ships and infrastructure without fundamentally changing their political system to spread the burden across the wealthy elite. Victories at Mycale and then the Eurymedon river enlarged the economic base of Athenian seapower, creating an empire that could sustain the navy. Athens had become a seapower by defeating the vast resources of the Persian Empire. This new-found wealth was shared with the people, through festivals, often involving large distributions of meat, state employment, full pay for oarsmen and other benefits that welded the people to the new identity. Money and democracy enabled populist Athenian leaders to impose a new identity on the state, altering the political balance of power, and alarming the armoured horsemen who feared the socially levelling consequences.

Wealth and power prompted an ambitious attempt to separate Egypt from Persian rule in the 450s. By sending aid to Egyptian rebels Athens attempted to translate seapower into great power. Opposition within the League had been crushed, Sparta stood aside. Reviving an independent Egypt would create a great-power ally, distract Persian military power, and secure strategic resources. Athens understood that only an independent Egypt could balance the Persian hegemon.

The dramatic expansion of Athenian imperial power within little more than a generation made continental powers anxious. More concerned with stability and order, they feared the destabilising politics of levelling democracy, delivered by Athenian naval might. For Thucydides such fears were a prime cause of the Second Peloponnesian War.[43] Success fed Athenian ambition – and arrogance. Having resisted Persian invasions not once, but twice, Athenians spoke of taking the war to Persia or conquering Carthage. It was hardly surprising that Sparta became fearful – the removal of her aristocratic allies, Ephialtes' reforms and the 'Long Walls' enhanced Athenian security, while success in Egypt would magnify it abroad and promote the democracy.

Pericles, son of Xanthippus, believed Athens could defeat Sparta and maintain her grip on Ionia and the Aegean. By the time he became effective head of state in 461 BC an unparalleled growth of wealth and prestige, intimately linked to the sea empire, had changed Athens. He controlled the unrelentingly aggressive demos by humouring the voters with promises of plunder and profit. Twice he accepted war with Sparta, which had good reason to be profoundly alarmed by Athenian ambition, rather than challenge the citizens.

The First Peloponnesian War (460–445 BC) tested the Athenian democratic state, the cohesion of the Delian League and sea power strategy. The conflict would be dominated by a single strategic factor. Athenian control of Megara and the critical pass at Geraneia blocked the Spartan route into Attica, while Athenian warships operating from Megara controlled both sides of the Isthmus of Corinth. While the Athenians held Megara the Spartan army could achieve little in Attica. Some Athenian aristocrats had planned to open the gates to the Spartans, to restore the old political order, but the occasion never arose. Spartan land power failed to inflict a serious blow, while the island of Aegina, Athens' old enemy, was conquered, disarmed and compelled to join the League. Athenian fleets ravaged the coast of Laconia in 456–455 BC, destroying the Spartan naval base at Gytheum. Yet sea power was not decisive: the key to Athenian success lay on land.[44] Failure in Egypt in 454 BC changed everything, although Thucydides exaggerated the scale of the defeat, and the number of Athenian troops and ships involved, to foreshadow the Sicilian disaster.

At least the Egyptian debacle introduced a note of realism into Athenian politics; the democrats recalled the aristocrat Cimon from ostracism to negotiate peace, relying on his reputation as a friend of Sparta. Ultimately, Athens abandoned pretensions to a mainland empire in return for Spartan recognition of her sea empire, and promised not to recruit members of the Spartan-led Peloponnesian League. Critically, Megara returned to the Spartan camp. While the Egyptian disaster caused dissension within the League, Persian plans to counter-attack left Athens with little choice but to increase the cohesion of the League, turning it into an empire. The spectacular double victory over Persian fleets off Cyprian Salamis in 451 BC led to the Peace of Callias, which excluded Persian ships from the Aegean and southern Anatolia. The Persian Treaty and the Athenian-Spartan Thirty Years' Peace provided international stability, enabling Athens to consolidate the empire and Athenian democrats to consolidate domestic power. Peace removed the justification for a Delian League of allies, but the creation of an empire enabled Athens to 'remain great' by harnessing their resources.[45]

The Athenians emphasised their power by embellishing the city. Marvellous buildings and spectacular ceremonies made a virtue of the devastation wrought by Xerxes, as a symbol both of the willingness to leave the physical city while remaining Athenian and of their unique human resources. Their city was made of men, not stones. 'Themistocles had, in effect, freed their city from physical bonds. Even if the city were razed to the ground, the polis would still continue in the minds of the Athenians themselves.' The survival of Athens as an ideal, a concept, a city of the imagination, owed everything to this spirit. Historians examined the ideas that made Athens great, while philosophers debated the best form of government, because they recognised the vital role of choice in the emergence of their city. Salamis became the touchstone of Athenian identity, a city so bold that it had abandoned the physical for the moral and won a stunning victory. The phrase 'to go on board ship' encapsulated the dynamic expansive Athenian spirit.[46] After Salamis, Athens, hitherto an inland city of landowners, was reconceived as a sea city: 'Long Walls' linked it to the Piraeus, while the new temple complex provided a grandstand view of the battlefield, and triremes became a standard device on coins and pottery. The men who ruled Athens used shipsheds and harbours, temples and other public works to reinforce the new identity. Art reinforced policy choices at every level from architecture to graffiti scratched on potsherds.

The process began at the top. Pericles used funds from the Delian League to rebuild the Acropolis, devastated by Xerxes' troops, sustain the democracy and reinvent Athens as a grand seapower capital. Work began as the First Peloponnesian War ended, increasing peacetime state employment, ensuring skilled workers depended on state pay, not aristocratic benevolence. Elite Athenians believed imperial dominion had a 'corrupting' effect on the city, reinforcing the grip of the people on Athens, and of Athens on Attica. Democracy and seapower had already created a substantial naval 'party' among citizens who relied on state pay, and consequently backed both democracy and empire.[47] This powerful citizen body, which dominated the ports, consistently rejected attempts to restore oligarchic rule.

The democracy celebrated victory with a colossal thirty-foot-high statue of Athena, later dubbed 'Promachos' (who fights in the front line), funded by Persian booty collected at Marathon. Athena, the warrior deity of the city, had been chosen long before the seapower turn. Set up around 456 BC the statue commemorated two great Athenian achievements, Marathon and the Peace of Callias, the first and last acts of the Persian War. The monument occupied a prominent place on the Acropolis, between the Propylea and the Parthenon, an external pair for the massive ivory and gold statue of Athena inside the greatest building in the Greek world. The goddess of the city, of warriors and of wisdom, stood armed and helmeted, shield by her side, spear to hand. Equipping the deity to serve with the heavy infantry demonstrated that Athenians still measured glory in the older currency of hoplite combat; they celebrated Marathon, not Salamis.[48] Athena presided over the resurgence of the democratic state in the fourth century BC, only to be taken many centuries later to Constantinople and destroyed during the Fourth Crusade (1202–4), the triumph of Venetian seapower.

Athena victorious was a warning to any who dared contest Athenian imperial might, on land or sea. She also served as a seamark, guiding the visiting ships to the city. The geographer Pausanias noted: 'The point of the spear of this Athena and the crest of her helmet are visible to those sailing to Athens, as soon as Sounion is passed.'[49] Athens had erected another great seamark at Cape Sounion, a Temple to Poseidon, begun in the mid-440s as a commanding celebration of seapower, and a naval station, complete with shipsheds.[50] These costly monuments reflected the economic success of the League as it morphed into an empire, with the entrepôt of the Piraeus at the heart of the system.[51] They were at once emblems of power and tools for seafarers. In a significant design change the Athenians realigned the

Propylea of the Parthenon complex to emphasise their seapower identity. The new alignment ensured that everyone who left the Parthenon complex had a panoramic view of Salamis, the fountainhead of seapower imperialism.

With new public memorials and seamarks in hand, along with important trireme shipsheds at the Piraeus and other Athenian harbours, Pericles, undisputed leader of the state, set out on a peacetime cruise to 'show the flag' around the Euxine. The voyage demonstrated the might and majesty of the great sea empire, deterred conflict, supported democratic movements and secured trade. Behind the fleet lay a polity bent on dominion over the seas and the trade that flowed across them. Rampant economic imperialism prompted the Megarian Decree: Megara was punished for remaining outside the Athenian Empire by excluding her ships from 'League' ports. The intention was to evade the terms of the Thirty Years Peace with Sparta by resorting to economic sanctions, rather than war, to recover this vital strategic position. Many considered the decree the primary casus belli of the Second Peloponnesian War. It was a serious threat to Spartan power. At the same time the activities of the Athenian fleet under Phormio in the Gulf of Ambracia challenged Corinthian authority, even before the dispute with Corcyra in 435 BC.[52]

Democratic Athens was spoiling for a fight. Having defeated the Great King, overtaken Sparta, the old regional hegemon, and turned the Delian League into an empire in the space of two decades, the Athenians created a grand imperial city, one that consciously outstripped Sicilian Syracuse as the wonder of the Greek world. By the 440s Athens possessed an unrivalled concentration of great architecture, symbols and statements of power. The city sought the cultural leadership of Greece with the same determination it had demonstrated in acquiring an empire; cultural pre-eminence would reflect 'the growth of Athenian power and wealth' and impress the other Greek states.[53] The contrast with 'humble' Sparta was obvious. Although Thucydides thought such outward display vulgar, it has fascinated the world ever since. As war approached, Athens made no attempt to avoid the clash, merely switching the construction effort from temples to walls and naval facilities. The people were ready for war, drowning out the voices of reason. War completed the process of transforming the League into an empire.[54]

Debating the prospect of war, the Spartan king Archidamus recognised the Athenians were prepared to use land overseas as compensation for any damage his army could do in Attica, while the fortification of the city and of the Piraeus enabled the Athenians to become a naval people. Themistocles had valued the port above the city, calling on the people to abandon the city in the event of a war and rally there. This was truly radical, perhaps deliberately so: to avoid having to make such a dramatic choice the Athenians built the 'Long Walls' in 457–8 BC, rendering Athens insular, despite its continental location.[55] The walls enabled Athens to withstand the Spartan invasion that Themistocles had anticipated soon after the Athenian victory at Platea.

With the walls complete, an empire under control, and a uniquely capable professional navy in hand, Pericles faced the prospect of a second war with the Peloponnesians with confidence. Democratic, maritime and wilfully expansive Athens had the money, naval might and experience to use the instrument Themistocles had forged. The Peloponnesians could not match Athens at sea, because only the Athenians had continued costly training after the Persian War.[56] Pericles urged the Athenians not to be slaves to the land, but to trade naval blows for military, and rely on their overseas possessions to sustain them. This asymmetric strategy made seapower 'of great importance'.[57] Pericles emphasised the point, observing that if the Athenians were islanders they would be even harder to defeat, a line that reminded them why the 'Long Walls' had been built. Sea power strategy also sanctioned the destruction of everything outside the walls. To stress that this was not a novel strategy Pericles deliberately employed the Salamis catchphrase 'to go on board': he viewed the 'city' as Themistocles had in 480 BC. The linkage was deliberate: Themistocles was the intellectual precursor of the Athenian seapower imperialism deployed by Pericles, son of Xanthippus, victor at Mycale and Sestos. As stressed by the unnamed Athenian commentator known as the 'Old Oligarch', author of the 'Constitution of the Athenians', such a radical step was far easier for those with little or nothing to lose: it emphasised divisions within the city. In his 'Funeral Oration', Pericles told the polis that this vision of a city, defined by ideas rather than fabric, was the key to success. He glorified the idea of Athens, the character of the people, emphasising a vision of the city over the reality. Athens was wherever the Athenians were. When he encouraged them to look to distant, uncertain things, rather than the security of the city and Attic land, the 'unlimited empire' he imagined was a seapower.

Pericles reminded the Athenians that as rulers of the sea, thalassocrats, they could go where they pleased, and defy the Great King. Their seapower stretched far beyond their allies, and was more valuable than lands or houses, which he dismissed as 'mere baubles'. While Thucydides repeated Pericles' mantra, that if Athens was content to uphold the navy, secure the city and not add to the empire it would defeat Sparta, he did so as a critique, attributing primary responsibility for the final defeat of Athens to populist leaders and Athenians more generally, who allowed ambition and avarice to deflect them from this policy. Yet the ideology that marked the route to Sicily, encouraging the people to abandon Attica and their ancestral lands for new territory, was no more than a misguided continuation of Pericles' agenda.

Pericles adopted a limited, maritime strategy of sea control, attempting to seize key Cretan naval bases to cut Peloponnesian trade with Egypt, and attack coastal towns and trade. His approach continued the coercive economic and military strategy that Athens had used against her 'allies' for decades,[58] while relying on the defensive strength of the heavily fortified city to deny the Spartans a 'decisive' victory on land. Pericles admitted the war would be expensive, and long drawn-out, but had no doubt it would succeed, if Athens avoided the temptation to extend the empire. The experience of the First Peloponnesian War provided some support for his analysis. However, he underestimated the impact of losing control of Megara, the need for an alliance with a major military power to neutralize the Spartan army, and the inevitable 'friction' of war. Bringing the population of Attica inside the city resulted in a devastating outbreak of typhoid, which killed Pericles himself and around one-third of the Athenian population.

Despite the relative failure of Pericles' strategy, the startling amphibious success at Sphacteria secured favourable terms in 421 BC at the Peace of Nicias (named after the Athenian general who helped negotiate the terms). Sphacteria also prompted a reassessment of the imperial tribute, including plans to enlarge the empire in Sicily and the East. Peace, as Thucydides observed, merely encouraged the ambition of the Athenians: 'Periclean Imperialism had generated too much energy and appetite for the Athenian demos to settle down to a stable peace.'[59]

When war resumed the Athenian general Alcibiades, like Themistocles and Cleon, recognised that sea power strategy required allies on land. He signed an alliance with Argos, hoping to keep the Spartans busy in the Peloponnese, and perhaps seize Megara, blocking the strategic Isthmus of Corinth. This approach came very close to success, but Spartan victory at Mantinea in 418 BC broke the alliance, and removed the democratic government of Argos.

Rather than prompting any serious strategic reflections, defeat at Mantinea led the Athenians to focus on Syracuse, long an object of envy and ambition.[60] Sicily would be a disaster of overambition, encouraged by the arrogance built into the fabric of Pericles' marvellous city. Yet the disaster at Syracuse also revealed the underlying strength of the Athenian state. Operating in a sea power theatre dominated by Athenian naval bases, the democracy won a series of victories that persuaded the Spartans to offer peace. Yet the underlying strength of Athens was exceeded by the arrogance of power. Having mobilised hitherto unparalleled naval might, the radical demos failed to understand how fragile their advantage was, compounding the error by executing the victorious commanders from the battle of Arginusae without good cause. Such hubris led to disaster. Athens lost the war at Aegospotami in 405 BC, defeated by a Spartan fleet funded by Persia. Anxious to keep the Athenian fleet off their coasts, and suppress the democracy, the victorious allies replaced Athens' democracy with an oligarchy, reduced the fleet to twelve ships, and tore down the Long Walls. While these terms proved to be temporary, losing the sea empire, and the resources it provided, meant Athens was no longer a great power. As Martha Taylor observed, 'far from exemplifying Periclean wisdom Thucydides seems to use the speech to highlight how many of Pericles' predictions proved false. The Spartans did learn to fight at sea, they occupied Attica and they won the war, with Persian support.'[61]

The shattering defeat at Aegospotami severely weakened the naval political body, enabling the oligarchic 'Thirty' to seize power and attempt to reverse the democratic process. They began by altering or removing democratic symbols; the assembly on the Pynx was moved to face inland, rather than towards the sea, and the oligarchs planned to destroy the shipsheds. Their hatred of the navy and of the Piraeus, home to the most radical democrats, was obvious.[62] This was not mere sentiment, nor simple terrestrial aversion to sea culture. It was a profound hatred of the democratic levelling that sustained the navy, and the empire. The people of the Piraeus led the democratic counter-revolution.

Imperial tribute had enabled Athens 'to maintain a large enough fleet to ensure command of the seas'.[63] Athens had become a great power by adopting a seapower identity, and creating a resource-rich sea empire to sustain that identity. Seapower relied on sea control and law courts, cruisers and lawyers. Peacetime constabulary services, dealing with piracy and other low-level challenges, justified imperial taxes and laws. As the first thalas-socracy of the historical era Athens could be forgiven for mistaking seapower for real strength. Without a significant continental ally Athens could only defeat a land power of similar weight by economic exhaustion, a hard task when the enemy despised money and gloried in close-order infantry battle. The ablest Athenian statesmen recognised this dilemma, and shaped their diplomacy accordingly. Others were willing to risk every-thing, including the sea control that sustained the empire in the quixotic search for a sea-based knock-out blow.[64]

The destruction of the expeditionary force at Syracuse enabled the enemy to challenge the Athenians at sea, and, however many times the Athenians won, they lacked the military power to turn naval success into a durable peace. The war effort remained limited. Sinking ships and drowning hired oarsmen was never going to defeat Sparta. By contrast a single naval defeat collapsed Athens' seapower empire. Given the choice Greek cities and islands preferred freedom to the economic and security benefits of Athenian rule. Local oligarchic polities proved difficult opponents, as they would for all seapowers. Leaders whose interests were primarily landed and local drove the dissolution of sea empires, from the Athenian to the British, as an elemental clash of cultures.

The link between inclusive politics and seapower requires restatement. All seapowers have been created and sustained by inclusive political systems, oligarchic republics.[65] Relative political inclusion has been critical to the construction of seapower states, pre-dating the assumption of seapower identities. By contrast there is no connection between political inclusion and sea power as strategy. Naval strength can be created by any state, under any political system, with the necessary will and wealth. Persia was a far greater naval power than Athens, but neither Herodotus nor

Thucydides ever described the Persian Empire as a seapower. The construction of a seapower required political, social and fiscal changes, including inclusive politics, culminating in a distinct cultural identity. In Athens the change from oligarchy to democracy, the core of a new identity, preceded the cultural shift. The trireme faced Greek cities with a hard choice. Most, including many with impressive naval reputations, were unable to fund the new standard of naval power, primarily because they were unwilling to make the necessary political change. Only democratic Athens was able to sustain the new navy and, through a second political revolution, become a seapower empire. The naval power of most Greek states faltered at exactly the point when Athens expanded. The example of Hellenistic Rhodes sustains this analysis. The Rhodian aristocracy, like their Venetian successors, became intimately engaged in naval activity, alongside the wider populace.[66] Rhodes maximised the power of the state in a dangerous world by focusing on sea-based security and economic development, sharing power and profit across the political structure. Although too small to be a seapower, democratic Rhodes proved remarkably durable.

The creation of a seapower necessitated a major transformation of the state, to secure the funds needed to build and maintain state warships, in state arsenals, operating from state harbours. This necessitated greatly enlarged state revenues, and the employment of a large naval population, a social revolution that has gone largely unnoticed. Although 'the shock was absorbed by the great commotion of Xerxes' invasion, this ought not to blind us to the magnitude of the change'.[67] Athenian democracy obliged the rich to pay the running costs of the fleet, prompting prolonged, bitter political struggles, and a powerful literature. Funds were secured through the office of trierarch, the commanding officers responsible for the running costs and maintenance of a trireme. This obligation was performed by the elite, the same group of rich men who funded drama, civic projects and other liturgical functions. They accepted the burden to avoid public disgrace and protect their class from the levelling tendencies inherent in the evolving Athenian political system. Men were appointed annually, once the number of ships to be mobilised had been settled; exemptions were made for those who could demonstrate that others were better equipped for the role.[68]

Although the elite accepted trierarchy, maintaining status by a combination of courage and generosity, political strife generated by the high costs of long-term conflict prompted a shift away from the concept of an individual task to a national mission shared by an entire class. This maintained the myth of aristocratic valour so precious to elite Athenians. Over time, trierarch payments were standardised, turning a unique role, one that could result in unexpectedly high costs, into something far closer to a regular tax, spreading the burden. Having overthrown the oligarchy, the victorious democrats allowed cotrierachy, as a concession to an aggrieved class. This had the added benefit of widening the pool of potential trierarchs to between 1,200 and 1,500 individuals.[69] Using this system Athens became a seapower, a democratic, tax-raising, warfare state capable of sustaining a powerful navy, rebuilding the social, political and economic foundations of the state in only eighty years. It was scarcely surprising that these changes prompted considerable civic strife.

The effective long-term management of the tax base was critical to sustaining seapower. Increased costs, associated with new, larger warships, 'fives' and 'sixes' – rowed by two men to each oar, in place of the individual oarsmen of the trireme (see pp. 87–9) – required Athenians to widen the class base in the 350s, extending the use of appeals for voluntary public contributions when state funding failed. The state needed money to pay for men and stores – they had plenty of ships. In the 340s, Demosthenes adjusted the system so that men paid into a trierarch fund on the basis of their individual wealth, a more equitable tax base, reforms that widened participation. These changes adjusted the relationship between the demos and the monied elite, while providing a major, if fluctuating, proportion of state funding, ranging from 60 to 70 per cent in the mid-fourth century to 20 per cent in the 340s. Trierarchs demanded recognition.[70] That did not mean they welcomed the obligation.

In the wake of defeat came reflection. The first sustained analysis of seapower, written by elite Athenians, tried to balance patriotism with pressing political agendas. Pericles' bombastic declarations of faith in seapower did not convince Thucydides, who recognised some of the realities that Clausewitz would later stress as reflecting the true nature of war – friction, chance and human failings – which had denied Athens the ultimate success. The imperial tribute system proved fragile, the loyalty of subjects no more than a reflection of power, sustained by violence, an oppressive system that enabled Sparta to pose as the defender of freedom. Thucydides contrasted Pericles' arguments with longer-term realities. The cultural, political and strategic ideas that sustained seapower created enemies, so they were dangerous and destabilising. Themistocles' aggressive promotion of democracy threatened the Spartan system, while Athens had supplanted Corinth as the leading maritime state. Pericles' success only emphasised the catastrophe that must follow when lesser men took control. Ultimately, Spartan power and Persian gold proved more durable than ships and control of the seas. Seapower failed the ultimate test, because Athens did not recognise its strategic limitations. In defeat Athens demonstrated astonishing resilience, but little political insight.

Thucydides was no advocate for Athenian seapower imperialism.[71] While he praised Pericles' leadership, he did not regret the end of the Athenian Empire, because he opposed the mass democracy on which it was built and the cultural assumptions that it sustained. Pericles had been the prisoner of a polity built by Cleisthenes and Themistocles, a popular assembly that expected success and, in the arrogance of power and glory, lacked the insight to recognise its fundamental weakness, preferring to execute generals who failed and subjects who revolted.[72] Thucydides' text was a sustained critique of democracy, imperialism and seapower. Furthermore these ideas, a synergistic form of state power, had proved impossible to control. His policy recommendation was bleak: break the links. In little more than a generation Athens went from a heroic city-state that defied and defeated an over-mighty universal monarchy to an ocean tyrant, a modern Minos. In speaking truth to the deluded men of Athens both Herodotus and Thucydides challenged the process and explained the looming catastrophe. Athenian seapower was tyranny, with the Melian dialogue, the ultimate imperial dilemma, as its dramatic core. While some readers recognised the argument, many more were content with simpler messages about the merits of sea power strategy, torn out of context and deprived of subtlety.

Thucydides' emphasis on the wider consequences of seapower was wilfully misread by nineteenth-century historians who assumed Athenian seapower had been a strategic choice. The continental assumptions of German scholars obscured the deeper reality that Athenian seapower was far more than a strategy. Eduard Meyer, one of the eminent *Flottenprofessoren* of Imperial Germany, explained Miltiades and Themistocles as if they were contemporary statesmen in Berlin, demanding the addition of a great navy to a dominant army, while condemning Athenian democracy as 'permanent anarchy'.[73] He ignored the reality that democracy pre-dated seapower. Like many of his contemporaries Meyer considered war a historical necessity, hated democracy and stressed the role of great men, free will and chance over more programmatic analytical tools.[74] Making post-480 BC Athens a precursor of Wilhelmine Germany was singularly dishonest. He must have known that Britain, a state he detested, was the modern Athens.

In the quarter-century that separated the battles of Marathon and the Eurymedon river, Athens was rebuilt as a seapower empire, creating the political and fiscal structures needed to sustain a trireme navy that outstripped all other Greek fleets in size and quality, defeated the Great King in Ionia, and challenged his imperial sway in Egypt. Athens essayed nothing less than the defeat of the very universal monarchy that Wilhelmine *Weltpolitik* aspired to create.[75] Furthermore democracy, the political basis of Athenian seapower, empowering an urban population without the land and wealth, was anathema to the leaders of the Wilhelmine state.

While the reconstruction of Athens as a seapower, supporting a costly specialist navy, had been driven by fear of a Persian universal monarchy, Thucydides questioned whether this was a sound basis for the development of a Greek state.[76] The shift to democratic politics empowered those without a stake in land or property, and encouraged leaders to delude the demos with visions of future prosperity. Obliged to work with this political structure, Pericles had little choice but to create an identity that encompassed all of the citizens, one built on the prosperity secured by maritime and imperial activity, rather than internal measures of levelling economic redistribution, which risked social strife and permanent stasis. The Spartans were alarmed by the culture of democracy, discord and daring that created Athens' seapower empire. Sea power strategy was merely the vector for the diseases of the seapower state. In victory Sparta imposed oligarchic government, destroyed the Athenian fleet and demolished the 'Long Walls'.

Thucydides provided a sustained critique of both the creation of the seapower state and Pericles' sea power strategy in the opening stages of the Peloponnesian War. Pericles directed the Athenians' gaze away from the traditional city in Attica, defined by walls and surrounded by land, towards the sea, of which they were the masters. He claimed that sea power and empire would compensate for the devastation of Attica by Spartan armies. Thucydides disagreed, attributing Athenian defeat to the stasis caused by civil strife between land-owning oligarchs, who had much to lose in a war with Sparta, and the landless urban demos, who did not. One consequence of the new identity was that 'the Athenians feel particular ownership over islands (and coastal places that the Athenians could imagine were islands), perhaps even those not in alliance with Athens'. Athenian interest in islands foreshadowed both the Melian and the Sicilian campaign.[77] The same insular obsession existed in the mental worlds of Carthage, Venice, the Dutch Republic and Britain. Seapowers considered territory and possessions that were insular or maritime, by location or function, worth fighting for, and that all islands were their property.

At the time of Pericles' death in 429 BC the Athenian seapower identity remained dominant. The demos looked to the sea for power and profit, forcing his successors to continue his methods. Pericles' skilful engagement of the demos in national policy encouraged later populist leaders to promise them wealth and luxury in return for votes. City dwellers reliant on trade and imported grain had little stake in the old values of land and agriculture, and less hesitation accepting the new vision. Thucydides blamed seapower culture for strategic over-extension. Athenians were bold beyond their power, because they were willing to travel, and considered the desire no sooner formed than executed. They did not respect the property of others, or recognise the limits of their power. Moving from city-state to seapower converted the Delian League into a 'tyranny', made the massacre at Melos the logical response to an insular challenge to imperial authority, and ultimately led to the catastrophe in Sicily – attempting to conquer an island larger than the Athenian state. In the last battle at Syracuse, Nicias tried to rally a demoralised army with the idea that they were the 'City'. Thucydides preferred the walled city in Attica and the land that lay beyond. So did Plato.

During the Peace of Nicias the Athenians seriously overestimated the strategic weight and reach of sea power, considering every island however large was their possession. The attack on Melos in 416 BC was a consequence of this arrogance. It was conquered because it was an island, and islands belonged to Athens. The use of extreme violence emphasised Athenian power to other major states. To do anything else would have looked weak, leaving Athenian sea power strategy at a discount. When the Athenians failed at Mantinea they chose to attack Syracuse, rather than defend Attica, abandoning the older landed value system.[78] This may have been a response to the Spartan strategy of Brasidas, who met the disaster at Sphacteria by attacking Amphipolis, an outlying city that supplied vital timber and naval stores. By Pericles' reckoning this imperial/naval town was more 'Athenian' than Attica and, as Brasidas had expected, the Athenians were prepared to fight for it. Thucydides was disgraced for failing to hold the city and the populist leader Cleon died in battle trying to recover it. However, the Athenians had been looking at Sicily for years, even thinking about Carthage beyond. They had, as Thucydides observed, 'become mad lovers of the far away'.[79] This was an obsession typical of seapowers, and in marked contrast to the distinctly parochial outlook of the Spartans and other continental peoples.

Besotted with the Periclean vision of a city that stretched across the sea, the Athenians chose war with Syracuse as an indirect strategy to crush Sparta. It was an obvious strategy for a seapower. Thucydides pointedly objected to the vulgar display when the fleet set sail, along with the immense resources of men and money committed to the enterprise, reflecting his sense that the real city lay in Attica, not across the ocean. Athens needed an ally to deal with the main enemy on land, to prevent the obvious counter-stroke, namely Spartan armies ravaging Attica, a reality recognised by Alcibiades, Pericles' most talented successor.[80]

Themistocles' Salamis gambit, taking the people out of the physical city, set a course that could not be reversed, making Athens bold, outward-looking, dynamic and aggressive. It transformed Athens into a state of mind, a sense of belonging, not a physical structure, ideas that were radically unsound. Thucydides gave the Syracusans the last word on Athenian seapower: descended from seafaring Corinthian settlers they dismissed the Athenians as mainlanders who only took to the sea under the threat of a Persian invasion.[81] This profound observation established Athenian seapower as a conscious choice, not a geographical inevitability. The element of choice had consequences. The seafaring skills of Athens were not unique: they could be acquired by anyone.

While the 'Long Walls' made Athens into a veritable island they also ensured 'the permanent domination of the democracy'.[82] As Thucydides observed, their construction had been opposed by aristocratic elements within Athens, who preferred to negotiate with Sparta rather than render democratic control permanent. The destruction of the walls would be the symbol of Spartan victory – because they were so intimately linked to democracy.[83] Ultimately, seapower as culture and identity depended on popular politics and a tax-raising warfare state, something that had been blindingly obvious to all those engaged in the Peloponnesian War. Modern strategists who treat the Athenians as mere exponents of sea strategy ignore the deeper reality that strategy was only one aspect of the debate.

Thucydides knew better, attributing the defeat of Athens to stasis, internal strife, rather than enemy action. This was deliberately ironic. His audience knew that the defeat of 404 BC, the end of the Second Peloponnesian War, had been inflicted by external forces: Spartan troops still occupied their defenceless city. He used irony to compel his fellow citizens to accept their democratic responsibility for defeat. Periclean seapower, which focused on 'the empire, the fleet, and power' rather than the Attic city, had led to defeat, not victory. Far from critiquing Pericles' successors for failing to implement his policy, Thucydides argued that they followed the same trajectory, but lost control of the process to a populace who believed in seapower. Ultimately, he attributed the downfall of Athens to the greedy pursuit and conquest of an empire, at the expense of Attica and the city: 'Thucydides identified the fall of Athens with its rise; he saw the downfall in the pursuit (and conquest) of empire itself.'[84]

Thucydides' examination of seapower must be read as a warning, not an endorsement, a necessary corrective to the naval vision of Themistocles and Pericles. His clinching argument was the response of the Athenian fleet at Samos to the oligarchic coup in Attica in 411. Forced to choose between the physical city and the Periclean seapower vision, the 'democratic' fleet elected not to attack their own city, because that would have given Sparta the opportunity to cut off the food supply through the Dardanelles. That they chose to defend the physical city was the enduring lesson that Thucydides wanted to teach. He did not mention the final naval defeat at Aegospotami, or the arrival of the victorious Spartan fleet at the Piraeus. They were by-products of the real disaster, the shift to a dynamic, aggressive seapower identity that set Athens on a collision course with Sparta and Persia, an alliance it could not defeat.

The astonishing resilience of Athenian seapower, as cultural phenomenon and strategic force, established a pattern. The linkage between commercial prosperity, democratic politics and imperial power, once established, dominated and defined Athens. Cultural seapower quickly acquired deep roots.[85] Despite defeat in the Peloponnesian Wars, Athens recovered, rebuilt and resumed the imperial course, not once but twice. Ultimately, the city, without the resources of the Periclean Empire, was overwhelmed by continental military power. Philip II of Macedon skilfully seized Athenian bases and naval resources in the Aegean as he brought mainland Greece under military control. The strategy of crushing seapower from the land would be copied by his son Alexander the Great,[86] and essayed by Napoleon Bonaparte two millennia later.

News of Alexander's death in 323 BC prompted another surge of Athenian naval expenditure and political ambition: the Hellenistic successor states finally crushed Athenian seapower culture, and with it the unique and original ideology that had sustained it for two centuries.[87] Athens' rich cultural legacy, originating in the heated debates of the trireme era, was recorded in histories, philosophy, theatre and even the concept of modern democracy. Athenian seapower would be recovered time and again by cities, states and thinkers across succeeding ages. While a handful of states adopted the concept, many more, from Rome to the United States, despite brandishing the emblems of Athenian naval glory, and rephrasing Thucydides, signally failed to become seapowers.

Surviving classical writing on seapower is dominated by critiques of the political and cultural consequence, composed by elite authors. How far alternative voices were actively suppressed and how far simply silenced by the passage of time is impossible to estimate, but the vehemence of the elite critique implies, at the very least, the existence of powerful pro-democratic opinions favouring seapower. The elite authors assumed their readers understood the mechanics of creating and using sea power strategy, and focused on seapower as a corruption of the Athenian people by Themistocles and Pericles. Recognising the connection between structural change and seapower they advised abandoning the sea in order to recover political stability. Stesimbrotus of Thasos may have been the first to make the point, his home island bore the scars of Athenian imperialism, but the 'Old Oligarch' and Plato developed the argument. The pursuit of seapower prompted an Athenian population explosion, including seafarers and all the essential support workers, from architects to whores, and required the rebuilding of the port at the Piraeus. The 'Old Oligarch' provided an ironic commentary on the rise of a seapower society:

> It is only just that the poorer classes and the common people of Athens
> should be better off than the men of birth and wealth, seeing that it is
> the people who man the fleet and have brought the city her power. The
> steersman, the boatswain, the lieutenant, the lookout man at the prow,
> the shipwright – these are the people who supply the city with power
> rather than her heavy infantry and men of birth and quality.

In Athens, he observed, 'we become slave of our slaves'. He was not alone in
thinking that Themistocles had degraded the city with the rowing pad and
the oar.[88]

Thucydides, in all probability responding to the 'Old Oligarch', acknowledged the divisive nature of the imperial maritime agenda.[89] Indeed his treatment of seapower in Pericles' 'Funeral Oration' can be read as a relatively new
line of argument, consistent with the introductory treatment in Book 1,
where he stressed the superiority of sea power, the key to empire, over the
trifling consequences of land warfare. Seapower made Athens rich, but it led
to the defeat of 404 BC. Although empire appeared successful and glorious, it
was a form of tyranny and required hard choices, exemplified in the Melian
dialogue. The Second Athenian League re-energised the debate. In 355 BC
Isocrates condemned seapower as tyrannical and demoralising, the cause of
tyranny, injustice, indolence, lawlessness, avarice and covetousness. It was the
obvious consequence of handing political power to men of low status who
earned a living from the state by pulling an oar.[90] With typical aristocratic
disdain for the sweaty labour of the oarsman, Xenophon claimed Athenians
could stay at home and profit from manufacturing, rather than pursue
seapower. Plato took these ideas to their logical conclusion in the Laws, where
he advised that a city aiming at peace should not be within sight of the sea:
ports made people shifty and distrustful, because naval warfare was cowardly,
in contrast to Hoplite combat. He discounted the victory at Salamis.[91] While
he acknowledged the dangers that alarmed Plato, Aristotle recognised the
strategic and economic advantages of a coastal location. He suggested
creating a clear break, a firewall, between the city and the port, effectively a
cordon sanitaire to prevent the dangerous contagions of trade and foreign
intercourse from reaching the spiritual heart of the polis. While he considered seeking to become an island city ruling the sea morally wrong, sea power
was still important. Aristotle's model reflected contemporary reality; in the

Hellenistic era naval forces supported the military activity of autocratic continental states, rather than offering an alternative cultural and strategic concept.[92] Shorn of her empire, Athens had been overwhelmed by Macedonian military might. Athenian democracy and rhetoric were no match for phalanxes and siege engines – because there was not enough money to buy allies or employ a great fleet. Hellenistic authors understood sea power, but the Hellenistic world had no seapowers. Rhodes, for example, the most important Hellenistic sea state, was too small.[93]

The Romans would echo Greek critics of seapower: Cicero attributed the corruption and misfortune of Greece to the fact that most Greek cities were close to the coast. This anti-Carthaginian propaganda was repeated by Livy. Comparing Rome and Carthage, Polybius stressed the moral superiority of land power, but did not examine the concept of seapower. It is an open question how far this Greek exile, writing to explain the rise of Rome to a Greek audience, shaped his words to suit the new masters.[94] The Romans used Plato's critique in their cultural denigration of Carthage; his demand that the city be a certain distance from the sea was their war aim in 150 BC, leading to the Third Punic War. These events prompted Appian to create a speech in the Senate condemning seapower, either from a lost volume of Polybius or directly from Plato.[95]

Greek hostility to seapower had been shaped by dim ideas of a 'Golden Age' before navigation, and an obsession with individual honour, defined by heroic infantry combat, driven by the anti-democratic bias of elite authors, including Thucydides. Seapower supplied food without the need for agricultural labour or landed estates, it fed the people, and enabled them to work in maritime industries. Herodotus had the great advantage of writing at a time when all Greece was implicated in the glory of Salamis and the liberation of Hellas from the Persian threat. But even the father of history recognised and critiqued the consequent imperial sea tyranny of Athens. The two great histories survived down the ages because they contained universal arguments about power and identity, arguments that had been common currency among their original audience. Textual evidence emphasises just how closely Athenian authors engaged with their predecessors. They did so as part of a dynamic, progressive society that had become obsessed with itself and how it was understood by others; it continued to debate these questions long after the brief efflorescence of imperial glory had passed. These texts were not the static lists of Mesopotamian and Egyptian rulers: they were living, breathing reflections of what it meant to be a seapower state. The evidence from other such states suggests that these debates were a critical part of that identity. This was why the Romans chose to destroy the literature of Carthage.

Athens was the first significant state that chose to become a sea state; her precursors were islands, small cities or marginal players operating in worlds shaped by continental great powers. While the Athenians borrowed ideas and methods from Phoenicia, their approach took a more militarised form. Already part of a democracy, the Athenians used a sudden windfall of silver to build a war fleet, which secured their independence, before acquiring an empire to sustain their fleet. This made the city a seapower great power. The combination of democratic politics and naval might gave seapower enormous cultural consequence and terrified contemporary land powers. Stunning victories at Mycale and the Eurymedon river reinforced the Spartan anxiety that Thucydides considered a primary cause of the Peloponnesian Wars. To sustain a sea power strategy Athens needed a sea empire, to fund the enormous cost of a professional trireme navy, subverting the Delian League from an Athenian-led mutual security pact into an imperial 'tyranny'. While this lacked moral justification, it was essential to Athenian seapower. Having tasted the fruits of seapower – empire, glory, prosperity and status – the Athenians were unwilling to relinquish them. The oligarchic coup of 411 BC, prompted by the economic demands placed on the elite by long periods of naval warfare, was defeated by the naval population of the Piraeus. Seapower states became imperial to secure the resources they needed to compete with contemporary proto-universal monarchies, and, although their rhetoric focused on defence and survival, in reality they were equally imperial, equally bent on conquest and exploitation. Athenian imperialism allowed the Spartans, the arch imperialists of ancient Greece, to claim that they were fighting to make Greece free, apart, of course, from Laconia and Messenia. That freedom was purchased with Persian gold, and it did not endure.

CHAPTER 3

Burning the Carthaginian Fleet

Carthage, the second great seapower, had always been a sea city. Established as a deliberate act of policy by Tyre, after the submission of the city to the Assyrian ruler Shalmaneser III in the mid-ninth century BC,[1] the Phoenician founders arrived by sea, not on horseback. They created a maritime hub, midway between Tyre and Tartessos, not a terrestrial military outpost. The politics of Carthage would reflect the overriding importance of maritime trade, trans-Saharan routes only being developed later. The evolution of the Carthaginian state would be shaped by conflict over control of trade routes and resources, against Greek and then Roman competitors with distinctly different land-based militarised cultures.[2]

The Tyrian founders of Carthage sought strategic and economic advantage at sea. They measured success in terms of commercial control, not arable acres; rather than attempt to conquer the hinterland they paid tribute to local rulers for the restricted area they had occupied. For several centuries food was imported from Sicily, Sardinia and beyond. Controlling the sea route from the Levant to Iberia mattered far more than acquiring land in Africa because the Phoenician economy relied on metals from Gadir.

Dido Building Carthage, J. M. W. Turner's 1815 allegory of the defeat of Napoleon's hegemonic ambition

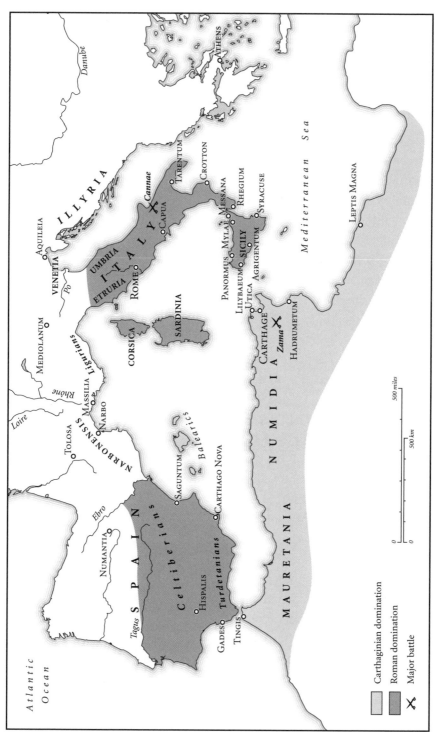

Rome and Carthage during the Second Punic War

Carthage followed the Tyrian model, acquiring insular naval bases such as Motya on the coast of Sicily, linking Carthage and Utica to control trade using the straits between Africa and Sicily. Bases on the south coast of Sardinia closed the northern route into the Alboran Sea.[3] Any challenge to Carthaginian thalassocracy prompted a swift reaction.

Located on an arrow-headed peninsula, and easily defended on the land side, Carthage possessed excellent beach and harbour accommodation. As Cicero observed, it was surrounded by harbours and connected by canals. Natural anchorages in the Lagoon of Tunis were superseded by monumental artificial harbours.[4] Over time the city acquired a regular grid, consciously creating a civic architecture of grandeur. At its heart lay the Agora and the Senate, situated between the harbour and the temple.[5]

The growth of Mesopotamian power on the Levantine coast, notably the Assyrian siege of 671 BC, prompted Tyrian emigration to the west. By 550 BC Carthage was effectively independent, possessed a significant fleet, dominated the route to Iberia, and was the acknowledged political, economic and religious leader of the western Phoenician colonies. Between 540 and 535 BC Carthage and the Etruscans defeated Greek attempts to occupy Corsica in a series of naval battles that secured allied control of the Tyrrhenian Sea and ended Greek access to Spanish mines. However, dramatic events in the east kept Carthage engaged with the wider world. In 525 BC Cambyses conquered Egypt, equipping the Mesopotamian superpower with a Phoenician navy, which the Persians envisaged using against Carthage. Tyrian refusal to sail against their 'children' removed the threat. By 509 BC Carthage was signing treaties with Rome.[6]

The gradual loss of contact with Tyre resulted in the evolution of a republican form of government. Two magistrates or suffetes were elected to lead the city each year, with a Senate to settle the big questions of war and peace. Citizens had significant political influence, and public protest was not uncommon. The Senate's preference for limited wars, commercial agreements and mercenary armies was entirely consistent with that of other seapowers. As a constitutional republic Carthage possessed the checks and balances needed to sustain relatively representative government. Aristotle considered the Carthaginian constitution a success: it evolved and endured, unbroken by tyranny or mob rule, in victory and defeat.[7] While Phoenician cities relied on commerce for their wealth, and were necessarily responsive to merchant oligarchies, the evolution of Carthage from colony and trading post to city-state, and then an African power, created a competing landed interest that complicated decision-making. Although landed families became a distinct class, they could only envy the monopoly on power possessed by their Roman peers. Rival maritime and terrestrial interests clashed over the direction of the First and Second Punic Wars, but the landed elite consistently chose limited defeat over unlimited war. The people assumed increasing significance in these patrician debates, as they did in Athens.

As a sea state Carthage bore the imprint of many cultures; Greek and Egyptian influences distinguished Carthaginian culture from its Phoenician origins. The city grew by assimilating immigrants, and Carthaginians had no ethnic or class restrictions on intermarriage, building a new society with strong north African, Greek and Italian connections. Women had property rights, and were economically active. Slaves were widely owned.[8] Carthage increasingly looked landward, to Spain and its own hinterland for resources, a shift of focus reflected on Carthaginian coins, where horses, palm trees and goddesses replaced ships.[9] These symbols reflected a state in transition, from seapower to continental empire.[10]

Carthaginian strategic culture reflected a commercial/maritime focus, a concern for stability and prosperity over conquest and territory, the combination of wealth and a weak manpower base that emphasised the need for allies and mercenaries, and above all a willingness to compromise to preserve the state. As 'the first truly extensive intra-Mediterranean empire' using islands as 'vital articulating points',[11] Carthage was an obvious precursor of Venice, and Britain. Territorial competition with the aggressive, land-hungry Greek settler states of Sicily, and then the Roman Republic, resulted in wars that Carthage was ill-equipped to win. It had no answer to the ruthless military cultures of such rivals, and generally failed the test of battle. Yet these contacts resulted in Carthage becoming increasingly Hellenised, nowhere more so than in the military sphere.[12]

Although the Carthaginians adopted Hellenistic military methods they did not absorb the all-consuming military culture of citizen soldiers, sacrifice and honour. Like their Tyrian founders they preferred to fight with ships, money and mercenaries. Even Hannibal lacked the killer instinct. His strategic/political model of limited victory leading to a balance of power and equipoise was better suited to a second-rank trading republic such as Tyre than a great power. Carthage was more likely to respond to aggression than initiate conflict, and raised armies with great reluctance. Political realism was a watchword: Carthaginian leaders were quick to abandon defeated allies and strike deals. As a seapower Carthage looked to the navy as the primary arm of the state. It waged limited maritime conflicts, usually for control of critical trade routes, island bases and resources, combining fleets built and manned by Carthaginians with expendable mercenary armies. Carthage responded when aggressive, land-hungry Greeks and Romans pushed into vital resource areas, but it did not pursue a conscious drive for territorial empire.[13]

When Greek settler states threatened to secure the productive lands of Sicily, Carthage launched a major operation. After a heavy defeat by Syracusan Greeks at Himera in 480 BC, the Carthaginians did not return to eastern Sicily for seventy years.[14] Himera prompted major social change, new government structures and an increased focus on domestic production. Carthage became isolationist. This process was closely linked to the growing wealth and political power of the landed elite. Landed wealth valued stability and long-term accretions of power, in contrast to the unstable, fluid rewards of sea trade. Carthage became an ancient Venice, an aristocratic republic, well ordered and disciplined, one that excited the admiration of Aristotle. Oligarchic politics were echoed in the spread of Hellenistic culture and new deities, many of Sicilian Greek origin. Although wars with Syracuse proved costly and indecisive, Carthaginian sea control secured the tax revenues required to fund the city and the fleet.[15]

Ultimately, Carthage needed Sicily: control of the sea routes to Iberia using galleys depended on bases there. After defeating the Athenians in 410 BC the city of Syracuse dominated Sicily, prompting renewed Carthaginian intervention. However, Carthage was not prepared to mobilise the military effort required for victory, allowing the conflict to run for decades. It did not want to conquer the island, for securing the naval bases and political influence was enough. An attempt to secure a decision failed catastrophically in 340 BC when a large Carthaginian army, including the elite citizen Sacred Band, was ambushed and almost annihilated. This ended the tradition of sending citizen soldiers abroad. Henceforth Carthage would restrict its aims and commitments, relying on naval power and mercenary troops to win limited victories. In 310 BC Agathocles, tyrant of Syracuse, changed the nature of the conflict, landing an army in north Africa for a 'decisive' battle. Although the invasion failed it caused a seismic shift in Carthaginian politics.[16] At this time Rome and Carthage were allies against the Greek states of the west.

Carthage held the key Sicilian naval bases, but failed to control Greek Sicily, becoming increasingly Hellenised through long-term contact. It also expanded into the African hinterland, a new emphasis on agriculture reflected in the introduction of the Greek goddess Demeter in 396 BC and Mago's famous agricultural encyclopaedia. Olives, wine, fruit and fish sauce became key exports, along with such Phoenician standards as purple dyes, leather-work and pottery. As Carthage expanded the domestic food supply became a core concern for the political leadership, anxious to avoid popular unrest.[17] The city accumulated massive reserves of precious metals, gold from west and sub-Saharan Africa, and silver from Carthago Novo (Cartagena) in south-eastern Spain. This wealth fuelled the economy of third-century BC Carthage, and paid the Barcid armies that conquered southern Iberia.

Around 300 BC Carthage, like a handful of other great cities, escaped the limits of merely regional competition. Rome, Carthage, Alexandria and Antioch, capital of Seleucia, had populations in excess of 100,000. By the second century BC the Mediterranean basin contained between 35 and 50 million people, approximately double the level of the eighth century. This growth was especially noticeable in thinly populated areas.[18] The consequent struggle for resources would reshape the Mediterranean. Carthage was rich in everything but manpower, grain and timber. Despite attempts to rectify these weaknesses through denser and more permanent patterns of settle-ment and the development of local sources for food and raw materials, Carthage's dependence on foreign troops, Sicilian grain and Sardinian timber led to ruin.[19] As it evolved from a Tyrian commercial outpost into a landed state its resource needs brought it into collision with Rome, the other rising power at the edge of the Hellenistic world. The question for the future was how the powers that dominated the Mediterranean in the third century BC, Rome, Carthage and the Hellenistic monarchies of the east, would interact. All had strengths and weaknesses, but only Carthage was a seapower. The city entered the contest with immense wealth and great maritime strength, but proved to be no match for the militaristic Italian republic.

Rome was not a maritime city: it controlled a strategic river crossing, and, although Roman territory reached the sea shortly after 640 BC, the Romans remained land-bound, far behind their seafaring neighbours, including the Greek city-states in Sicily and southern Italy, in naval capability. Rome acquired its first warship, and its first coins with warship images, in 394 BC.[20] There was no turn to the sea. Rome was focused on the Italian peninsula, recognising Carthaginian maritime dominance and control of the great islands of the Tyrrhenian Sea. In a sacred Treaty of 348 BC Rome agreed not to trade to the west of Carthage or in Sardinia, and by renewing the Treaty in 306 BC it recognised a Carthaginian 'sphere of interest' that included Sicily. In return Carthage stayed out of Italy. These treaties were recorded on tablets of bronze. Although the balance of power between the two states changed across the centuries, there remained a clear distinction between Roman land power and Carthaginian seapower.[21] In the decade after the last Carthaginian Treaty the Romans pushed into the toe of Italy. Their relationship with Carthage began to change after the capitulation of Tarentum in 272 BC completed Roman control of the Italian peninsula, and provided a fine harbour. Rome concluded a treaty with Ptolemy II to isolate Carthage: consequently, Egypt rejected a Carthaginian request for a loan of 2,000 talents during the First Punic War (264–241 BC).[22]

When the great historians of the nineteenth century addressed the wars between Rome and Carthage they unhesitatingly adopted the Roman explanation of their causes, the only ones recorded in ancient histories. Ignoring the possibility that the Carthaginians might have taken a different view from that expressed in Greek and Latin texts, Thomas Arnold, Theodor Mommsen, Eduard Meyer and their followers accepted the 'orientalist' argument that Carthage, an effete 'eastern' power, was culpable. Roman claims had been validated by victory. At the centre of the Roman version was the contention that Rome had suddenly found itself at war with Carthage, a war that was unwanted and unexpected and for which it was unprepared. The contemporary audience for these specious claims had been the powerful Hellenistic states of the east. In reality Rome did not stumble into the First Punic War. Pyrrhus' attempt to establish Hellenistic primacy in Italy and Sicily obliged the Romans to think beyond the peninsula, while conquering the grain and resource-rich island was an obvious follow-on to the conquest of southern Italy. Roman forethought was obvious. They possessed an impressive fleet when they declared war in 264 BC, complete with effective administrative and command structures, shipyards and stores. This navy was essential to project military power into Sicily.[23]

The Roman myth of naval incompetence was created to obscure pre-war planning and the bad faith behind the wholly fabulous 'navy from nothing' story that a new fleet had been built after the outbreak of war, by copying a Carthaginian wreck. Not only was the claim absurd, but Roman warships were modelled on heavily built Syracusan 'fives', not light, agile Carthaginian types, vessels known as 'fours'. The Syracusan design deliberately shifted the balance of advantage in naval battle from Punic seafaring skill to infantry combat power. The Roman fleet was largely built and manned by allied cities with maritime traditions, while the Roman sea cities of Ostia and Antium (Anzio) were excused from military conscription to supply the fleet with ships and men.[24] The seizure of the Sila Forest, a major shipbuilding resource, from the Bruttians in 267 BC provides compelling evidence that Rome was planning for naval conflict.[25]

Rome prepared for war and chose the moment to begin: to have entered a war on an offshore island without a fleet would have been idiotic. However, the construction of a powerful navy did not make Rome a seapower. It remained a military state, using a navy to extend the strategic reach of the army, the main strike force. The heavy losses that Roman fleets suffered during the First Punic War, from storms and stress of weather, reflected heavier warships, inexperienced commanders, the weight of the fabled but soon abandoned *corvus* (a spiked boarding ramp), and above all the dominance of the army over the navy. The arrogance of generals caused many naval disasters, but the Romans learnt quickly. By the end of the First Punic War they could execute classic ramming attacks and had dispensed with the *corvus*. Several continental military powers have created effective navies, while some navies, including those of Rome, Germany and the United States, became highly proficient. The main question for land powers was not naval professionalism but their willingness to sustain the fleet in the long term, as a core concern of the state. The Romans never took the navy to heart. Bereft of honour, glory and plunder, the sea lacked the social cachet and prestige of military service; it was 'not popular with the Roman elite', who 'hated and feared the sea'.[26] The Roman fleet could project Roman military power from one continent to another, but it was not a war-winning weapon, or an especially useful way to represent Roman power. Rome would rule the ocean by conquering the land around it.

One of the more unpleasant legacies of the Sicilian wars was the continuing presence on the island of large groups of unpaid mercenary troops. When Italian Mamertine mercenaries seized Messina, massacring the adult male inhabitants, the Carthaginians tried to remove them. Rome quickly seized the town, the vital bridgehead for an invasion of Sicily, breaking long-standing treaties that placed the island in Carthage's sphere. After completing the conquest of the mainland the Romans were ready to secure new commercial openings, desired by the Romano-Campanian aristocrats running the Senate. Having fought for more than a century to maintain market access and strategic naval bases in Sicily, Carthage faced a new challenge, from a power seeking total control. Having signally failed to secure Sicily during 140 years of war, the Carthaginians were self-evidently not a military threat to Rome. They had shown neither the capacity nor any intent to invade Italy.

The Roman Consuls elected in 264 BC chose war, seeking glory and profit. While Carthage was the obvious barrier to overseas expansion, the First Punic War was fought alongside a war against the Gauls in northern Italy, indicating that personal ambition and imperial expansion overrode sound strategy, and that Carthage was not considered to be an equal.[27] The avowed Roman *causus belli*, the worthless claim of Mamertine thugs, was the pretext for premeditated aggression. The real reasons were ambition, personal and imperial, perhaps mixed with Thucydidean anxiety about Carthage's growing wealth and power.

With Carthaginian maritime/commercial wealth a prime target, the Romans looked to overthrow and despoil the enemy, and their appetite grew with the eating. Rome's other neighbours were poor, and therefore less attractive targets for aggression. The Romans simply ignored the terms of a treaty into which they had freely entered, inscribed on tablets of bronze and deposited in the state archives. To cover their malfeasance they mounted a sustained propaganda offensive that remained effective two thousand years later. Nineteenth-century nationalist historians adopted Rome as their model, condemning Carthaginian bad faith, when the oath-breakers were Roman.[28]

Carthaginian war aims were defensive, and they demonstrated no interest in changing them. Their limited, defensive strategy was no match for the

ruthless, relentless, remorseless methods of Roman territorial aggrandisement and the enrichment of the senatorial class. Roman resources may have
been impressive, but the political will to win proved more significant.

Sicily, a large island where both sides depended on sea transport to
deliver troops, animals, food and supplies, was a classic maritime strategic
theatre. Command of the sea was critical to military success, and the First
Punic War witnessed the largest number of fleet battles in ancient history.
Carthage was the regional naval power while Rome, which had recently
created a fleet using the resources of southern Italy, lacked experience. After
an initial defeat the Romans won a series of victories using the *corvus*, which
enabled Roman Marines to capture Carthaginian warships. The *corvus*
stands as a metaphor for the Roman militarisation of maritime conflict and
the new, larger warships that had evolved in the preceding century.

The trireme had been the weapon of seapower, a vessel of simple design
that used speed and skill to ram and disable enemy ships. It depended on
skilled helmsmen and rowers. However, the Syracusans in the Great
Harbour had demonstrated that heavier warships with more embarked
infantry could neutralise maritime skill by frontal ramming. Dionysius I of
Syracuse developed the five specifically to counter Carthaginian naval skill.
In a five the top two levels in a three-level rowing system were double-
manned, taking the oar crew out beyond 300, without adding to the number
of skilled men. The five was designed to defeat triremes by direct, bow-
to-bow or frontal ramming, minimising the requirement for skilled
helmsmen. The first dated example appeared in 397 BC.[29] However, the five
was slower and less manoeuvrable than the trireme. Anxious to retain these
important maritime attributes the Carthaginians developed the four, a
double-banked ship with each oar pulled by two oarsmen, using fives as
flagships. At the battle of Mylae the Romans used 100 fives and 20 triremes.
They ignored the four.

Despite their frequency and cost the naval battles of the First Punic War
were strategically indecisive. As long as both sides retained local naval bases
they could replace lost ships, mobilise fresh crews and return to the fray.[30]
In 256 BC, with both sides tiring of a strategic stalemate, Consul Marcus
Atilius Regulus revived Agathocles' strategy, clearing the sea passage to
north Africa in a major naval battle, and landing an army close to Carthage.
A 'decisive' victory on land would force the Carthaginians to evacuate Sicily,

Corsica and Sardinia, and disarm their fleet, reducing Carthage to a vassal, like the mainland cities of southern Italy.

Rejecting Regulus' demands, the Carthaginians hired a Spartan soldier, Xanthippus, who taught them how to defeat the Legions. Xanthippus realised that fighting on broken ground played to Roman strengths, negating the Carthaginian phalanx, cavalry and elephants. Regulus was defeated and captured, his army annihilated, yet the Roman war effort was essentially unaffected. Regulus' campaign, and the Libyan peasant uprising he provoked, seriously damaged Carthage, which may explain why political power shifted from merchants to landowners. The landowners preferred to focus on Africa, running down the war at sea and in Sicily. In a rare naval victory at Drepanum in 249 BC, when the Carthaginians had enough sea room to use their manoeuvring skill, they took ninety-six Roman galleys. At the same time the new general in Sicily, Hamilcar Barca (father of Hannibal), fought a skilful defensive campaign with a small professional army. After losing a large convoy in another naval defeat, the Carthaginian leadership made peace on relatively mild terms.

Carthage had lost the political will to fight, while senatorial ambition and superior manpower resources sustained Rome's wars of plunder and conquest. Carthage paid a high price for peace, initially the evacuation of Sicily, a war indemnity of 2,000 talents and a promise not to attack Syracuse. Carthage became a Roman ally, which suited the political ambitions of her oligarchic leadership. The limited nature of Roman victory meant Carthaginian forces were not restricted.[31]

After the peace Carthage failed to pay disbanded mercenary units loitering around the city, provoking a revolt that nearly destroyed the state.[32] The levelling social threat posed by this conflict alarmed the Romans, who refused to support the mercenaries, lest the contagion spread to Italy. Instead they supported the Carthaginian landowners, cultural allies in the struggle to keep political power in elite hands. Even Heiron of Syracuse sent food and money to his erstwhile enemies. In 238 BC the Romans refused to accept the island of Sardinia from the rebels. Clearly the Romans had no fear of Carthage, which they preferred to the chaos and instability of popular uprisings. They feared the radical politics of people power, *demokratia*, not *thalassokratia*.

Profiting from Roman forbearance Hamilcar Barca crushed the mercenaries and secured power. He quickly supplanted the landowner-led

Council of Elders with a new assembly, building a political base for a Barcid state fuelled by nationalist populism. The combination of levelling inclusive politics and a successful general prompted a rapid reversal of the Roman position. In 237 BC the Romans seized Sardinia and Corsica, in violation of the peace treaty, blocking Carthaginian plans to reoccupy Sardinia. At the same time they demanded an additional indemnity, the threat of war adding insult to injury. Carthage was in no position to resist. Although the ousted oligarchs found an audience in Rome, Barcid reforms were upheld by the popular assembly: Carthaginian citizens possessed significantly more political power than their Roman contemporaries. Roman ambition was not satiated by Sicily and Sardinia. They conquered Liguria, before moving into Illyria and Greece, on equally flimsy pretexts.[33]

Having lost the island bases that had sustained the old sea-control strategy, Hamilcar shifted Carthaginian power from sea control to an Iberian land empire. The new empire would fund the war indemnity, rebuild the war chest and generate a large army for future conflicts – without undue interference from Carthage. Profoundly influenced by Alexander the Great, Hamilcar rebuilt the Carthaginian army with elephants and battle-winning cavalry. His son Hannibal, who grew up amid the endemic frontier warfare of Iberia, recognised that, unlike Rome and Macedon, culturally acclimatised to employing their citizens as armoured infantry, military glory and death in battle was not the Carthaginian way. Hamilcar also switched his religious allegiance, worshipping versions of the Greek deities Zeus and Heracles. Melquart/Heracles became the patron of his Iberian state, and closely identified with his family. This Hellenistic linkage between man and god, which had no precedent in Phoenician religion, saw images of Barcid rulers dressed as the deity on silver coins minted in Spain, coins that combined Syracusan design with Punic script.[34] Back in Carthage, Hamilcar's supporters exploited growing hostility towards Rome, which led to anti-Italian riots, fuelled by cheap Campanian imports. Despite Roman threats popular hostility remained politically potent.

The expanding Iberian Empire of Hamilcar and his son-in-law Hasdrubal caused concern in Rome, prompting heavy-handed warnings and a regional barrier treaty to restrain Punic expansion south of the River Ebro. Gilbert Picard suggested the Treaty actually restricted Carthaginian territory to a line south of the Jucar, rather than the Ebro. This placed the town of Saguntum under Roman protection, making their subsequent declaration of war perfectly logical. The Romans had already supported the aristocratic faction at Saguntum, helping them massacre the popular party.

This local provocation was merely one element in a Roman policy of economic and military aggression that threatened every other state in the Mediterranean. Hannibal, newly installed as head of the Iberian state, saw the growing unrest within the Roman world as an opportunity to reverse the result of the First Punic War. Even the Campanians, Roman allies in the first conflict, were beginning to doubt the wisdom of tying themselves to a state with unparalleled, expansive military, political and economic power. Hannibal saw an opportunity in the Greek cities of southern Italy, which were alarmed by Roman universalism. He knew Carthage could not defeat Rome single-handed; only a broadly based coalition could restrain the over-mighty Republic, a new Delian League to restrain the new Persia. He would begin the war in Iberia, then use his battle-hardened troops to smash the Roman armies, their centre of gravity, and encourage other states to join his coalition. He relied on popular politics to bring cities and states over to his side. Rome, like Persia, always backed the aristocratic party. Far from being the 'war to the death' extremist of Roman propaganda, Hannibal was a rational statesman, far closer to William III than Alexander the Great or Napoleon.

As the last champion of the classical world, this Hellenised outsider recognised the existential threat posed by the ever-advancing Roman military state, a state that deliberately broke treaties simply because it could, despoiling other states of territory and wealth. While we cannot prove that Hannibal knew the writings of Herodotus or Thucydides, the probability is high. He spoke and wrote Greek, as did most elite and commercial Carthaginians, while relations with Greek-speaking Ptolemaic Egypt were close. His approach to war, diplomacy and policy is best understood in the Greek tradition, resisting the rise of a universal monarchy. The Greek 'Official Historian' on his personal staff, the Sicilian Silenus of Calceate, wrote to influence opinion across the Hellenistic world. Such writing would be a critical element in Hannibal's project to build anti-hegemonic coalitions. He employed seapower strategy against Rome, waging limited coalition war to restrain an over-mighty hegemonic power and restore balance. Rome feared that a coalition of Carthage and the major Greek states, sustained by populist assemblies, linked by control of the seas, could wear down its resources.

For too long the classical world had mistaken Rome for just another political actor, unable to comprehend a culture that combined militarised savagery, inexhaustible greed and a lust for conquest. Hannibal realised that, as long as Rome existed, no city, state or empire was safe. Well aware that his tactical genius would not enable Carthage to defeat Rome single-handed, Hannibal looked for allies. He wanted to dismantle the Roman Empire in Italy by exploiting disaffection among subject peoples and building a coalition of major powers. Lacking statesmen of Themistocles' insight the Hellenistic kingdoms of the east went to their doom one by one; they did not mass their fleets under one admiral, nor their armies under one general. Mutual mistrust barred the way to a Grand Coalition of Carthage, Macedon and Seleucia that might have restrained Rome.

Polybius attributed the outbreak of the Second Punic War (218–201 BC) to the Roman seizure of Sardinia and the extra indemnity, Hamilcar Barca's anger with Rome, and Roman concern about Carthaginian success in Spain. Hamilcar had good reason to be angry: the Romans were untrustworthy, oath-breaking imperialists, bent on world conquest, unable to tolerate the idea that another state might also be powerful, especially a seapower built on maritime wealth and political inclusion. Hannibal knew that Rome had to be stopped if Carthage was to survive. Correctly anticipating that the Romans had already decided on war, he seized the initiative before they could act, sacking Saguntum, their Iberian satellite.[35]

Alfred Thayer Mahan's famous argument about the influence of sea power on Hannibal's strategy missed the key point. Galleys were very different strategic tools to the sailing battleships that Mahan studied. Their slender wooden hulls, densely packed with rowers, needed water and food for 250 men every day, and periods hauled out to dry on the beach to remain effective.[36] Control of the seas by galleys depended on a secure local base. Hannibal could not use the large, effective Carthaginian fleet to invade Italy because he had no suitable bases. The loss of Sicily and Sardinia crippled Carthaginian naval activity in the Tyrrhenian Sea, restricting the fleet to fleeting visits to the Italian coast. It could not support a full-scale invasion.[37] Hannibal's strategy revolved around securing a naval base in southern Italy. After his victory in 216 BC at Cannae in Apulia he did not attempt to overthrow the Roman Republic, which was beyond his strength, nor lay siege to Rome, which was too heavily defended. Instead he marched south to secure a naval base, the key to a Carthaginian strategy of limited maritime war and coalitions. Philip V of Macedon recognised the opening, signing a treaty drafted by Hannibal, which had the aim of reducing Rome to a satellite within an Italic confederacy under Capuan leadership and Carthaginian tutelage.

However, the Romans refused to accept defeat or political compromise. Rome, a fully mobilised warfare state, had the resources to fight on, despite the catastrophe at Cannae. It proved to be a far more resilient politico/ economic structure than older agricultural states, which could be coerced by a few ravaging campaigns. The Roman fleet prevented Carthage and Macedon from combining forces, because Hannibal could not secure an Italian naval base. Naples held out, and even when he seized Tarentum the Romans retained control of the harbour. Similarly, when Syracuse joined the alliance the Romans quickly blockaded the city by land and sea. Throughout the war the Roman fleet remained dominant on the Italian coasts, with the Carthaginians avoiding battle. Control of the seas gave Rome the strategic initiative, isolating Hannibal in Italy from Iberia, Carthage and Macedon. Naval command of the Adriatic kept the Macedonian army in Greece, giving Rome the luxury of choosing where and when to fight. The first Roman offensive conquered Barcid Iberia in 206 BC, the second secured a 'decisive' victory in Africa in 202 BC.[38]

In 209 BC the Romans recovered Tarentum, thereby denying Hannibal his best chance to acquire a naval base. Without allies he could only hope that Rome would lose heart and accept peace terms, although he was well aware that such an outcome was highly unlikely. Instead the Roman general Scipio shifted the focus to north Africa, reprising Regulus' strategy, with more power and greater skill, while offering moderate terms that split Carthaginian politics. The popular party looked for Hannibal to return and save them, whereas the oligarchs favoured a deal. The oligarchs were on the verge of success when Hannibal returned, the treaty was torn up, and a new army assembled. Defeated at Zama, near Carthage, in 202 BC, Hannibal had no option but to bring the war to an end.

Scipio exploited his victory to revisit the terms offered the year before. The Peace of 201 BC doubled the war indemnity and halved the fleet that Carthage was allowed to retain. The post-war Carthaginian fleet would consist of ten triremes, cruisers for constabulary work, not fours or fives for fleet battle. Scipio believed Carthage, disarmed and reduced to client status, would live in peace with Rome under an oligarchic government that shared Roman fears of populist politics. He looked to the oligarchs to transform Carthage from Mediterranean seapower into agricultural province. Scipio did not destroy Carthage after Zama because he did not think it necessary, and the massive city defences would have required a long siege, allowing a political rival to replace him as Consul and reap the political and economic rewards.[39]

Once the peace had been signed, Scipio made a bonfire of Carthaginian seapower. 'Scipio ordered the ships to be taken out to sea and burnt. Some authorities state that there were 500 vessels, comprising every class propelled by oars. The sight of all those vessels suddenly bursting into flames caused as much grief to the people as if Carthage itself were burning.' There could be no mistaking the message behind this piece of theatre. Burning the fleet in front of the city demonstrated Rome's victory over seapower to the people they really feared, the Carthaginian demos. It was little wonder they wept.[40] The Romans knew what they were doing. Land power had triumphed, leaving seapower disarmed, desperately vulnerable to the knock-out strategy of Agathocles, Regulus and Scipio. Without a fleet Carthage could be deterred, coerced or bullied without the cost of mobilising legions or moving them to north Africa. It could be blockaded by sea, a terrible menace for a vast metropolis that relied on imported food. The Carthaginian oligarchs understood that political chaos would follow any interruption in the food supply, an anxiety shared by political leaders in seapower democracies across the ages.[41] It was the ideal discipline for a landed oligarchic government.

Hannibal accepted Scipio's terms, physically intervening in the assembly to stop an intemperate speech against Rome. This was political wisdom, not love of the enemy. Like his father, Hannibal used defeat to rebuild the state. Elected suffete in 196 BC, while Rome was busy fighting in Macedonia and Seleucia, he re-energised the popular political base, breaking the power of the oligarchs by reforming the tax system and exposing elite corruption. His opponents went to Rome, where the specious claim that he was preparing for 'revenge' found a ready audience. Rome had no reason to fear a military attack, instead they feared 'people power' mobilised by a talismanic leader.

Hannibal was the obvious figurehead for any servile or plebeian move for freedom or political power. Upsetting the oligarchy in Carthage threatened the social order of the aristocratic republic on the Tiber. Hannibal had to be removed and, having long anticipated the danger, he made a swift exit in 195 BC, heading east to Seleucia.[42] He fought for Seleucia against Rome in 192–189 BC, without success. To ensure his brand of populist politics would not be revived anywhere in the Hellenistic world, the Romans hunted him down. Yet the threat he represented did not end with his suicide sometime between 183 and 181 BC in Libyssia on the shore of the sea of Marmora. Hannibal was the last leader of Hellenistic resistance to Rome, Zama the last battle that might have stopped the universal monarchy. He fought to return the world to balance, and create the space in which his home city could survive and prosper as a seapower, a culturally distinct polity.[43] While his name and his home city remained, Rome would never be secure.

Two Punic Wars had taught Rome how to deal with seapower. Beginning with Scipio's peace terms Rome systematically destroyed the navies of defeated enemies. Without rivals Rome could rule the seas cheaply. The Washington Treaty of 1922 provided an echo of this approach, using diplomacy to bring the seapower navy down to a level that the continental/military United States was prepared to sustain.

Despite a second defeat Carthage remained the greatest Mediterranean port city, a vast metropolis generating prodigious wealth. It was not predisposed, by origin, location or culture, to subside into the sonorous rhythms of agricultural production. At the heart of Carthaginian identity were two monumental, man-made harbours. The original artificial harbours, filled in during the fourth century BC as the city expanded, were replaced by larger works that dominated the sea frontage during the Punic Wars. Between city and sea, majestic walls, built on massive rock foundations, were ready to resist the ocean and the enemy.[44] These colossal walls presented Carthage to the world, and channelled trade through the sea gates, structures that combined ceremonial, commercial and military functions, mighty militarised customs houses that taxed trade.[45] The final harbour system comprised a rectangular commercial harbour leading to a circular inner harbour, housing an immense naval arsenal, with sheds for 170 galleys. This unparalleled structure occupied the outer circuit of the harbour and the inner island, which also housed the naval headquarters. It was the most imposing architectural construction ever built for the prosaic function of servicing a galley fleet. Three centuries after it had been destroyed, the very stones robbed out to build another city, memories of the circular harbour still inspired awe. In the *Punic Wars* Appian testified to the enduring impact of a unique seapower statement. He stressed the homogeneity of the design, the combination of shipsheds, storehouses and an all-seeing command centre, while the height of the walls and the narrow entrance prevented outsiders seeing what was going on inside.[46] Few accounts of Carthage resist the temptation to show the circular harbour, as an artist's reconstruction, or a photograph of overgrown ruins. It remains the iconic image of ancient seapower. David Blackman and Boris Rankov summed up its meaning:

> For the great powers, the monumentality of the shipsheds was an impor-
> tant feature – indeed a target. This was intended to convey a political
> message: a threat to potential enemies as well as a matter of civic pride;
> it was also at times probably a sign of internal political rivalries within a
> state ... the visual effect would have been considerable: visitors arriving
> by sea (as many would have done) would have been impressed by the
> shipsheds.
>
> The threat expressed by the construction of such complexes must
> not be underestimated ... it was in part the construction of the massive
> shipshed complex at Carthage, regarded by Rome as a threat to her
> dominance, that led to the Third Punic War and the final destruction of
> Carthage.

The naval harbour was 'intended to impress visitors with the wealth and power of the state'.[47] Originally built with wooden sheds in the late third century BC, before the Second Punic War, the harbour was rebuilt in stone, half a century later, to a sophisticated design combining mass and symmetry, conveying power and order as the ultimate symbol of Carthaginian pride and ambition. This statement of Carthaginian power and identity was completed only a few years before a Third Punic War erupted. It mattered little that there were few warships to place in these magnificent buildings; they demonstrated Carthaginian intent.[48]

Although the Romans understood the circular harbour – they had read Athenian texts that treated shipsheds as political and cultural icons – they made no attempt to match the Carthaginian statement. There is no archaeological evidence of Roman shipsheds. The only other shipsheds of the Hellenistic era are at Rhodes, a small, insular sea state. Boris Rankov believes that there must have been Roman shipsheds which have been covered by later structures,[49] but it is equally likely that the Romans, who did not invest galley fleets with the cultural significance accorded them by seapowers, did not bother. Brick and stone shipsheds were costly investments, and the Romans, like most great continental military powers, did not treat navies as permanent institutions, at least until the imperial era. First and foremost Rome did not rely on the fleet as a symbol of power, so there was no need for an imposing architectural statement of naval might. Rome could not be defeated at sea, and was never going to lose a war in the short term. There would be ample time to build new ships and train new crews. The Romans preferred to build new ships when required rather than maintain existing units. They possessed fine stands of timber and ample human resources. Literary evidence of Roman shipsheds may refer to prosaic short-term wooden structures that would leave little or no archaeological evidence. Fundamentally, the message conveyed by monumental shipsheds was not one that Rome wished to repeat. In Roman eyes shipsheds and inclusive populist politics were the twin pillars of the Carthaginian menace, levelling ideology delivered by sea. The Romans created a very different symbol, the rostral column, after Caio Duilio's victory at Mycale. Duilio's column, studded with the rams of captured galleys, represented a victory over seapower, rather than a statement of naval glory. The rostral column became the naval motif of choice for continental opponents of seapower. They can also be found in Paris, St Petersburg and Washington.

However, Rome had misjudged the Carthaginians. They did not accept the finality of their defeat, or acknowledge Roman dominion. Nor did they revive the failed military strategic model of the Barcids. Hannibal had abandoned the military option after Zama, urging his countrymen to accept peace, and rebuild their state around inclusive politics and economic power, a true seapower. His success prompted the Carthaginian oligarchs to conspire with their Roman peers, united by a mutual fear of populist politics, to remove him. The initiative was Carthaginian, and it had nothing to do with appeasing Rome.

Hannibal recognised Carthage's future lay in recovering and developing maritime trade, the commerce that funded the city, and ought to sustain a seapower navy, a constabulary force to secure the sea lanes. It was no accident that Scipio left the Carthaginians with ten triremes; by this time triremes were powerful cruisers, not battlefleet units. The resilience of Carthaginian seapower culture reflected the critical role of maritime commerce in the life of the state, the enduring Phoenician heritage and the growing awareness of their connection with other seapowers, past and present, not least Athens. After a brief dalliance with Macedonian military glory, armoured manpower and elephants, Carthage returned to maritime trade and manufacturing.

The Carthaginian economy recovered quickly after the Second Punic War; trade and agricultural exports made the city rich, funding a fresh round of major civic works. These grand projects symbolised the success of post-war reconstruction; they represented Carthage, and included the great naval harbour, a defiant statement of wealth and pride, built by the popular Assembly of a revived state. The circular harbour combining scale, elegance and power humbled the shipsheds of thalassocratic Athens, and stood ready to house, service and sustain a mighty naval force. The fleet, which the Romans had so publicly destroyed, was the ultimate symbol of Carthaginian power. The sheds tantalised and bewitched the imagination of all who arrived at the city by sea.

Enduring hostility after Zama, the 'Carthaginian Peace' and the death of Hannibal demonstrated that Rome's real concerns were political, not strategic. Rome did not fear sea power strategy, in any shape or form, and did not consider Carthage to be a significant military power. The fear that grew after the Second Punic War was social and political. The Senate judged seapower Carthage to be the epicentre of a levelling political tendency that threatened to destroy their class and their privileges. Having smashed the Hellenistic great powers in the decade following Zama, Rome was at liberty to finish off Carthage. A decade after the final destruction of Macedon the Senate was looking for another war of conquest and plunder. Carthage remained one of the richest states in the Mediterranean, perhaps the richest, completing a fifty-year war indemnity in 152 BC. It had given Rome no cause for anxiety. 'Roman pretexts for war were extraordinarily thin,' but the prospect of plunder attracted ambitious senators and ensured troops were easily raised. As William Harris observed, the Third Punic War of 149–146 BC 'was a ruthless attack by an overwhelmingly more powerful state on one of its neighbours'. Polybius noted that the Senate was anxious not to advertise the real reasons, because they did not want to be seen to have started the war.[50] They still cared about the opinion of the Hellenistic world, anxious lest Hannibal's populist coalition should revive. However, the Roman decision was driven by more than imperial expansion and personal greed: this existential conflict aimed at nothing less than the annihilation of an alternative culture. The only rational explanation is that Rome so feared Carthaginian seapower politics that it decided the city must either become an agricultural backwater, ruled by aristocrats, or be annihilated.

There was no evidence of Carthaginian military revanchism. Carthage had not broken the treaty, raised an army or rebuilt the navy. Indeed the pliant Carthaginians, who had quietly accepted their demotion from the ranks of the great powers, and the end of their sea empire, were ready to make yet more sacrifices to preserve peace. Rome deliberately set out to expand its empire for profit and create a monoculture. Harris concluded that 'a war against some enemy or other, with some "justification" or other, the Romans expected and intended almost every year'.[51] It would be hard to conceive a more profound dichotomy between the Roman continental approach and the commercial concerns that propelled the seapower worldview. Carthage demonstrated that trade was a remarkably effective method of acquiring wealth, but the model only worked in states that adopted an inclusive political culture.

Hemmed in by the ambitious Numidian King Masinissa, and prevented by the Treaty with Rome from mobilising significant naval or military power, the Carthaginians were left to emphasise the shipsheds, looming behind the massive commercial harbour, as the symbol of their identity, the basis of their existence as an independent state. Yet for all their symbolic power the shipsheds posed no challenge to Roman naval control. There is no evidence that a battlefleet was built; even the Romans only claimed to have heard rumours of timber stockpiles. Any Carthaginian warships used in the Third Punic War were extemporised, and manned by amateurs.

In 155 BC the people's party took control of Carthage, propelled by nationalist rhetoric, tired of Roman interference, and ready to act now that five long decades of war reparations had been paid. They expelled political rivals who favoured Rome, and incited Libyan farmers to resist Masinissa's oppressive rule. His centralising policies were opposed by tribal leaders and farmers alike, enabling Carthage to undercut his authority by offering better terms. As the regional hegemon Rome sent delegates to arbitrate, then signally failed to do so. Among their number was Cato the Censor, an elderly veteran of the Second Punic War. Clearly alarmed by what he saw, Cato returned to Rome, where he began declaiming the mantra 'Carthage must be destroyed', despite the opposition of the Scipio clan. They argued that without the discipline of a comparable external power the Roman populace would reject aristocratic authority.[52] Despite famously brandishing fresh Carthaginian figs in the Senate, Cato cannot have been alarmed by Carthaginian agriculture; he had read Mago's famous agricultural encyclopaedia and, like many another elite Roman, exploited its wisdom. Similarly, the balance of trade between the two cities was hardly significant. It is more likely Cato had seen the majestic new naval harbour, whose elegant Ionic columns spoke volumes about the wealth and ambition of the democrats, and heard the growing hostility to Rome. The radical populist Gisco, elected suffete by the Carthaginian Assembly, openly incited hatred of Rome. Cato found Carthage roused to passion, and increasingly hostile. Carthaginian aristocrats and landowners encouraged his fears. Having persuaded himself that Carthage was bent on revenge Cato brandished the figs to show his fellow senators how close the city was to Rome. Under Gisco's leadership the Assembly voted for naval and military rearmament, and aided a rebel prince to assemble an army to conquer Numidia. The Romans concluded that 'a virulent revolutionary centre was being formed on the most northern tip of Africa, close to Sicily and to southern Italy'.[53]

This was no isolated occurrence. It occurred amidst a general crisis of government and social stability across the late Hellenistic world, raising fears that the levelling populist movements of Carthage and Greece would infect the Roman body politic. Levelling politics were a serious threat: King Attalus III of Pergamum had concluded that the only way to preserve the aristocratic social order was to hand over his kingdom to Rome. Macedonia rose in revolt in 152 BC, Syria and Egypt were in social disarray, while a slave conspiracy at Setia in Italy in 198, sparked by enslaved Carthaginians, was only the most spectacular of a seemingly endless succession of violent protests and uprisings by the underclass, their ferocity and extent fuelled by the legacy of human misery that flowed from the Hannibalic and Macedonian wars, a tide that threatened to overtop the defences of aristocratic Rome.[54]

Having smashed the old political and social order, and a centuries-old multi-polar state system, largely for personal aggrandisement, the Roman aristocracy had to confront the chaotic consequences of their actions.

The Roman vision of social order was collapsing right across the Mediterranean world. In Greece the Achaean Confederation, a conservative ally of Rome since the Second Macedonian War (200–197 BC), suddenly shifted course and became a centre of populist nationalism, confiscating the property of the rich and espousing anti-Roman views. 'They relied mainly on Corinth, which had once more become a great commercial and industrial centre containing a vast working-class population with extremely advanced ideas.'[55] In 150 BC the Romans felt they needed a pretext for their cold-blooded decision for war against Carthage. Four years later they began the Achaean War without any such flummery. They deliberately provoked the Achaeans into war in order to wreck the most powerful Greek state, which had become alarmingly democratic, before it could generate a pan-Hellenic confederacy. Rome was not driven to war by defensive fears, unless the very existence of a multi-polar state system, or of any other state, was a legitimate cause for concern.

Carthage was the obvious place to begin the process of restoring order. It was big, rich, visibly angry, alarmingly close and directed by a popular Assembly. The new naval arsenal symbolised a latent military threat, border troubles with Numidia provided an excuse, and the city's wealth a lure for consular and legionary avarice. Having accepted limited defeat in two wars the Romans assumed the Carthaginians would buckle before a threat. Rome based her demands on the threadbare pretext of alliances. In place of the Mamertine thugs and Saguntum came Numidia. In 150 BC Masinissa's raids into Carthaginian territory, backed by Rome and exiled Carthaginian oligarchs, finally provoked Carthage to act. The presence of the oligarchic exiles reinforces the argument that Rome's real fear was the threat from an alternative cultural/political system.

Rome responded to the Carthaginian revival by demonising their populist politics, religion, maritime culture and commercial methods. Building on the litany of insults generated by Hellenistic Syracuse, Roman leaders incited a suitably xenophobic Senate to declare war on a defenceless state. The object was, as Cato so aptly said, to 'destroy' the very name of Carthage, the physical city, the people and above all the culture that it represented.

This would be a war of extermination – the ultimate response of continental hegemons to the seapower challenge.

When the Romans began to mobilise, the Carthaginians quickly removed Gisco and the other populist leaders, killing many of them. They hoped to stave off disaster by handing power back to the aristocrats and disarming. Throwing themselves on the mercy of Rome, they handed over 300 children from elite families as hostages, along with their weapons and warships. It was all in vain: Carthage's willingness to compromise had limits. These were crossed in 150 BC when Rome demanded the physical destruction of the city and removal of the populace 8 miles inland.

Some argue that the Roman demand was merely an attack on Carthaginian commerce.[56] This reading ignores the influence of Plato's anxiety about the 'corrupting sea', and his advice that the answer to levelling politics was to level the city and move its inhabitants 8 miles away from the 'corrupting sea', to live as farmers.[57] Their aristocratic leaders would see eye to eye with their Roman peers. Recognising reality the Carthaginian people replaced their leaders with more resolute men and fought to the bitter end.

The Romans did not expect that the Carthaginians would destroy their city and move inland. They knew that Carthage, although no longer a seapower, remained a significant sea state, dominated by the economics of maritime trade. Rome deliberately set out to annihilate seapower culture, an act of policy reflecting a profound fear of inclusive politics and maritime trade. The destruction of Corinth in 146 BC confirmed 'the destruction of Carthage was not caused by manic enmity such as only a threatening neighbour could produce'.[58] Neither Carthage nor Corinth posed any strategic threat to Rome. Both were strikingly successful maritime economic centres, with popular assemblies, and they offered alternative cultural models to the wars, armies and aggression of oligarchic Rome, either through peaceful trade or by funding anti-hegemonic coalitions and alliances, trading wealth to obtain strategic weight – the classic seapower strategy of limited war.

It should be no surprise that Censorinus, the Consul who delivered the Roman ultimatum to Carthage, was a Platonist. He believed cities by the sea were suspect: trade gave them unstable souls and uncertain customs.[59] Plato's ideal society was landed, dominated by peasant labour and aristocratic control: it promised a future that was solid, worthy, stable – and dull.

To this end Rome demanded Carthage commit economic and cultural suicide, as an alternative to being annihilated.[60]

The Carthaginians could not 'return to the land'; they had arrived from the sea and remained a maritime people. A 'sea city' from the start, Carthage had been built by the very people Plato identified as the vectors of corruption. Rome feared the exemplary power of the Carthaginian demos and the political power of seafarers and artisans who they believed supported 'the most extreme form of democracy'. Fearful Roman senators sought a stable society of rank and deference, purging Mediterranean sea cities of their threatening maritime/populist culture. Neither Carthage nor Corinth posed a military threat; instead the example of Athens fuelled Roman fears. Athenian resistance to Persia, Sparta and Macedon had been driven by ever more inclusive, radical politics, associated with seapower, naval might and the discipline of the oar bench. Naval arsenals provided physical evidence of these ideas and their ultimate symbolic form. Little wonder the Romans were alarmed by the combination of a great naval harbour and the radical, anti-Roman politics of the Carthaginian demos.

Ultimately, the last Punic War was a shattering clash of cultures, land against sea, a landed aristocratic oligarchy against a populist civic assembly, military empire against merchants. The Roman demand that Carthage be uprooted and moved inland sparked popular fury: Italian residents were massacred, the democrats restored to power, and the city began to rearm. In stark contrast to the preceding conflicts this would be a war to the death, because the cause of the conflict was not territory, trade or power, but identity and culture. The city would be defended with fatalistic resolution: many of the Carthaginian leaders were extreme democrats. Unlike the first two conflicts this war had no great battles or campaigns. It consisted of a single siege, lasting three years, and the outcome was all too predictable. The only naval action was a brief, indecisive Carthaginian sortie from the circular harbour.

The outcome was never in doubt: Rome had the military might to crush Carthage and Corinth in a single campaign season. Having worn down the defenders by hunger and bombardment, Scipio Aemilianus launched a massive assault through the military harbour, symbol of Carthaginian might, and into the city beyond. No one was spared. The citadel held out for six days: 50,000 people inside were sold into slavery. Death or slavery summed up the nature of Roman victory. Rather than face Roman justice, Roman deserters and Italian mercenaries chose to die in a burning temple. The entire city was destroyed, smashed and burnt to ensure populist politics and seapower would never rise again. Legend had it the Romans ploughed salt into the ground, a classical sign of desolation. Such measures were unnecessary, and would have required unfeasibly large quantities of salt.

Polybius recorded how Scipio, his former tutee, wept as the city burnt, reflecting on the consequences of his actions in terms that stressed a Hellenistic cultural heritage and the political realism that characterised his family. Both men knew that the destruction of Carthage, which had already surrendered, was an outrage to classical norms, literally blasphemous. The Carthaginian envoys had stated as much when confronted with the demand to destroy their own city.[61] Scipio quoted the passage from the *Iliad* where King Priam reflected on 'the inevitable fall of cities, peoples and empires', and admitted that he foresaw the fall of Rome: Rome would be destroyed, not by seapower, or populist politics, but the enervating corruption of absolute power, the city sacked by a barbarian horde that sailed from Carthage.

The fate of Carthage reflected Roman cultural anxiety. While they carried home the treasures of Greek civilisation, the Romans denied the Carthaginians the same status, annihilating their city, works of art and words in a furious, existential rage. Carthage, a thoroughly Hellenised city, was demonised as eastern, corrupt and effete. Amidst the destruction the Romans plundered anything of monetary value, but paid little attention to Carthaginian art and cultural artefacts. No great libraries came back to Rome, any books that survived were handed over to African kings, while plundered statuary was recorded as 'Greek' rather than Carthaginian. Carthaginians had long been collectors of statuary: Hannibal's famous collection included a fine bronze Hercules by Lysippus.[62] Any statues that were not returned to their original Sicilian owners quickly lost any connection with Carthage. Although Greek art looted at Corinth fared better, the meaning of both cultures was lost.

The mass art theft and large-scale destruction of cultural icons by the Roman army, echoed later by Napoleon and Hitler, was intended to diminish the status and self-worth of the defeated enemy; placing these treasures in the capital of the new ruler enriched the claim to rule. While many items of plunder had intrinsic artistic merit, the purpose of transporting them back to Rome was not to make Rome even more cultured, but to destroy the culture of Carthage, Greece, or anywhere else that fell under Roman sway. Looting, as Robin Waterfield argued, was 'a tool of imperial suppression'; statues had cultural and religious power alongside their intrinsic monetary value. The Royal Library of Macedon, a prize from the Third Macedonian War (171–168 BC), of immense importance to the history and culture of the state, was seized by Consul Aemillius Paulus. In this way Rome destroyed the intellectual remains of the state shaped by Philip II and Alexander the Great.[63] Rome had no interest in the other side of the argument; it was a continental military power, bent on universal monarchy. By contrast seapowers remained curious, not only open to new ideas, but anxious to preserve the record of other pasts, maritime and continental. The role of Athens in the development of geography, as the primary audience for the 'Universal History' of Herodotus, and a fascination with the world beyond Greece, was echoed by the Carthaginians. The sketchy, second-hand remains of Carthaginian geography provide compelling proof of a curiosity so insatiable that it fascinated the Greeks, whose texts contain the bulk of the surviving material. In their turn Venice, the Dutch Republic and Britain took a very similar view of the world beyond their borders, contemporary and historical, propelled by economic interest and cultural curiosity.

Ultimately, Rome created a monoculture, the lightly Hellenised world-view of a senatorial class whose overriding concerns were military power, land and wealth. It was hardly surprising that later Roman writers lamented the decline of public morality, which they attributed to the incursion of 'Eastern Luxury'. In truth any luxury was willingly acquired, and the Romans, like the Spartans before them, quickly fell under the spell of imported ways. Their cultural contribution was the unprecedented savagery that shocked the Hellenistic world. Republican Rome did not make peace: it used war to secure the complete subjugation of the enemy.

After the capture of Corinth, 'the Senate ordered that the city should be razed to the ground so as to terrorise the revolutionaries', by which they meant democrats.[64] The same fears propelled the annihilation of Carthage. Desperate to erase civic populism the Romans wiped out two great cities, a sophisticated civilisation and the culture of seapower in a single year. These were gestures of appalling power, designed to intimidate rivals into submission. Rome would acquire an empire in the east through the implosion of existing states, paralysed by the spectre of Carthage, something Oswald Spengler termed a 'deficiency of resistance'.[65] The armies of Antiochus III of Seleucia and Mithridates of Pontus, vast assemblies of men, horses and elephants, were designed for show, not service. When they came face to face with the Roman legions they collapsed under the weight of their own irrelevance. Their navies were no better. Rome's universal monarchy emerged in a political vacuum.

Rome wiped Carthage, Corinth and the seapower challenge from the face of the earth. That challenge had never been especially powerful: only the cultural meaning of seapower terrified Rome. In the process a fragile Mediterranean balance between land and sea was shattered, creating a universal monarchy, flooding Rome with cash, treasure and slaves. The sudden accession of wealth and servile manpower fatally damaged the Republic, and ultimately wrecked Roman power.

Within four decades of the destruction of Carthage, the Roman navy, no longer required to deal with major powers, had withered, facilitating an upsurge in piracy.[66] Lacking a sea sense, Rome ignored the constabulary core of seapower, fatally weakening Rhodes, the last sea state that recognised the need to protect maritime trade. When Pompey addressed the pirate question he did so in a suitably Roman manner, landing troops and driving the 'pirates' the approved Platonic distance inland, to take up the morally superior calling of farmer.[67]

Although they chose to destroy seapower the Romans read and valued Herodotus and Thucydides. Their interest did much to ensure that their texts were transmitted across the ages. This was critical to the intellectual history of seapower, a process of recovery, reuse and reimagination. The insight and understanding of the ancient world would survive a millennium in which seapower was in abeyance, and energise new debates. While it is generally accepted that the intellectual heritage of the ancient world inspired the dramatic development of Western humanism in the Renaissance, few recognise how this learning was transmitted by sea, from Constantinople to Venice, from whence it spread across Europe. Venetian printed editions enabled Greek texts of Thucydides to reach the Netherlands and England early in the sixteenth century. The impact of this text in cold, dark countries, very different from the Aegean homeland of the author, helped shape the last great seapowers.

Newly published Roman texts retailed a profound cultural hostility towards the very idea of Carthage at the humanist turn, ensuring the Punic Wars became the ultimate clash of cultures, the definitive total war. Livy's chilling account of the destruction of the Carthaginian fleet at the end of the Second Punic War and Polybius' gloomy prognosis on the durability of Roman imperium after the Third joined the Greek masters as standard elements of elite Western education. From the Renaissance to the Cold War the classics were read, translated and absorbed as the Western mind grappled with its own mortality. Nowhere was this process more significant than in the new seapowers, as they faced new versions of Roman imperium, be it Ottoman Turkey, Habsburg Spain, Bourbon France or Petrine Russia, while the French Revolution and the Napoleonic Empire brought the whole process full circle – as the self-styled new Rome consciously set out to anni-hilate the modern Carthage.

While the wars between Rome and Carthage are often represented as a contest for dominion over the known world, in reality the two states fought for very different worldviews. The Romans sought more land, wealth, power and control. By contrast, seapower Carthage sought a stable, balanced world in which it could secure trade routes and profit from an expanding Mediterranean economy. When the Roman command economy threatened their 'informal empire' of trade, the Carthaginians were prepared to resist, despite the obvious disparity of means and methods.

If the First Punic War was about naval bases and resources, the Second was an attempt to restrain Rome within a multi-polar state system, harnessing the power of the Hellenistic East and the smaller Italian states to balance the military colossus. Hannibal did not plan to annihilate the enemy: he believed that Rome, reduced to a suitable size, could be a useful member of the international system. In the Third Punic War, Rome annihi-lated Carthage, lest it become the focal point for pan-Mediterranean popu-list movements, while enriching a senatorial class greedy for the rewards of victory. The annihilation of Carthage and Corinth was driven by a deep-rooted fear of cultural difference, which could only be solved by imposing a monoculture and calling it an empire.

In 146 BC Carthage and Corinth were systematically destroyed, their books and inscriptions, art and statuary ruined or removed. Carthage was wiped off the map and denied a history. It became a grand morality tale, coloured by lurid stories of an inferior 'Eastern' civilisation, separated from the Graeco-Roman tradition by Punic perfidy and child sacrifice. The good Romans had triumphed over evil. Hannibal became the model anti-hero, brilliant but morally flawed. He suffered the ultimate indignity, reinvented by Rome as a cunning, bloodthirsty exponent of 'war to the death' when in reality he was a classic seapower statesman, a cool, calculating realist with a preference for treaties and compromise. Carthage and Corinth would be rebuilt, as Roman trading centres, corporate pastiches of a once great past, serving the interests of a military colossus, not a maritime people. Separated from its inclusive political and economic roots seapower would not be used for a millennium, an age in which the core concerns of sea states – maritime specialisation, commerce, political inclusion and a constabulary navy – were at a discount.

CHAPTER 4

Trade, War and Ceremony

THE VENETIAN SEAPOWER STATE

Although a millennium passed without a seapower state, trade and navigation continued, and continued to be taxed by littoral states, especially those
that controlled choke points such as the Bosphorus and the Danish Straits.
Similarly, the sea remained profoundly relevant to strategy, armies moved
by sea, from the barbarian invasions of England and Byzantine operations
in Italy and Africa, to Arab and Russian attacks on Constantinople and the
Norman Conquests. But the sea as a space remained marginal in a world of
monotheistic faiths unnerved by the ocean and wars fought for territorial
control over taxable land. Most battles were fought on land or in coastal
waters, where ships became platforms for land fighting. Warships abandoned the ram, the ancient ship-killing weapon, because there were few
professional naval forces, and even fewer chances of a battle between great
fleets. Consequently, weapon systems that demanded high levels of professional skill were replaced by infantry combat or land weapons, such as
Greek fire-throwing devices and siege engines.

Ultimately, no states or statesmen saw an advantage in the asymmetric
shift of focus from land to sea, none suffered from the external resource

The Ceremonial Gates of the Arsenale, Venice

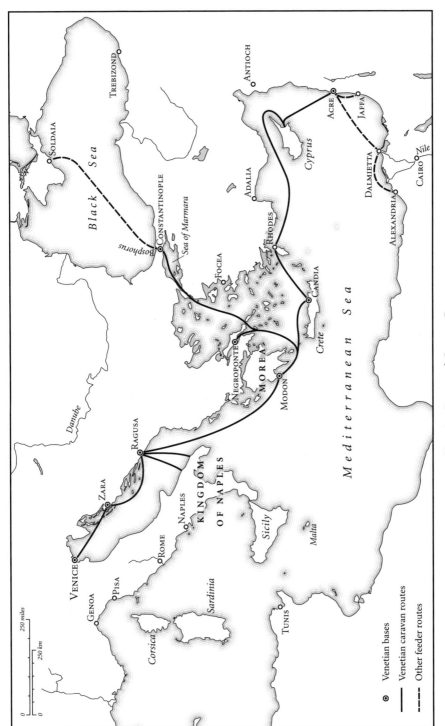

Venetian Bases and Caravan Routes

dependencies that had propelled rich and powerful city-states such as Athens and Carthage to make that choice. Furthermore the intellectual heritage of seapower had been lost; a few copies of key texts lingered in Byzantine monasteries or in Muslim libraries, deprecated by clerics who detested the ocean.[1] When these ancient texts were disseminated by war, conquest and the willingness of Europeans to challenge religious and political orthodoxy, they provided new seapowers with ideas, techniques and above all political precedent from the ancient world. It was no accident that Greek thought escaped the Catholic ban on heathen texts in heterodox Venice and the Protestant seapower states of northern Europe, which were open, inclusive and inquisitive societies that emphasised the sea to sustain worldviews at odds with the Roman mainstream.

The absence of seapower states created an opening for maritime cities, operating on the margins of landed empires, either as clients of major powers or agile, evasive operators, acting as intermediaries between antagonistic polities separated by culture and distance. One of these marginal states would become the first modern seapower, not because it was strong, but because it was weak, and consciously chose to be different.

From the outset both the identity and policy of Venice were moulded around maritime prosperity. In the absence of taxable land the state relied on customs dues, taxes on salt and wine. Critically, Venice stood outside the overarching systems of secular and spiritual control that shaped the rest of Italy. Although it espoused the Catholic faith, the City kept the Church under control, because Roman Catholicism, especially the more strident, authoritarian forms that banned trade with infidels, and disapproved of seafaring, was incompatible with seapower culture. In the secular sphere Venice maintained historic links with Byzantium, and never recognised the authority of the Holy Roman Empire. These choices enabled the self-defined imperial state of Venice to arbitrate between Emperor and Pope, from an insular base beyond the temporal authority of either.[2] Venice endured because it adopted an inclusive, oligarchic political structure, relying on elections, checks and balances to secure the Republic against dynastic rule and dramatic shifts of policy. Unique among Italian republics, Venetian government was dominated by a powerful bureaucratic and highly legalistic structure. The system bound men to the state, rather than clans and factions, avoiding the civic strife that punctuated the history of Genoa, until the closure of the aristocracy entrenched privilege and leadership. The head of state, the Doge, was elected by his fellow aristocrats, and from the tenth century his powers were strictly limited. Acting in concert with his Council and the Senate the Doge embodied the state, but if he attempted to act for himself he could be obstructed, or even executed. Political stability enabled Venice to prosper and survive for a thousand years.

The political structure of the state restricted the power of individuals, and prevented the emergence of dynastic rule. The need for such safeguards was obvious, given the civic violence and regime change that punctuated medieval and early modern Italy, as warlords, dynasts, *condottierri*, radical republicans, Spanish kings, Holy Roman Emperors and even popes battled for control of cities and states. Alongside a complex system of interlocking offices and restrictions the Venetians erected an official pageantry of government, from the 'Wedding with the Sea' to Church processions, backed by full granaries and cheap food to keep the lower orders content. The stability and durability of Venice was built on sound foundations, while elite Venetians thought their constitution the highest achievement of the state, the ultimate Venetian work of art. The ruling elite closed ranks against nobles from the *terra firma*, foreigners and the lower orders. Churches were central to that stability, but the Papal See, which excommunicated Venice more than once for trading with the infidels, never controlled Venetian religion. Although devout Catholics, Venetians were not bound to the Roman See. The parallel with Henry VIII's repudiation of Roman authority is significant.

Venice was always going to be different. The sea isolated it from terrestrial developments, shaped its social structure and provided the parade ground for its ceremonies. While the myths surrounding Venice claimed the city had emerged serenely from the seas, by divine providence, effortlessly assuming dominion over them, the reality was very different. Venetian seapower, like that of every other seapower state, was not 'natural'; seapower identity was consciously created, and endlessly reworked, by an aristocratic elite that never lost sight of the importance of maritime trade sustained by naval power. Having chosen to be a seapower, privileging maritime trade over terrestrial expansion, it was inevitable that Venice would acquire an insular empire of some form. The nature of that empire was settled by the logistics of conducting trade with the eastern Mediterranean and Black Sea in galleys. These small, manpower-intensive vessels needed frequent stops at secure ports, no more than two days apart by oar, to refresh their crews. Without those ports Venetian trade would depend on the goodwill of others. The empire was created as Venice became a great power. As a great power, in wealth and resources, rather than men and territory, Venice stretched out onto the adjacent mainland, to secure the resources needed to sustain naval dominion and control key trade routes through the Alps. This turned the maritime republic into a land power, generating hostility among other states, which feared the Republic's wealth and unique political system.

The physical city began as an assembly of tiny local communities on man-made islands, a character it retained into the twentieth century. It was connected by boats, not roads, with footpaths unsuited for horses and wheeled traffic. This was a deliberate act of policy, one that had fundamental cultural consequences. Before the sixteenth century the Venetian elite built houses on the canals, handling trade on the ground floor, or sea storey, with accommodation on the upper levels, on compact ground plans that demanded upward extension.[3] These narrow frontages were used for overt display, developing distinctive secular and spiritual architectures to express an identity defiantly at odds with the cities of the mainland.

Down to AD 1000 Venice was a local actor, dominated by coastal, riverine and lagoon commerce, mostly barge traffic; locally produced fish and salt along with imported luxuries were exchanged for agricultural produce to feed the mud-bank city. This trade was convoyed, defended by armed men. Thereafter armed seafaring took hold, creating a unique political structure that valued the freedom to trade, secured by political and religious independence. The city evolved to sustain sea-going shipping, processing imported goods to add value, while securing strategic resources, especially shipbuilding timber. Venetian sea power was funded by trading revenues. In 992 Venice earned Byzantine favour by sending warships, and took their reward in reduced customs dues. Venice ruthlessly exploited Byzantine weakness to control trade, to the consternation of rulers and ruled alike. Stripped of customs revenues by Venetian and other Italian merchants the once great empire declined rapidly. The great navy that had secured Byzantine trade was allowed to rot; the empire failed the seapower test.[4]

Yet Byzantium remained the obvious model for Venice, as the old hegemon and core trading connection. Long after Venice had ceased to be a Byzantine satellite it maintained cultural links with the East as powerful, enduring statements of difference. Eastern identity, island location and naval power kept the rest of Italy at arm's length. The Byzantine connection inspired the distinctive twelfth-century Basilica of San Marco, a consciously archaic Orthodox building, decorated in Greek style, based on Justinian's 600-year-old Church of the Holy Apostles in Constantinople.

In political terms Venice looked beyond Constantinople to an older Rome, manipulating the republican heritage and reusing Roman artefacts and architecture to sustain state and aristocratic identities. Another east provided apostolic bodies, icons and architectural references. From Islamic Egypt came St Mark, winged lions, pointed arches and the Doge's Palace, modelled on a Cairene Mamluk audience chamber.[5] Such borrowings drifted into historical texts, art and architecture over the generations, becoming official truth for a unique state. Yet Venice was the only Italian city without a Roman heritage.[6] That the history-less Venetians were obsessed with the past is one of the minor ironies of their condition.

Venetians began to shape their own history in 1177 when they hosted and reconciled the Pope and the Holy Roman Emperor. This political land-mark was celebrated in the annual 'Wedding with the Sea' ceremony on Ascension Day, the Doge being rowed out of the lagoon on the ceremonial state galley, to cast a golden ring into the sea. Behind the ceremony lay a classic Venetian power play. The Emperor's inability to control northern Italy allowed it to control Adriatic commerce. By this time Venice was a powerful sea state, a regional actor of naval and maritime consequence, heavily engaged in trade with Byzantium and the Muslim powers. It became a great power through an act of war. In 1204 Doge Enrico Dandolo master-minded the diversion of the military forces of the Fourth Crusade, intent on recovering the Holy Land from Islam, to conquer two Christian cities. The Crusaders paid their fare to the East by restoring Zara (near the former city of Zadar) to Venetian control and overthrowing the Byzantine Empire. The Latin Empire, erected on the wreckage of Byzantium, provided Venice with rich hauls of booty, including famous *quadrigia* installed on the pediment of the Basilica San Marco, fabulous trade privileges and the chance to purchase a chain of island bases linking the Adriatic and the Aegean from Frankish warlords lacking any sense of the sea. Dandolo's victory transformed Venice 'from a small state into a superpower: she had multiplied her territorial holdings, was the leader in Mediterranean trade, and claimed hegemonic rights over Byzantium.[7] The use of violence to secure trade was nothing new. In 886 the Venetians had sacked the rival port of Commachio, stressing an absolute commitment to the extension of trade. From the start that trade included selling strategic materials, weapons, metals and shipbuilding timber to Muslims, despite a succession of papal interdicts.[8] The city would be excommunicated but Venetians never let faith interfere with trade. Down to 1204 the Venetians fought for trade; thereafter they fought to retain it, using the island empire and naval power. Wealth, power and a new set of historical artefacts reshaped the Venetian past. Links with Byzantium could be emphasised, because they no longer carried any hint of political dominion.

To exploit the opportunities created in 1204 Venice created a maritime economy, by legally blocking alternative outlets for capital, including land. Intended to ensure the elite remained in the city this legislation survived until the sixteenth century.[9] At the height of its relative power, in the medieval era, Venice possessed a stable political system, not yet ossified by the closure of the aristocracy, while other powers were in turmoil, both internal and external. Although seapowers rose through piracy, slave trading and war, once established, as Frederic Lane observed, they became 'more concerned with maintaining transportation services and the benefits of peaceful exchange'.[10] Stable Venice avoided piracy, which would alienate critical customers; unstable Genoa lost markets because it could not control Genoese pirates.[11] Ultimately, 'the Venetians sought sea power, not territorial possessions from which to draw tribute'.[12] They fought to improve conditions for Venetian trade, usually at the expense of commercial rivals, rather than the major land powers, who they served as seafaring middlemen. When two major powers collided the Venetians would support whichever was least likely to damage their commerce or provide the most lucrative trade privileges. Other people's wars made Venice the greatest medieval sea state and, briefly, a seapower great power, one that combined the reality and the representation of ships of war and trade to create a language of seapower.

Windfall profits from the Fourth Crusade enabled the city to rise above a group of competitors, buying 'an Empire of Naval Bases' across the eastern Mediterranean.[13] These linked the Adriatic with Crete and later Cyprus, ideal offshore insular possessions for a seapower state trading with the greatest trade hubs, Acre, Aleppo, Alexandria and Constantinople. Doge Dandolo established a standard coinage, essential for international trade, to replace discredited Byzantine money. Banking systems evolved to support costly voyages, while bills of exchange eased the movement of funds. Venice regulated trade, excluding competitors to maximise profits from a relatively static commerce.

Venice worked hard to maintain a diffuse market with multiple sources of supply, and to prevent monopolistic suppliers pushing up prices and squeezing margins. It did not allow religious difference to interfere with business, trading with Byzantium and Mamluk Egypt. The recovery of St Mark from Alexandria in AD 828 reflected close economic ties with the Abbasid governor.[14] Both Venice and Egypt, which also controlled Syria, profited from the spice trade, opposing Turkish warlords and Mongol emperors. Little wonder that Cairo, the largest city where they traded, influenced Venetian architecture.[15]

The development of navigational science, using charts and compasses, opened up the Mediterranean for winter and night navigation in the years after 1300, doubling the number of annual Greek convoys. As Venetian trade stabilised, merchants residing in foreign ports established regular communications. Commerce was capitalised, while publicly funded state debt was created in 1262, obliging Venetians to subscribe to provide stable incomes for the charitable guilds that helped sustain social cohesion and sponsor cultural projects. As with all seapower states the main revenues came from customs dues, not land taxes.

Venice, the dominant eastern Mediterranean entrepôt, linked Asia, the Middle East and the Mediterranean with northern Europe via the adjacent Alpine passes and later through state galleys sailing to Flanders. The entrepôt model increased revenues: goods could be taxed on entry and departure. German merchants, who brought silver to purchase goods in Venice, silver the Venetians used to fund purchases in the Levant, were granted their own trade centre in 1228.

Venetian trade relied on using two types of ship. Great merchant galleys carried rich trades in spices and silks, using oars to maintain schedules or avoid capture. The oarsmen and crew, paid Venetian professionals, ensured high performance and sustained a body of skilled oarsmen for war. However, that resource was limited, and vulnerable. Regular, secure transport enabled the Venetians to control trade, retaining their position as the entrepôt at the heart of a system that reached as far as London, Bruges and Antwerp, and avoid French trade barriers. The northern galleys returned with local wool and tin. Sailing ships carrying bulk cargoes, grain and raw materials became larger and more seaworthy over time. They were escorted by war galleys.

By the 1290s a century of almost unbroken success had introduced a note of unreality into Venetian thinking. The arrogance and ambition of a city at the peak of its relative power was reflected in the suggestion that long-term economic success would be secured by placing a Christian Fleet in the Indian Ocean, breaking Muslim control of the spice trade.[16] After 1300 Venetian economic imperialism survived rebellions in subject territories and defeats on the Italian mainland. Trade privileges and control of the Adriatic ensured the money kept flowing. Genoa, a dynamic maritime republic on the Ligurian coast, emerged as a serious economic rival after 1250, exploiting a more flexible, less statist political structure. War with Genoa diverted Venetian attention from Constantinople, where a return to Greek rule in 1261 enabled Genoa to acquire Venice's commercial privileges. Further losses followed the fall of Acre, the last Crusader Kingdom, in 1291 and defeat by the Genoese in the Adriatic. By the end of the century Venice had recovered control of Byzantine trade, forcing Emperor Andronikos II to concede duty-free access to the imperial market.

As a small, densely populated port Venice was profoundly vulnerable to epidemic disease. Devastating outbreaks of the plague in 1347–9, 1575–7 and 1630–1 arrested economic development and changed the city. The first plague literally halved the population; the others were only marginally less destructive. Trading links with the East were the vector for the disease. Human losses were replaced by a constant stream of migrants, but, while the immigrants were dynamic, they were not Venetians, nor were they seafarers: economic development following the plague took on a more industrial character, processing raw materials for export, notably chemicals, glass, metallurgy, paper-making and luxury goods. While these industries were a by-product of maritime trade, they were also an alternative: 'Never again was Venice so largely a maritime nation as it had been in the thirteenth century ... Venice could still compete as a naval power second to none, but increasingly its strength lay in the wealth of its craftsmen and merchants rather than in its large reserve of ships and native seamen.'[17]

For Frederic Lane this development was pregnant with the seeds of dissolution, as two more inconclusive wars with Genoa, for control of the sea routes to the Aegean, the Black Sea and Egypt, challenged the social order of the city and exposed the alarming weakness of post-pestilential Venetian galley crews. Allies had to be hired and diplomacy did more to secure a drawn outcome than naval skill. In an attempt to rebuild shattered civic pride Doge Andrea Dandolo created a humanist history of the state. His successor, Marino Faliero, read the lessons of recent history in a very different way. Faliero attempted to overthrow the Republic, with the support of middle-class maritime economic actors who blamed the old system for the latest defeat and the loss of their markets. Faliero's move echoed a trend for elected rulers to seize power across Italy. In a striking testament to Venetian political stability Faliero was tried and beheaded on the steps of the Doge's Palace, his portrait expunged from the record of his peers. Despite decisive action at home the Venetians continued to suffer overseas. The King of Hungary seized Dalmatia while the Genoese, invited into Cyprus by Venetian settlers, secured control of Famagusta. Public debt grew ten times in thirty years.

Endurance, diplomacy and money kept Venice afloat. In 1379 Genoese forces entered the Lagoon, and threatened the city, but the Venetians fought back and outlasted the enemy. Henceforth money became the dominant strategic tool. Venice bought vital ports from local rulers and defended them against the encroaching Ottoman Turks. Venetian troops were mercenaries, as were their commanders, while the best sailors were increasingly recruited from Greece and Crete. The Republic bought insular Corfu in 1386 to replace continental Ragusa, creating a fortified position to secure the Adriatic. Argos and Nauplia were bought in 1388, Durazzo and Scutari in 1396.[18] The Dalmatian coast was recovered in 1409, once again with money not warships.

While the imperialism of purchase exploited Venetian strength, the new emphasis on fortresses revealed an underlying reality: the era of effortless naval dominance, built on quality and quantity, had passed. Despite a series of naval defeats Venice monopolised the high-value trades between East and West, especially the spice trade, exploiting the openings created by divisions within the Islamic world. While Mamluk Egypt and the Ottoman Sultanate competed for trade, Venetians could hold down prices. The

Republic still faced east, nobles had naval and commercial careers, and the Basilica of San Marco was festooned with ancient stonework brought back from the East by ship captains anxious to make a statement of patriotism and munificence. Byzantine detailing remained central to Venetian Gothic architecture.

Over time Venetian civic architecture emphasised three areas: the Piazza San Marco developed as a theatre for power, faith and politics; the Rialto became the commercial centre; while the Arsenale, home of the galleys that carried Venetian trade, and fought her battles, gave its name to every other military workshop in Europe. After 1204 the Arsenale, begun as a naval workshop and storehouse at the seaward end of the city a century earlier, became a warship-building factory, the centre of state shipbuilding. At the end of the thirteenth century it was expanded to become the communal shipbuilding centre, with a massive new rope-works. Infantry weapons and siege engines were also manufactured and stored there. In 1326 the dockyard was pushed outwards into the marshy areas at the northern end of the city, to facilitate the construction of large sailing ships. To build and maintain trade galleys, and mass-produce war galleys, the Republic retained a regular workforce, the famous *Arsenalotti*, ready to meet maritime emergencies, long before other European states had national shipyards. They had a privileged place in the state, combining critical citywide roles such as fire-fighting with ceremonial duties. It was highly significant that the Doge retained the right to conscript all the shipbuilders in the Lagoon to work at the Arsenale in an emergency. Successive construction campaigns at the Arsenale defined the relationship between the Republic and the navy.[19]

In the mid-fifteenth century Venice aspired to become an empire, despite its weakness, to eclipse Athens by sea and Sparta by land, and to emulate Republican Rome. In an attempt to deter rivals the old Venetian moderation and discretion were replaced by theatres of power and overt bombast, represented by the Roman Triumphal Arch, the emblem of classical glory.[20] Nor was it accidental that the first part of the city to adopt the new language was the Arsenale, where extensive reconstruction began soon after the Ottoman conquest of Constantinople. The new land gate, the first humanist work in the city, echoed a Roman triumphal arch in the *terra firma*. It was intended to impress. A decade later houses that obscured the view were compulsorily purchased and demolished to create a 'wide and beautiful street' for the annual ceremonial visit of the Doge, accompanied by representatives of foreign powers. This was the first triumphal way in Venice.[21] The ceremonial water gate, the land gate and the high brick walls were calculated to impress and to deter foreign powers. They were the talk of Europe, and were used to represent Venetian power to elite visitors.

Yet access to this space was strictly controlled. The Arsenale walls, 'the first serious attempt to give monumental Venice a plausible Roman presence', had no military utility. They imposed order on the *Arsenalotti* and kept out foreign agents. The Venetians had long known the importance of recovering information and keeping secrets. Secrecy and obsessive intelligence gathering became defining characteristics of Venice, essential tools for a seapower state facing far larger foes. As a knowledge-based state Venice modelled and mapped the world, the better to locate itself and project its power.[22] In 1547 a new shipshed and storehouse were built for the state barge, the *Bucintoro*. Michele Sanmicheli's design would be reused for the doorway to the arms depot in 1591.[23] Both were created to impress foreign visitors, adding another layer to the ceremonial of power of the Arsenale.

If Venice was, as Iain Fenlon has argued, a 'ceremonial city', then the *Magna Porta* of the Arsenale placed seapower at the heart of that process. The Venetians knew that they stood in a line of succession stretching back to Athens and Carthage; they had read the classical texts, inspected the ruins of ancient Greece, from Agamemnon's Mycenae to Homer's Delos, and surveyed the site of Carthage.[24] They placed ancient stone lions recovered from Greek islands outside the Arsenale, under an inscription that turned the mythic foundation of the city in AD 421 into fact. Combining Greek and Roman material emphasised Venice's status as a great power in Italy, as well as *domino maris*.[25] Such claims would be thrown into sharp relief within a decade, when war broke out with the Ottoman Sultan.

Beyond the architecture of display lay real wars, and after 1470 these would be dominated by the relentless advance of the Ottoman Empire, a continental hegemon with astonishing reserves of manpower and material, driven by a political system that made endless conquest the price for internal stability. These wars were fought for territorial control, trade and money: religion was a useful propaganda tool, not a motive.[26] Ultimately, this was a conflict between contrasting imperialisms: between a seapower and a continental hegemon. However, in contrast to older existential conflicts between Athens and Persia, Carthage and Rome, both sides had an interest in keeping the conflict limited, because both faced serious threats in other quarters, and the Venetians never lost sight of the trade imperative. While Venetian naval hegemony was not an existential threat to the Ottomans, Venetian control of Levantine trade damaged Ottoman revenues, which were critical to their imperial security.

The Venetian overseas empire, or Stato da Mar, was an extension of the city, strikingly similar to that of the other seapower states. It was dominated by a chain of fortified ports, combining galley harbours with naval facilities that included galley sheds, workshops and arsenals with space for large sailing ships. These towns were fortified on all sides, against local people and potential foreign invaders. The key positions were Corfu, the southern gate of the Adriatic, Modon (Methoni), at the south-western tip of the Peloponnesus, and Candia (Heraklion) in Crete, the pivot point of the entire eastern Mediterranean, on the main routes that linked Venice to Constantinople, Aleppo and Alexandria. Between 1211 and 1669 Crete was run as an aristocratic Venetian fiefdom, to avoid the cost of maintaining a mercenary army. Three fortified cities on the critical north coast of Crete reflected the reality of Venetian interest, the capital Candia and regional centres at Chania and Retimon. All three harbours were developed. Candia could hold fifty war galleys. In the mid-fifteenth century new fortifications were erected to meet the looming threat of Ottoman siege engines and strategic isolation.[27] The extraordinary costs were justified by the hope they might deter an attack that Venice could not defeat and preserve the trade network.

Despite their preparations and intelligence networks the Venetians failed to anticipate the fall of Constantinople in 1453, because their attention had been drawn to the mainland. Exploiting a relative power vacuum Venice became a major power in northern Italy. These wars drew resources away from the sea and the trading networks that had funded the Republic, just as the Ottomans achieved hegemony in the Middle East and the Balkans. The risks inherent in this shift of focus would have been obvious to classically educated statesmen from Thucydides' account of the Sicilian Expedition, but access to Greek texts lay in the future. It has been argued that the move to the *terra firma* was wise, or even inevitable.[28] Whatever the rationale the decision had a significant, and wholly adverse, impact on neighbouring states. Once Venice began to act like a 'normal' state its wealth and power threatened every other state in the peninsula, while the stable, successful republican system posed an ideological challenge to both secular and spiritual governments. Although Venice fought its Italian wars with mercenary armies, under mercenary generals, they distracted the city from a fundamental threat to their command of eastern trade. Surprised by the Ottoman conquest of Constantinople, Venice had to seek an accommodation with the new hegemon, one that held the upper hand, and adopt a new strategic model, one that would resonate with the leaders of all seapower states. Constantinople would not be the high-water mark of Mehmet II's challenge to Christendom: that would come on the Italian mainland, within sight of Venice.

The strategy of Venice would be the strategy of Pericles: 'to maintain control of the sea, to defend cities that could be protected from the sea, to pick up more when that was easy, and to retaliate for Turkish acts of aggression by seaborne raids'. Contemporary continental powers, propelled by faith and terrestrial ambition, consistently failed to destroy the Ottomans in battle. Venice carefully avoided giving the Ottoman Sultan secular or spiritual pretexts for deploying 'the full power of the Turkish army' against them.[29] This was consonant with the interests of a maritime trading nation, and above all wise. Yet such hard-earned wisdom needed occasional refreshment. Lured into a religious war by a dying Pope Pius II, Venice was abandoned by Italian allies, suffering serious territorial losses in 1479, losses it had to accept to preserve trade.

The drift to the shore was well underway by 1500, when one-third of Venetian state revenues came from mainland cities, one-quarter from overseas territories, and another quarter from local sales taxes. Critically, while Venice's overseas possessions cost as much to run as they paid in taxes, the mainland estates consumed only one-quarter of the revenue they provided.[30] Venice had to consider the purpose of terrestrial expansion, and how to create the army it needed to secure its terrestrial possessions, without surrendering political power to the landowners and populations of the terra firma. These questions had been raised in Athens and Carthage: they would recur in the Dutch Republic and the British Empire. It was at this time that the Palazzi of the elite ceased using the sea storey for trade: old buildings were modified, new ones dispensed with a design feature that explained why the great families ruled the Republic.[31]

A second Turkish war led to the loss of Modone and Corone in 1499, the essential eastward-looking eyes of the Republic, while Ottoman raiders burnt villages within sight of Venice itself. While Frederic Lane identified these events as the turning point in Venetian history, the beginning of 'decline', such judgements reflect an older sense of how states operate, tinged with the American historian's search for exemplars of his own country. After 1500 the maritime hegemony that created and sustained an empire of sea lanes and trade was held on the sufferance of a far larger power, one that had its own Arsenale on the Golden Horn, and a supply of seafaring subject peoples to match that of Xerxes. Fortunately for Venice the Ottomans were more concerned with land than trade, enabling the Republic to retain much of the commerce of the East, but defence costs necessarily rose.[32]

While the loss of the two eyes of the Republic weakened Venice's grip of the Aegean, the disgraceful behaviour of the fleet sent to save them raised more fundamental questions. Had the very culture of Venetian seapower begun to decline? After centuries of relative stability in Mediterranean naval warfare, large cannon and massive sailing ships brought new elements to battles hitherto resolved by anti-personnel missile fire and hand-to-hand combat, techniques at which the Venetians excelled. The war of 1499–1500 would be the first in which heavy cannon were used as ship-killing weapons. Their arrival had been signalled in 1453 when Ottoman cannon sank Venetian galleys off Constantinople with massive stone shot. In 1470 Ottoman artillery deterred Venetian attempts to relieve the port of Negroponte. In 1499 these weapons were mounted on heavy sailing ships of up to 2,000 tons. Integrating such lumbering behemoths into galley fleets posed major problems. At the strategic level fast, agile galleys moved between closely connected bases, limited by water stowage and crew endurance. They lacked the firepower of lumbering wind-dependant sailing ships that could operate without shore support for weeks on end. In battle tactical cohesion between wind-powered and oar-propelled craft required extraordinary seamanship and tight discipline. An emerging consensus suggested sailing ships should take up advanced positions, to fire on advancing enemy galleys, breaking up enemy formations before the oared craft engaged. This required admirals to wait for the wind to favour their plans, or tow their argosies into place. Both were time consuming, and uncertain. Smaller sailing ships were more agile, but less imposing.

Venetian naval power had, reached a high point in the 1490s: Genoa had been distracted by the French invasion, and, although the Sultan had used a fleet to seize Negroponte, his commanders avoided combat at sea. When he mobilised a new armada in 1499 Venice assembled a powerful force under Captain General Antonio Grimani, including twelve grand galleys, forty-four standard war galleys, four massive carracks, ten large sailing ships and fourteen more sailing vessels off Modon on the south-west coast of the Peloponnesus. The Venetian base lay close to ancient Sphacteria, where the Athenians had humbled Spartan pride, a bay the Venetians called Zonchio, but known today as Navarino.[33] The Ottomans had to sail past Modon to bring heavy artillery to besiege the Venetian fortress of Lepanto in the Gulf of Corinth. While the Ottomans had more ships, their galleys were lighter, as were most of their sailing ships, apart from two monster ships packed with elite Janissary infantry.

Confident that his superiority in heavy sailing ships and galley expertise would prevail, Grimani held station off Coron and Modon, waiting for the chance to strike. The Ottoman Admiral Duad Pasha would not risk battle on the open sea, bringing his fleet into Zonchio. On 12 August, Duad put to sea, hugging the coast, supported by Turkish troops on shore. Grimani attacked with the wind astern, ideal conditions to open the attack with his big sailing ships. Antonio Loredan attacked the largest Turkish ship with two of the Venetian carracks. After an exchange of cannon fire, and heavy close-quarters fighting, all three were consumed by fire. At this point the Venetians were well placed to destroy a shaken enemy fleet and secure their strategic objective. Instead the Venetian ships held back: after taking a few Ottoman vessels the sailing ships and great galleys abandoned the pursuit, to the consternation of the galley fleet. They had been unnerved by cannon fire. Amidst the sound and fury a small Venetian sailing ship had been sunk, and senior officers killed by round shot. Rumours circulated that Grimani had deliberately failed to support Loredan, a younger and more popular commander. That said, the initial failure was recoverable, but when Grimani ordered another attack the great galleys once again held back, and the sailing ships were unwilling to board the enemy. After this inconclusive skirmish the Turks entered the Gulf of Corinth, and Lepanto fell, a strategic disaster.

Venice met the defeat with characteristic resolve, disgracing and impris-
oning Grimani. Grimani blamed the cowardice and disloyalty of his subordi-
nates. Alvise Marcello, commander of the sailing ships, had entered the fray,
only to pull back after two members of his staff were killed by a massive stone
shot. His actions emphasised the profound psychological effect of these
missiles. In turn Marcello blamed Grimani's poor tactics and confusing orders.
The captain-general had failed to co-ordinate his forces, leaving them unsure
of the larger plan. Grimani had been following the Senate's orders, which did
not reflect the new circumstances. Critically, all the senior commanders were
positioned towards the rear of the fleet, unable to lead by example or respond
to opportunities. Loredan had provided exemplary, inspirational leadership,
but no one emerged from the fleet to replace him. A year later another battle
near Zonchio exposed similar lack of discipline. Modon, Coron and Zonchio
fell to Ottoman armies, and the Sultan withdrew his fleet to Istanbul. The two
failures off Zonchio reflected poor tactics, ineffective leadership and faltering
recruitment, and they ended Venetian dominion at sea.

After the Turkish fleet withdrew the Venetians secured vital offshore
bases in a series of impressive amphibious operations. Benedetto Pesaro
allowed his crews to loot captured towns, executed unsavoury Ottoman
leaders, and disgraced or executed captains who failed the test of battle,
however well connected. His actions renewed discipline among officers,
rebuilt lower-deck morale and improved naval recruitment, largely restoring
Venetian prowess.[34]

Although the psychological effect of heavy guns was profound, the
massive Turkish bombards were almost impossible to reload in action. At
Zonchio the fight between the great sailing ships had turned into an
exchange of missiles and edged weapons which the Venetians were winning.
In desperation the Turks resorted to incendiary devices, setting fire to all
three carracks.[35] The scale and significance of the battle made this one of
the first naval battles (if not the first) to be represented in a contemporary
woodcut and sold across Europe.[36] The introduction of heavy cannon
coincided with a new age of brutality. Albano d'Armer, captain of the
second Venetian ship lost at Zonchio, was sawn into pieces at Istanbul, on
the orders of Sultan Bayazet II.

After Zonchio, Venice reinforced the fortifications of the sea empire, but
this strategic system began to unravel when the Ottomans created a single

hegemonic Islamic Empire, conquering Mamluk Egypt in 1516. Now the Sultan combined naval resources with control of the spice trade. The Venetian overseas empire, like that of Barcid Carthage, would be overwhelmed by superior land forces when the hegemon was dominant at sea. Some outposts fell quickly, the island of Cyprus was overwhelmed in a single campaign, but the defences of Crete worked well. Candia withstood a long siege and only fell in 1669 because Venice lacked the naval power and money to sustain the defence. The heroic defence of an isolated port city became a standard of Venetian warfare from 1470, when Mehmet II took Negroponte, until the successful defence of Corfu in 1716; this fortress was relieved by fresh troops who were landed after a naval victory, aided by a Habsburg land offensive. The Venetian fleet had kept the seas open off Corfu.[37]

A decade after the debacle at Zonchio, Venice's terrestrial ambitions received an equally profound shock. With Italy beginning to dominate Venetian policy, defeat at Agnadello in 1509, a battle fought far closer to Milan than Venice, marked a high-water mark of terrestrial ambition. The opposing force belonged to the short-lived League of Cambrai, an alliance between France, the empire, the Pope and other Italian states. After Agnadello the Venetian land empire collapsed with startling speed. Yet the more important point, often overlooked, is that the greatest European alliance of the age had been created to oppose Venice, because Venice terrified the crowned heads, secular and spiritual, of half a continent. The League reflected Venice's great-power status. The speed with which the Republic recovered most of the lost territory, a process completed by 1516, reinforced the message. The League collapsed, but Venice endured. It also learnt a lesson. After 1529 it espoused a policy of neutrality, 'self-confidence was gradually replaced with the growing realization that the Venetian role in international affairs was less than before, and that the foreign invasions of the 1490s had placed control of the [Italian] peninsula in the hands of the Habsburgs and the French'. When the Pope and Charles V made peace at Bologna in 1529 they ignored Venice, 'a watershed between the age of Venetian militant triumphalism and the new realities'.[38] Henceforth Venetian survival depended on balancing and manipulating French and Spanish interests.

Unable to fight back, Venice adjusted the past to meet the new situation, applying a Roman cultural veneer. An official historiographer was appointed in 1516, and a new civic architect a decade later, to impose more recognisably Roman facades. Lacking the classical footprint of other Italian civic centres, Venice reinvented urban space for political, liturgical and artistic effect. The Piazza San Marco and the Piazzetta that linked it to the lagoon, alongside the Doge's Palace, were refashioned as a Roman Forum, redolent with imperial power and civic majesty. This space would impress foreign powers and the *popolari*, transforming Venice into the new Rome, Jerusalem and Constantinople.

While Venice's Roman identity was largely invented, it served the useful function of normalising Venetian power, rendering the distinctive Republic in recognisably terrestrial form. Old Republican virtues were an excellent tool to control the lower orders. This recasting of identity emphasised stability and the avoidance of risk. It also served the agenda of the oligarchy that had taken control of Venice during the war with League. The ruling class had split, power fell to an elite group of older ruling families, marking the final step in the ossification of the Venetian elite as 'a small, closely united group, which kept in its hands all decisions about the life of the inhabitants and the policy of the Republic'.[39] At the same time the oligarchs released themselves from the ban on terrestrial investment. The turn towards a Roman past, and Roman public architecture, reflected reality: Venice was no longer a seapower.

Venice rebuilt the texts and images of the past, for internal and external audiences. New arts, oil painting from the Netherlands and Italian humanist literature conveyed the power of the state. Vittorio Carpaccio, 'the first great marine painter', used galleys and sailing vessels to represent Venetian particularism and power: 'in no other painter do ships have so important a part'.[40] Carpaccio captured contemporary ships in great detail.[41] His work addressed an age of anxiety, as Ottoman expansion and Italian wars challenged the Venetian model. The established political and social order needed reinforcement, while the state was anxious to display longevity and power. In the absence of kings, armies and extensive territories, the Venetians had emphasised civic grandeur, ceremonial display and the creation of a suitable, evolving 'Myth of Venice'. Foreign visitors were overwhelmed by the scale and luxury of these productions.

In 1516 Carpaccio created *The Lion of St Mark*, an allegory emphasising the security of the city and its commerce, for a government office. The apostolic lion stood half on land, half in the sea, carrying the message of peace, which was necessary for trade, represented by a fleet of trading vessels in the background, while the Ducal Palace represented stability, government and law.[42] The timing was significant. Carpaccio's image, a 'Myth of Venice', appeared shortly after the catastrophe at Agnadello and the loss of key elements of the Aegean trading network to the Ottomans. Anxious for peace with the eastern potentate and western rivals, Venice worked hard to impress both with symbols of power and a reinforced navy, symbols that faced in both directions, and helped maintain civic pride and social cohesion.

The closed social structure established in 1297 obliged the ruling elite to secure the consent of the lower orders through civic gestures, ceremonials and festivals. In the late fifteenth century the emerging charitable founda- tions, the Scuole Grandi, created communities across the old social divisions, bolstered by charity, and represented by historical and religious imagery. They bound individual communities and groups around a shared location or vocation, where leading roles were taken by the citizens and *popolari* in miniature republics that gave the lower orders access to civic leaders. Their meeting halls, decorated with historical and religious art, emphasised the Venetian past and the role of the divine in its flourishing condition.

History paintings were designed to be read as documents, emphasising civic and familial glory. Patrician donors purchased art that glorified their families. These images reinforced texts, rare in the era before printing, and were meant to be understood as literal truth. Images on the walls of major public buildings were frequently cited as historical evidence, because the men who had commissioned them were truthful and close to the events represented. Old pictures were copied, because they possessed a powerful documentary quality. Not only did Venetian historians cite images, but they consciously shaped their arguments to include them, pioneering illustrated history. Such works constituted a powerful visual element in the official version, upholding the reputation of the state and justifying past and present actions. This was especially important for a relatively small seapower state operating at the margins of two worlds. Humanism shifted Venetian perspectives westward, onto the land and ever closer to a Roman past. The acquisition of former Roman cities on the *terra firma* gave Venetians a taste for the architecture of imperial grandeur. As the Ottoman threat loomed,

Jacopo de' Barbari's *View of Venice*

and *terra firma* imperialism roused the hostility of other Italian states, Venetian intellectuals hurriedly reorganised their past: Marcantonio Sabellico's official history of 1487 was closely modelled on Livy's Roman history.[43]

Jacopo de' Barbari's colossal woodcut of Venice of 1500 emphasised the critical role of the ship, accurately rendered, as the symbol of the Republic in an image that celebrated the city's fame and its unique nature. This was not so much a map as a statement of Venetian primacy in trade between East and West, as the greatest maritime power in Europe.[44] Barbari filled the waterfront with outsized three-masted merchant ships, while an accurate account of the Arsenale, complete with galleys, stressed naval power. No longer generic background decoration, ships had become symbols of hope at a dark juncture in Venetian history. They spoke of fame, glory and profit at a time when all three were in short supply; they helped sustain the illusion of greatness and maintain social cohesion.[45]

Alongside the art of seapower Venice adopted the latest methods of literary exposition. The University of Padua, on the Venetian *terra firma*, supported scholarship in law and the practical arts. The rise of humanist learning was greatly aided by the presence of Petrarch and a growing engagement with Greek, the key to humanism. Greek scholars fleeing Constantinople and the other Byzantine territories came to the city with the largest Greek merchant community in the West. Cardinal Bessarion donated his exceptional library of Greek manuscripts to the Republic in 1468, to save

Greek culture and learning from the catastrophe of 1453.[46] His manuscripts sustained a rich tradition of humanist scholarship, prompted by émigré Greeks, and of Greek printing by the pioneer publisher Aldus Manutius, who brought these ancient texts to the Western world.[47] In 2016 the Marciana Library, belatedly built to house Bessarion's bequest, celebrated Manutius's work with a display of his editions of Greek classics.[48] Thucydides was published in May 1502, four months before Herodotus. The title page of the copy of Thucydides in the exhibition was endorsed with the English word 'Library' in a bold, old hand. Like many another copy of the core text of seapower thought, this book had once belonged to an Englishman. Manutius's English friends included the humanists William Latimer and Thomas Lynate, who taught at Oxford and Cambridge respectively, and copies of his books can be found at both universities.

Venice introduced seapower to the West as an intermediary between two worlds, and two epochs. The publication of Thucydides, the master text of seapower, proved to be timely. Sixteenth-century Venice faced a range of challenges that exposed the weakness of her seapower identity and resource base. In the eastern Mediterranean an expansive Ottoman Empire controlled all the terminals of the Asian trade, removing Venice's room for manoeuvre. Monopolistic suppliers waging expensive wars tended to push up prices. This focused attention on the Italian mainland, to which Venice looked for food, strategic raw materials, labour and control of the routes to the north. The temporary loss of this Italian Empire after the catastrophe at Agnadello shattered Venetian ideas of invulnerability. Beaten on land and sea, stripped of critical naval bases and landed estates, it seemed that Venice was finished, reduced to the old island and a few petty outposts, a shrunken relic of what had been but sixty years before one of the glories of the Western world. It was inevitable that ideas of decline entered the minds of the Venetians. In 1512 Pietro Aretino reflected on the impermanence of all things, ships, states and human ambition. Two months after Agnadello, Doge Loredan condemned the costly, disastrous policy of *terra firma* expansion, deploring the reliance on mercenary armies:

> this does not happen with affairs at sea, since there we are masters over all, and we conduct our own affairs alone, with true zeal. Nor does one know what stupidity ever drew us away from the sea and turned us to

the land, for navigation was, so to speak, an inheritance from our earliest ancestors and has left us with many reminders and warnings that we should remain intent on it alone.[49]

Loredan's Venice had been built by men of the sea, so their example should be followed. His reading of recent disasters privileged the idea that Venetian seapower was consciously and deliberately constructed, rather than the work of God, or geography. Although such anxieties were temporarily stilled by the recovery of the *terra firma* over the next eight years, they remained significant. Venice was no longer a great power, even on an Italian peninsula where the imperial sack of Rome in 1527 reflected the overwhelming nature of Habsburg power.

Classical art and architecture dominated the Venetian response to this challenge. In 1529, the year in which the Treaty of Bologna demonstrated Emperor Charles V's dominance of Italy, the Tuscan architect Jacopo Sansovino was appointed to oversee the Piazza San Marco, the ceremonial heart of the city, created in the late twelfth century by filling in a canal and knocking down a church. He would serve Doge Andrea Gritti's agenda of restoring Venetian prestige through culture and commerce, wisdom and justice, virtues expressed through architectural renewal. Only classical architecture could convey these ideas, and Sansovino, who had fled the Habsburg sack of Rome two years earlier, was ideally equipped. His Loggetta, Marciana Library and Mint framed the view of the Basilica and the Piazza, adding majesty to the prospect from the sea, the obvious line of approach to Venetian buildings. These symbols of wisdom, wealth and power replaced the meat market, which moved to the Rialto. The Marciana, a 'temple of Renaissance learning', a new Alexandrine Library, emphasised the wisdom in the Doge's Palace. Monumental figures of classical gods echoed giant figures outside the Doge's Palace.[50] The city granaries remained, alongside the Mint, as a key tool of social control. The new architecture positioned Venice as an island of internal peace and stability, detached from a peninsula dominated by foreign armies, where the Florentine Republic had been overthrown and Rome sacked by Lutheran soldiers.

The Loggetta, an elite viewing platform for outdoor rituals, carried elaborate panels representing Venetian imperial power, alongside the wisdom, preparedness and harmony of Venetian government. Over time the loss of

Cyprus and then Crete changed the meaning of the panels. Classical references penetrated the Doge's Palace, where Sansovino topped the ceremonial Stair of the Giants with monumental figures of Mars and Neptune, the gods of war and the ocean respectively, the twin pillars of the Venetian state. Here successive Doges completed their investiture, and here Doge Faliero had been beheaded.[51]

By 1550 Venetian architecture was dominated by classical and Baroque models, reflecting an agenda of civic magnificence as deterrent. However, the language was subtly modified to sustain a distinctive Venetian message. Vitruvius' ancient Roman text was published in Venice in 1556, with the assistance of Andrea Palladio and his humanist patrician Daniele Barbaro. Barbaro and Palladio were connected to the *terra firma* city of Vicenza and the Roman Church.[52] Palladio's new designs carried these ideas into a city hitherto defined by a unique and eclectic architecture. His two great churches, San Giorgio Maggiore and Il Redentore, carefully expanded the sightlines of the Piazza San Marco to bring the Bacino into the ceremonial space of the city. The three equidistant points framed the maritime theatre, as the Piazza San Marco did for terrestrial events. At a time when Venetian relations with the Papacy were confrontational, Palladio subtly employed the maritime setting and Venetian themes to subvert the Roman element of the Baroque. The architecture of classical power, which Palladio developed from Vitruvius, was welcome in Venice, once shorn of Roman connections. Descended from a gondolier family in nearby Mestre, Palladio exploited the maritime setting to resist papal interdicts. The final pieces in the watery space, the Dogana and the Santa Maria della Salute, provided a suitable combination of secular and spiritual focal points for the vision that Venice wished to project. By the time the last element was completed in 1631 the Bacino San Marco had become 'a space of dense spiritual and political meanings, a theatre of Venetian mythology'.[53] The identity of Venice was bound up with the sea, it was best seen from the sea, and those in Venice were drawn to look to the sea.

Venice provided the ultimate example of a constructed identity. Not only did the Venetians invent their history, borrowing ideas and artefacts from many sources, but they turned their watery location into an exercise in the architecture of splendour. Critically, the Venetians used every artistic tool to enhance their power: architecture, art, literature and music were blended into a myth of divine creation, transforming the fragile floating world of the city-state into something altogether more durable. Not only did the Venetians use canals and boats to demonstrate their difference, but they shaped their watery spaces to highlight the city's unique culture. Medieval and early modern Venice encompassed the lagoon *as well as* the city proper. This body of water, populated by fishermen, salt farmers and those travelling to the mainland, 'contained some of the city's most venerable monasteries'. Skilfully exploiting insularity the Venetians controlled the way in which visitors experienced their city. The four water routes to the city were controlled by the government, which used architecture to keep elite visitors guessing, before revealing vistas of civic magnificence that overwhelmed the senses. The most impressive route stretched from the port of Chioggia to the south. After a disorienting 13-mile passage through the featureless lagoon, visitors entered the narrow Canale San Giorgio, alongside the great church. Then the Canale opened out into the Bacino San Marco, a 'climactic revelation of the principal civic and religious monuments of the city', the Ducal Palace, Piazzetta, Campanile, Clock Tower and Basilica, along with Sansovino's Library and Mint. It was little wonder that many were overwhelmed.[54]

The direct route from the sea was marked by Michele Sanmicheli's impressive fortress of San Andrea, a masterpiece of allegorical masonry representing stability and power, tied to the sea.[55] The Venetians deliberately prolonged the experience of arriving by depositing visitors for the night on one of the smaller islands, to absorb the scale and grandeur of the city from a distance.

Venetian bell towers also served as leading marks for lagoon pilots and navigational beacons for ships at sea. The Campanile of San Marco was topped with a gilded statue; others were rebuilt in white stone, or featured fire and smoke beacons. They enabled navigators to calculate position and distance with accuracy.[56] A visiting Englishman, Thomas Coryate, had no trouble identifying the Campanile as a seamark.[57]

The synergy between the Venetian and other seapowers' exploitation of architecture as seamark, statement of power and ceremonial space is obvious. The Parthenon complex, Carthage's Circular Harbour, Amsterdam's Dam Square and massive naval magazine, along with the highly elaborate approach to London along the Thames – the Fortress at Tilbury, the Dockyard at Woolwich, crowned by the Baroque magnificence of Greenwich

Palace – addressed the same agenda. All five seapower states created architectures of maritime power, aggressively connecting maritime trade, naval might and secular identity.

The impact of ceremonial Venice was captured and transmitted in images that emphasised the unique, maritime nature and commercial focus of the city. The English ambassador Sir Henry Wotton acquired a large painting of the city, dated 1611, which he donated to Eton College.[58] Prominently displayed, it offered a powerful visual reference for generations of elite youths, future statesmen and civic leaders, a vision of La Serenissima as a city to visit and a model to emulate. Some would make the Grand Tour, collect Canalettos and understand the synergy between seapower states past and present as commercial republics focused on trade, empire and naval power.

In 1516, the year the empire of the *terra firma* was largely restored, the thirteenth-century law that had blocked investment in land became ineffective.[59] This should be understood as a response to the loss of critical maritime outposts in Greece. The new legal structure removed the Venetian aristocracy from overseas trade, shaping a landed elite with extensive *terra firma* estates. As they shifted their power base from trade to land they built Palladian villas along the canalised River Brenta, which linked them to the sea city. A simple, self-interested change in the law had undermined the critical synergy between trade, power and identity.

The return of peace to the Peninsula in 1529, under a Habsburg aegis, opened a new age of Venetian civic magnificence in the Roman manner. The galley, instrument and emblem of Venetian power and prosperity, was consigned to the background of a medal struck to celebrate the ducal reign of Andrea Gritti, architect of the new Roman display. Venice had chosen to wear borrowed clothes, clothes that had profound implications for Venetian identity. Ancient Rome had been the sworn enemy of seapower states; the inheritors of that autocratic, continental *imperium* were Ottoman sultans, Habsburg emperors and Roman pontiffs. Venice, the greatest commercial emporium in the Mediterranean, was a new Carthage. Obvious as such a connection must have been to any reader of Livy, whose work was well known to Venetian humanists, the city still chose a Roman identity.[60]

Despite the shift of focus to the land Venice sought new trades to replace lost eastern markets. As the new oceanic world opened in the late fifteenth century the old rival Genoa turned to the west, joining the Spanish American project as a favoured client. In a testament to Venetian commercial acumen the state organised the collection and dissemination of the latest knowledge, through the dynamic print industry. In the 1550s Giovanni Battista Ramusio, a Secretary to the ruling Council of Ten, published the first major collection of travel narratives from the ancient Greeks to the latest expeditions. His critical methodology served the needs of practical men.[61] The text was an official document, disseminating ideas and authorities to support the revival of Venetian maritime enterprise.

Fortunately for Venice the spice trade did not collapse after the Portuguese rounded Africa's Cape of Good Hope; Lisbon monopolists preferred to keep prices high, allowing Venice to remain competitive for another century. The Venetian spice trade ended when the Dutch seized the Spice Islands early in the seventeenth century, monopolising supply from plantation to market. Soon Venetians bought their spices in Amsterdam, and shifted to other trades, including exporting wine and dried fruit from their remaining Greek islands to northern Europe. However, falling returns on maritime enterprise encouraged investment in the more profitable *terra firma*. By the seventeenth century, Venice was effectively self-sufficient in food, which 'reduced the extent to which the wealth of the Serenissima depended on the sea'.[62] Now Venice no longer needed to be a seapower.

At the same time the patterns of trade were shifting. The staple trades in state-run merchant galleys, carrying high-value, low-volume cargo, spices, silks and luxuries, folded in the 1530s. This reduced the value of the Venetian 'system of interlocking bases, patrols, and trading convoys' and the role of the state. The great merchant galleys had been state assets; they were replaced by privately owned sailing ships that hauled bulkier commodities, food and raw materials. Increasingly sophisticated three-masted rigs enabled them to replace galleys, and open new routes. Here the Venetians faced stiff competition from heavily armed English sailing ships, as ready to plunder as trade. The English were propelled by commercial imperatives, the emerging seapower ideology of the Elizabethan state, and a growing taste for Ionian currants. With Venice no longer the sole arbiter of East–West trade, revenues were seriously reduced. The state responded by imposing higher customs dues, which encouraged smuggling and collusion with English traders. In the decade after the great victory at Lepanto (1571) the eastern sea empire began to crumble.[63]

Venice met the mid-sixteenth-century cycle of war, fire and plague, widely believed to herald an impending catastrophe, and the more immediate reality of economic decline, with new civic and religious ceremonials, binding all levels of society to an identity driven by markedly increased religiosity. The drama began with the Ottoman assault on Malta in 1565, an event that divided Venetian opinion. Some thought another Turkish war inevitable, others were anxious for peace with the Sultan, to retain the Eastern trade. The synergy with Dutch attitudes, and those of Carthage, is obvious. Venice was powerful because it was rich, and that wealth was based on trade; therefore it was necessary to trade with the enemy. Recognising that war would be costly, and offered little hope of success, only a direct attack would bring the Venetians to war. In 1570 the Turks struck Cyprus, at the eastern end of the empire, confidant that a major fire in the Arsenale had weakened Venice. Antonio Bragadin's heroic defence of the naval base at Famagusta bought the Republic time to mobilise, while his terrible fate made the stakes clear to all. Having surrendered on terms, including safe conduct, the garrison was subsequently massacred. For two days the Turks tortured Bragadin, who had cost them dearly in manpower and time, outside the city gate. Then he was flayed alive. Within weeks an eyewitness account was in print.[64] Although the Republic had little faith in Roman pontiffs and Habsburg monarchs, it joined Spain in Pius V's Holy League, as the last hope of preserving the overseas empire.

The war would be fought with new weapons. After Zonchio heavy cannon were mounted on galleys, a ship-killing weapon system. These gun-armed galleys were central to Mediterranean warfare, dominated by bases, fortresses and amphibious operations, long after heavy sailing ships had become standard in the Atlantic world. Galleys could operate close inshore, engage land defences and disembark troops. Venetian galley design and construction were improved by access to ancient texts, a typically practical Venetian use of humanist learning.

By 1560 Mediterranean galleys carried a powerful forward-firing battery of five cannon, a powerful central weapon and two pairs of lighter artillery. Venice retained professional rowing crews who were armed, free men with an eye for plunder. Ottoman and Spanish ships were rowed by shackled slaves. The introduction of *a scaloccio* rowing in the 1550s, using multiple men pulling each oar, reduced the demand for skilled oarsmen. One skilled man could direct four raw recruits. This system enabled the galley to grow and carry more soldiers. Artillery and larger rowing crews enhanced the galleys' tactical power, at the expense of strategic mobility, and greatly increased their cost. At the same time the falling cost of heavy guns made sailing ships more efficient warships. The massive logistical demands of great galley fleets were already being serviced by sailing ships; it was but a small step to put the guns and soldiers onto the new platforms. Furthermore the end of commercial galley trade meant Venice no longer generated expert oarsmen.

Sixteenth-century war galleys were finely tuned to the strategic and tactical thinking of their owners. Venetian galleys, used to relieve fortresses and chase pirates, were faster and carried relatively few troops, relying on superior guns and gunners. Venetian commanders were the most skilful, and determined, well aware that disgrace, or worse, awaited cowards and fools. Spanish galleys, the most powerfully armed and manned, were designed for amphibious assault, sacrificing speed and agility, while Ottoman craft carried troops and guns for strategic operations against islands and coastal territory, emphasising agility and acceleration for evasion because the Sultan sought territory, not control of the sea.[65] Yet just as the tactical power of the post-1550 galley fleets peaked, it was neutralised by cost and strategic immobility. Galley fleets only met in battle in the very unlikely event that both sides wanted to fight.

By this time Venice had been outmatched at sea by the Ottomans and the Habsburgs, empires that commanded vast resources and numerous maritime subjects. Much like the ancient Persians, the Ottomans dragooned seafaring subjects into war fleets, while the Habsburgs relied on clients such as Genoa, possessions such as Naples and domestic centres such as Barcelona. Furthermore, Venice faced a terrible dilemma. It had no friends: the Habsburgs threatened Venetian independence, the Ottomans their empire and trade. Balancing these threats in the sixteenth century cost Venice most of its sea empire.

Down to the 1570s the Ottomans held the initiative; their centralised empire proved more effective at mobilising and deploying power than the fractious Christian world. Having conquered Cyprus in 1571, Sultan Selim changed Ottoman strategy, ordering his admiral, Ali Pasha, to destroy the galley fleet of the Holy League, the combined forces of Spain, Venice and the Pope. The two fleets, both over 200 strong, met off the former Venetian port of Lepanto in the Gulf of Corinth on 7 October.

In the last and largest galley battle the fleets engaged head on. Both sides tried to maximise their advantages, cover their deficiencies and exploit enemy weaknesses. The Holy League, commanded by Don Juan of Austria, bastard half-brother of Philip II, planned to smash the Ottoman centre with a heavy concentration of outsized flagships, or lantern galleys, while his wing squadrons blocked Ottoman outflanking manoeuvres. The Venetians were given the inshore station, as the most skilful operators with the lightest draught galleys. The Christians had more ships and more soldiers, and generally fought from higher decks. The Ottoman plan relied on superior tactical agility to turn both allied flanks.

Having learnt to value firepower the Venetians converted redundant trade galleys into galleasses, large, heavily armed oar-and-sail hybrids, each carrying more cannon than five galleys. Six were deployed ahead of Don Juan's line, two for each division, to break up the advancing Turkish formation. Four got into position, on the Christian centre and left wing, where they sank some galleys and disordered the Ottoman advance. Despite that the Ottoman right wing crept around the Venetian flank. Once the Turks were committed the Venetian admiral Agostino Barbarigo skilfully pivoted his line and crushed them against the shore with artillery and close-quarters fighting, in which Barbarigo and many more Venetian officers were killed.

Ali Pasha had launched a furious assault on the Christian flagship, pinning the allied centre, while his wing squadrons developed the decisive flank attacks. Here Don Juan's heavy ships paid dividends. Once they had fired their bow guns, normally at point-blank range, both sides were committed. Any ship that tried to turn away would be destroyed. With their ships literally locked in battle soldiers exchanged missile fire from the tightly packed decks and attempted to board, while fresh soldiers were fed onto the main platforms from other galleys. Finally, Spanish infantry, many wearing armour and using powerful muskets, surged onto Ali Pasha's flagship. Hit by a musket ball, Ali was captured, dragged to Don Juan's flagship and summarily beheaded. The Turkish centre collapsed.

The two galleasses covering the allied right wing failed to reach their station, which helped the Ottoman commander Uluj Ali to outmanoeuvre

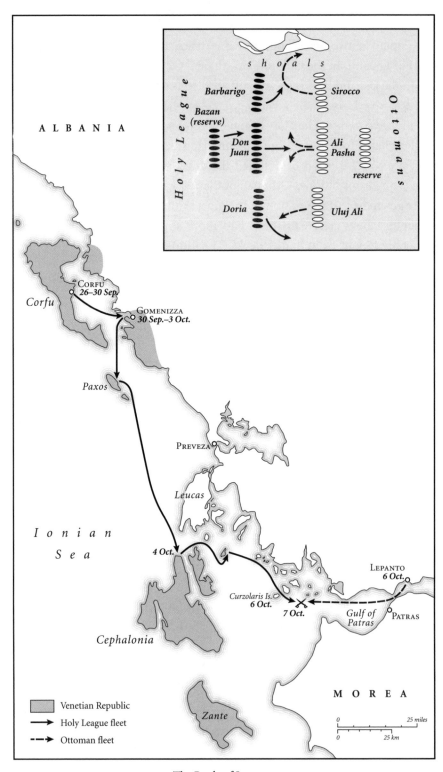

The Battle of Lepanto

the pedestrian Genoese Admiral Gian Andrea Doria. Constantly threatening Doria's exposed right flank, Uluj drew the Christian squadron out of position, detaching it from the centre. Once a suitable gap had opened he darted back, heading for Don Juan's flank. He reached the main battle just as the Ottoman centre collapsed, and ran into a fresh allied reserve. With the battle lost and his admiral dead, flight was the only option. The thirty galleys Uluj led away were the only coherent Ottoman force to escape the catastrophe.

More than 60 per cent of the Ottoman ships were taken, at least 30,000 men, half the fleet, were killed or captured, and many Christian galley slaves were liberated. At one level the Christians did very little with their victory, because the campaign season had almost ended, and they had not agreed on higher policy. However, the real result became obvious in 1572. An Ottoman fleet of over 200 hastily constructed galleys reappeared in Greek waters, but Uluj Ali carefully avoided battle, waiting under the guns of Modon, where the allies did not dare attack. Although the Ottoman galleys had been replaced, the skilled archers, marines and above all petty officers and pilots proved irreplaceable. The new fleet was only a shadow of the one that had fought at Lepanto. The Venetians and the Spaniards ensured the damage done that day lasted for decades by executing all the skilled mariners. Turkish soldiers made good galley slaves, but Turkish mariners were too dangerous to be left alive.

Victory at Lepanto saved Corfu and Dalmatia from Ottoman attacks, but it could not recover Cyprus. Voltaire began a long tradition when he dismissed the battle of Lepanto as an empty spectacle, barren of any results, an argument that misunderstood the mental world of sixteenth-century Venice and Christendom. Lepanto had an immense, uplifting psychological impact on the Christian West, ending decades of Turkish success in a fashion that could be attributed to divine intervention. In Venice it ended a prolonged crisis of confidence dating back to Zonchio, assuming enormous symbolic significance as the Republic rebuilt its identity for a diminished future.[66]

Venice deployed Lepanto to regild their naval prowess, celebrating naval heroism and relief that the Republic still knew how to fight. The heroic leadership of admirals Sebastiano Venier and Agostino Barbarigo was venerated at Roman triumphs, complete with captured slaves. All levels of society had a stake in the battle, aristocrats, shipwrights and oarsmen celebrating their seapower identity in a series of events that merged the secular and the spiritual. Naval glory was a common currency when so much of the populace was engaged with the seas.

However, Venice could not live on glory: it needed to trade with the East, and that required an accommodation with the Grand Turk. Caught between the upper and lower millstone of Habsburg and Ottoman power, the Council of Ten secretly opened peace talks. Venice needed an accommodation with one of the great continental powers: Turkey was the better economic option. While the Senate favoured continuing the war, older, wiser men decided otherwise. This 'nation of ship-keepers' had little option. The war had been phenomenally expensive; operating the entire galley fleet consumed Venetian resources at an alarming rate. Realising that peace would be an unwelcome surprise for a highly motivated populace, the government hastily shut down the Lepanto celebrations.[67]

They were also closing the era of Venetian grandeur. In 1572 and 1573 Christian and then Ottoman amphibious fleets captured and recaptured Tunis, the last major operations by fleets of war galleys. They would not be mobilised again. Venetian galleys went back to anti-piracy work, while those of their erstwhile Spanish allies failed to get into the English Channel in 1588. The Mediterranean war galley was, as John Guilmartin stressed, 'an evolutionary dead end', created for a theatre of short distances and high concentrations of force, studded with the fortified naval bases they needed for sustained operations. Galleys and their crews needed safe access to the shore every few days, their fighting efficiency declined rapidly if their hulls were not regularly cleaned and greased and the rowers rested, fed and watered. Furthermore the skills needed to row a galley had ceased to be relevant to any economic activity, while men were becoming expensive, as slaves or free men, and strategic power could be delivered by more durable, mobile and sustainable sailing ships. Oared warships remained useful for inshore and riverine work, but the race-built galleon changed everything.[68]

It was no coincidence that the waning of the war galley coincided with that of Venetian great power and the centrality of the Mediterranean world. Ships, states and ocean voyaging had expanded far faster, and more fundamentally, than the city-state of Venice. Once again the growth of proto-hegemonic land empires reduced seapower to marginal status. The last seapowers would be larger states, commanding wider oceans, but they too would be overwhelmed by continental hegemons.

Although they had passed their prime, galleys still had their uses. In 1574 King Henri III of France visited Venice on his way home from Poland. The festivities that marked the occasion highlighted the Venetian switch from Habsburg to French alliance; the show of seapower culture was intended to impress an ally, not deter a rival. Henri entered the city through a temporary ceremonial arch and loggia at the Lido. Designed by Palladio and based on a Roman arch built for Septimius Severus, the arch was decorated with history paintings by Tintoretto and Veronese.[69] It framed the king's initial view of the city, focusing attention on the carefully contrived ceremonial area around the Piazza San Marco. Parallels could be drawn with Henry VIII's use of the Thames between Gravesend and Greenwich to impress Charles V in 1529, as well as the view from the Acropolis and the Great Harbour at Carthage. The ceremonial of power was a major asset in the seapower arsenal. Venetian welcoming ceremonies were packed with ships of trade and ships of war, but this would be a last hurrah for the galley as the Venetian icon. The Doge arrived to greet Henri III in the gilded *Bucintoro*, which ferried them both around the city. Henri was accommodated in the Ca' Foscari, halfway along the Grand Canal, the better to appreciate Venetian difference. The Arsenale was a central feature of the ceremonial. Workmen assembled a galley while the king ate lunch, a demonstration that left a lasting impression on the French. A century later, when Colbert began building Louis XIV's battlefleet, the Arsenale remained the exemplar of best practice.[70] Neither minister nor monarch recognised that such concentrations of naval resources were only possible in a seapower state. The visit justified all the hard work and expense, providing Venice with a powerful ally against Philip II, one that was allied to the Sultan.

Having purchased peace and trade at a heavy price the Republic rebuilt its defences to deter further Turkish aggression. Obliged by the 1573 Treaty with the Sultan to limit its fleet to sixty galleys, Venice mass-produced frame timbers, so that many more could be built when required. This technology, developed from ancient methods, had been demonstrated to Henri III. The Arsenale, as the workshop and symbol of state power, was upgraded: winged victories were added to the main gate, and a massive new ropeworks was built in the most severely practical style. These would be displayed to high-status visitors, along with the *Bucintoro*'s elaborate ship-shed and the arms store, whose classical porticos paraded state ideology. As places of strength their architecture echoed Sansovino's Mint.[71] These measures may have helped deter the Turks, although Ottoman offensive capacity at sea had been gravely weakened at Lepanto. A new ceremonial shipshed for the *Bucintoro* marked the point at which galleys slid into marginal roles, a fitting metaphor for the ebb tide of Venetian great power.

It was fortunate the war had ended. Venice suffered another devastating outbreak of the plague between 1575 and 1577, in which a quarter of the population died. Fresh liturgies and ceremonials were followed by the construction of the Palladian Church of Il Redentore, celebrating the passing of the pestilence. In 1577 Sebastiano Venier, the hero of Lepanto, became Doge, a tribute to his heroic status rather than his suitability for office. Naval might and divine protection, represented in art, architecture and output from the Arsenale, helped Venice manage disease and decline.

Once the crisis of the 1570s had passed, Lepanto was triumphantly restored to the centre of Venetian iconography, despite the fact that Spain and the Papacy had become enemies. This dramatic, divinely ordained, victory suggested that the Venetians were the new Israelites, the chosen people, marking a further development of the Myth of Venice, adding new ideas to a necessary past that was constantly evolving to sustain continuity and order. In the years that followed, major public spaces inside the Doge's Palace, the cult centre of Venetian seapower, which had recently been ravaged by fire, were redecorated by the finest architects and artists, illustrating the long seapower history of the Republic that had culminated in the glory of Lepanto and the visit of Henri III, symbols of continuing consequence:

> as so often in the history of the Republic, the Venetian elite carefully adjusted the rhetoric of the Myth of Venice so that it remained effective as both an expression of Venetian self-confidence as well as a means of social control, while still taking account of the lessons of recent history. For all of its shaky foundation, the mythology continued as Venice slid into terminal decline.[72]

Although relative decline could not be avoided, the Venetians managed the process with remarkable skill. Venice avoided the fate of Athens and

Carthage, surviving as a trading power for another two centuries. The Dutch and the British would follow similar trajectories, and they found much to emulate in the Republic, not least the manner of its retreat from power. In a world dominated by ever-larger powers, ones bent on continental hegemony, possessing the resources to overwhelm the naval efforts of seapower states and the economic weight to crush their trade-dependent systems, Venice had to tread very carefully. Beyond a certain level of resources, size and weight overwhelmed the asymmetric advantage of seapower, stripped away the empires that funded the seapower project, and demoted them to second- or third-rank status. The creation of large hegemonic empires condemned an unchanging Venice to relative decline: 'Venice stayed the same, while the world around it changed.'[73] In one critical area, commercial shipping, decline was absolute. Frederic Lane, who knew a great deal about US merchant shipbuilding and subsidies, made a telling analogy with Venice: both republics began as seapowers, but slowly morphed into something very different, losing their comparative advantage in shipbuilding and ship-operating. Both states resorted to protectionist legislation: the United States evolved into a continental military hegemon, but Venice lost ground to more efficient Dutch and English shipping. Tariff barriers could not keep them out of the market.[74] Adriatic piracy, by local actors and ships from the North Sea, imposed additional costs on Venetian shipping. Ultimately protectionism failed: dominion over regional trade was more important to Venice than the maintenance of a domestic shipping industry.

Defending the sea empire against the proto-hegemonic Ottoman Empire in the century after 1560 devastated the Venetian economy and the trading network. After the loss of Crete in the mid-seventeenth century, Venice's Eastern trading network, the reason for the sea empire, became uneconomic. Although the remaining insular possessions had little economic potential, Venice remained obsessed with their defence, adding to the heavy debt burden of an exhausted state. Markets were lost to more agile rivals, amongst whom the English became increasingly significant.[75]

Overwhelmed at sea, and stripped of key Eastern bases, Venice's economic focus shifted to the *terra firma*, where returns on investment were higher, and more secure. Venice was fast becoming just another Italian state, even if the legacy of maritime connections provided useful opportunities and rewards. Manufacturing expanded, in part to fill gaps created by war and unrest in other Italian centres. The slow shift from entrepôt to manufacturing town was well underway as Venetian power ebbed away. Industry and capital, processing to add value, and loans for interest, replaced the carrying trade. By the end of the sixteenth century, as Fernand Braudel observed, Venice was 'the foremost industrial city in Italy'.[76] The explosive growth of cloth manufacture employed the urban poor, while high-grade glass dominated the scientific and luxury markets of Europe.

As private trade waned the state became a major employer, finding work for the aristocracy in embassies, the Church, the navy and the administration of the cities of the *terra firma* and the sea empire. By the beginning of the seventeenth century, Venice had paid down the state debt: taxes declined, enabling many elite families to live off the state. Banking developed along lines pioneered elsewhere in Italy, although the chartered and joint stock companies so important to Dutch and British seapower imperialism would not be adopted for many years.

During the thirteenth century Venice had deliberately created a maritime economy, blocking alternative outlets for capital, including land. The first capitalist economy would be sustained by consistent state intervention, which included measures to boost trade, including marine insurance, convoys and naval patrols. Reversing the ban on alternative investments in 1516 largely removed the Venetian aristocracy from overseas trade. By the seventeenth century, wealthy merchants were a separate group, including foreigners, lacking direct access to the levers of power.[77] State support for costly naval activity declined.

In decline, Venetian culture became a critical element in the European milieu; different aspects of the city gripped visitors from across the continent and the British Isles beyond. The English had begun to see something of themselves in Venice before 1500, when men of learning came to buy Greek texts from Aldus Manutius. These texts educated the men of power, who brought them into their libraries and their policies. John Dee, geographer, astrologer, navigator and inventor of the term 'British Empire', owned three copies of the Aldine Thucydides. Francis Walsingham and William Cecil had copies, Sir Walter Raleigh used it, and Thomas Hobbes translated it into English. At the same time Walsingham and Cecil's son Robert supported Richard Hakluyt's great voyage compendium, *The Principal Navigations, Voyages and Discoveries of the English Nation* (1589), which was inspired and informed by Ramusio. These borrowings were avowed, conscious and deliberate, shifting the locus of seapower from the Lagoon to the Thames.

There was an obvious synergy between these seapower states. Both were dominated by 'great commercial centres highly dependent on maritime trade, with similarities also at the level of urban administration ... London and Venice dominated the states of which they were capitals, and this lack of real urban competition set them apart from most of their European counterparts.'[78]

Venice moved away from a seapower identity just as the English began to imagine and then shape their own. The Commonwealth interregnum empowered the London merchant elite, and after the Restoration of 1660 their concerns remained significant. In 1688 they grabbed a share of power in the new Constitutional Monarchy, helping to create a synergistic landed/ commercial oligarchy of money and influence. The Venetians had anticipated these developments back in the 1610s: they could see both Dutch and English merchants copying their economic ideas and breaking into their markets. English success was both a source of pride and a reason to urge the recovery of Venetian seapower. It was singularly ironic that Sir Henry Wotton, James I's ambassador, should remind the Senate that both England and Venice relied on the sea for prosperity and power, and that trade and statecraft were intimately connected, blissfully unaware that his audience knew far more about such subjects than anyone in England.[79]

By the 1650s Venice was facing a critical problem. Too weak at sea to meet Ottoman aggression it hired armed sailing ships from English and Dutch contractors. These ships helped win battles, but they were the harbingers of economic ruin. Venice gazed longingly at the English Commonwealth's mighty navy and the direct way it was used to support the expansion of English commerce. It was all too reminiscent of Venice in the age of Doge Enrico Dandolo. The English might be simple folk, but they were very strong, and would make fine allies. The Venetians recognised that the English Navigation Laws of 1651 had been developed from Venetian legislation of 1602. However, the Venetians had been trying to shield a waning asset from competition, while the English were promoting a dynamic, expansive sector.[80] Just as the Venetian leadership lost sight of the sea, the newly empowered merchant elite of the English Commonwealth used the navy to grab a growing share of Levantine trade, the old staple of Venetian commerce. That they did so through an overt act of conscious emulation demonstrates how closely London had observed La Serenissima. David Ormrod argues that the English Navigation Acts were a 'staggeringly ambitious' drive to create an 'overarching national monopoly within which English shipping and long-distance trade could develop', based on Venetian models.[81] That policy required commanding naval power, the synergy of state, sea and strength to ensure the Navigation Laws would be sustained by a seapower culture and an ideology that connected London merchants with political power.

As trade fell away in the seventeenth century, Venice concentrated on securing the Adriatic. State administration remained in the hands of the nobility, with no thought of democracy. The elite that ran Venice abandoned commerce and found a new vocation: too proud to trade, and too Venetian to farm, this tightly knit group of rich and powerful families monopolised the great offices of state and Church, hierarchies that, in turn, preserved their self-esteem and civic status. More adventurous nobles found roles in the navy, although not the army, and in colonial government. These could be springboards to high office. The decision to move out of trade, into land and state bonds, would be a common response to wealth in seapower states.

At the turn of the eighteenth century, the English classicist, essayist and politician Joseph Addison blamed the decline of Venetian trade on an aristocratic regime more concerned with privilege than profit. Contemporary Venetian nobles thought trade undignified, and newly rich merchants were quick to follow their example.[82] As an educated Englishman, Addison assumed it obvious that trading nations must remain open to novelty and change. He also accused the Venetians of neglecting their strength at sea: 'they might, perhaps have all the islands of the [Aegean] archipelago in their hands, and by consequence, the greatest fleet, and the most seamen of any other state in Europe'. It seemed the Republic existed merely for the sake of existing.[83] Yet the English found things to admire in Venice, because it was an elegant, antique mirror held up to reflect their emerging sense of a seapower self. Something of that understanding can be seen in their preference for the precise sparkling artworks of Canaletto over the more artistic output of his contemporary Francesco Guardi, images that satisfied Venetian taste.[84]

The move to the *terra firma* preserved commercial fortunes, but a maritime republic that depended on aristocratic leadership to sustain dynamic growth suffered. The stately aristocracy of Venice chose to live quietly; some wrote histories, to inform the political process and promote the image of the state. These histories echoed the great art cycles created for the Doge's Palace. At the same time the Venetian aristocracy rejected external control: as Paolo Sarpi made clear in 1606, the Venetians were not papal Catholics. They rejected any universal authority, especially one tinged with unbecoming excesses of territorial imperialism. When the Pope allied himself to Spain at the head of Catholic reaction, the Venetian elite kept the Catholic shock troops, the Jesuits, out of the city.[85] For Venetians, the state, not the Church, was the ultimate object of public veneration, an ideology reflected in a service culture that outlasted the glory days of seapower. By 1700 those ideas had become ossified. The magnificence remained, with ornate gilded palazzi, fine art, music and theatre expressing a sense of self that maintained their social distance from the lower orders, and fascinated tourists. The Venetian elite became an attraction.

Plague, war and debt left Venice too weak to operate as a great power in an era of expansive continental military empires. It turned to diplomacy, neutrality and costly fortifications, because it lacked the political dynamism to undertake fundamental change. After 1718 the Republic remained neutral, relying on Austria for protection from the Turks. France sent warships into the Adriatic in 1702, prompting the cancellation of that year's 'Wedding of the Sea', a decision that 'symbolised the end of Venetian pretensions to control the operations of foreign warships in the Adriatic'.[86] Waning naval power and prestige mirrored weakened authority, customs dues went uncollected, and Austria developed Trieste as an alternative Adriatic link to Germany. It seemed that a moribund sea state would be sustained by the profits of land and industry, that seapower had become a vanity project, a residual legacy that helped to market the Republic, rather than a strategic or economic reality. Yet although the economic value of the maritime empire crumbled, the image of seapower remained deeply embedded in the Venetian identity.

As Venetian horizons shrank the attractions of *terra firma* grew. The last imperial outposts of Venice were the Ionian Islands, fortresses and naval bases of limited economic significance. Corfu, once the gateway to the

Levant, became a defensive bastion to secure the Adriatic. Critically, neither the Stato da Mar nor the *terra firma* were ever integrated into the Venetian political system. While Venice retained all the pomp of seapower, the cost of the sea empire exceeded the economic returns. Yet Venetian leaders expressed no interest in the obvious alternative, turning to the *terra firma,* building a 'normal' state, and sharing power with the mainland provinces.[87] Venice remained a maritime city-state, defiantly different from the rest of Italy, independent and unique. To the very end Venetian perspectives took in the world. Their heroes were travellers, traders and admirals: seven hundred years of sustained interaction with the East had created a culture apart from Italy and Europe.

Critics affected to see nothing but corruption and decay in the Republic's final century, but there was another version of the story. By preserving peace after 1718, Venice managed to halve the mountain of state debt incurred in the previous century, and adjust to the reality of being a second-rate regional power. Late-eighteenth-century Venice underwent a small but significant naval/maritime revival with an increase in commercial activity, even if the capitalists and the ship captains were no longer exclusively Venetian. Venice's merchants were the first Europeans to open a business at the Red Sea port of Jeddah, trading coffee from 1770; the city was a major player in Levantine commerce.[88] This new energy may have reflected the reopening of the aristocracy, which enabled wealthy merchants to buy a place at the top table.

Despite the reality of relative decline and the loss of naval dominance Venice survived. It remained a major entrepôt and economic centre; signs of decline were matched by resurgent commerce. By the 1780s trade with north Africa was booming, shipbuilding had recovered, and the port was busier than ever. Furthermore, Venetian naval forces were active on the Barbary Coast, upholding treaties and a newly recodified set of maritime laws. Venice had a future in a balanced, multi-polar world: it remained a unique example of stable, secure republican government in a world of monarchs and misrule. Beneath the froth and frippery of Carnival and the pleasures of theatre and concert, there remained a set of ideas and images that helped to shape other sea-based identities.

The Venetian navy was revived in the eighteenth century, combining seventy-gun ships of the line and galleys. It was no longer dominated by Venetians; many of the officers and crew were hired, replacing an aristocracy that had abandoned the ocean, and a lower order content to work at home. In the absence of major wars the navy supported commerce, combating pirates and corsair states. The economy continued to grow, especially textile industries, while the Republic had food to export. Even the proportion of the population employed at and around the sea was growing. This suggests that, once wars and plagues had been factored out, the underlying reality of Venetian populations was that they grew steadily and maintained a maritime focus. Venice remained a profitable sea state, even if great-power status was but a hazy memory.

Admiral Angelo Emo's attack on Tunis in 1785 provided Venetian aristocrats, who numbered Emo among their number, with a sensational demonstration of the continuing strategic consequence of sea power. Disciplining corsair states reduced the risk and cost of maritime commerce. A worthy heir of Enrico Dandolo, Emo re-energised the Arsenale and shipbuilding programmes. Yet, in a curious reversal of chronology, Emo's monument, commemorating the last event in Venetian naval history, commands the entrance to the Venetian Naval Museum.[89]

In 1792, Venice, a leading port and shipbuilding centre, and possessing an effective navy, was ideally placed to profit from the wars that would convulse Europe and to recover its seapower identity.[90] Five years later the Republic was overwhelmed. Unable to comprehend the meaning of a new world dominated by radical, violent change, and fearful for their extensive estates on the *terra firma*, the elite caved in without a fight at French dictation. On 12 May 1797 La Serenissima abolished itself, allowing French troops to occupy the Piazza San Marco, where no invading army had ever stood before. Napoleon emptied the Mint and ransacked the Arsenale, sending ships to join the French fleet, laden with guns and stores. Venetian emblems in the Arsenale were defaced, and the *Bucintoro* was ceremonially burnt on Isla San Giorgio, in a conscious echo of Scipio's destruction of the Carthaginian battlefleet. Napoleon had updated Livy: his bonfire marked the end of Venetian independence, oligarchy and above all seapower.

Although the substance of seapower had long since departed from the Lagoon, Napoleon incinerated the symbols, because he hated everything that they represented. He systematically annihilated Venice's name and reputation, much as the Romans had done to Carthage, stealing the archives and art treasures that defined Venetian identity. Five months later he gave the plundered ruins to Austria, only to take them back to build a new naval base in 1805. Whereas Antwerp and Den Helder built fleets that carried heroic local names and identities, the fleet reconstructed at Venice ignored the past.[91] Perhaps Napoleon feared the message it would convey. He spent the rest of his career attempting to apply the flaming torch of continental imperialism to the last of Venice's successors.

Napoleon systematically defaced the city: filling in canals and opening public gardens, best known today as the location of the Biennale art festival. His work, like that of Scipio Aemillianus, ensured French, Austrian and mainland Italian regimes would not be oppressed by reminders of a far greater past, one that that had shaped global consciousness, a past that continues to pose awkward questions. When Napoleon fell, the Austrians continued his work, bringing central European soldiers and their military bands to the sea city, building a causeway to destroy everything that made Venice special, the easier to exert control. Ironically, the final ruin of Venice as a port came at the hands of the British. Their blockade of Napoleon's Italian Empire devastated regional trade, redirecting Venetian traffic into different havens.

Venice's unique nature, a former Byzantine satellite that consciously chose to become a seapower, was sustained through the construction of a foundation story that combined divine intervention with an invented Roman heritage in an endlessly evolving myth that served as a tool of civic prestige and communal cohesion. However, such mythologies attract counter-narratives. Habsburg Spain, an imperial hegemon, created a 'Black Legend' of Venice as a tyrannical oligarchy of spies and torture, a moribund sink of vice. One suspects they had some help from their Genoese clients. Napoleon deployed this 'Black Legend', directing a tame historian to update the Spanish story from captured Venetian archives. Pierre Daru, the former military logistician, concluded: 'The victim richly deserved her fate.' By the time Daru's book appeared, between 1815 and 1818, the fate of the city had been settled. The Congress of Vienna handed it to Austria, a state with little interest in the ocean. Napoleon read Daru's book in exile on St Helena; his notes on 1797 were added to the second edition of a text that assuaged the guilt of an age that upheld Napoleon's destruction of the Republic. By condemning the idea of a seapower state, Daru served the continental great powers. The book was soon discredited: Leopold von Ranke exposed the use of forged documents, and it was not translated into English.[92]

Greatly reduced by French and Austrian occupation, its absorption into Italy finally crushed the very essence of Venice – the beating maritime heart of a region that stretched far beyond the territorial limits of the modern state. The self-centred metropolis of the ocean became just another city, and a small one at that, in a continental state dominated by Rome, Turin and Milan. The sea was no longer central to the polity that ruled Venice. Italy completed the ruin that Napoleon had begun, homogenising Venice, a unique sea-city, into a continental whole dominated by industry and agriculture. Venice has been shorn of its commerce, while outsized tourist ships dwarf the most beautiful of all seascapes, pumping the tiny streets full of indolent bodies. The process had been paralleled by the stripping away of the sea from Venetian cultural history, as if the city on the Lagoon made up the whole of Venice. This is a common approach when old sea empires are reimagined for post-imperial presentation. Grotesquely diminished by this process Venice has been reduced to a decorative attraction on a mud bank at the blunt end of the Adriatic, the wonderful cultural treasures seemingly assembled at random. There are no ships: the *Bucintoro* and the Wedding of the Sea are but memories: Church, state and soil have overwhelmed a unique seapower identity. Modern Venetian Catholicism is Roman and terrestrial, where once it was defiantly local and maritime. The modern emblem of the city is the humble gondola, a water taxi, not the great galleys of war and trade, nor yet the heroic galleass of Lepanto. The Arsenale should echo to the sound of axe and adze, shaping a replica galley, to show the world that Venice, once ruler of the seas and emporium of the oceans, was the fulcrum of modernity, and a beacon of stability and order in a region blighted by war, insurrection, conquest and chaos.

Civic magnificence, ceremonial pomp and classical symbols instructed visitors in the purpose and power of La Serenissima – a place apart. The great architecture of the seapower state in Venice, and across the maritime empire, faced the sea, carefully designed to impress approaching visitors, connect the state to older examples of strength and stability, and proclaim the impregnability of vulnerable imperial possessions. The ceremonial spaces of the Piazza and Bacino San Marco celebrated the city and the business on which it depended. Today an endless stream of visitors look but do not see; they are close to the sea, but unaware of the intentions of the men who made Venice the mistress of the Adriatic. So alien is the very idea of seapower that the elegant, inconsequential Venetian amusements developed for eighteenth-century tourists have come to define the city. The brooding Arsenale lies off the beaten track, a quiet place for those who care to reflect how easily the meaning of history can be obscured.

While the Venetian seapower state managed the competing attractions of maritime trade, secured by control of the sea, and terrestrial expansion on the adjacent Italian mainland, these were never the simple either/or alternatives posited by contemporary commentators and historians, Venetian or outsider. Venice achieved great-power status on the margins of a disordered world, operating in a period when the larger states of the Mediterranean were focused on terrestrial issues. When that situation changed, proto-hegemonic land powers built navies to control trade and extend their imperial sway. To meet this challenge Venice expanded its terrestrial base beyond the Lagoon, to secure the timber, manpower and food it needed to sustain an ever-increasing level of naval power. Only a dominant navy could secure the overseas commercial empire and the chain of insular bases that serviced merchant shipping and the galleys that protected them. Insular empires sustained Athenian and Carthaginian seapower, resource-rich areas providing men, money, food and raw materials. When rich, dynamic seapower states began acting as land powers they alarmed continental rivals.

The Venetian empire of trade relied on a network of naval bases and islands, linking the city to the major ports of the Levant. These ports were separated by no more than two days at cruising speed under oars, a requirement for low-endurance trade galleys. Venetian territorial possessions, both overseas and on the Italian mainland, served connected commercial and strategic needs. They were interconnected and interdependent.[93] Although Venice combined land and sea empires it remained a seapower: only the asymmetric strategic and economic advantages conferred by seapower could enable a small, weak city-state in northern Italy to operate as a great power. From first to last Venice was defined by the sea. The sea ceased to be the main source of wealth in the seventeenth century, but still dominated Venetian identity, ceremonial and culture.

Continental hegemons built navies to counter the threat posed by Venetian wealth and ideology; Venice responded by upgrading the fleet and the Arsenale as a deterrent, and ensured these symbols were understood by presenting them in classical cultural forms. Venice created a diplomatic service to provide advance warning of danger, using wealth to build alliances and secure political support. These measures delayed the inevitable: Venice could not sustain great-power status, and refused to integrate the land and sea empires into the political structure. Ultimately, the critical question for all seapower states was how to retain their distinctive culture as they expanded to distant islands and continental territory. Territorial possessions threatened to change or dilute the core identity. Most seapowers chose to ignore the political concerns of such territory, either ruling them directly or through subcontractors, as aristocratic fiefs or company possessions. Venice used all three models. As the standards of great power rose, Venice, unlike Athens and Carthage, chose managed relative decline. It was fortunate that the expansive energy of the Ottoman Empire had ebbed, while other regional powers were focused elsewhere. Eighteenth-century Venice remained a significant regional actor, although increasingly industrialised and intent on terrestrial possessions. The Dutch Republic would follow the same trajectory. The parallels between Venice and Amsterdam in decline were profound, rather more so than in their great-power days. Both remained rich, commercial and maritime, until they, along with Genoa, were wiped out in a grand bonfire of European sea states in the late 1790s, by the new proto-Roman hegemonic empire of Republican France. In 1815 the Congress of Vienna ratified Napoleon's decision to incorporate Genoa and Venice into continental states, but Britain restored and reinforced the Dutch state, to serve its strategic interests. Some in Britain wished to revive Genoa, but Venice had been damned by Spanish and French propaganda. It would take the British several decades to untangle myth and reality in their understanding of the first modern seapower state.[94]

Venice was a true seapower, a great power sustained by an empire of maritime trade, connected by sea and secured by naval power. Empire and Navy sustained the self-esteem of the state, supported by monumental civic architecture.[95] However, like every other seapower, Venice also exploited mainland territories, the *terra firma*, bringing it into collision with continental hegemons. The two empires financed Venice's freedom and power, without political representation. Seapower was far more than control of shipping lanes: it was an identity that shaped the state and the way the state ruled over colonial and conquered territory. Venice centralised the economic activity of the empire around a dominant entrepôt whose customs revenues funded the entire project. The critical role of seapower as culture and identity was emphasised by the long, agonising defence of the insular empire against overwhelming odds, the maintenance of a great navy long after the economic value of seapower had waned, and the striking resurgence of the sea in the last decades of independence. The 'Myth of Venice' may have exaggerated reality, but it had solid foundations.

Venice occupies a critical place in the intellectual history of seapowers, the bridge between the classical and modern worlds, between East and West, and the exemplar for seapower successors. Both the Dutch and the English ransacked Venetian culture and identity to shape their own seapower projects. Nineteenth-century Britons installed Venice among their precursor states, grasping the underlying reality of a city that had become little more than a ruin, crumbling back into the sea from whence it had first risen. In 1851, the year of the Great Exhibition, John Ruskin's eccentric examination of Venetian culture employed the city as a salutary warning of impending doom.[96] Ruskin's analysis of the Republic's loss of vitality remains significant, not because it is accurate, which it is not, but because it recognised the reality of a city where public and private culture reflected the unique seapower identity that had been constructed to sustain Venetian power, and did so in an extraordinarily provocative metaphor.

CHAPTER 5

'To What Great Profit Are We Opening the Sea'[1]
THE DUTCH SEAPOWER STATE

The Dutch Republic, a nation with extensive economic activity at sea, fishing, whaling and carrying trades, and extensive empires in Asia, Africa and America, backed by a successful navy, has commonly been identified as a seapower. But that identity was a brief anomaly. The Republic only operated as a seapower for twenty years, and the identity was never taken to heart by the nation at large. The idea of seapower persisted long after the identity had faded, as part of a debate that lasted until Napoleon abolished the Republic. When the Dutch seapower state collapsed in chaos it left the English to assume the mantle of seapower, an identity they had aspired to for two centuries. In the process the English profited greatly from ideas and methods pioneered by the Dutch, the first northern European seapower. The dramatic uptake of Dutch ideas, methods and merchandise in England, together with a significant movement of bankers and skilled artisans, reflected a fundamental change, one that can best be understood as conscious emulation. This process was accompanied by three essentially naval wars, the only time two states competed to become the seapower.

Seapower temple: the Amsterdam naval magazine and headquarters

The Dutch Empire

The Low Countries had a long maritime tradition, dominated by major rivers and the ports of Bruges, Ghent and later Antwerp. The divergent interests of a region dominated by local agendas were unified in opposition to the centralising regime of the Emperor Charles V, successor to the Dukes of Burgundy.[2] Self-interested local resistance formed a significant part of wider protests against Habsburg rule that led to the Dutch Revolt. Holland, unlike its Flemish neighbours, refused to fund warships to protect the herring fishery, preferring instead to pay for safe-conduct passes. Amsterdam, Gouda, Haarlem and Leiden objected to Charles's attempt to impose taxes, only conceding when the imperial regent banned fishing.[3] Further attempts to raise taxes in Holland in the 1550s played a significant part in sparking the Dutch revolt, and it would be relaunched from the sea by Calvinist privateers who seized the port of Brielle in 1572. Amsterdam, an old opponent of maritime taxation, belatedly joined the rebels in 1578, one of many towns to make a conscious choice. That choice reflected the economic self-interest of an expanding commercial centre, rather than the political and religious convictions that arrived with the Calvinist refugees who fled Antwerp in 1585.

Tax receipts from the seventeen pre-revolt Burgundian provinces show the seven northern provinces, which became the Dutch Republic, had been marginal economic actors. Holland paid less than half the tax of Flanders and Brabant, Amsterdam had 4 per cent of the Netherlands export trade, while Antwerp had more than 80 per cent. The main international trade of pre-Revolt Amsterdam was with the Baltic, largely importing grain for domestic consumption. The Dutch Revolt changed that balance, as Amsterdam inherited powerful networks of trade and finance from Antwerp refugees, linking the city with Iberia and the Mediterranean. The new Republic depended on imported food, including fish, grain and salt, along with key raw materials, timber and iron, for shipbuilding and industry. Between 1585 and 1610 the old trades were reinforced by Asian, Caribbean, Brazilian and Arctic business. There were good reasons to become a seapower. Yet there remained another Republic, landlocked, agricultural and anxious about exposed continental borders, one that saw no reason to follow where Amsterdam and Holland led.[4] These differences mattered in a region heavily influenced by local agendas, where provinces and cities jealously guarded their privileges. The rebel provinces' focus on the sea gave their particularism a distinctive character. The state depended on the support of powerful economic actors who shared power with a quasi-regal princely house and landed aristocrats. This inclusive relationship distinguished the new state from autocratic Spain and France: it gave capitalists a share in power, something that they used to advance their interests through the 'disproportionate leverage over the ultimate deployment of state resources'.[5]

However, the Republic had to be created on land: the political will to win led diverse interest groups, landed and maritime, to pool their resources, accept a military leader and fund a professional army and massive fortifications for wars that required it to outlast Habsburg Spain, the most powerful state on earth, in a war of human and economic attrition. While naval activity played a useful supporting role in the Revolt, it could neither secure nor guarantee the territorial integrity of the new state. By contrast insular England secured territorial integrity by essentially naval means. The Armada campaign of 1588 had significant implications for the Dutch, but they finished fighting for independence sixty years later. Between 1600 and 1609 the overwhelming priority of land warfare, and the attendant costs, left the Dutch with no option but to rely on private-enterprise naval methods. That said, there is no reason to believe that they would have created a standing navy even without the land war. The Republic was not a seapower: it was dominated by the Stadholder, a prince of the House of Orange-Nassau, serving as Captain General, a warrior leader halfway between a Venetian Doge and a King. The Prince also held the office of Admiral General, but never commanded at sea, and left the administration of the fleet to others. The Stadholders secured Dutch independence at the head of armies, not fleets. After 1609 successive Stadholders sought hereditary status, relying on the army to secure that position. Such princely ambition was opposed by the proto-city-state of Amsterdam and the Province of Holland, which favoured a peaceful commercial policy, secured by the powerful navy of a seapower Republic. Far from becoming the accepted national identity Amsterdam's seapower agenda remained a contested option in bitter political battles that split the Republic. The struggle between these diametrically opposed concepts of the state shaped Dutch politics in the seventeenth century. Power shifted from land to sea, from Prince to Republic, while maritime trade and empire created a brief 'Golden Age' of expansive wealth and cultural sophistication.

Amsterdam's argument reflected the reality that ships and trade dominated the economy: over 40 per cent of the labour force worked directly or indirectly in the maritime sector.[6] For two centuries the Republic protected its shipping in peace and war with a cruiser navy, directly linked to trade by local taxation. Yet it never managed to fund the force properly: taxes were avoided or evaded, while 'the fissiparous character of Dutch society constantly obstructed action on a national scale'.[7] The Dutch state, consisting of seven provinces, never accepted seapower as a core national project.

Before 1650 the Republic did not attempt to acquire strategic sea power, the ability to command the sea, it did not build a battlefleet to control the seas, and it did not act as a seapower. It acquired those ambitions and instruments as a direct response to the challenge posed by English control of the Channel, and then only after the Stadholderate had been suspended by a republican oligarchy dominated by Amsterdam.

Between 1653 and 1672 the Stadholderless 'True Freedom' Republic acted as a true seapower, an exceptional great power in the European system, defined by relatively inclusive politics and naval power. The cost of the battlefleet exposed the reality that, while the three maritime provinces consciously chose a seapower identity, the four landlocked provinces did not, so the ideological and cultural core of the Republic remained in flux throughout the years when it operated as a seapower great power. This 'Golden Age' of proto-hegemonic economic power ended in the disastrous year of 1672. A French invasion prompted the restoration of the Stadholder and his armies, a belated recognition of strategic reality. As a continental state with limited territory and inadequate manpower the Republic had to focus on terrestrial concerns, primarily the long land borders. These required costly fixed defences and a standing army, not a battlefleet. The following four decades saw the seapower battlefleet sacrificed to the forts, armies and alliances that would ensure the survival of the state. The Dutch abandoned seapower for security.

In 1579 the Union of Utrecht that created the Republic was a defensive alliance of seven provinces against Spain. It protected their rights and delegated authority to a national States General, the Council of State with around twenty-five members, in which all seven provinces were equally represented. This structure reflected the old structures and separations of power that had been upheld by the Revolt, preserving local exceptionalism in a unique political system, linked by a shared 'national' desire to resist Spanish centralisation. In theory the system obliged cities, provinces and the state to negotiate and compromise, promoting sound decision-making, but Holland's economic and political leverage, largely secured by loans to less prosperous provinces, gave it a dominant voice. The system limited the role of central government, it could co-ordinate but not control the separate provinces. In contrast to contemporary absolutist monarchies the flexibility of the system created stability by integrating different interests, especially the sophisticated balancing of trade and taxation that propelled the economy.[8] The States General met in The Hague, the capital of both Holland and the Republic, every day of the week to direct war, foreign policy and federal taxes. Positive action required unanimity. The Hague was also the seat of the Stadholder. The Republic combined a representative core, directed by local oligarchies, with the overall guidance of an elected head of state. It also enshrined Holland's dominance of the Republic, and Amsterdam's dominance of Holland. Cities held eighteen of the nineteen votes in Holland's Provincial Government, the nobility had one. The system facilitated consultation and negotiation, leading to the aggregation of interest groups.

With the support of England and France the 'bourgeois fiscal-military state' had achieved effective independence by 1588, and created the first modern economy. The defeat of the Spanish Armada by Anglo-Dutch forces enabled the Republic to focus on reducing the threat of maritime predation by Flemish privateers, using aggressive patrolling, convoys and a developing insurance market. Blockading the Scheldt Estuary crushed the economy of Antwerp and the southern provinces; it also stopped Spain bringing troops by sea. Privateering flourished, exploiting investment opportunities and available capital. Relative security at sea focused attention on maritime trade, as did the cash-strapped Republic's decision to delegate overseas naval operations to joint-stock companies that evolved into quasi-national empires.[9]

An obvious expression of the Dutch state, the navy reflected the complexity of domestic politics and a dynamically changing international context. Created in a market-oriented society that solved strategic and organisational problems by economic and contractual methods, the navy grew organically from pre-Revolt convoys and fishery patrols and the 'Sea Beggar' privateers of 1572. It solved strategic problems by controlling critical coastal and inland waters, providing amphibious lift, supported sieges, blockaded Flemish rivers and choked Spanish trade, alongside the core missions of convoying merchant shipping and fishing fleets, a constant demand from the commercial sector.[10] The convoy and licence money had been settled in 1572. Relentless demand for ships, men, money and supplies made the navy one of the most complex organisations in early modern Europe, and that experience filtered out into the wider economy, where large trading companies operated impressive fleets. These missions required a large force of cruisers, many of them hired from local merchants, while Asian and Mediterranean trades required larger ships that could fight. Many of the ship-owners who profited from hiring ships sat on local Admiralty committees. This 'Old Navy' of armed merchant ships, privateers and chartered companies defeated the remnants of Spanish naval power.[11]

The navy was directed by the States General, with the Admiral General (when a Stadholder held that office) and five separate admiralty colleges providing day-to-day administration. The College system, which evolved over the space of twenty years as a response to the divergent interests of commercial elites, was agreed in 1597 as a temporary measure. It lasted until 1795 because it enabled local interests to control local taxes.[12] Three colleges were located in Holland, at Amsterdam, Rotterdam and a shared college for the North Quarter, alternating between Hoorn and Enkhuizen; the others, at Middleburg and Dokkum and after 1645 Harlingen, served Zealand and Friesland. Much of their work was economic. The commercial elite that ran the Admiralty boards were also involved in the administration of the great trading companies, the VoC and the WIC. Consequently, 'Merchant companies had a stake in the organised use of violence to back up their commercial interests, and to varying degrees entertained the right to exercise such violence on their own behalf.'[13] Controlling the collection of convoy and licence money gave local merchant elites significant political power, and ensured the state protected their shipping.

The merchants who directed the admiralties used the navy to escort their merchant ships. The persistence of the cruiser navy, long after the Republic had fallen back into the second rank, reflected the economic importance of maritime activity. Peacetime commerce protection was funded by local convoy fees and licences for privateering and trading with the enemy, along with import dues raised in the inland provinces. These funds were never adequate, leading the four inland provinces to demand that Holland and Zeeland cover the shortfall. In war additional taxes were raised by the States General and by public loans on the Amsterdam capital market, used as subsidy payments by the local Admiralty boards, which lobbied the provincial assemblies to secure more funding.[14]

Often derided as inefficient, the regional Admiralty system sustained a successful seventeenth-century navy by exploiting links between trade and war common to all seapower states. These Admiralty committees had every reason to be effective: not only were they run by men with a background in shipping and trade, they also had access to the largest concentration of maritime resources in northern Europe. Self-interest ensured sound decision-making. An entrepôt economy placed a priority on the safety of shipping, and convoys, in use long before the Revolt, remained the preferred method.[15] Convoys took precedence over fleet battle, cruising and blockading the Flemish ports.[16]

Viewed 'collectively and institutionally' as a defensive seaborne militia, the navy was 'less intimidating, and more national than the army'. Successful admirals became national heroes, the publication of individual and collective biographies helping to cement their status.[17] Yet seamen and officers generally backed the Orange faction, not the 'seapower' States Rights Party. Few officers came from patrician backgrounds. Michiel de Ruyter's States Rights politics, and his friendship with Johan de Witt, poisoned his professional relationship with the Orangist Admiral Cornelis Tromp, and threatened the combat effectiveness of the fleet in 1672.

Before 1650 most Dutch warships were small hired merchant types, stiffened by a handful of medium-sized warships, cruisers rather than capital ships. Battles were fought without tactical order, a series of melees dominated by boarding. Seamanship and energy were privileged over the cohesion and control that Prince Maurits imposed on the army to such good effect. The Dutch would learn a new way of war at sea from the English, who took Dutch military methods afloat in the 1650s.

The limits of Dutch naval power were exposed in 1598, when Philip III switched from land operations to economic warfare. State-funded campaigns against Spanish and Portuguese commerce and colonies failed, paralysing provincial admiralties with debt, leaving the Republic to rely on non-state actors, privateers and the new East India Company, the Vereenigde Oostindische Compagnie (VoC), for oceanic warfare. The States General harnessed these efforts with financial incentives and helping to unify the diffuse elements that became the VoC. In 1602 the Court of Directors provided their ships with privateer commissions to seize Portuguese shipping, both to establish Dutch economic primacy in Asia and to weaken the Habsburg Empire. At least thirty Portuguese carracks were taken, a single carrack seized by Jacob van Heemskerck in 1604 provided plunder valued at four million guilders, prompting the VoC to hire legal expert Hugo Grotius to justify a problematic capture.[18] The VoC developed bases in Asia to sustain the maritime impulse, but, like all such establishments, since ancient times these seapower footprints evolved into distinct territorial entities, focused on resource extraction.

When England made peace with Spain in 1604, English privateers moved to Dutch ports, doubling Dutch activity, and forcing Spain to begin peace talks. In 1607 a national fleet under van Heemskerck, heavily supported by the VoC, annihilated a Spanish fleet in Gibraltar Bay.[19] These efforts crippled Spanish trade, by keeping Iberian carracks tied down in Europe while the Dutch opened Asia, secured access to the Mediterranean, and provided a suitable naval core for the republican narrative of power and profit that Amsterdam set up as a contrast to the Stadholder's sterile, costly military campaigns. Yet the sea remained secondary: independence had been secured on land, only an army could prevent a hostile invasion. This reality may explain why the Republic ignored the large prestige warships built by the monarchies of Denmark, England, France and Sweden. These intimidating tools, built to assert dominion over the oceans rather than fight for trade, were of little interest to a Republic that relied on superior commercial acumen and private violence.

The post-1588 maritime economy created a strong service sector, industrialisation and large-scale urbanisation. Amsterdam's population rose from 50,000 in 1600 to 200,000 in 1650.[20] The Twelve Years' Truce with Spain of 1609 served Amsterdam's interests, releasing Dutch maritime enterprise from wartime restraints. The Stadholder's decision to resume the war in 1621 exposed Dutch commerce to Flemish privateers, forcing the Republic to increase naval activity. Although Maerten Tromp's annihilation

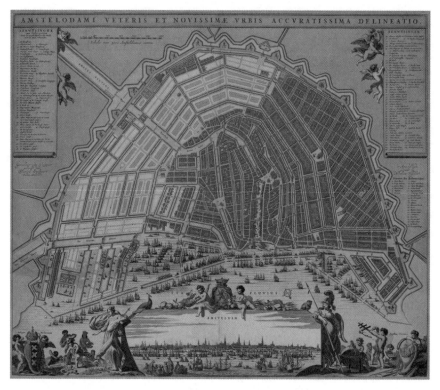

The seapower city, a fortified bastion of commerce: Daniël Stalpaert's
map of Amsterdam in 1662

of a Spanish troop convoy at the battle of the Downs on 21 October 1639
effectively ended the conflict, Flemish privateer activity only abated after
the French captured Dunkirk in 1646. Spain finally recognised the Republic
in 1648, but Dutch shipping had been critical to the Spanish economy for
decades. The costly, counterproductive war reinforced the Amsterdam
oligarch's preference for peace.[21] Despite a growing threat from English
privateers many warships were sold in 1649, to reduce the financial burden.
Neither independence nor peace had settled the identity of the state,
although they had raised the stakes.

In a deeply polarised polity the Stadholder and his Orangist supporters
favoured war, the army and hard-line Calvinist faith. The States Rights or
post-1650 True Freedom party disagreed fundamentally on all three issues.
These opposing concepts of the state dominated seventeenth-century
Dutch politics. Initially, the republican system restricted the Stadholder's

authority, but Prince Maurits' *coup d'état* of 1618 purged city councils, provincial assemblies and civic militias of political opponents, significantly increasing his personal authority and the prospect of dynastic rule.[22] The violent separation of political power from the economic sector that sustained the state caused friction. The political structures of seapower states had to include the men of trade and money. Maurits' assumption of control over external policy, war and diplomacy alienated the burgeoning city-state, as did his decision to resume the war with Spain in 1621. After 1625 his successor Frederick-Hendrik 'steadily increased his influence in the States General, over which he presided . . . Only the Province of Holland, dominated by the merchant aristocracy of Amsterdam, could restrain him, by withholding money. The city's maritime interests were not served by the Stadholder's policy'.[23] The rivalry between Prince and City reached a crisis as the war with Spain drew to a close. Frederick-Henry attempted to secure dynastic rule through a French alliance, ambitions mirrored in French architecture and decorative arts. In 1641 he attempted to capture Antwerp, as the key to assuming royal power. Thwarted on the battlefield Frederick-Henry discussed exchanging Maastricht for Antwerp, an initiative that did not pass unnoticed on the Amstel, because reopening the Scheldt would ruin Amsterdam. Frederick-Henry's death in 1647 enabled Amsterdam's leaders to impose their agenda on the Peace of Munster the following year.

Heavy shipping losses in the second war with Spain encouraged Amsterdam and Holland to oppose the Stadholder. They favoured a different political model, one that was linked to a seapower identity. Peace prompted a dramatic restructuring of the Dutch economy; profits from Baltic shipping services and domestic agriculture fell, while those from the 'rich trades' in luxuries rose, benefiting from England's distraction and a war between Venice and the Ottomans to acquire much of the Turkish trade with Europe.[24] This economic boom shaped investment patterns, propelled a 'Golden Age' of Dutch culture, and funded the True Freedom seapower state. The opportunity for political change arose by chance. In 1650 the young Stadholder Willem II had recovered the authority of his office by sending troops to intimidate the cities of Holland.[25] His sudden death a few months later gave Amsterdam and Holland the chance to reshape the Republic.

This struggle reflected tensions inherent in all seapowers, between land and trade, aristocrats and merchants. In the Republic, Amsterdam was *primus inter pares*, not a hegemonic city comparable to Athens, Carthage or Venice, cities that dictated the politics, economics and culture of the state. In the Dutch case a struggle for identity pitted a seapower proto-city-state against agricultural provinces that had no interest in the ocean.

The Dutch never bought into the True Freedom seapower identity that Amsterdam and other coastal towns in Holland, Zeeland and Friesland attempted to impose upon them. It remained a veneer, obscuring a land-minded polity. The Republic was never insular, although Holland, relatively safe behind the 'water-line', may have seen itself as a semi-insular version of Periclean Athens behind the 'Long Walls'. By 1600, as the tide of war ebbed, Amsterdam sought peace and prosperity in place of war and anxiety. Over the next forty years the rich city imagined itself as a northern Venice, complete with canals, an imperial city-state whose commercial concerns in Asia, the Baltic and the Mediterranean should dominate national policy. The Amsterdam elite wanted to restrain the Stadholder, reduce the army and build an empire of trade without taxes. These aims were promoted through a seapower identity built on old traditions, new heroes and economic might.

The political struggle for the soul of the Republic would be bitter and bloody. As seapowers grew in power and wealth the city-state assumed increasingly imperial attributes, the evolving embodiment of empire. Built and decorated to impress, seapowers arranged tokens of distant watery triumphs and imperial territory to bolster their status and sell seapower to taxpayers, voters and visitors alike. The artistic competition for the cultural high ground mirrored political tensions, and proved equally fraught. In Amsterdam architecture shaped a new vision, a Republic of commerce, naval might and a class-less society. The opening shot in the cultural conflict was an elaborate monument for Jacob van Heemskerck in Amsterdam's Oude Kirk. Heemskerck had died in the great battle off Gibraltar in 1607, humiliating Spain, opening the Mediterranean and securing Asian markets and the Twelve Years Truce. His victory marked the emergence of the Republic as a major naval power.

After a decade without major Dutch victories on land or sea this heroic death caught the popular mood.[26] The memorial challenged the hitherto dominant military narrative of land campaigns and Stadholders, and it pre-dated any memorial for Maurits' father, the founding Stadholder Willem the Silent. Holland Pensionary Johan van Oldenbarnevelt used the opportunity to promote a seapower ideology of peace and trade secured by the navy.[27]

Oldenbarnevelt and Amsterdam supported the navy as a largely self-funding national force promoting and protecting trade, in contrast to the tax-eating, largely mercenary army. He persuaded the States General to fund a state funeral and public monument. The hero cult of admiral, established in post-Lepanto Venice and Elizabethan England, became party-political propaganda. A state funeral, the first since that of Willem the Silent, challenged the uniqueness of that event, while the monument was unprecedented.

The Oude Kirk was Heemskerck's church, that of the Amsterdam Admiralty and of seamen generally. The monument linked Heemskerck with Hercules, using a Florentine iconography that stressed the republican agenda, along with a Latin epitaph that admired his 'Herculean courage ... in the Straits of Hercules'. Heemskerck had broken the Spanish grip on the Pillars of Hercules, the emblem of Habsburg Spain. The monument replaced one for the Emperor Charles V, while the iconography reflected the title-page of Lucas Jansz Waghenaar's famous 1584 pilot book, *Der Spieghel der zeevaerdt*, known to the English as *The Mariner's Mirror*.[28]

The States General commissioned other artworks dealing with Gibraltar, including a monumental picture by the pioneering marine artist Hendrick Vroom, which it presented to the Stadholder. This iconography challenged the assumption that only elite soldiers had virtues that could be rewarded by fame. The Amsterdam civic history of 1611 used Heemskerck's monument to establish a seapower identity.[29] It celebrated the deeds of a famous admiral to legitimise the commercial and political agendas of an Imperial city-state. This overt propaganda prompted an Orangist counter-attack, which culminated in the execution of Oldenbarnevelt in 1619.

Heemskerck's monument would be the first of a series erected to honour naval officers and inspire future generations, secular monuments in religious settings. They adorned the otherwise stark walls of Calvinist temples, recording lives given for the nation. Yet the cult of the naval hero also carried an international message, through a Latin text that could be read by pan-European elite audiences, and circulated as text and image. When the cult of naval heroism ended sixty years later the monument to Michiel de Ruyter in Amsterdam's Nieuwe Kirk would be a lament for a lost identity.

Amsterdam, the most dynamic commercial and industrial city in Europe, had good reason to strike for control of the state. Relatively isolated from the land wars, Amsterdam merchants focused on the profits of seaborne commerce, rather than the risks of European invasion. Amsterdam developed an entrepôt trade model that favoured maritime enterprise and related industries, prompting Dutch seafarers to develop economical ships and shipping services. They would carry much of the trade of Europe, and in turn fund the state. During the eighty-year war for independence the Dutch tax burden, already the highest in Europe, increased four times. Tax receipts were dominated by Holland, the richest province, and, within Holland, Amsterdam, the richest city. Holland paid 58 per cent of national taxes, Amsterdam alone contributing 25 per cent of the total. The other maritime provinces, Friesland and Zealand, paid 12 per cent and 9 per cent respectively, while the four landlocked provinces produced no more than 6 per cent. After 1582 the States General also levied a standard import tax, which went directly to the five admiralties.[30]

The creation of public debt tied capitalists to the state, their proximity to the commercial sector ensuring that they recognised the interests of those without political representation.[31] Local control of taxes and naval finances ensured that long-term trends in naval funding were neither arbitrary nor random. Merchant elites carefully balanced cost and benefit. Joint-stock companies and banks financed trade and war, while new credit mechanisms improved the flow of trade. The model for the Amsterdam Bank was Venetian, as was much else in the new state. It became the central clearing house for global finance: smaller banks served small traders and artisans.[32] The joint-stock principle also applied to canal-building, drainage projects, harbour construction, ship-owning and marine insurance, spreading ownership, profit and risk among the merchant and working classes. These developments occurred at a time when rivals were distracted by wars and occupation, enabling the Dutch to acquire a large share of maritime trade with startling speed. Shipping services turned resource dependency into strength. Amsterdam became the hub of an expanding global trade system, moving and redistributing goods and services, secured by a navy funded from customs dues and shipping fees.

As Jan Glete observed, the Republic proved highly effective at promoting economic interests, and more efficient at mobilising military, naval and economic power than any contemporary autocratic state. It sustained disproportionately heavy fiscal-military burdens through a complex financial system combining local and national taxes with loans:

No seventeenth century state was able to surpass it in resource mobilisation for war, if the size of the population is taken into account. Dutch chartered companies, organised for trade and warfare overseas, were also effective against enemy forces organised by states.

Critically, the Republic could maintain very high levels of taxation for decades, without significant resistance, because the inclusive political system, like those of other seapowers, provided the men of commerce, who paid the bulk of taxes, with significant political power.[33] They voted to ensure their taxes were used to protect their interests. Secure on land and sea, dynamic commercial growth funded additional naval power, to expand the boundaries of commerce. Financial stability reduced interest rates, enabling the Republic to wage war more efficiently than absolutist rivals with poor credit ratings. Effective tax-raising enabled the state to secure the loyalty of soldiers, sailors and contractors through regular pay. The state was sustained by consensus, not imposed by royal diktat, but that consensus was fragile.

Before the Revolt the Dutch provinces had willingly exchanged relatively high taxes for relevant security, but objected to distant wars, attempts to centralise the administration and reimpose Catholicism. The Revolt shifted the financial centre of the region from Antwerp to Amsterdam, which used sea power strategy to crush the old master city, and tried to repeat the process against the rising threat from London. This model was challenged by successive Stadholders, who favoured a 'normal' continental state reliant on military force.[34]

The Stadholders had a good case. Maritime forces played a useful auxiliary role in the war of independence, accounting for only a quarter of defence spending. This was primarily a military struggle, waged by a professional army created specifically to fight inside the Republic without destroying it. The soldiers were highly disciplined, professional and tactically innovative; they were influenced by classical texts, rather than their Spanish foes. The army was far larger per capita than the French, while many recruits were foreign, and cadres of Dutch officers and non-commissioned officers ensured it remained under control.[35]

The Republic, perhaps from bitter experience, was largely immune to the lure of military pomp and swagger. Armies were necessary evils, needed to secure the land borders, not symbols of national pride or power. Nor were such views restricted to the elite: Dutch military art of the 'Golden Age' emphasised boredom, licentiousness and waste.[36] Armies posed a serious threat to liberty: Stadholders used troops to overthrow civil government in 1619 and 1650. Little wonder the merchant oligarchs of Amsterdam pushed a seapower identity to reshape national policy.[37] Their 'True Freedom' Republic dispensed with costly soldiers, putting their faith in civic guards, militias of the worthy and the well connected. In the hour of need these ideological armies would fail.

Ultimately, the Republic faced a classic seapower dilemma: it was nowhere near large enough, in land or manpower, to become a conventional great power, but it needed a powerful army simply to survive. The fiscal and political costs of that army militated against the emergence of a seapower state. When the army was fully mobilised to secure the frontier there was little money left for the navy, while high taxes inhibited maritime activity.

The sudden death of Stadholder Willem II in 1650, shortly after his army had threatened the gates of Amsterdam, enabled the States General to leave his office vacant. Reversing the outcome of the power struggle three decades earlier, when Oldenbarnevelt had been executed for treason, Amsterdam assumed power in the Republic. Setting aside the Stadholder's posthumous son, the 'Great Assembly' of 1651, dominated by republican agendas, enabled the provinces to recover the authority they had recently lost.[38] As power shifted from the Stadholder's Palace to Amsterdam Town Hall, the Republic consciously chose to become a seapower, to protect the economic interests of Amsterdam and the other maritime towns, replacing the Prince and the army with politicians and a larger navy. The decision was driven by the disasters of the war with England, which Amsterdam exploited to secure an increase of one-third in the convoy and licence payments, significantly improving the liquidity of the five admiralties. Amsterdam's dominance of the state was reflected in overseas trade: those that it dominated, the Baltic, Asian and Mediterranean trades, prospered, at the expense of Zealand interests in the Caribbean and Brazil.[39] The True Freedom regime, led from 1653 by the Pensionary of Holland, Johan de Witt, was in essence Amsterdam on horseback. Having developed the federal/brokerage state to secure independence on land, the post-1648 regime redeployed the model to secure maritime economic hegemony.[40]

De Witt, the son of a Dordrecht councillor imprisoned by Willem II, had personal and political reasons for suspending the Stadholderate. In 1651 de Witt joined the Holland Naval Committee, alongside Lieutenant Admiral Maarten Tromp, beginning a lifelong engagement with naval affairs, including art and strategy, and ensuring he placed naval power at the centre of an external policy. His brother Cornelis joined the Rotterdam Admiralty in 1652, and married into the city elite.[41] Both brothers would go to sea with the fleet.

Within months a militant English Commonwealth tested the new Republic, forcing it to fight for command of the sea. England asserted dominion over the Channel, the windpipe of Dutch prosperity, demanding a salute from passing ships of war and trade. The salute, lowering topsails and ensigns to English warships, was both a symbol of English dominion, which could be turned into cash payments, and a tactic that left Dutch ships vulnerable to attack. The Republic rejected the claim, asserting the Grotian doctrine of 'free seas', and prepared to fight. Ultimately, the war was driven by mercantilist economics. English merchants and ship-owners wanted the Commonwealth to use the powerful fleet, purchased with their taxes, to seize trade from the Dutch. As one Dutch pamphleteer observed, 'The English are moving against a golden mountain, but we on the contrary against one of iron.'[42] This would be a naval war, no soldiers were required.

When war broke out de Witt took control of the Holland Naval Committee, responding to Tromp's well-founded complaints about the inadequacy of Dutch fleets, largely composed of hired merchant ships. Not only were such vessels too slow to keep station with purpose-built warships and too weak to withstand heavy artillery, but their merchant officers proved unsteady. After the war small hired merchant ships were replaced: the navy used large VoC ships in the Second Anglo-Dutch War, but not the Third.[43] In 1652–4 the Dutch had no answer to a battlefleet, built to control the Channel. England forced the Dutch to fight for their trade, defeated them in battle and blockaded Amsterdam, where grass grew in the streets. The True Freedom regime faltered.

Commonwealth England posed a new challenge. Unlike Spain it shared the True Freedom agenda of creating a commercial seapower state, and was prepared to fight for primacy. Realising that the Republic needed a costly battlefleet, as well as the existing cruiser force, de Witt hesitated. He anticipated political problems in a state far from unified behind the seapower identity. Facing economic ruin and political turmoil de Witt created a battlefleet by diverting funds from the Republic's primary strategic systems, the army and border fortresses. In October 1652 further naval defeats prompted the States General to build thirty new ships of the line, using war taxes and loans. Soon afterwards de Witt became Councillor Pensionary of Holland, and effectively head of state as Raads Pensionary in July 1653. Two years later he married into the prominent Amsterdam oligarchy family of Bicker, and in 1659 he took a coat of arms, complete with a helmet, and had them emblazoned on his coach.[44] De Witt and his republican supporters linked the state and seapower, making the new battleships national rather than provincial property, to ensure the local admiralties did not sell them after the war. This 'New Navy' would be a permanent, professional battlefleet.

In the First Anglo-Dutch War the Republic had to defeat the English fleet to survive, and blockade London into submission, much as it had blockaded Antwerp. Long before the new ships could be built, Tromp's death demoralised the navy and the populace, while a brief English blockade threatened economic ruin and undermined the authority of the new regime. Economic hardship sparked domestic unrest, empowering advocates of the Stadholder. It required considerable diplomatic skill to minimise the consequences of defeat.

Defeat exposed the fleet's fragile morale. Around half of the sailors were foreigners, the States General offered lower wages than commercial shipping, and admiralty colleges were notoriously slow to pay and provided poor food. Mutinies were not uncommon.[45] The Dutch, unlike the English, did not allow impressment, the forcible recruitment of seafarers.[46] Discipline among seafarers of all ranks was a serious problem.[47] A decade later de Witt confessed to the British ambassador Sir William Temple that in defeat at the Four Day's Battle of 1666 English sailors had 'gained more honour to our nation, and to the invincible courage of our Sea-men than by the two other victories'. He admitted the Dutch sailors would not have stood to their guns on the second day, let alone on the fourth.[48]

Defeat 'convinced Johan de Witt of the importance of a strong navy'.[49] The costly 'New Navy' that emerged after 1654 combined a professional officer corps with a standing fleet of purpose-built warships to secure sea control in battle, using the new gunnery tactics.[50] It would occupy a central

1 Celebrating the dawn of seapower: Minoan imagery like this fresco from Santorini emphasised the ships, ports and fishing that shaped the first thalassocracy.

2 Pericles, leader and theorist of the Athenian seapower state in the early years of the Peloponnesian War. His fame was cemented by Thucydides' immortal history, a work that stressed the totality of such an identity, and the political problems that flowed from democracy.

3 An iconic vessel: the replica Athenian trireme *Olympias* under sail, the oars having been brought inboard for strategic movement. In battle, Athenian warships emphasised manoeuvre and ramming: their bronze rams would smash through their opponents' lightweight hulls, leaving them half sunk. After the battle, the prizes would be towed ashore and repaired.

4 Seapower city: this modern reconstruction emphasises how Carthage was dominated by the circular naval harbour, the connection with the sea, and the maritime prospect from the walls and the temple complex on the hill.

5 The battle of Lepanto, 1571, at once the crowning achievement and culmination of Venice's great-power status, as Venetian skill with oars and guns was rendered irrelevant by the vast resources of the rival continental hegemons, Ottoman Turkey and Habsburg Spain. Nevertheless, the battle lived on as an icon of Venetian greatness, the greatest galley battle of all, and a symbol of Christian success.

6 Sebastiano del Piombo's masterful study (copied here by William Henry Furse) of Gian Andrea Doria, master of the Genoese sea state, mercenary and *admiralissimo* of Charles V, captures the depth and subtlety of the man who transformed the endemic chaos that weakened Genoa and who reshaped the economy. The absence of decoration speaks volumes.

7 Amsterdam Town Hall: classical palace of the Dutch seapower state, bastion of republican virtue and the global economic domination that funded the Dutch Navy. Between 1650 and 1672 the True Freedom regime focused the nation on the ocean, with disastrous consequences.

8 Within a generation the Dutch seapower state would be violently overthrown, replaced by a quasi-monarchical regime determined on defending the land frontiers. In 1686 Willem van de Velde the Younger created an elegy for Dutch seapower: *Cornelis de Tromp's Former Flagship the 'Gouden Leeuw' on the IJ in front of Amsterdam*. Tromp was out of favour with the new regime, and his famous old ship was on her way to be broken up.

9 Portuguese bastion, British shipping. The Tower of Belem, a cross-encrusted barrier against Muslim raiders, symbolised the profoundly terrestrial concerns of the Avis dynasty. The image was created by British artist John Thomas Serres to celebrate British control of the Portuguese economy, and the reality that Lisbon was a British naval base.

10 While Peter the Great built a new capital on the sea at St Petersburg, as well as a major navy, he retained the terrestrial focus of his ancestors. The definitive symbol of Russia's response to seapower was the fortress complex at Kronstadt, the largest collection of sea defences in the world.

11 If Peter the Great feared the sea as a vector for inclusive politics and British fleets, other more religious Russians feared it as a catastrophic portent linked to the biblical flood – a sensibility expressed in Ivan Aivazovsky's *The Ninth Wave*.

12 Although he fought on land, and preferred military heroics to the oceanic effort, William III, as Dutch Stadholder and English king, used seapower to prevent Louis XIV from establishing French hegemony over continental Europe. In the process he united the two seapowers under his rule and oversaw the transfer of that power from Amsterdam to London.

13 Whereas Kronstadt and Belem were always barriers, the old castle and harbour at Dover quickly became a symbol of British expansive enterprise, an open door for trade and communication. Richard Wilson's *Dover* of 1747 presages the many images of the town that would be created by J. M. W. Turner.

14 The British followed the Venetians in making naval workshops a window into the soul of the nation. Woolwich, the smallest of the five great dockyards, built many of the great First Rate ships that defined British power, from the *Henry Grace à Dieu* to the *Royal George*. Such images of naval industrial power fascinated foreigners who were curious to understand the mechanics of seapower.

15 The capital ship as holy relic: J. M. W. Turner's triptych of HMS *Victory* at Spithead, bearing the mortal remains of Lord Nelson. For Turner the great ship was the essence of Englishness, an approach he would develop as the wooden walls faded away with the coming of steam.

16 Although no longer a great power, Britain, like many another modern inclusive liberal state, still depends on the free movement of shipping and global trade. In this way it remains connected to the seapower identity of previous centuries. In 2018 the Royal Navy took delivery of its largest ever warship, the 65,000-ton aircraft carrier HMS *Queen Elizabeth*. The ship is projected to remain in service for fifty years.

17 Modern naval might remains fixated on hardware and imagery. In this official photograph of the latest examples of high-technology warfighting capability, the carrier-borne F-35 Lightning II flies over the stealthy 15,000-ton destroyer USS *Zumwalt*.

18 In the absence of a seapower great power, since 1945 command of the sea has been exercised by the United States, despite the challenge of the Soviet Union and now the rising power of the People's Republic of China. The question for the future is whether these continental states can share the seas. Joint naval exercises such as that pictured suggest co-operation may be possible.

role in the ideology of the 'True Freedom' Republic, a seapower state anxious to establish an exceptional great-power identity, distinct from the monarchical and terrestrial concerns of other European powers and the displaced Stadholderate.[51] This new fleet would require a major increase in funding, as an addition to the cruiser force. While the battlefleet transformed the Republic into a seapower great power, funding it through the States General, rather than cash-strapped local admiralties, proved divisive. Shifting defence funding from land to sea alarmed and alienated the inland provinces.[52] Furthermore the great-power implications of the battlefleet and associated navalist propaganda raised concerns abroad when de Witt deployed his 'New Navy' to secure commercial access to the Baltic in 'the interests of Amsterdam'.[53] De Witt's armada, like Pericles' triremes, wielded a weapon more formidable than cannon. They were branded with 'the mark of freedom', a threat that every autocrat understood.[54] While overt economic imperialism pleased Amsterdam, French observers linked the battlefleet with Dutch aspirations to dominate world trade, anxieties enhanced by the 'impertinence' of a Republic in a world of monarchies.

The First Anglo-Dutch War left de Witt anxious to avoid another conflict, relying on the deterrent effect of the 'New Navy' as part of a complex Cartesian calculation to sustain the Republic, block Orangist claims and secure trade. As a satiated seapower the Republic had little need for war, but it would fight for national survival and essential trades. However, less prosperous rivals viewed such modest objectives as overbearing ambition.[55] In seeking deterrence through costly defence preparations de Witt missed a critical reservation. Only rational actors can be deterred. When it came to de Witt's Republic neither Charles II nor Louis XIV were unduly interested in logic or reason: personal prestige, reputation and respect were more consequential concerns. Like the English Commonwealth the new republican regime changed the national flag, replacing the standard of the House of Orange with a republican tricolour, and renamed warships to reflect their ideology. In 1639 Tromp's flagship had been named for the Stadholder's wife; in 1666 de Ruyter sailed in the altogether more prosaic *de Zeven Provincien*, backed by suitably virtuous adjectives of freedom and liberty, and local place names. These dull descriptors were no match for the English *Sovereign of the Seas*, a boast backed by a hundred cannon.

Using money and resources to avoid war through an overt display of superior force had always been a key element of seapower diplomacy. Naval parades, the Athenian ship-sheds, the Great Harbour at Carthage and the Arsenale at Venice all served that role. States that depended on maritime exchange needed to keep the seas free and avoid the costs of wars, while limited populations and, in the Dutch case, weak borders made war especially undesirable. Those borders were weak because the True Freedom regime funded the 'New Navy' in part by cutting expenditure on an army it believed to be wasteful and a political threat. While Amsterdam merchants objected to paying for an army that might crush their freedom, inland provinces objected to using national taxation to fund the battlefleet.

In 1619 Stadholder Prince Maurits had executed Oldenbarnevelt for treason. Thirty years later the True Freedom leadership, understandably anxious to avoid the same fate, adopted the 'New Navy' as an ideological pillar, building on foundations laid by their precursors, the men who erected Heemskerck's monument. In an attempt to justify the new political system de Witt refined Pieter de la Court's radical tract of 1662. *The Interest of Holland* openly advocated Holland's separation from the other provinces, to avoid the cost of defending land borders, and, as de la Court stressed, the 'shame of paying for an army'. A republican system was the best guarantor of trade, fishing and manufacturing, while a powerful fleet could secure neutrality and free trade, defend shipping and deter war. Mediterranean convoys protected Dutch trade against Barbary corsairs, leaving the ships of less fortunate nations exposed; prosperity was central to the Dutch identity that the True Freedom wished to create. The fleet was, of course, at once republican in politics and republican in purpose. However, de Witt knew another conflict with England could be ruinous.[56] While the Orange faction stressed military strength and centralised authority, the True Freedom party followed Oldenbarnevelt's concern to uphold the sovereignty of the individual provinces, a mechanism that enshrined the dominance of Amsterdam, the economic centre of the Republic.

Hitherto the Republic had operated as a sea state, lacking a battlefleet to contest control of the seas. Defence spending was dominated by an army under the control of the Stadholder, a system that most Dutch people accepted. After the military coup of 1650 Amsterdam and Holland had 'determined never to sacrifice the strength of the navy for a reinforcement of the army, which they feared might again be used to intimidate them into political capitulation'. Having taken control of the Republic the True Freedom administration had been taught the potentially fatal consequences of naval weakness by an English battlefleet. Suitably chastened, the state funded a national battlefleet, designed to secure access to the oceans, greatly enhancing the political weight of the Republic and its ability to secure oceanic trade. The battlefleet expanded the navy's strategic role from defensive patrolling to serving 'the economic interests of the province of Holland' and the altogether more ambitious task of 'maintaining the balance of power in Europe'.[57] The Republic acquired the tools of sea power which, de Witt argued, was 'an indispensable condition of commercial prosperity' in a seapower state. He deployed naval power to ensure England and France understood that the cost of any war would be 'prohibitively high'. He could only hope that naval power would reduce the need for an army that could threaten domestic liberty.[58] Such elegant calculations ignored the realities of seventeenth-century international relations and the predominantly Orangist populace's desire for the return of the Stadholder. Seapower identity remained contentious: the inland provinces rejected the maritime focus, Zealand felt the Baltic and Mediterranean interests of Amsterdam took priority over its Caribbean concerns, and de Witt's aggressive use of the new battlefleet navy to secure the commercial interests of Amsterdam did much to bring about the Second Anglo-Dutch War of 1664–7.[59]

Circumstance and contingency enabled the Dutch republican leadership to invent a seapower culture and identity, and they did so with a clear eye on the needs of the moment: to meld the people of the seven provinces, a rich and shifting mix of incomers from the southern provinces, Germany, France, Scandinavia and England, into a nation, while sustaining dramatic economic expansion. The process began as a decisive break with the past, yet it would enshrine key elements of older realities.

The Republic had been defined by the long struggle for independence from Spain: soldiers and sieges, triumph, tragedy and grinding endurance dominated its identity. It would be a nation, but not a state, strongly suffused with Old Testament values and Roman connections. Yet amidst traditions of martial prowess one important constituency within the Republic consciously crafted an alternative identity, shaped around the sea, commerce and naval power. In 1610 the humanist polymath Hugo Grotius developed a suitable identity from myths of Batavian resistance to Rome, a legal justi-fication for the revolt and of rule by oligarchy.[60] His work reflected the choices made by the City of Amsterdam and the province of Holland. The great seapowers of the past had been city-states, and Amsterdam, the economic powerhouse that dominated national policy, had many of the same characteristics. Amsterdam Town Council debated international rela-tions, war and peace alongside local government and charity, well aware of their seapower precursors.

The city's canal system had been built to make Amsterdam the new Venice, while the Athenian clash of cultures between an aristocracy in thrall to landed property and military renown, and the energetic men of sea commerce, between elite and bourgeois, would be played out all over again on the Amstel, with much of the same rhetoric, and considerable violence. Between 1600 and 1672 the cultural high ground was in flux and successive Stadholders advanced Roman concepts of centralised authority and mili-tary power, while men of money and trade fought back with naval glory, heroic admirals, commerce and exploration. The past became a battle-ground of ideas: political manoeuvres were explained through classical allegory, and represented by public magnificence, tools that the Amsterdam men knew Venice had used.

In theory Amsterdam had less authority in the state than Athens, Carthage or Venice, but in reality it dominated the United Provinces. It controlled peace negotiations between 1645 and 1648 and, having secured control of the state, used the 'New Navy' to force Denmark to reduce the Sound Dues, a tax on a core Amsterdam trade. The Amsterdam elite ran the state and the VoC, controlling an empire in Asia.[61] These classically educated men were uncommonly well travelled and, like their Venetian counterparts, engaged in trade. Not only did patrician Amsterdamers know their ancient and modern history, but they used it in print. Nicolas Witsen's study of shipbuilding looked back to ancient texts, while P. C. Hooft urged the value of history to those who would rule. Others published maps and pilot books, while the city retained an Italian official historian, to project its civic virtue across Europe.[62] Johan de Witt's humanist education included Greek.[63] He was familiar with Themistocles and Pericles, heroic leaders of the first seapower state. His Republic would be strikingly similar to the older seapowers.

Where Venetian aristocrats had prided themselves on a rather forced Roman past, both civic and personal, bourgeois Amsterdamers developed a youthful pride in the novelty of their republican experiment, while cultural struggle between land and sea confused their approach to the past. Amsterdam's leaders adopted the supposedly freedom-loving Batavian ancestors they found in Tacitus, and affixed Latin epitaphs to their tombs, yet Scipio Africanus was a popular reference. One early-seventeenth-century pamphlet urged reprising his strategy against Carthage to defeat Spain in the West Indies.[64]

Much of this cultural conflict was waged through architecture, painting and print. Newly separated from Antwerp and Brussels, long the cultural capitals of the region, the new Republic had little expertise in the fine arts. This omission had to be addressed quickly, both to deliver a national message and to fill glaring gaps created by the widespread destruction of religious art by Calvinist iconoclasts during the Revolt. The result was a new art, built on traditions and expertise from the Burgundian-Flemish era, but stripped of Catholic agendas. Fortunately, old cultural links survived the caesura. While Peter Paul Rubens, the greatest artist of the age, remained in Antwerp, working for the Habsburgs and the French, he kept in contact with the new Republic. By the mid-seventeenth century a dynamic Dutch art market had emerged, supported by middle-class rather than elite or royal patrons, an audience that placed the sea at the centre of Dutch identity.[65] Pictures became familiar items of private display, portraits hanging alongside images of vessels. Amsterdam's emerging seapower culture combined elite patronage for public consumption, notably Heemskerck's Monument, with pictures suitable for bourgeois domesticity.

The art of pre-Revolt Flanders had featured the sea, and demand grew, keeping pace with maritime enterprise and naval glory.[66] Unlike much Dutch art, which refined existing models, realistic seascapes and ship portraits, empowered by the Reformation, were novel. Pre-Reformation maritime images had been stylised, but when the Republic needed to celebrate the naval side of the Revolt in the mid-1580s the Haarlem artist Hendrick Cornelisz Vroom (1562/3–1640) developed realistic seascapes. His early masterpieces addressed the Spanish Armada, notably in oil paintings and tapestry cartoons for Lord Howard of Effingham, Lord High Admiral of England. The cycle had been inspired by the Tunis Tapestry cycle of the Emperor Charles V, which Howard had seen in Brussels, images of power, wealth and glory suitable for a monarch.[67] Howard's cycle linked naval battle with maps and charts, and adopted a novel sea-level perspective. Vroom also pioneered townscapes, a genre to celebrate the United Provinces' rising civic centres.

Vroom's art attracted customers, his prices attracted emulation. Marine art became a recognised specialisation, a significant body of self-defining artists. The correlation between the seapower culture of the True Freedom era and marine art was striking. Between 1650 and 1675 the number of marine artists in Amsterdam doubled, from ten to twenty, and then fell back to ten. The collapse in Haarlem and Rotterdam was even more precipitous. In Antwerp, which still supplied the Dutch and Italian markets, the collapse was delayed until the 1680s, by which time the regional total had fallen to less than a quarter of the high point in the 1660s.[68]

Alongside high art in oils and tapestry, for public display, a dynamic print culture emerged, another format that Vroom mastered.[69] In 1651 the dissemination of naval imagery, a central motif of the True Freedom regime, entered the monthly newspapers. *Hollantsche Mercurius* began illustrating reports with prints of naval events, influencing national iconography, sustaining a generation of skilled artists and engravers. Monotone prints served a growing audience for seapower imagery, although it is likely most consumers were connected with the sea, a very large proportion in Amsterdam, significantly fewer in Gelderland. Furthermore these images travelled across Europe, exciting interest and emulation wherever seapower was discussed.[70]

The States General recognised the diplomatic value of art, presenting foreign princes with new Dutch work and Old Masters, acquired through Amsterdam art dealers. Vroom's pictures were especially appropriate gifts for an English court that had long consumed Flemish marine art. Their purpose may be inferred from the decision of the States General to present Henry, Prince of Wales, with a copy of Vroom's *The Battle of Gibraltar* in 1610, only a year after the original had been created for the Stadholder.[71] The English understood: King James I purchased the Armada tapestries from Lord Howard in 1612, and 'displayed them in the Banqueting Hall to receive the Spanish Ambassador. It has been suggested that in so doing perhaps he could pursue dialogue with Spain without the appearance of weakness'.[72] The overtly triumphalist Banqueting Hall hang ensured the

Spanish ambassador feigned illness – to avoid being confronted by such images, and humiliated by references to them in royal speeches.[73]

Vroom would record the English fleet entering Flushing in 1613, carrying the Princess Royal and Prince Frederick of Bohemia, and then in 1623 as it returned to Portsmouth from Spain. These were potent emblems of royal naval magnificence.[74] Such images were seen by English audiences predisposed to seapower imagery by a century of royal collecting. Henry VIII had acquired Flemish images in the 1540s, to promote an aggressive seapower ideology, images that shaped English taste.

When the War of Independence resumed in 1621, Dutch artists lost access to key pigments, and their art took on a more sombre hue.[75] Willem van de Velde the Elder (1611–93) replaced Vroom's opulent palette with a new method, monochrome pen paintings that represented ships and battles with startling precision, part technical record, part artistic creation. These costly monotones were commissioned by the States General, regional admiralties and elite individuals, including admirals and foreign dignitaries. Van de Velde also produced engravings celebrating Tromp's victory at the Downs in 1639. For the post-1650 True Freedom seapower state, marine art became an ideological weapon, a critical representation of national identity, projecting Dutch naval prowess to the world. The Republic employed Van de Velde as an official war artist. In 1653 he carried messages to Tromp, before providing eyewitness accounts of battles as art and text. He sailed into battle on at least six occasions during the Anglo-Dutch wars.[76] This was no accident. Van de Velde worked closely with Johan de Witt, the architect of seapower culture.

The presence of marine pictures in both public arenas and private residences reflected the economic and political realities of the Amsterdam elite; they profited from trade, and travelled on ships, while the densely packed harbour made such views a commonplace.[77] Alongside smoke-shrouded images of naval glory Amsterdam harbour provided a recurrent statement of maritime economic power, a profusion of ships of war and ships of trade, set against the backdrop of a great merchant city. They were inspired by images of Venice and Genoa, the latter a familiar haunt of Low Countries artists, images that exemplified the seapower synergy of trade and defence, with ships of state, commerce and war linked to an imperial city-state. Their propagandistic purpose was obvious and, once reduced to an engraved print, they reached significant domestic and international audiences.[78] Harbour and shipping scenes filled town halls and private residences. In 1686, long after the restoration of the Stadholderate, the Amsterdam Harbourmasters commissioned Willem van de Velde the Younger's superb *'Gouden Leeuw' on the IJ in front of Amsterdam*, featuring the one-time flagship of prominent Orangist Admiral Cornelis Tromp.[79] The picture hung in the Harbourmaster's Office, a semi-public space, where they met and engaged with the wider maritime community. Yet the image was more elegiac than boastful, the warship it featured was on her way to the breaker's yard in the year the picture was completed, following de Witt's seapower state into the world of memory.[80] Perhaps the famous old ship was used to convey a political message, that Amsterdam supported the new regime, rather than representing Dutch seapower. This was fitting for the last great Dutch sea piece. Willem III's invasion of England two years later proved to be the last hurrah of the seapower navy, and the art that it had inspired. After 1688 the English bought the pictures.

While marine art embellished public and private spaces the capital city of a seapower great power required civic grandeur. The Parthenon, the Great Harbour at Carthage and the Piazza San Marco set a standard that combined majesty in scale, decoration and functionality. Amsterdam met the challenge of representing seapower in monumental architecture by marking the triumph of their agenda in the Treaty of Munster of 1648, an 'eternal' peace to facilitate trade. The Town Council of Amsterdam, the Empire City at the heart of the Republic, the dominant politico-economic assembly, celebrated peace and the reduction of taxes by rebuilding the Town Hall, and the surrounding space, in a new architectural language. The new building would accommodate the greatly expanded business of a city that had acquired empires of trade and territory, and counter the cultural influence of palace-building Stadholders. The decision to create an ensemble to rival the Ducal palaces of Genoa and Venice reflected a local addiction to pomp and circumstance, a love of opulence and display that stretched back to the Burgundian era. The building would celebrate many humanist virtues, but humility was not among them. It appalled monarchs, who believed such swagger to be their birthright.

The Town Hall was a statement of imperial power expressed through architectonic town planning: 'a single statement of a most complex kind, extended in space beyond the limits of the building, and cumulative in its effect'.[81] The new building dwarfed the Stadholder's Palace and the adjacent Nieuw Kirke, combining politics, trade, banking and justice in a single overwhelming ensemble. It was never going to please the warlike Orange faction or Calvinist hardliners seeking a 'Godly Republic'. The men who voted for the building would suspend the office of Stadholder after the death of Willem II, putting their trust in a 'true' Republic.

When the foundation stone was laid in October 1648 the poet Joost van den Vondel employed architectural and imperial comparisons with Athens and Rome to emphasise Amsterdam's dominion over world trade, before making potent comparisons with the civic buildings of Venice and Antwerp, mighty cities of trade and money. To reinforce the visual power of the building a suitable space was cleared, consciously integrating building, location and decoration to transform the humble Dam at the head of the harbour into a new Piazza San Marco.[82] Katherine Fremantle observed that the Town Hall introduced classical architecture to Holland, a decision that can be understood in the same way that Ruskin read the Venetian Baroque, an alien import marking the end of native dynamism. Hitherto Dutch public buildings had been brick-built Gothic products of Flemish tradition.[83] Rubens' 1622 engraving of Genoa, an ideal sea republic, played a significant part in converting the Dutch to classical forms. His friend Constantijn Huygens, Secretary to the Stadholder, had visited Inigo Jones's Banqueting House, complete with Rubens' fabulous ceiling, the Queen's House at Greenwich and the Palladian buildings of northern Italy. He owned key architectural texts in several languages. Dutch classicism was heavily influenced by the French taste of Huygens' master, Stadholder Frederick-Henry. In the 1630s both men created classical residences in The Hague and reshaped the city centre. The first large-scale urban reconstruction in Dutch history used the languages of modernity, power and prestige to create a capital suitable for an important state, and a dynasty.

Recognising the proto-royal message, Amsterdam borrowed the new architecture, even if there were more appropriate architectural models, such as the republican severity of Rome or the elemental democratic majesty of Athens. Instead Amsterdam subverted the Baroque, the language of the Counter-Reformation, much as Palladio had done at Venice, in a decorative scheme informed by Rubens' learned Genoese classicism.[84] The carved-relief work and statuary were executed by Antwerp craftsmen. Although dominated by classical iconography, the new building contained biblical references that highlighted the unfitness of clerics for secular government. The maritime theme, conveyed in costly imported stone, art and statuary, boasted of present prosperity and future riches, while the inlaid marble floor of the ground-floor Burgerzaal featured two hemispheric maps showing the extent of Amsterdam's trade, including Abel Tasman's newly located New Holland. The space demanded visitors contemplate Amsterdam, the world power of global trade, while councillors were reminded of their responsibilities. 'Only St. Peter's, the Escorial and Palazzo Ducale in Venice could rival it for scale or magnificence.'[85]

On the walls Neptune calmed the waves, while the Fall of Phaeton offered a powerful warning of the risks of vaunting ambition, aimed at the House of Orange, an image reproduced on a medal marking the death of Stadholder Willem II in 1650. Soldiers were shown being demobilised, with peace reigning in their place. Yet the City Fathers, aware that their seapower vision would be contested, loop-holed the ground floor for the 12,000 muskets stored in a purpose-built armoury.[86]

The language and icons of seapower were generic. The Bell Tower, based on the Athenian Temple of the Winds, carried a Cog wind vane, a motif retained from the old Town Hall. The new structure, which celebrated trade, was built with imported German stone and Italian marble on a foundation of Norwegian timber piles to stabilise the muddy location.[87] A medal struck for the inauguration of the building in 1655 featured Jason's *Argo* bringing the Golden Fleece into Amsterdam Harbour, subverting a critical emblem of Habsburg imperialism. The carefully contrived realism of the ancient ship emphasised the rebirth of Athens on the Amstel, while the Latin motto – 'To what great profit are we opening the sea' – laid bare the heart and soul of the city, and the ambition to rule a seapower state. This was 'a single statement of a most complex kind, extended in space beyond the limits of the building, and cumulative in its effect ... worthy of her status and of the virtues of her government, which might declare her greatness within the city and to the admiring world'.[88] The contrast with contemporary French readings of Roman history, leading to Universal Monarchy, was profound, and revealing. A century later the British went one step further: not only did they create a secular seapower temple at Somerset House, in the heart of Imperial London, but the building housed the navy's administration.

The iconography of the Town Hall was dominated by the western pediment, where a female representation of Amsterdam received the trade and homage of the world, surrounded by images of the sea, trade, global navigation and wealth, under the Arms of the City. These featured the Imperial Crown, awarded by Emperor Maximilian, a device that made Amsterdam an 'Empire City'. Four continents paid homage to Imperial Amsterdam, in a building that celebrated peace and prosperity.[89]

Alongside the public headquarters of the new empire emerged a naval storehouse as wondrous and potent as the shipsheds of the Piraeus, the Great Harbour of Carthage and the Arsenale of Venice. If the Imperial Town Hall reflected Amsterdam's ambition, the construction between 1656 and 1661 of the Admiralty building and a naval magazine, on an architectonic scale, highlighted the power that secured the city's trade. Built to handle the stores and supplies of the greatly expanded 'New Navy' after the First Anglo-Dutch War, and to dominate the sight lines of the harbour, the great brick building consciously echoed the imposing façade of the Town Hall, cementing the seapower identity of the city-state.[90] As Vondel observed, the new building would enable the navy to fit out 'fleet after fleet with more tranquility than ever before', 'installing fear in tyrants at sea'.[91] His audience knew the tyrants were English. The other admiralties did not follow Amsterdam's example.[92] The two great public buildings of Republican Amsterdam were tools of power: they impressed visitors, excited emulation and heightened the sense of the unique and exceptional.

The primary threats to the True Freedom came from France and England. French continental hegemonic imperialism and religious zealotry threatened the survival of the Republic, while Colbert's mercantilist command economy, anxious to control Spanish trade, threatened Dutch prosperity. While England had no interest in annihilating the Republic, which had been a useful ally against Spain, it asserted a maritime dominion incompatible with Dutch policy, attempting to continentalise maritime space to tax Dutch fishing in 'English' seas and secure a flag salute from Dutch ships. The claim, based on John Selden's *Mare Clausum*, was backed by a powerful battlefleet, including the emblematic *Sovereign of the Seas*. With three decks of mighty bronze cannon the *Sovereign* gave English claims a terrifyingly real stamp; Dutch sailors nicknamed it 'The Golden Devil'. The Commonwealth created a purpose-built sea-control battlefleet to secure the seas against continental supporters of the monarchy, and protect English trade. In 1652 they closed the Channel to Dutch shipping, basic economic warfare, forcing them to fight for maritime economic primacy. Even in victory the English did not secure the advantages that mercantilist thinkers imagined, because Dutch seapower had deep financial reserves. Ultimately, the Dutch would fight to survive as an independent state, even if it cost them the great-power status and the dynamic economy of the seapower era.

At the restoration of Charles II in 1660, Amsterdam suggested sending the king a sumptuous gift, to secure his friendship. The States General readily concurred, seeking a defensive alliance and trade concessions. Charles thanked the States General for the gifts, which included a yacht, pictures and other artefacts, but no alliance resulted. Charles's subjects would not allow him to accept Dutch terms.[93] This mattered because the naval financial settlement of 1653 was no longer adequate for the 'New Navy'. The tax base had become deeply contentious, the French envoy anticipating the end of de Witt's system. To avoid the loss of trade that might spark an Orange restoration, de Witt secured an increase in naval taxes and rebuilt the battlefleet as a deterrent.[94] The new ships had no effect on English decision-making in 1665, they failed to deter an English war, and then suffered a major defeat at Lowestoft. Desperate to forestall internal disorder de Witt prevented the fifteen-year-old Prince of Orange from visiting the returning fleet. He could not allow the Prince to challenge the ideological link between his regime and the navy.[95]

The naval policy of the True Freedom regime served sectional rather than national interests, primarily focused on countering Orangist internal challenges rather than English warships and legal opinions. The fleet was both a physical and an ideological tool, representing the triumph of seapower culture over continental military alternatives, a clash that occurred in all seapower states. The survival of Johan de Witt and the True Freedom seapower state depended on an unbroken run of success.

In three Anglo-Dutch wars the Dutch defended their commercial interests against an ambitious centralised commercial state, still primarily defined by land. England's powerful navy, created for insular security, was slowly reconfigured to fight for trade, enabling the English to assume a seapower identity a few decades later, when the Republic laid down the burden of being a great power.

English policymakers understood the maritime, economic bases of Dutch power. Sir William Temple, an observant and sympathetic envoy at The Hague, considered de Witt's Republic a distinctive seapower state, too small and weak in human resources to be a continental military power, yet prodigiously wealthy, and very much a great power. Furthermore he saw the parallel with Venice, another republican seapower state that relied on mercenary troops, and long, limited wars of economic exhaustion.[96] Ultimately, its limited population crippled the Republic's ability to act as a great power. In the wars that raged between 1688 and 1713 most of its soldiers, and around half the sailors, were foreigners, as they had been for decades.[97]

Temple reinforced his seapower analysis with an early example of geographical determinism, claiming lack of land and dependence on imports had forced the Dutch. Once at sea they had generated a vast trade and merchant fleets, equal to the rest of Europe combined, without the obvious local resources of shipbuilding timber, iron and other materials, and despite dangerous harbours. For Temple the critical advantage lay in the Dutch system of government: trade decayed under arbitrary or tyrannical rule. These were, of course, de Witt's views, and almost certainly reflected discussions between the two men. George Downing, who was less well disposed to the Republic, was equally clear on the synergy between trade, de Witt's state and the navy. The synergy of politics, trade and war, exemplified in the financial base of the Dutch Navy, was critical. 'The Convoys of Merchant-Fleets into all parts, even in time of Peace, but especially into the Streights [of Gibraltar], which give their Trade security against many unexpected accidents, and their Nation credit abroad, and breeds up Sea-men for their Ships of War.' While the sources of Dutch wealth were unique, the English might emulate their methods, including living frugally and re-exporting luxuries. He condemned mercantilist thinkers at the Restoration Court, notably the Duke of York, who believed naval victory would transfer wealth across the North Sea. The end of Dutch hegemony would profit many trading nations, and the Republic would rather rejoin the Holy Roman Empire than submit to the English. He cautioned the war party to wait: the tide of Dutch power was ebbing, they were becoming luxurious, and their trade had begun to slide as England, France, Sweden and Denmark pushed into extra-European markets. A fall in the price of grain reduced the sale of Asian goods in northern Europe, and the carrying trade to southern Europe. The reduction in bulk cargoes impacted on Venice, Genoa and the Dutch, shifting Mediterranean trade into English hands. Temple traced the history of commercial pre-eminence from Venice to Portugal, and then from Antwerp to Amsterdam.[98] His judgement proved sound: commerce and power passed from Amsterdam to London when the True Freedom regime was overthrown, the Republic reverted back to a terrestrial stadholderate, and England became a 'Republic'.

While England and the United Provinces contested the dominion of the seas, French statesmen feared that, if either acquired a monopoly of global commerce, they would prejudice Bourbon imperial projects. France had no desire to be a seapower, but it had a serious appetite for Spanish land and wealth, and a deep distrust of the republican political model of seapower states. In an attempt to balance the Second Anglo-Dutch War (1665–7), France acted as a faint ally of the Dutch, but, despite crushing defeats at the battles of Solebay and St James's Day, the triumphant Medway Raid by the Dutch Navy in June 1667 demonstrated such aid was unnecessary.[99]

Recognising the resilient ideological challenge posed by de Witt's victory, France launched a full-scale assault on Dutch commerce before peace had been signed at Breda in the late summer of 1667. English naval operations had limited impact on the Dutch economy, but French tariffs quickly choked Amsterdam's lucrative sugar trade. The Dutch trade that France tried to destroy was dominated by Asian and Caribbean produce, and Spanish demand for shipping services. King Louis XIV used punitive tariffs to block this trade at the Customs House. At the same time his troops occupied part of the Spanish Netherlands. De Witt halted their incorporation into France with the 1668 Triple Alliance, the Republic, England and later Sweden, combining to restrain France within the 1659 borders. Thwarted of his prize Louis, who valued land and fortresses far higher than trade and colonies, redoubled his efforts to crush the Dutch.[100] The Triple Alliance was a public humiliation, one that Louis never forgave. Within months Louis and Charles were planning an attack.

The delicate balance that de Witt created to sustain the seapower oligarchy against an Orange revival depended on a French alliance for terrestrial security while the Republic operated as a seapower great power. Having annoyed Louis XIV, the Republic needed to restore the army, which de Witt's regime could not do without handing power to the House of Orange.

Colbert, Louis XIV's mercantilist naval, colonial and commercial minister, was equally clear. French hegemony had been built on the ruins of Spanish power, but it required the annihilation of Dutch commerce to bring the project to completion: 'so long as they are masters of trade, their naval forces will continue to grow and to render them so powerful that they will be able to assume the role of arbiters of peace and war in Europe and to set limits on the King's plans'.[101] That was all a seapower state could hope to achieve against a Universal Monarchy. Dutch money and ideology consti-tuted a standing threat to the Sun King's vaunting ambition. Colbert rejected the Dutch economic model, creating a command economy, combining protectionism with a large battlefleet to secure trade by force. French tariffs inflicted serious damage on the Dutch economy, and Colbert had 'long-term ambitions for Antwerp'.[102] In 1648 the Treaty of Munster closed the Scheldt to trade, but the closure only applied while the Southern Netherlands remained Spanish. It would not apply if they became provinces of France. If France opened the Scheldt for trade the Republic would be ruined. In 1701 Louis used this threat, hoping to deter the Republic, but only succeeded in unifying the Dutch behind the Stadholder.[103]

Amsterdam's worldview was dominated by ocean-going trade, domi-nated by the Baltic and the VoC, which was rapidly evolving into a territor-ial empire in Asia. Although independent of national government the company was controlled by the men who dominated national politics under de Witt. It had been built by war, driving the Portuguese out of Asia and dominating the Indian Ocean and the Indonesian archipelago, by harnessing private capital to the War of Independence.[104] Authorised to conduct Asian trade, attack Spanish and Portuguese shipping, build fortresses, sign treaties and make defensive war, the VoC was, as Charles Boxer observed, either 'a state within a state' or a semi-detached empire'.[105] Sir William Temple believed it to be effectively a sovereign state, with forty or fifty 'warships' and 20,000 soldiers, commanding the trade between northern Europe and Asia, exchanging Asian goods for Baltic produce, grain, timber and iron. In a compelling demonstration of the synergy between state, empire and busi-ness, dependence on Indian saltpetre gave both the Dutch and the English East India Companies massive leverage with their governments.[106] The VoC model was applied to all Dutch overseas holdings. The state subcontracted the empire, a key element of its economic and strategic structure, to a company that shared many attributes of the local and regional government, and the same leaders. Limited liability protected both the state and investors. The VoC became a staple of the economy, and company stock was central to the Amsterdam exchange, the bell-weather of the economy, paying dividends of between 12 and 50 per cent.

The Amsterdam elite were also heavily represented in the governance of the West India Company and the Society of Surinam, linking the governments of Amsterdam, Holland and the Republic with a commercial empire.[107] Surinam was highly profitable, but the WIC never escaped its early dependence on the state for funds and military support. Attempts to unify the VoC and WIC into a single national trading empire in the 1640s were blocked by the VoC, which objected to the imposition of an Iberian 'tributary' model of empire, in which the merchants were excluded from political power. This would have broken the central plank of the Republic's seapower identity: political inclusion. De Witt used the system more sympathetically during the Second Anglo-Dutch War, securing loans from the company and other forms of support. In return the VoC was represented at the peace talks, and their interests were upheld. The company was always looking for tax breaks.[108]

If Amsterdam, the city-state at the heart of Dutch seapower, was a modern Carthage, then the semi-detached Asian fiefdom of the VoC mirrored Barcid Iberia. Once established in the Indonesian archipelago the company became continental, emphasising territorial control and monopolies of supply. Rather than extending maritime trade into new markets it expelled rival European traders and crushed local resistance.[109] As George Downing observed, Dutch concepts of 'freedom of the seas' only applied to British seas; the seas of Africa and Asia were closed by force. In Asia the VoC imposed *mare clausum*, in sharp contrast to the *mare liberum* line the Dutch took over herring fisheries in the North Sea.[110] Having replaced the Iberians as imperial actors the Dutch adopted their methods. This closed trading system became inefficient, pushing up costs, the very antithesis of classic seapower.[111]

After 1688 the VoC consistently lost money on Asian trade: costs rose three times more quickly than revenues in the 'Golden Age', despite rising volumes of trade.[112] Dutch pepper often sold at a loss. After 1713 the VoC and the subsequent national empire in Asia existed on the sufferance of more powerful states, a galling situation that did nothing to improve relations with Britain.[113] Unable to compete at sea and no longer in control of a staple trade, corruption, incompetence and the growing costs of running a distant territorial empire combined with a weak financial base, reliant on loans to cover operating costs, meant that for the VoC disaster was inevitable. Like the Republic it traded on reputation and image, building an enormous Amsterdam warehouse, a statement of enduring power and consequence that collapsed in 1822.[114]

The decline of the VoC reflected deeper trends in the post-1672 state. The governing council, the Heeren XVII, came from a merchant elite shifting from trade to government service and landed interest to stabilise familial power bases. The names that dominate Peter Burke's analysis of the Amsterdam elite recur with striking frequency in Femme Gaastra's history of the VoC, alongside their portraits and possessions. Many were also engaged in the Levant trade and the government of Amsterdam, which, by extension, included those of Holland and the United Provinces. Having created a new oligarchy these men gentrified the VoC. Excluding merchants from the Amsterdam Chamber after 1690 created a hereditary elite divorced from trade just as the economy peaked and the Republic became normalised in the European state system.[115] This process can be traced in all seapower states.

After 1713, debates within the Heeren XVII lost sight of the sea, focusing on costly territorial expansion. This was an obvious response to the end of the seapower state, and of strategic sea power. After 1713 the British pushed into Dutch Asian markets, planning the peaceful destruction of their once-mighty precursors.[116] The Dutch Empire on the Indian mainland ended in 1783, the year the VoC granted the British East India Company free access to Asian waters, ending the spice monopoly. A decade later the British seized the strategic naval base at Trincomalee, to pre-empt the French. The base secured control of the Bay of Bengal, the Malayan coast and the Malacca Straits. The VoC was nationalised in 1796, and wound up in 1800.[117]

Few would have predicted that outcome at the high point of the Dutch seapower state, in the autumn of 1667. Just as everyone else accepted the Second Anglo-Dutch War would peter out in a patched-up peace, with both sides distracted by domestic issues, with peace talks already scheduled, Johan de Witt delivered a seapower masterstroke, one he had been planning for more than a decade. He needed to win the war, avoid commercial losses that would harm his supporters in Amsterdam, and above all forestall rising enthusiasm for the sixteen-year-old Prince of Orange, whose Stuart heritage gave Charles II leverage in Dutch politics.

With the English fleet laid up, for want of money, Michiel de Ruyter and Cornelis de Witt led a Dutch Fleet into the Thames Estuary, smashed the new fort at Sheerness, and seized or burnt five major warships in Chatham Reach, including the iconic *Royal Charles*. This was Johan de Witt's victory, his ideas, his energy and his vision: he reckoned it the 'best plenipotentiary of all' at the peace talks, reinforcing his diplomacy by keeping the fleet at sea until peace had been ratified.[118] The Medway Raid and the subsequent Treaty of Breda sustained the True Freedom regime against rising Orangist enthusiasm.

While contemporary pamphlets linked victory on the Medway with the 'Eternal Edict' of June 1667 that restricted the role of the Prince of Orange, the measure had been forced on a reluctant de Witt by an emerging centre party that ruptured the Amsterdam/Holland elite seapower consensus. De Witt's Bicker in-laws had lost their dominant position, replaced by former allies Coenrad van Beuninghen and Gillis Valckenier, who combined with Haarlem Pensionary Gaspar Fagel to thwart the Grand of Raads Pensionary, the most important civil official in the Republic in the absence of the Stadholder. The Edict was double-edged, abolishing the position of Stadholder in Holland, and later Utrecht, but effectively ensured the Prince of Orange would become Captain General when he came of age, thereby guaranteeing a renewal of partisan strife.[119]

At Breda, Charles II sought recognition of his sovereignty of the seas, though his tangible claims against the Dutch were relatively minor. The symbolism of power and prestige was vital for the restored Stuart monarchy, as it was for de Witt's Republic. Both men were engaged in a complex three-sided game, one in which Louis XIV held most of the best cards. De Witt knew that an alliance with England to resist French hegemony would be fatal to the True Freedom regime and great-power status, because the Dutch would be 'forced by the exigencies of war to assume the principal burden of land combat, while the English took on that at sea'.[120] Insular England would always be a more effective seapower than the continental Republic, but shifting defence spending to the army would hand power to the Orange party.

However, such concerns lay in the future when de Witt and his supporters exploited the Medway Raid, the high-water mark of Dutch seapower, for political advantage. Their propaganda, primarily intended for domestic consumption, was pushed to extremes: Dutch words and pictures deeply offended the English monarchy. Cornelis de Witt commissioned from Jan de Baen, an artist whom Charles II admired, a great image for Dordrecht Town Hall, featuring himself, fire, smoke and a Dutch flag fluttering over Sheerness. Cornelis Bisschop created a similar allegorical image, bedecked with symbols of peace, justice, freedom and unity. They were only the high points of a torrent of words and pictures that represented Dutch success. Such was Dutch dominance of the means of design, production and dissemination that this offensive left the English speechless. Charles II recognised that he needed to secure the ability to reply, to acquire the art of seapower. His declaration of war in 1672 specifically demanded that de Baen's Dordrecht image be destroyed, and highlighted the humiliation of the *Royal Charles* being used as a fairground sideshow. Once these demands became common knowledge it was hardly surprising that the offending image was lynched by an Orangist mob in Dordrecht.[121] Ultimately, the consequences of the Medway were so damaging that Stephen Baxter posed the question, 'was it wise to attack Chatham?'[122] In the Medway the Dutch Republic state overstepped the bounds of what seapowers were allowed to do. It humiliated a major monarchy in deed, word and image, an insult reinforced by publicly boasting of power and consequence. Five years later the regime had been swept away.

By the time the *Royal Charles* was quietly broken up in 1673 the Dutch art market had collapsed. Orders dried up, pictures flooded onto a satiated market, prices fell and many artists moved abroad. Neither market nor prices ever recovered, while hack work and half measures replaced sophistication and insight.[123] Artists with a market outside the United Provinces left, notably the artists of seapower Willem van de Velde father and son. They moved to London, and took 'the King's shilling'.[124] The son's greatest work lay in the future. Under a restored Orange regime Dutch taste moved away from the sea, while architecture abandoned the civic agendas of republican seaports for the landed domesticity of the nobility.[125]

That seapower states consistently attracted the hatred and fear of absolutist/continental/military regimes was not a question of naval power, or ships, but the existential challenge their political structures posed to the legitimacy of other, less inclusive forms of government. When seapowers broadcast the superiority of their system, primarily to secure internal cohesion, counter-propaganda mocked their commercial values, cowardice and unreliability. Napoleon's 'nation of shopkeepers' was only the last in a long line of insults stretching back to Spartan jibes about Athenians. The 'True Freedom' Republic had overplayed the seapower agenda after the Medway Raid for domestic reasons, alienating England, the obvious ally against French hegemonic ambition, while ignoring the need to improve military forces, and the reality that the seapower identity had not taken root in the population. The Amsterdam elite were detested by the middle and working classes, who believed they exploited power for personal advantage. Unable, or unwilling, to satisfy the agendas of an Amsterdam elite that had lost faith in his leadership, de Witt tried to balance France and England without an army, while keeping the Prince of Orange out of office, in defiance of public opinion. His system collapsed in 1672, when the 'New Navy', the costly instrument funded by national taxes, failed to deter war.

Sir William Temple highlighted the constant tension between the Orange and State parties, divided on religious and political grounds, which 'made the weak side of this State; and whenever their period comes, will prove the occasion of their Fall.'[126] Domestic support for the Raads Pensionary ebbed as the Prince of Orange reached maturity. Many looked to exploit the coming change. Even republican probity proved a handicap. Key figures in Amsterdam resented de Witt's overtly even-handed treatment of political and economic issues.[127]

De Witt attempted to sustain the Republic's international position and domestic stability through the Triple Alliance in 1668, a security pact that forced Louis XIV to retire from the Spanish Netherlands and blocked his return. This humiliated the Sun King, whose support de Witt needed both to resist English claims to sovereignty of the seas and to avoid the need for a large army. He needed English support to make the Triple Alliance effective, to restrain Louis's continental ambition, but his supporters feared they would lose trade to their allies. Unable to work closely with either England or France the Republic fell back on diplomacy, but without allies it was too weak to control events or deter war. The True Freedom party could not balance these conflicting concerns. The triumphs in 1667 and 1668 were rapidly undone by French money and Stuart ambition to rule without Parliament. In 1670 the secret Treaty of Dover wrecked the Republic's

diplomatic position, Charles and Louis agreed to satisfy their mutual resentment of a Republic whose very existence challenged royal authority.[128] Yet
the allies were not of one mind: Louis took a Roman view, the new Carthage
must be destroyed, whereas Charles wanted more trade, and a reliable, that
is Orange, ally in The Hague against France. Ultimately, these divisions
would save the Republic, but not the regime.

The Treaty of Dover placed de Witt on the horns of a dilemma: unless the
Republic reverted back to a Stadholderate under a half-Stuart Prince, it would
be attacked by England and France. In either case the True Freedom was
doomed, seapower would pass to the English, and de Witt might follow
Oldenbarnevelt to the block. Although many erstwhile supporters were ready
to sacrifice their principles, he held firm. This was unwise: the crisis found
the Dutch army and navy in disarray. After 1667 the admiralties paid off
ships and men, to rebuild their credit, while the English rebuilt their fleet. In
January 1671 de Witt secured an increased naval and military budget in the
States General, hoping a fleet of seventy-two capital ships would deter
Charles. In November he accepted that war was inevitable and mobilised the
navy. De Ruyter prepared for a pre-emptive strike to block an English invasion, and success at the battle of Solebay bought the Republic twelve months.[129]

However, Solebay proved to be irrelevant: the Republic was not an island.
Louis declared war on 6 April 1672, as the campaign season opened, because
to wait any longer 'would diminish his glory'. The very existence of de Witt's
exceptional Republic had become an affront to his royal dignity. Louis
wanted to humiliate the Dutch before the world, force them to abandon
their government and the connected seapower identity, and get them to
conform to continental norms while he erected a new Roman Empire on
the ruins of Amsterdam. The obnoxious Protestant Republic would be
annihilated, for having the temerity to behave as a great power. Unwilling,
or unable, to comprehend the depth of Louis's animosity, de Witt attributed
the war to a more prosaic cause: 'Dutch interference with Louis's desire to
occupy the Spanish Netherlands'. Louis had not mentioned this issue when
declaring war, to avoid triggering the 1668 Triple Alliance.[130]

The seapower Republic had been living in a fool's paradise. Many recognised Louis's agenda, none better than the Dutch artist who represented the
hostile coalition, France, England and Munster, as the three heads of
Cerberus, the monstrous guard dog of the underworld. Cato's motto

'delenda est Carthago' appeared on the beast's collar.[131] Within weeks French troops had occupied the country as far as Utrecht, reviving bitter divisions between unoccupied Amsterdam and Holland and the rest of the country. Without a friend in the world, or an adequate army, the True Freedom regime crashed in ruins at the first shock of war. De Witt's navy won the war at sea, but that was never going to save the Republic's four terrestrial provinces. Instead de Ruyter's brilliant performance in 1673 covered the abolition of a state that he had loyally supported and the shift of resources from sea to land that saved the United Provinces.[132]

The process of normalising the Republic began with the murder of de Witt and his brother, a necessary political act, albeit one of unprecedented savagery.[133] With much of the country under occupation, his system in ruins, and wounded by an assassin, de Witt had resigned; weeks later he and his brother Cornelis were ripped to pieces in a street in The Hague. The collapse of the True Freedom state saw Willem III assume the Stadholderate on 7 July 1672. Willem quickly mobilised the fiscal and strategic resources of the state, rebuilt the army and created a pan-European coalition to defend the European state system upon which Dutch survival and prosperity depended.

Louis, like Xerxes, had underestimated an enemy he despised; his armies were unable to break the water line, or even hold their ground once the Austrian Habsburg-led empire entered the conflict. Willem III sacrificed seapower exceptionalism for endurance, his quasi-royal status deflecting and diminishing the ire of kings, and attracting substantial support in England. It was emblematic that Willem sacrificed de Ruyter to the new realities of the Orangist state, sending him to fight a hopeless campaign, in a secondary theatre, with an under-strength fleet, while he recovered all seven Dutch provinces. Willem secured domestic control by sending troops to purge the town councils, as de Witt had feared.[134]

The change of regime, and the long, bitter fight back against Louis XIV, fundamentally changed the Republic. It ceased to be, and more significantly ceased to claim to be, something unique and different. Willem replaced de Witt's exceptionalist True Freedom seapower with a continental military state that resisted French hegemonic ambition in alliance with England, Spain and the Habsburg Holy Roman Empire. Louis XIV may have failed to destroy the Republic, but de Witt's death ended the seapower state. Willem III would resist Louis's ambitions of Universal Monarchy for the rest of his life, but he did so as a conventional head of state and fought on land.[135] His best ally would be the French king. Amsterdam opposed Willem's policy for a decade, but the Revocation of the Edict of Nantes in 1685, and a fresh French tariff war in 1687, released the revenues Willem needed to invade England in 1688. The prime beneficiary of Willem's policy would be England, which was far less exposed to French military might.[136] Much as Louis had feared, Dutch failure merely cleared the way for the assumption of seapower by England, the culmination of a two-hundred-year process, heavily impacted by ideas, images and methods from the Low Countries.

In 1688 Willem reversed the politico-strategic balance shaped by Louis XIV, deposing his father-in-law and creating an Anglo-Dutch alliance to preserve the security and prosperity of the Republic. Louis XIV's ambition to create a new Roman Empire and a command economy trumped Anglo-Dutch trade rivalry and memories of recent wars. Alliance with the Royal Navy enabled Dutch traders to take short-term profits at the expense of long-term interests.[137] As is often argued trade followed the flag, the flag flying on the largest fleet. Willem's two states became 'the seapowers', sustaining extraordinary military commitments for twenty years in order to restrain France. Already past its economic peak the Republic had to dig in and resist, much as it had under Willem the Silent, in costly land campaigns of endurance.

Three major wars between 1672 and 1713 eroded the economic base that had sustained Dutch seapower in the 'Golden Age' of the True Freedom. During the first war, 1672–7, the 'overseas trading system, and the main towns, were seriously damaged and a long term decline ... set in'. After a brief revival in the 1680s, 'the permanent, irreversible decline of Holland as a maritime and industrial power commenced only in or around 1688 with the onset of the Nine Years War and its many harmful consequences for the Dutch economy'. Relative decline became absolute decline after 1720, with the loss of the Spanish domestic market, and then the Baltic grain trade. Baltic trade had been weakened by the 1688 alliance: the English became the dominant naval power in the region, enabling them to undercut Dutch insurance rates, and block profitable Dutch exports of Baltic naval stores to the enemy.[138]

The Dutch paid a heavy price for their territorial integrity, accepting a subordinate role at sea after 1688. Spending on troops and forts increased, reducing the navy to a secondary role. Between 1652 and 1713 Dutch battlefleets, 'operating in the interest of Dutch state policy, were financed by the States General'. De Witt managed this 'without constraining resources, as the army could be kept at peacetime strength ... the battlefleet was paid for by taxes serving the interests of the federation and the territorial state; and the cruiser fleet paid for by customs dues and serving the interests of trade'.[139] Focused on the need to restore the European state system to balance, Willem III used the navy as a diplomatic counter, pushing the battlefleet up to 100 ships of the line, including 15 first-rate three-deckers.[140] These increases were forced onto the Zealand and Friesland admiralties, greatly increasing their indebtedness. After Willem's death in 1702 the navy drifted back to the core task, defence of trade. The Republic's new leader, Pensionary Antonie Heinsius, 'never really took the Navy to heart; leaving battlefleet operations to the English, and allowing the regional admiralties to reassert their independence'.[141] After 1702 the States General focused the naval effort on purely defensive missions.[142] There was little risk: Louis XIV's battlefleet fell into sharp decline after 1692, while French armies remained on the Republic's exposed borders and French privateers flourished. Having waged the War of the Spanish Succession on credit, rather than raising taxes, the Dutch state carried a mountain of debt in 1713, 'paralysing diplomacy and crippling naval spending'. The debt burden exacerbated provincial disputes about policy and funding. Post-war economic revival depended on recovering trade with Spain, Spanish America and the Mediterranean. This would only happen, as Amsterdam City Council stressed, by keeping the French Bourbon candidate and his command economy methods out of Spain. The failure of that agenda left the city demoralised. Too weak to shape the Peace of Utrecht the Republic had to accept an Anglo-French deal. The Barrier Treaty secured the Franco-Belgian border, but this served British rather than Dutch strategic interests. There was no economic windfall to recoup wartime expenditure: war had failed to pay.[143] After Utrecht there were no more national taxes to fund the battlefleet; the 'New Navy' drifted into memory, and instead it became what Jaap Bruijn termed a 'Second Rate Navy', one that fulfilled the functions of the pre-1652 'Old Navy'. It protected Dutch commerce and ensured convoy and licence fees were paid. Pepijn Brandon critiqued the term 'Second Rate', emphasising the conscious decision by the merchant elite to focus on a lean and efficient convoy escort cruiser fleet that served their interests, and to abandon the costly sea-control battlefleet. While the post 1713 navy remained excellent it was small, consciously freeloading on British naval dominance (much as the West is currently freeloading on American naval dominance). Problems only began when the commercial interests of the Dutch sea state became seriously antagonistic towards British dominance of global trade. Such opposition required a sea-control battlefleet, but the decision to create one came too late to prevent the disastrous losses of the Fourth Anglo-Dutch War of 1780–3. The cruiser navy was brushed aside by British reserves while the Royal Navy's main fleets dealt with France and Spain. As Pepiyn Brandon demonstrated, regional Admiralty boards trimmed customs dues on rising trade volumes while peacetime state subsidies increased, before rocketing upwards after 1780.[144] Dutch naval weakness after 1713 was a matter of conscious choice, a choice made by merchant elites increasingly divorced from the realities of oceanic trade.

The glory of the Chatham Raid, the apogee of Dutch seapower, proved short-lived. Willem III returned the Republic to its default setting, a quasi-monarchical military state with powerful commercial and imperial assets that were operated as chartered companies by the men of Amsterdam. In reality the 'decline' of Dutch seapower was merely the recontinentalisation of the state after the failure of de Witt's seapower project. By 1692 the trident of seapower had been gripped by Britannia, a goddess modelled on a mistress of the king so deeply humiliated in 1667. After 1713 a shrunken navy escorted a static trade across oceans it no longer attempted to command, in words or pictures, let alone deeds. Dutch seapower culture soon faded, the best artists moved to England in 1672, following the market for marine art, as the Regent class – the self-perpetuating oligarchy that ruled the cities – abandoned maritime iconography for cows and fields.[145]

The Dutch seapower state, briefly a great power, ended not with a bang, but with a heartfelt sigh of economic relief. The 'normalised' Republic needed decades of peace to rebuild its finances, and began by cutting the funds of both armed services.[146] It became an object lesson in decline.[147] England moved in the opposite direction, becoming a United Kingdom, incorporating Scotland and Ireland to create a domestic base capable of sustaining a far greater seapower empire, one that persisted until the middle of the twentieth century, while the significantly smaller Dutch state could not sustain the effort after 1713. Scale has always been a critical aspect of seapower states: too large and they inevitably become territorial empires of continental scale, too small and they remain sea states, like ancient Rhodes and medieval Genoa. The standard of that scale shifted across time, although never in a crudely linear manner, to meet the challenge posed by contemporary land powers.

The Republic followed Venice into managed decline. Prosperous oligarchic elites abandoned the unique model of a combined seapower and great power to preserve their Republic. That choice, like the initial decision to become a seapower, was conscious, and rational. Johan de Witt's True Freedom had been an experiment in full-blooded state seapower, bolder than Venice, treading a fine line between arrogance and annihilation. De Witt relied on deterrence and a diplomatic balancing act to preserve his Republic from two proto-hegemonic states, Louis XIV's continental France and Charles II's maritime England, enabling the Republic to operate as a great power, a status that it could not achieve on land. He stressed Dutch exceptionalism in ways that were deeply provocative, and ultimately unsustainable. Willem III recognised that in order to survive the Republic would have to join the system and accept the limits of national power inherent in its location, scale and population. Willem's diplomatic skill enabled the Republic to act as a great power, but the Republic was not a great power, as it would discover after his death.

The reality of decline can be traced in the economic activity of the Regent class. Having secured the key offices of state they became rentiers, breaking the link between merchants and naval defence. After 1700 they invested in provincial bonds, not risky sea voyages. There were no seamen on the Admiralty committees, prompting merchants to create their own pressure groups, which emphasised cruisers to defend trade, ending the national approach to naval policy and sea power strategy. England became the seapower.[148] As the commercial impulse slipped away, land-owning and rentier economics became the norm. In 1618, 33 per cent of the Amsterdam elite had no occupation and 10 per cent had country houses. By 1748 the respective figures were 73 per cent and 81 per cent. As Adam Smith observed, all merchants want to become country gentlemen. A dynamic economy required a steady supply of fresh merchant families. Immigration sustained the entrepreneurial spirit in Amsterdam down to 1680; thereafter the economy slowed, and so did social change. By 1720 public debt provided an attractive investment. While the Venetian elite moved from trade to land, their Amsterdam counterparts moved from trade to bonds. In both cities full-time roles in government completed the ossification of once dynamic mercantile elites.[149] In 1795 the old Republic was overwhelmed by the French Revolution, the federal-brokerage state was replaced by a centralised unitary state, ultimately presided over by Napoleon. This structure would be inherited by the post-1815 kingdom of the United Netherlands.

The United Provinces became a seapower under the True Freedom regime, after the treaties of 1648 ended Spanish regional hegemony. It was able to make that choice because the men of money and trade had been integrated into the political process, ensuring 'bureaucrats and capitalists interacted on a much more equal footing'. This can be contrasted with the situation in the autocratic, continental Roman imperial monarchies of Spain and France.[150] The Dutch had developed inclusive structures to fund the terrestrial War of Independence, structures that enabled de Witt's seapower state to emerge. However, the threat of continental military aggression remained: two decades later the regime and its self-proclaimed seapower identity were destroyed by the hegemonic ambitions of Bourbon France, which detested its political model and prosperity. It passed unmourned from a monarchical world in which no one outside Amsterdam believed it had any right to exist. Those who admired the regime lacked the power to help. The True Freedom leadership consistently overrated the threat posed by English demands for 'Sovereignty of the Seas' and the damage it could do to Dutch economic hegemony, and underrated the existential threat posed by Louis XIV. De Witt tried to balance the two monarchies, while reducing the army, to prevent an Orangist coup, and fund a sea power battlefleet to control the seas. The self-identifying 'exceptional' republican regime collapsed in 1672, long before it could become an established national identity. The totality of that defeat has been obscured by the fact that it occurred in the geo-strategic context of European power politics, rather than a naval battle.

The Dutch seapower state was a short, failed, experiment, one that never appealed to working people; even the sailors who manned the fleet remained loyal to the Orange regime. The republicans used naval victories to develop a distinct, new, national identity, but they could not sustain the regime. The harder that republican propagandists worked to maintain domestic support, the more they alienated and alarmed potential allies, especially England. England desperately needed a stable alliance partner to help restrain the proto-hegemonic power of France. On this point Cromwell and Charles II were in accord, and both were disappointed. Amsterdam counted the economic cost of an English alliance, but ignored its absolute necessity. Dutch trade was hardly affected by English measures, as the Republic carried very little of England's trade.

Dutch great-power status in the age of de Witt's True Freedom regime reflected a regional power vacuum, not an underlying reality. When France, the empire and England reached their true potential the tiny republic could not compete. Willem III admitted as much when he sacrificed Dutch interests to create the coalitions that blocked Louis XIV's 'Universal Monarchy', but his wars still bled the Republic white.[151] He defeated French ambition, managed Dutch decline and smoothed the transfer of seapower from Amsterdam to London. Ultimately, the cost of defending the Republic overwhelmed the state, forcing it to abandon a seapower identity that had, briefly, made it a great power. When faced with a choice between destruction or decline the underlying political wisdom of the United Provinces was obvious.

The seapower state had been funded by Dutch primacy in world trade, itself a product of relative peace after the Treaty of Westphalia (1648). Rampant prosperity and overt display excited envy, while the representative commercial oligarchy that sustained seapower alarmed absolute monarchies, especially Louis XIV's France. From the late 1660s French tariffs and industrial protection closed Dutch markets. Spain, a central plank of regional economic activity since before the Revolt, was lost in 1702, breaking a complex commercial system that relied on the interaction of Baltic grain and lumber, Dutch fish, American sugar, tobacco, indigo and furs, Asian luxuries and southern European markets, supplemented by a large carrying trade and growing industrial output. The demands of war between 1688 and 1713 overtaxed Dutch finances, money and credit ran out, and the leadership chose decline over destruction. They would live on the proceeds of domestic debt, land and VoC stock. Peter Burke demonstrated how these men and their Venetian counterparts, families made by enterprise and risk, evolved into rentier landlords and bond-holders.[152] Simon Schama argued that the aristocratisation of the Amsterdam elite, and the 'normalisation' of the Dutch state within the international system, after the shattering experience of 1672 had demonstrated the existential risks of uniqueness, were timely concessions to the limits of a small state. Once it stopped posing as a seapower great power the Republic found allies to uphold the status quo against the hegemonic ambition of Louis XIV. Contemporaries noted the analogy between the Republic in 1672 and Venice at the time of the League of Cambrai (1508).[153] The Dutch 'choice' to abandon great-power status was conscious, and entirely consistent with the decision to become a seapower in 1650. The logic was simple. After 1713 the Dutch economy declined relatively, although not absolutely, because it lacked the markets and resources to continue growing dynamically, and without a battlefleet navy it could not command the seas, as it had under the True Freedom regime. Both population and European territory remained static while those of rival states expanded. It was no coincidence that the men who opted for stability and order had already presided over the VoC's drift away from seagoing enterprise into territory and crops. After 1713 trade stagnated and Dutch capital flowed into London, where interest rates were higher and investment opportunities greater. Dutch money helped develop the British seapower state.[154]

The attempt to emulate Venice on the Amstel failed. The Republic was only briefly a true seapower, during a period when the True Freedom regime aspired to be the arbiter of Europe, hegemon of world trade and the political model for all mankind. It left a powerful legacy for the last seapower state.

CHAPTER 6

Sea States and Overseas Empires
A PROBLEM OF PERSPECTIVE

Being deeply engaged with the sea, or possessing overseas empires, did not make states seapowers. Some were sea states, too small to aspire to great-power status, whereas others, continental powers, saw overseas possessions as useful adjuncts to their core concerns. While sea states shared much of the seapower identity, they were too small to be great powers. Continental states acquired sea empires without changing their culture or aspiring to be seapowers. Ancient Rhodes, early modern Genoa and Imperial Portugal provide opportunities to refine the definition of seapower and the impact of changing international contexts on the ability of states to adopt and develop sea-based identities. Rhodes and Genoa found distinctive ways to exploit the sea to enhance their wealth and security without challenging the great powers. By contrast Portugal and Spain, which are commonly listed as seapowers because they acquired large overseas empires, had no interest in becoming sea states, let alone seapowers. The Iberian empires endured for centuries, but their cultural cores remained impervious to the ocean. Monarchical absolutism, the Roman Church, terrestrial ambition, aristocratic privilege, monopolistic economic models and a sustained

Seamark and symbol: *The Colossus of Rhodes* by Johann Bernhard Fischer von Erlach

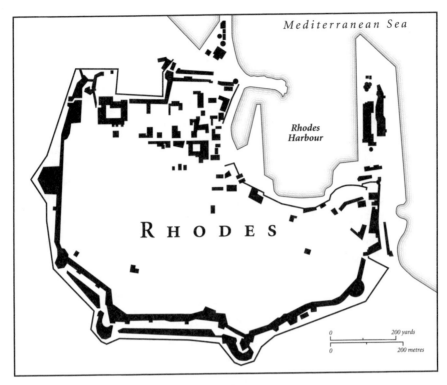

Rhodes

contempt for seafarers, oceans and new ideas ensured they remained profoundly continental. After a brief period of effectively unchallenged naval dominance the Iberians allowed Genoese and Dutch contractors to administer, transport and bankroll their trade. When rivals challenged their control of the seas they fell back on land defences, and alliances with seapowers and sea states, to secure their commerce. Their colonies of settlement evolved into new states, dominated by the same combination of militarism, authoritarian politics, the Roman Church and peasant taxation that had stultified the home country. The Iberian sea empires remained rooted in the Reconquista, and Roman symbols of power.

While Athens and Carthage evolved from sea states into seapower great powers, provoking the hostility of continental rivals, other sea states avoided their fate by recognising their weakness and reining in such ambitions. These sea states retained the core elements of the seapower model, relying on commerce and fleets, and relatively inclusive oligarchic assemblies dominated by the commercial elite, and they avoided conflict with great land powers. They adopted a realpolitik of restraint, concession and coalition-building. Their armed forces were dominated by cruisers, to protect trade, rather than battlefleets.

Rhodes was one of many ancient sea states, small, weak and self-aware trading cities. The largest of the Dodecanese islands, located off the coast of Asia Minor, Rhodes was ideally placed to control the trade routes between Egypt and Phoenicia to the south and the Dardanelles and the Aegean to the north. The Greek-speaking islanders had been Persian tributaries, fighting for Xerxes at Salamis, until liberated by Athens. Local oligarchs switched to Sparta, before the Peloponnesian Wars saw the island return to Persian rule. In 409–408 BC the structure of the island changed and the three small trading ports pooled their resources, shifting economic and political power to a new fortified port city at the northern end of Rhodes.[1] After some internal dissension this created a far stronger Rhodian maritime identity. Sea state culture generated the economic resources to create some of the most impressive fortifications in the Greek world, surrounding state-of-the-art port facilities. The republican constitution, widely considered among the best in the ancient world, avoided the excesses of oligarchy and populism, providing the stability needed to develop maritime trade. Social harmony was enhanced by sharing the benefits of trade, the needy were fed by the state, and wealthy citizens undertook ambitious liturgies. Similarities with contemporary Athens were more than coincidental. Rhodes was amongst the most cosmopolitan cities of the age, with striking public and private buildings, and impressive art collections.

The navy secured the island and the carrying trade that paid for imported grain and shipbuilding timber, exploiting seafaring skills and a central location between the Levant and the Aegean. Rhodes shaped regional commerce, and controlled the critical Egyptian grain trade. The naval dockyards were guarded, while warships were built and manned by Rhodians. The majority of male citizens had naval experience, and many were engaged in trade. While eminent Rhodians boasted that they had served as common sailors, military service was ignored. The army, deployed in continental possessions, was largely mercenary. Few Rhodians were prepared to abandon trade for soldiering, unless their city was besieged. The fleet admiral, or *nauarch*, combined naval command with high political office and the authority to conclude treaties. The navy focused on the suppression of piracy, and Rhodian maritime law was widely followed.

After the death of Alexander the Great in 323 BC his empire was divided into three contending continental empires: Macedon, Seleucia and Egypt. This enabled a small, rich insular polity to establish independence. The Macedonian garrison was quietly expelled, ending tribute payments and focusing on trade. This 'freedom' was strikingly similar to later Genoese and Dutch political models. Rhodes became the centre for banking and finance, an international business hub, a vital feature of Hellenistic economic activity. It was the centre of a trading network, dominated by grain, spanning the Greek-speaking world, including the Nile, the Black and Tyrrhenian seas, from Pontus to Carthage, with Egyptian grain a Rhodian monopoly. Pontic grain shipments obliged Rhodes to take a close interest in the Dardanelles, the choke point for Black Sea trade. Domination of the most important bulk trade of the ancient world suggests positive action. It made the island rich, but vulnerable. Any threat to the staple trade could ruin the economy, bankrupt the merchants and destabilise the political system. Too small to compete with great powers Rhodes relied on diplomacy and the mutual animosity of the great powers to continue trade. So important was the island to the Hellenistic trading system that when it was devastated by an earthquake in 228 BC all the great powers sent aid.

Rhodes became rich, using money to obtain strategic advantage, supporting allies with cash, weapons and supplies, and buying off hostile powers. In an age dominated by large-scale land warfare Rhodian wealth had significant strategic leverage, which it used to support the balance of power and protect economic activity. The war against pirates was 'unrelenting', while Egypt, the key to Rhodian wealth, occupied a special place in any strategic calculations.[2] As long as the Hellenistic world remained in balance Rhodes would be secure, and prosperous.

Rhodes avoided binding alliances, although it favoured Ptolemaic Egypt, the main trading partner. However, Rhodes was an attractive target for ambitious powers, anxious to control regional trade and secure naval dominance. In 315 BC the Macedonian ruler Antigonus 'the One Eyed' needed a navy to attack Egypt, and coerced the Rhodians into providing a few ships. In 306 Antigonus wanted more, so his son Demetrius 'the besieger' subjected the city to a massive assault. Thwarted by Rhodian naval forces, stout walls and Egyptian aid, the attack failed. Throughout the siege the Macedonians protected Rhodian merchants across the Greek world and, along with a compromise peace, this suggests Antigonus wanted to keep on good terms with the islanders. The Rhodians celebrated their victory by selling Demetrius' fantastic siege machines to fund the 'Colossus', a 100-foot-high bronze statue of the sun god Helios, a striking statement of wealth and a majestic navigational beacon.[3] Rhodes would preserve its independence and prosperity for as long as Alexander's successors contested his legacy.

This advantageous situation ended when Philip V of Macedon destabilised the Hellenistic world, exploiting a period of Egyptian weakness. Desperate to restore balance, and control Macedonian-inspired piracy, Rhodes looked to Rome, hoping it would balance Macedon. Rome grabbed the opportunity, imposing outrageous, effectively illegal conditions on Philip. Carefully hedging their bets the Rhodians acquired the status of Roman friends, without any binding commitments. As Polybius observed, despite co-operation with Rome for 140 years the Rhodians never entered into an alliance. 'Desiring that no ruler or prince should lose hope of aid and alliance from them, they did not wish to bind themselves to anyone or be engaged by oaths and treaties, but preferred by remaining unencumbered to gain advantage from any and all.'[4] There are few better statements of how seapowers and sea states see the world.

As might be expected, Rhodes was anxious to bring the Second Roman-Macedonian War to an early end, to secure the mainland territories and above all to end the piracy that had been a key feature of Philip's war effort. The Rhodians hoped the region would remain a constellation of states, in which they could wield enough influence to secure commerce and resist the ambitions of Philip and Attalus of Pergamum. The primary war aim was 'freedom for all the markets and ports of Asia'. The islanders had no desire to damage Macedon, only to restore the old balance of power that had secured their trade against the restrictive, continentalising tendencies of the successor states.

Rhodes added very little to a Roman war effort dominated by large-scale land operations, conducting only a few sea-control missions and minor landings. It focused on anti-piracy campaigns against Philip's Cretan 'allies', leaving the navy only partially mobilised. Rome and Pergamum needed little help at sea, and Rhodes had few soldiers. Such self-interested sea state contributions were unlikely to secure much credit with a continental power.

When Rome went to war with the Seleucids, Rhodes skilfully secured additional mainland ports. Despite its limited strategic role Rhodes emerged with more territory, and control of the Cyclades, aside from Delos, where the Romans were active. The continuing weakness of Egypt meant the old three-power Hellenistic balance had been replaced by a two-power system dominated by Rome and Seleucia. The islanders could preserve their neutrality if the two great continental powers fought over territory, but only if they did not damage Rhodian trade. However, 'if one should defeat the other too decisively, the eastern Mediterranean could once again come under the aegis of a single state'. Then 'Rhodian diplomacy might for once find itself with nowhere to turn.'[5] Unfortunately for Rhodes a showdown between the two 'great' powers had become more likely in the absence of a third, balancing power.

When Antiochus III of Seleucia invaded Greece, and Rome counter-attacked, Rhodes remained neutral until the Roman fleet arrived at Delos, by which time the Seleucid armies had been defeated. Even now the Rhodians thought Rome, which had no history of remaining in the east, would simply punish Antiochus and withdraw. Rhodian naval skill secured major victories off Side and Myonessus in 191–190 BC respectively. In the first battle they defeated Hannibal's Phoenician fleet, in the second they rescued the Romans from their own incompetence.

With Seleucia defeated and disarmed, Rhodes and Pergamum argued over control of captured ports. The Romans imposed a clever compromise: Rhodes retained the coast of Asia Minor and the adjoining seas, but Pergamum held the Dardanelles, controlling Rhodes' Black Sea grain trade. Now Rome had become the Mediterranean superpower, 'Rhodes was independent and powerful in the east only through a kind of Roman dispensation. If the attitude of the Senate were to change, the Rhodians would be without a strong ally.'[6] The sea state existed at the whim of a continental hegemonic empire that did not share its concerns, nor value its unique skills. While the issues remained beneath Roman notice Rhodes could still operate, overturning a Pergamene blockade of the Dardanelles, but relations with Pergamum were damaged.

This tightrope walk ended when Rhodian warships escorted the Seleucid bride of King Perseus of Macedon to her wedding, a gesture of goodwill towards both Hellenistic monarchies rewarded with Macedonian shipbuilding timber and gold. The Romans chose to be offended, backing agitation for independence in Lycia, a province they had lately granted to Rhodes. At this juncture the normal calculating restraint of Rhodian diplomacy was upset by public opinion. Swayed by Roman arrogance and 'Greek' sympathies the Rhodian populace backed Perseus, who had cultivated them with signs of honour, while the Romans were insulting and overbearing. Rhodian leaders recognised that in a war with Rome, Perseus would lose, and had no desire to share his defeat, but populist agitators pushed a pro-Macedonian agenda. Consequently, while the balance of power had been settled, and there was no point joining Perseus on his funeral pyre, Rhodes did not send aid to Rome.

As ever Rhodian diplomacy in the Third Roman-Macedonian War would be shaped by economic interests. War disrupted the grain trade, obliging Rhodes to beg Rome for access to the Sicilian market. As economic damage mounted, Rhodes sent mediators to Rome and the Roman army in Greece. Arriving after Perseus had been decisively defeated at Pydna, the mediators were treated with contempt. Desperate to curry favour with Rome a hint was enough to see the pro-Macedonian faction butchered. Back in Rome ambitious senators, looking for plunder, demanded war. That option was not taken, but the Senate kept up the pressure for several years, denying Rhodes the alliance the islanders craved. After a century of neutrality and detachment Rhodes had run out of options: it could exist as a Roman satellite, or not at all. Rhodian neutrality relied on a regional balance of power, not Rhodian strength: 'the world in which such a neutrality was possible had finally expired on the field of Pydna'. Rhodes became a Roman client.[7] Once Rome had achieved universal monarchy in 146 BC, destroying Carthage and Corinth, there were no other options.

Rome developed Delos as a commercial rival, and revoked Rhodes' mainland territorial grants. Yet much of this apparent hostility was the carelessness of absolute power. During the widespread massacre of Italian merchants across the Greek world, sponsored by Mithridates of Pontus, Rhodes offered them sanctuary. Profoundly exposed to Roman power by its economic model and limited size, Rhodes would be the most loyal of subjects.

In truth Rhodes was let off lightly, because the sea state was too small to be a threat. It was not occupied or plundered, retaining the grain trade, a large merchant marine and a degree of freedom in regional affairs when an alliance was granted in 164 BC. To preserve economic prosperity in an age of

Roman universal monarchy that steadily absorbed the entire Mediterranean world, Rhodes chose submission. The decision was rational, the only choice for an island run by traders, bankers and middlemen. Roman peace was better for business than war, which invariably prompted an upsurge in piracy.

Although the history of Rhodes effectively ended in 164 BC, it remained nominally independent for another two centuries: the sheer scale of the Roman Empire rendered such tiny outposts invisible to the imperial capital. Left to grapple with Cretan piracy Rhodes joined Pompey's belated campaign. In AD 44 the island was swept up into the administrative province of Asia, and simply carried on trading. Trade had been in decline since the second century BC, but the city remained rich, a major educational and tourist destination, associated with philosophy and art, a living museum of Greek culture. It is, perhaps, no accident that the greatest Rhodian work of art, the *Laocoön* sculpture, represents a clash of cultures, the judgement of the gods and the destruction of a thriving sea state.

Rhodes' fate, swept up into a Roman province, was typical of sea states in ages of imperial rule and nation states. Amalfi, Genoa and even Venice would lose their freedom and identity in homogenised continental cultural models that hated and feared maritime states, ocean traders and their inclusive political systems. The experience of Rhodes would be reprised by other sea states. Few would escape those limits, and some of those that did, becoming true seapowers, chose the Rhodian solution when their power ebbed. Retreat and resignation were better than destruction.

In 1653 the Council of the Genoese Republic proposed that the four seapower republics, Venice, the United Provinces, England and Genoa, should become allies.[8] While nothing came of the proposal, as England and the United Provinces were then at war, it implied a connection between oligarchic republican politics and sea states. Republics, public governments bound by law, are not necessarily democracies. Montesquieu observed that republics could be ruled by aristocratic or oligarchic bodies, and this model can be applied to all true seapower. Montesquieu recognised that England became a 'republic' in 1688, when political power passed from Crown to Parliament, reducing the monarch to the status of hereditary figurehead.

Most late medieval and early modern European republics were commercial city-states, including Venice, Genoa and Florence, which developed classical explanations for their choice. Hansa and Flemish port cities adopted similar methods of government, but showed less interest in ancient history. These patrician republics, dominated by self-interest and specific forms of economic activity, were vulnerable to larger royal landed powers, which looked to tax their trade, and the riotous behaviour of those without a stake in the state, who sought to redistribute wealth. These republics faltered and fell when nation states and multinational empires emerged.

Five republics – Athens, Carthage, Venice, the Dutch Republic and Britain – became seapower states. Others made different choices, because they were too small, or too exposed to larger land powers. Hemmed in by mountains, without a major river to connect it to the hinterland, or enough fertile land to feed the population, medieval Genoa took to the sea in search of food and profit, exploiting overland access to northern Italy and France. The location became significant when the Roman road system collapsed. Briefly under Byzantine control, Genoa remained an economic connection until Constantinople fell in 1453. The Genoese created the capital to fund commerce through piracy, and in the absence of a regional seapower created an empire of trade stretching across the Mediterranean and into the Euxine, linked to Spain, northern Europe and the Atlantic. With a population base only half that of Venice, Genoa may have been too small to achieve seapower status. Even when Genoa defeated Venice at sea it lacked the internal stability and revenue streams to sustain control of the sea. Venice made the transition from sea state to seapower, carving an empire of islands out of the enfeebled carcass of Byzantium; Genoa lacked the internal cohesion and domestic resources. It fought Pisa and Venice for trade, seized Corsica to control the adjacent seas, and expanded into Liguria, buying land and incorporating local elites into the state.

In Genoa 'freedom' meant the freedom to trade, and freedom from the taxes inevitable in a centralised authoritarian state.[9] This small state agenda left Genoa prey to factional violence, lacking Venice's powerful centralising structures. When the national Bank of San Giorgio ceased trading in 1444, it continued to manage the city's debts, collect taxes, pay dividends to investors, and administer subject cities and colonies. The state was run by the shareholders of a bank. The Genoese carefully hid this fact from foreign rulers, to whom they frequently ceded control, using the bank to ensure real power remained with the oligarchy. Genoa was almost an anti-state, relying on private wealth, private naval forces and mercenary troops.

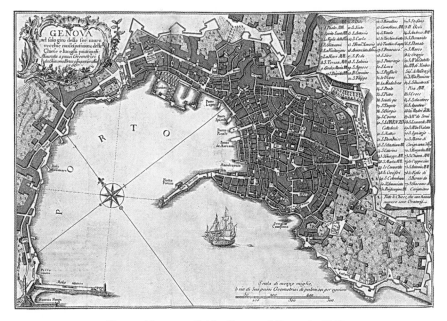

Giovanni Lorenzo Guidotti's map of Genoa in 1766

Between 1435 and 1528 the state was almost continuously contested by rival factions, leading to frequent, violent, destabilising change. Chaos was the only stability. French and Milanese administrators consistently failed to satisfy the economic demands of their commercially minded subjects, while native Doges were removed by rival factions. Little wonder the order and stability of Venice became a beacon throughout Italy.[10] In the half-century down to 1500 the fortunes of the two cities diverged fundamentally: Venetian trade grew to 750,000 ducats a year, whereas that of Genoa fell to a mere 125,000. The decline began with the Ottoman conquest of Constantinople in 1453, which ended Genoa's Black Sea empire, and Venice's recovery of Cyprus in 1474. Attempts to refocus trade on the western Mediterranean and north Africa met stiff competition from Iberian, English and French traders. Much of this trade was carried on large privately funded carracks, with no direct state intervention.[11] Genoese political incoherence meant commercial relations were constantly undermined by piracy. By contrast Venetian diplomacy and compensation secured vital markets, including the Mediterranean spice trade. One outcome was a dramatic decline in Genoese shipbuilding and the proportion of the population working on or about the sea. As Steven Epstein observed: 'Venice had found a way to preserve civic peace and Genoa had not.'[12] As domestic trade faltered Genoese bankers invested in foreign enterprises, including Portuguese Asian voyages, exploiting a significant Genoese presence in Lisbon, Seville and Cadiz to open new opportunities. The discovery of America by a Genoese navigator, Christopher Columbus, shifted the city's focus, just as the Ottoman Empire reorganised eastern trade. American bullion changed the Genoese economy. Iberian protectionism forced Genoese merchants to work within their systems, largely ignoring Genoa itself.[13]

Ferdinand of Aragon had recognised his dependence on Genoese banking and commercial networks in 1482. His centralising military state had crushed key economic actors in Aragon and Catalonia, as Castile mobilised military power to complete the Reconquista. He used Genoese naval and commercial power to secure trade links, resource flows and loans. Many of these functions were left to foreign contractors, rather than allowing any of Spain's quasi-independent regions to operate as a sea state – one that was run by merchants and bankers, not the landowners and warlords who directed the centralised Spanish state. Foreign, relatively distant and politically weak Genoa could be dispensed with if it became a problem.[14] This relationship reflected the development of Spain. Having captured Seville the Castilians wanted to control the Straits of Gibraltar; initially the 'officers and men employed in these naval operations were mostly, in the early days, Italian mercenaries, and for many years the traditional seaborne trades of Seville also remained in the hands of either Muslims, or of Pisans or Genoese'.[15]

While Genoa remained a sea state, governed by the basic maritime republican model, Venice created a culture to sustain the seapower ambitions unleashed by Doge Enrico Dandolo. Because it remained a sea state Genoa did not translate wealth into civic magnificence or public display. Without great-power ambitions, and therefore little need to demonstrate status and identity through art, Genoa did not develop a local school of artists to represent seapower culture. Genoese patrons hired Flemings and other Italians to produce generic works of art. Jacob Burckhardt emphasised Genoa's proverbial contempt for higher culture. 'The example of Genoa shows in a striking manner with what insecurity wealth and vast commerce, and with what internal disorder the possession of distant colonies are compatible.'[16] Ignoring the reality that Venice, with an incomparably greater sea empire, remained a well-ordered state, Burckhardt did not recognise the importance of the sea, or the consequences of being a sea state like Genoa. Rather than compete in the polite world of cultural display Genoese elites fought on the narrow streets of their clan areas. They created no images of themselves.

Although Flemish and Dutch artists, including Rubens, worked in Genoa, the majority served northern European patrons. The rocky coast of Liguria and the harbour of Genoa provided a generic backdrop for many Dutch sea pieces.[17] Overt elite display was familial, rather than statist. The Republic's Palazzo San Giorgio had a single grand room, displaying civic worthies in wall tombs, a model adopted by the Dutch a century later.

Where the Genoese sea state relied on private initiative, rather than state control, to generate influence, Venice, a seapower great power, was drawn into avoidable and ultimately unwinnable conflicts with larger terrestrial powers. With the Mediterranean divided between fewer, but more powerful regimes, Venice moved onto the land, alarming the great powers, but Genoa became a client of the Holy Roman Empire, France and then Spain. When Habsburg troops sacked the city in 1522, 'no event drove home more force-fully the real cost of foreign rule and the end of liberty'.[18] A mere pawn in the struggles of great continental powers, Genoa lacked the money and manpower to sustain independence and the freedom to trade. It had to choose sides, and create a stable government. In 1528 Genoa turned against the current overlord, the French King Francis I, because he was setting up a rival economic centre at the port of Savona, threatening Genoa's *raison d'être*. The parallel with Rome's development of Delos is striking. However, Genoa, unlike Rhodes, had choices because it operated in a multi-polar state system.

The patrician Genoese financier and military contractor Andrea Doria overthrew the French-backed government and formed an alliance with Charles V, Holy Roman Emperor and King of Spain. Doria secured Genoa's freedom to trade and profit without state intervention or high taxes. French rule had excluded Genoese merchants from Charles V's burgeoning empire, just as the American bullion began to flow. The new alliance served the inter-ests of the commercial elite. Charles agreed to respect Genoa's constitution and economic interests, hired Doria's galleys, appointed Doria to command his Mediterranean fleet and borrowed money from Genoese banks to pay for the fleet.[19] This arrangement made Doria rich, and secured his influence over the city. Genoese warships enabled Spain to deal with French and Muslim threats, while Genoese seafaring and banking expertise helped develop the New World. Doria maintained internal order through a new constitution that restricted political power to a closed oligarchy of aristocrats and rich merchants, removing the political rights of the rest, and reducing the leverage of foreign powers. The biennial Doge was a figurehead: the commercial class made all the big decisions. Finally, Genoa had achieved stability, as an oligarchic republic, the obvious sea state political model. Having recreated the Republic in the name of 'Liberty', the liberty to trade freely and pay as little tax as possible, Doria remained in the background, chairing the Supreme Court, upholding the laws that maintained the system. Carefully positioning himself as a servant of the people, Doria avoided taking high office.

With Doria as a financier and naval contractor to Habsburg Spain, Genoa was a client, not a state. The economic centre of gravity shifted west, as Genoa lost Chios to the Turks (1566), but Spanish gold flowed into the city, creating a profitable banking sector.[20] Genoa secured a major share in the trade and finance of Spanish America. As Robert Lopez observed, 'by the time of Philip II, the proud empire where the sun never set was almost an economic colony of Genoa'. In 1638 regulations excluding foreigners from Spanish America ignored the Genoese; they remained heavily engaged in the imperial system three hundred years later.[21]

Genoa's unusual political structure, and the reality that Andrea Doria commanded fleets of his own ships, significant personal capital assets, may explain his hesitancy in battle. His personal prestige sustained a Genoese regime that lacked real power. The state was Doria's business; the galleys were his capital assets. Where the public ceremonial spaces of Venice and the Dutch Republic spoke of the state, Doria celebrated his personal status in a palace built to entertain Charles V and emphasise his contribution to Habsburg imperium. Doria appeared as Neptune calming the waves, alongside a gallery of heroic predecessors, with Charles as Jupiter. A reference to the Golden Fleece linked emperor and admiral through the elite Habsburg decoration Doria had received in 1531.[22]

Doria's decision proved wise and timely. In an age of warring great powers there was no room for independent sea states. A long-term relationship with the most economically attractive great power sustained Genoa's economic activity. Forced to choose, it accepted Imperial/Spanish protection in return for banking connections and access to new markets. Genoa abandoned war and naval force as tools of statecraft, developing a wider maritime policy to sustain the economy and integrity of the city.[23] To avoid foreign occupation it acted as the client and agent of a continental great power. It had the freedom to choose because it operated in a multi-polar world. The emergence of a universal monarchy would have compelled Genoa, like Rhodes, to obey. Without a state navy, or statist territorial ambitions, the Genoese did not threaten Madrid's terrestrially focused worldview. Genoa's ideology was no threat to Spain because Genoa was a small, weak client, not a dynamic seapower state. While Genoa, like ancient Rhodes, maintained a small force of cruisers to defend trade and combat pirates, it relied on the mutual interest that many powers felt in upholding the 'freedom' of the city to avoid existential threats.[24]

The Genoese economy shifted from maritime trade to banking and financial services.[25] Although the Republic had no money, Genoa was rich, easily managing to fund harbour works, city defences and even wars. The decision to act without a state navy was conscious; the Genoese elite used other tools to exert international influence. The Spanish axis faltered early in the seventeenth century, when interest payments on royal loans were suspended and Madrid dismissed Genoa's claims of sovereignty at sea. Treating the Republic as a mercenary contractor suggests Imperial Spain no longer cared for efficient ships or long-term loans. At the same time the arrival of cheaper, more efficient Dutch and English shipping and convoys rapidly displaced Italian vessels.[26] These changes hastened Genoa's shift from ship-owning to banking, although it retained a few state galleys to carry specie between Spain and Genoa, for overland shipment to Flanders. Genoa replaced native shipping by turning itself into an entrepôt, with favourable tariff regimes drawing trade into the port. The city achieved international consequence without a navy or merchant shipping. Soon the harbour was packed with Dutch ships; the English used another free port, nearby Livorno.

As Spain faltered Genoa's position came under pressure. Bankers moved their money out of Spain and the Council rejected a Spanish alliance in 1635. As Venice declined to the status of a sea state Genoa survived by abandoning the sea altogether. It was too small, and too vulnerable, to make any other choice. Without a shared enemy, a universal monarchy that would outweigh their commercial rivalries, the republican alliance plan of 1653 failed. English and Dutch warships were fighting over trade just outside Livorno. It is unlikely the Genoese imagined fighting for control of the sea. Lacking the revenue and resources to compete with rising nation states, Genoa evolved into a free port to escape domination by a declining Spanish Empire, trusting to the wider economic system for protection against a great-power takeover.

Spanish decline exposed Genoa to the might of Bourbon France, French troops, French fleets and French ambitions to create a universal monarchy that had no place for maritime republics, be they great or small. Their very existence was an affront to Louis XIV's royal dignity. If Genoa wanted to continue trading and banking it would have to acknowledge its weakness. In 1684 a French fleet bombarded the city in a dispute sparked by the sale of a few Genoese galleys to Spain. Louis XIV forced the Genoese Doge to come to Versailles and publicly apologise for the impertinence of acting as an independent state. Genoa quickly disposed of the last remnants of its navy.[27] Louis captured the Doge's humiliation on a tapestry, which he sent to Rome, reminding the Pope where power resided in Catholic Europe. The Venetian Republic received a similarly hostile message when the French ambassador publicly celebrated the birth of a prince.[28] Louis's heavy-handed methods reflected a visceral hatred of republics and a profound distaste for seapowers. The Italian sea states had been warned against resisting the advance of French imperium.

Despite the humiliation Genoa remained independent because France was not the hegemon of the sea as Rome had been. Louis's power was limited by the presence of 'an English, a Dutch and a Spanish fleet active in the Mediterranean. The Republic's strength lay not in its squadron of galleys, which it could easily agree to disarm, but in the interests bound up in its port.'[29] Not only would Louis be defeated by the 'seapowers' but Genoa's apparently 'defenceless' approach preserved its neutrality for another century. Republican France, a true successor of the Roman Republic's universal monarchy, simply integrated Genoa into a continental super-state. Genoa did not recover its independence in 1815, because republics were at a discount and the British were anxious to deprive the French of a useful naval base.

While Genoa's experience emphasised the limits of sea states, it survived just as long as the Venetian seapower state. These oligarchic republics inspired political thinkers across Europe, notably the Dutch, and helped shape the northern European seapower states.

It is commonly assumed that Portugal was a seapower, an assumption that confuses the possession of a global maritime empire with cultural identity. Portugal, like its larger Iberian neighbour, remained profoundly continental, lacking the inclusive politics, economic dynamism and maritime focus to construct a seapower identity. The Iberian sea empires were directed by royal autocrats who emphasised religious faith over commercial success, continental expansion over sea control, and imposed monopolistic economic models that crushed initiative and enterprise. Iberian monarchs forced all economic actors to work within a system dominated by continental concerns.

Portuguese imperialism was driven by religious zeal, linked to the reconquest of north Africa, encouraged by food shortages and lack of cash. Portuguese empire-building began with the capture of Ceuta in 1415, a Moroccan city that remains in Iberian hands. Prince Henry, 'the Navigator', pushed voyages seeking sugar, slaves and gold down the west coast of Africa, to fund the expansion of this and other coastal enclaves.[30] When it acquired control of the Asian spice trade Portugal's centralised command economy ruthlessly exploited the opportunity to fill the royal coffers for domestic and north African projects. Royal monopolies kept prices high and trading volumes low, excluding private enterprise.

Royal control crushed initiative, slowed decision-making and burdened the empire with powerful religious agendas, crushing a nascent seapower culture. In 1511 Portugal captured the great Asian trade hub of Malacca, but religious prejudice, excluding Muslim merchants, and royal monopolies quickly rendered the port useless.[31] Portuguese rulers used the proceeds of overseas trade to fund a territorial and religious crusade in north Africa. The religious agenda prompted them to hand control of the empire, and its tiny Portuguese colonial population, to the Church. This royal/religious partnership, which dated back to 1319, left no space for merchants, while the mismatch of missionary work and mercantile trade compromised commerce with Muslims.[32] Prince Henry had funded pioneering voyages through the Order of Christ, of which he was treasurer. The ultimate emblem of the Portuguese imperial project were the ubiquitous red crosses that dominated

The Portuguese Empire

Portuguese Empire
Coastal explorations
Oceanic exploration
Trading posts
Sea trade routes
Areas of influence and trade

PORTUGAL
AZORES
MADEIRA
CAPE VERDE
BRAZIL
ANGOLA
MOZAMBIQUE
MAURITIUS
GOA
INDIA
CEYLON
PEGU
MACAO
TANEGASHIMA
MALACCA
SPICE ISLANDS
Hawaii

Atlantic Ocean
Pacific Ocean
Indian Ocean

the walls of the Tower of Belem and sails of Portuguese carracks. This was the badge of the Order of Christ, a crusading organisation with a powerful terrestrial agenda, one that came to a bloody denouement in Morocco. In the absence of alternative sources of capital Portuguese maritime trade was dominated by religious orders. The Jesuits sustained their overseas outposts through private trade which, along with the privileges they received from the Crown, necessarily disadvantaged ordinary merchants. The partnership of Crown and Church ensured Portugal did not develop the inclusive political institutions to harness national efforts to the sea. Kings excluded Portuguese merchants from political power and economic opportunity, while clerics aided them to advance their own agendas.

Without politically powerful merchants Portuguese overseas commerce depended on Genoese bankers, merchants and shipping to fund and move imports from Lisbon to Antwerp, another market dominated by Genoese banking.[33] It was no accident that the Portuguese century in Asia was ended by a true seapower, a republic shaped by the relatively inclusive politics and open economy needed to sustain maritime imperialism.

The mental world of Portuguese kings and princes, from Prince Henry to Dom Sebastian, was dominated by the chivalric quest for battlefield glory. The Aviz dynasty was obsessed with honour, crusading against the infidel and the expansion of Portuguese power. Recognising the financial rewards King John II had pushed maritime expansion. After his death in 1496, Manuel I, 'the fortunate', spent the proceeds on domestic prestige projects to enhance his status in Europe. Manuel, who 'dreamed of crowning himself king of all Christianity', married the eldest daughter of Ferdinand and Isabella. Their son, heir to every kingdom in Iberia, was the realisation of Aviz ambition.[34] When his wife and son died, Manuel used Asian wealth to centralise the state, increase royal power and attack Morocco. To court favour with Spain he expelled the Jews. Many moved to the Low Countries, demonstrating a fundamental cultural difference between a proto-seapower and a continental state. Manuel sacrificed a major source of maritime capital, navigational science, enterprise and activity to concentrate on continental ambitions, ensuring Portugal would never become a seapower focused on overseas trade and empire.

Asian wealth created an architecture of prestige: the Tower and monastery at Belem, and the palace at Sintra. The 'Manueline' style was dominated by ropes and armillary spheres, proclaiming Portugal's command of the sea. Although it has long been used to represent oceanic activity, Manuel's spectacular Tower was a cross-encrusted Christian bastion, guarding Lisbon against Muslim raiders, supported by a saintly fort across the Tagus river. The dominant symbol of Manueline architecture remained the cross, symbolising the synergy of royal and Church absolutism. Portugal celebrated seapower, but could not comprehend it. Manuel's regime was religious, absolutist and continental.[35]

At the heart of the problem, as John Elliott observed of Habsburg Spain, was a culture imbued 'with the crusading ideal, accustomed by the *reconquista* and the conquest of America to the quest of glory and booty and dominated by a church and an aristocracy which perpetuated those very ideals least propitious for the development of capitalism.'[36] Charles Boxer found further evidence in the history of commercial shipping:

> Although the Portuguese empire was a sea-borne empire if ever there was one, the mother country did not always have enough sailors and shipping to cope adequately with her own colonial trade, a part of which was sometimes carried in foreign (chiefly English) shipping.[37]

Despite trans-oceanic empires in Asia and America, Portugal retained an aristocratic terrestrial culture, where blood and land mattered far more than the undignified business of seafaring trade.

Portugal's relationship with seapower has been further confused by the role it occupied as a vector for old knowledge and new ideas that shaped the last two seapower states. Portuguese navigators mastered Greek, Jewish and Arab maritime science, connecting the Mediterranean and Atlantic worlds, shaping Europe's late fifteenth-century global vision.[38] Portugal pioneered the oceanic sailing ship, building large vessels for Asian trade, but design and productivity fell behind rival powers in the late sixteenth century. Portugal did not build many ships, commercial losses were high, and investment in shipbuilding and commerce dried up. Portugal also produced the first major text on naval warfare, *New Art of War at Sea* (1555) by the Dominican friar Fernando Oliviera. Despite his maritime experience, which included a visit to Henry VIII's court, Oliviera's text reflected the influence of St Augustine, architect of the Catholic Church's perception that the sea was a 'licentious' or corrupting place, even if it could be used to spread the word of God.[39] Like his royal and clerical masters Oliviera considered that proselytising was a major objective. Only one copy of his book survived, suggesting a short print run.[40] Little wonder the colonial prizes increasingly fell to more worldly states. Oliviera's time in London may have opened a connection that would flourish in the dramatic late Tudor maritime turn that exploited Portuguese seafarers, texts, charts and experience. Much of this material was obtained after 1580, through the exiled court of the pretender Dom Antonio. Having benefited from Portuguese navigators and ransacked Portuguese carracks for navigational and commercial intelligence, the English carefully obscured Portuguese input. The profound difference in approach between Oliviera and Sir Walter Raleigh, who worked closely with Portuguese seamen, is suggestive. While the Portuguese friar feared the corrupting sea, the ambitious Englishman anticipated an oceanic future.

By the time Raleigh began writing, Portugal was no longer an independent state. In 1578 King Sebastian used the proceeds of Asian trade to raise an army and invade Morocco, a terrestrial/ideological crusade that ended in disaster, for the country and the Aviz dynasty. Sebastian and much of the Portuguese nobility were slaughtered at the battle of Alcacer-el-Kebir, by a Moroccan army similarly unified by faith. The catastrophic loss of manpower, money and prestige saw Portugal subsumed into Philip II's Habsburg world empire in 1580. Once under Habsburg rule the Portuguese Empire was attacked by the Dutch.[41] Spain, like Portugal, extracted wealth from America and Asia to sustain European conflicts. Challenged by dynamic armed traders from the Dutch Republic and England, the Iberians abandoned the sea, falling back on territorial control and fortresses.

Portuguese weakness would be highlighted when the VoC, a joint-stock company, overwhelmed their Asian empire. The VoC was funded by Portuguese plunder and the Amsterdam stock market, supported by an oligarchic republican government and a community of former Portuguese Jews, who spread Portuguese expertise. Despite these losses Portuguese culture continued to prioritise territorial control and religious issues over oceanic commerce. Shipbuilding stagnated for want of capital, timber and skilled manpower. The limited supply of ships and sailors forced Portugal to abandon staple trade routes to northern Europe and the Mediterranean, focusing on the captive markets of Asia, Africa and Brazil, where foreigners also provided much of the shipping. The Portuguese war for independence drew scarce money and manpower away from the sea, leaving Portuguese merchant shipping moribund. The business fell to the Dutch, who were at war with both Iberian powers, skilfully profiting from capturing as well as carrying Portuguese goods.

The period of Spanish rule in Portugal, from 1580 to 1640, emphasised territorial settlements outside Europe and resource extraction, while limiting and controlling trade through royal monopolies. Castilian contempt for seafaring and an obsession with crusading glory and gentlemanly activity helped to ossify Portuguese attitudes. Having secured independence in 1640, Portugal needed protection from Spain and the Dutch. England provided security through an unequal alliance sealed by a royal marriage. The English mediated peace with Spain and the Republic, and in return acquired Tangier, Bombay and access to Portuguese markets.[42] Portugal finally became part of a seapower empire when it handed effective control of the maritime economy to England. English warships became a common sight at Lisbon, a naval base that secured the maritime flank of England's expanding oceanic empire. English naval stores and equipment were stowed in the crypt of King Manuel's great monastery at Belem, where a vacant niche still awaits the return of King Sebastian.

After 1640, Brazil revived the empire with sugar, tobacco and gold, traded as royal monopolies. After 1690, Brazilian gold dominated the economy, but much of it ended up in Britain, to purchase goods and services that Portugal could not provide, and sustain the European and imperial security guarantee. Portugal failed to create the naval force or the commercial shipping needed to service the empire on which its prosperity depended. Commerce was left to foreigners, while the 'Naval service in Portugal had no prestige'.[43] Secure behind British sea power, Portugal continued to exploit its colonies for another century, as its Asian empire crumbled under Dutch and English pressure. By 1740, Goa was a solitary reminder of faded Indian consequence. After 1700, Portugal's imperial focus shifted to Brazil, a terrestrial power base, and the west African slave trade posts that fed Brazil's plantation economy. Brazil absorbed the bulk of Portugal's colonising effort down to the 1820s when its independence reduced the empire to irrelevance.

The Jesuits exerted enormous influence in the empire after 1640, funding religious work through trade, with royal support.[44] Marquis Pombal removed them in the 1760s, seriously weakening an empire that lacked secular educators and administrators. Inefficient royal trade monopolies failed, while smuggling and illegal trade became the main economic outlets for a moribund empire. Profits inevitably fell to Britain, not Portugal. Finally, the colony of Brazil outstripped the mother country. In 1792 the British imperial envoy and administrator Lord Macartney concluded that Portugal's future depended on moving the capital to Rio de Janeiro. Portugal was a weak, vulnerable appendage of a dynamic colony. Macartney, en route to open the Chinese market, anticipated oppressive 'commercial regulations and restrictions' would prompt a Brazilian revolution. These monopolistic tools served continental agendas. Aggressive British trade and the Napoleonic conflict hastened the breakup of an empire that the Portuguese lacked the mindset and manpower to hold on to.[45]

The downfall of the oceanic empire only emphasised the reality that Portugal had never placed the sea at the centre of state policy or national identity. The sea belatedly acquired a prominent place in Portuguese culture in the late nineteenth century, part of a reworked past populated by heroic navigators and colonial administrators. This message culminated in the fascist monument that Salazar erected alongside King Manuel's Tower of Belem, a building that told a very different story. Down to 1580 Portugal had used imperial profits to fund terrestrial projects in European and north Africa, reflecting a deeply conservative culture where land and agriculture carried more prestige than trade: slave plantations were more 'gentlemanly' than seafaring. The empire could only be secured through an unequal alliance with a seapower great power that could protect Portugal's overseas colonies and its European borders. In return England secured commercial privileges, and the cession of key maritime hubs at Tangier and Bombay, which Portugal could not afford to defend. The character of Portugal's overseas empire would be shaped by peasant colonists, who willingly exchanged Iberia's rigid social order for the open spaces of South America. Unlike transient merchants they settled, integrated and developed a local, continental, identity that enabled Portugal to hold Brazil despite the loss of sea control.[46]

Portugal was never a sea state, let alone a seapower. It remained a centrally directed command economy serving an absolute ruler and an authoritarian universal Church. The proceeds of trade were used to increase royal absolutism and the power of the Church as an arm of state. There was no move towards the political inclusion of the merchant class, much of which was foreign. This ensured Portugal's primary military force remained the army, which defended the land border with Spain, and fought in north Africa. Aristocratic and terrestrial concerns outweighed oceanic engagement. While Portugal's agricultural colonies of settlement survived, most of the trade entrepôts fell to real seapowers, the states that controlled the trade.

Socially and politically ill-equipped to exploit the opportunities created by oceanic expansion, the Iberians remained focused on royal monopolies, missionary work and continental legal controls that closed the seas, restricting the development of their sea empires, with shipping and banking services provided by Flemish, Dutch and Genoese contractors. Like St Augustine they treated the sea as a dangerous place, across which the profits of mining and agriculture could be extracted. Their Asian and American empires were substitutes for the European and north African territories they craved. In sum Iberian sea empires were about land, not trade, faith, not commerce. Both remained fundamentally continental.

Although sea states and maritime empires have often been conflated with seapowers, their underlying realities were strikingly different. Most sea states did not aspire to become seapower great powers, with the notable exceptions of Carthage, Venice and briefly the Dutch Republic. Instead they operated successfully between continental great powers in multi-polar political systems. Too small, wise or fragmented to aspire to greatness, they remained absolutely dominated by the sea – their economic *raison d'être*, and the source of any political influence they possessed. Like seapower states they suffered in an era of universal monarchy, but they lacked a seapower's ability to resist.

Critically, neither sea states nor maritime empires were constructed identities: these cultural responses to the sea reflected older realities of location, faith and terrestrial culture. While overseas empires like that of Portugal no longer exist, the sea state has never been more important. Collectively, contemporary sea states sustain the vision that made seapowers great, the economic, political and intellectual agendas of progress. Without sea states the world would be a darker place, lacking the cultural diversity and exchange that sustains creativity. Louis XIV hated them, Napoleon wiped them out, but we should celebrate their continuing existence. Sea-state identity remains active, not least in the debate about the nature and future of Europe. Sea states reject centralising, continentalising restrictive economic and political models because they conflict with their core values.

CHAPTER 7

The Limits of Continental Naval Power
ABSOLUTISM, COMMAND ECONOMIES AND ONE-PARTY STATES

While Rhodes and Genoa remained outside the category of seapowers for want of scale and ambition, Portugal consciously rejected the inclusive political model that they adopted, in order to persist with continental absolutism and command economics. None achieved great-power status, because they lacked the capacity to become sea powers or continental powers. By contrast a significant group of continental military powers not only achieved great or even superpower status, but they also developed sea power fleets configured to contest naval hegemony. Several such states – Persia, Rome, the Ottoman Empire, Habsburg Spain and Bourbon France – have already featured in this book as opponents of seapower. This chapter shifts the focus to another such state, because today there are no more seapower great powers: John Ruskin's line of succession was broken in 1945. In their place continental military hegemons, superpowers, contest the command of the sea with navies dominated by the potential utility of Captain Mahan's sea power. The continental agendas of these hegemons clash with the maritime worldview of contemporary sea states, the residuary legatees of seapower.

The Russian Coast defence ironclad warship *Petr Velikiy*

This chapter uses the concept of the seapower state, a conscious cultural construction with generic political, economic and strategic elements, to examine the development of naval ambition in a continental military great power, to test the validity of the approach and the utility of the results. Such states do not share the limits and weaknesses of seapower states; they are large, mostly self-sufficient, and their primary strategic instrument is military. Both state and economy are centrally directed, with economic actors generally excluded from political power. While the obvious contemporary case is China, whose rising naval power has been confused with seapower, the best case study is that of Russia, another great land empire that endured Mongol invasion, internal disintegration and rapid reconstruction before making a conscious effort to compete with the 'West'.[1] Russia, like Rome and Imperial Spain, was a great land power that created a powerful navy as a strategic tool; it had no intention of becoming a seapower. While Russia or the Soviet Union remained serious naval powers, this reality was obscured by present-minded studies that emphasised Russian exceptionalism and alarmist geopolitics above underlying structures. Once the fleet stopped going to sea, and Russia was no longer a naval threat, the field was left to historians, who ignored anything present-minded.

Navies, as Jacob Burckhardt famously observed of the states that create them, are 'a work of art', a cultural construction with an infinite variety of forms, forms that reflect the nature of the state, and best understood by examining the place that navies occupy in national or imperial culture. Examining Peter the Great's naval project in the context of his revolutionary regime will explain why he created a powerful navy, and whether he attempted to impose a seapower identity on his landlocked people.

Russian interest in the sea was 'a final by-product' of links with the West. In the sixteenth century Russian expansion ran into a series of barriers that denied them access to the Baltic, the Sea of Azov and the Black and Caspian seas. The English sailed to Arctic Archangel to reach Moscow. Ivan IV thought about a navy and Boris Gudonov bought ships, while the early Romanovs built river fleets and an ocean-going vessel. However, such craft were technology transfers and administrative upgrades, not cultural transfusions. Sixteenth-century Russia had no interest in Western religion or secular thinking, only 'useful' knowledge.[2] Vulnerable frontiers were the strategic priority, while Russia's impressive roster of human resources included few seafarers. The bitter legacy of Mongol dominion, including autocratic rule and a powerful Church, gave the Russian state enormous authority over all aspects of life. A state with very low literacy rates, lacking an indigenous commercial middle class and liquid capital, did not provide fertile ground for new thinking and trade, let alone something as alien as a sea identity. Russia was always going to be a hard place to construct a seapower culture, yet it is often claimed that Peter the Great attempted to do so.

Peter I (1672–1723) built his navy, naval infrastructure and aspects of his state in emulation of Venice, the Dutch Republic and England. His navy was a permanent, state-owned force of warships, complete with the necessary dockyards, infrastructure, recruitment, logistics and administration to sustain them.[3] It was at once a tool and a symbol of state power; however, Peter built not one but three navies. The first two were small ship forces, focused on riverine and coastal operations in the Sea of Azov and the Gulf of Finland; the last included ships of the line with open-water capabilities. The first two were used aggressively, often successfully, in maritime/ amphibious operations, including sieges, linked to land campaigns. The last was essentially for show, emulating, but very wisely not engaging, British fleets sent to command the Baltic.

Before Peter, Russia had few maritime traditions, and few Russians had any desire to acquire any, especially if it required them to work on this alarming, alien, unholy wasteland. Nowhere in the whole 'Petrine Revolution' was Peter's input more important than in the nautical turn. Other tsars might have modernised, but only Peter, a true believer, took his country to the sea. He did so quite literally, being the first tsar to sail, to travel by sea, to learn nautical science and practical skills, to build ships, to command fleets and to risk the future of Russia on the ocean – placing a new imperial capital, a curious combination of Venice and Amsterdam, on the sea.

In the coda to his achievement, the Naval Statute of 1720, Peter created a suitable past for this project, tracing the dawn of Russian naval development to his father, Tsar Alexis. Alexis's project had sparked Peter's interest, and produced the handful of Western craftsmen who enabled the young tsar to study navigation, geometry and ships. Peter first encountered the sea at Archangel, then Russia's only port, in 1693, sailing out to the ocean with the departing Anglo-Dutch merchant fleet. After a second, longer Arctic voyage in 1694, Peter built a fleet at Voronezh for a war on the Don River and Sea of Azov, and in 1697 travelled to Holland by sea, to learn about the maritime world. The sea was central to his modernising agenda; he did not count the cost. When the Dutch could not teach him how to build a ship from paper draughts, a vital tool of technology transfer, he shifted to England. Between January and April 1698 he lived and worked at Deptford Dockyard, recruiting experts to build and sail his ships, teach navigation and create a modern navy. Peter's recognition of English maritime pre-eminence proved critical to the new navy, and left a powerful anglophile legacy in Russian naval culture, along with naval dynasties. Peter built ships in England, witnessed a mock sea battle at Spithead, the ultimate expression of English power, and observed the test firing of shells by a large mortar, a new warship designed to bombard coastal positions. At Deptford he spent time with progressive naval officers including the Marquess of Carmarthen and John Benbow, at the epicentre of the contemporary seapower state. At this time the Thames was dominated by public and private shipyards, a seapower microcosm of shipbuilding, science, naval skill and the new political system. The river was alive with great fleets of privately owned merchant vessels, the lifeblood of a dynamic commercial economy trading as far afield as India and China.

Peter's boon companion at Deptford, Admiral the Marquess of Carmarthen, advised him to recruit four types of skilled men in England: master shipwrights and high-ranking artisans skilled in the design, construction and outfitting of warships; a few 'ingenious English sea officers'; English sailors to show Russians how to become seamen; and navigation teachers. The numbers recruited remain uncertain, and some were spies. Carmarthen's reward was a tobacco contract, reflecting contemporary English interest in Russia.[4]

Peter famously trashed the garden and contents of Sayes Court, the house of naval administrator and navalist author John Evelyn, which he had sub-let from John Benbow.[5] William III found the tsar a difficult and rather dull guest, bored by Peter's incessant talk of the navy and carpentry, but he was astute enough to give the tsar a fine yacht, the *Royal Transport*, to sail home.[6] Peter acquired his first major portrait, by the English court artist Sir Godfrey Kneller, showing him as a modern Western man of war, in full armour, with naval themes prominent.[7]

Peter arrived in England shortly after it became a seapower great power, combining the victory at the battle of Barfleur-La Hougue in 1692 with a massive shipbuilding programme tied to the National Debt and the Bank of England. The wartime army had been demobilised in 1697. English ships were sailing in every sea, and the country possessed a reservoir of maritime expertise at all levels and in all aspects, while the political nation had accepted that it was insular, maritime and distinct.

How far Peter's experience of London influenced the construction of a fleet and the sea-city capital at St Petersburg can only be guessed, but within a decade he had completed the most remarkable 'navalisation' of a hitherto landlocked continental state in world history. It is equally significant that no other Russian ruler ever embraced the ocean in the same joyous, abso-lute way. Making the fleet a national priority, working on it with his own hands by way of example, and taking pleasure in mastering the new sea world at the heart of his reforms made Peter unique. It is inconceivable that another Russian leader would have boasted of his skill as a shipwright in a state document. Peter understood the sea, ships, navies and their power at all levels. Just how unique he was became evident soon after his death – his navy began to rot, its fabric, human resources and infrastructure neglected and forgotten. Even now, three hundred years later, Peter remains the greatest navalist in Russian history, a prophet without honour in most of the country he created. Vladimir Putin, a native of St Petersburg, might understand the issue, but his naval vision remains a paper project.

The naval project was a central element in Peter's transformation of Russia from a pre-modern, semi-Asiatic state into a modern Western great power, a process that fascinated the contemporary world, and continues to command attention. Most accounts emphasise the central role of the naval turn in the introduction of alien ideas, techniques and systems into Russia. Peter reshaped national culture to enable Russia to survive and prosper in a world dominated by heavily armed, expansive western European states.[8] He established the agenda in a single lifetime: the establishment eulogy of 1725 was illustrated by an engraving in which a modern military Peter, Kneller's heroic leader in full armour, offers a grateful Mother Russia, in traditional dress, warships, a great Western city and all the tools of modernity – technical and navigational instru-ments, printed works of science, terrestrial and heavenly globes.[9] The heavy allegory emphasised the sea as the essential modernising agent, and the artist was Dutch. Historians have accepted Peter's claim that the navy was central to his revolution, but most miss the role of contingency in the final outcome.

Peter was a very odd tsar: he liked ships, sailors and sailing, he learnt to sail as a boy, travelled to the West via Archangel, his only oceanic port, to learn more about the sea. On his return he created fleets of ships on the rivers of the south, and then the Baltic, working as a naval architect and shipwright. To suggest that his contribution to the Western turn was anything other than unique would be absurd. Seventeenth-century Russia had to modernise or perish, but the decision to build a navy was neither organic nor inevitable, and it was not dictated by the exigencies of the Great Northern War. Russia did not need to cross any seas to conquer states in central Europe, Scandinavia, the Caucasus or Persia. Furthermore the sheer scale of Russian naval development, which outstripped most existing navies within a generation, was unprecedented. In 1700 Russia had no access to the Baltic; by 1721 a Russian fleet dominated the sea, projecting imperial power all the way to Stockholm and Copenhagen.

Yet this process should not be read from Western or maritime perspectives. Peter had no desire to create a seapower state. Over a thirty-year period he created enough naval might, in various forms, to serve the national interest, but no more. While his engagement with the sea remained emotional and personal, the vision that drove his policy was strategic and functional. Logic and opportunity, not a boyish enthusiasm for ships, led Peter to create naval forces. He recognised the need for naval assets in 1695: his army could not capture the Ottoman fortress of Azov because the Turks retained maritime supply lines. In 1696 hastily built Russian ships isolated the fortress; it surrendered. Such pragmatic approaches shaped Peter's naval vision.[10] He celebrated the victory with ceremonial gates bearing a Russian version of Caesar's motto, 'Veni, vidi, vici', and a medal representing Neptune submitting to the tsar, the first of many examples of the classical naval symbolism that illuminated his reign. These alien emblems launched an aspirational relationship with the Roman past, culminating in the declaration of empire in 1721.[11] Posturing with borrowed symbols and classical languages was typical of regimes anxious to impress upon their subjects the merits of their work. Yet the design delivered a deeper message. Peter, like, the Romans, did not want to be Neptune: he wanted Neptune to submit to his imperial terrestrial sway.

Not that victory at Azov gave Russia access to the ocean. The fortress commanded the delta of the River Don, flowing into the shallow, landlocked Sea of Azov; the Black Sea lay beyond the heavily fortified Straits of Kerch, held by the Ottomans and their Crim Tarter clients. Unable to pass the Straits the Russian ships had limited strategic potential. Despite their symbolic importance Peter abandoned them and new towns at Azov and Taganrog after a military defeat on the River Pruth. Having discovered the limits of Russian power in the south, Peter switched his attention to the Baltic. He declared war on Sweden in 1700, one day after celebrating peace with the Ottomans.[12]

War served a vital role in Peter's project. Victory, the judgment of God, validated his reign and his radical measures. It was a circular process: the cost of Westernising Russia was war, which would only be successful if Russia Westernised. The legal justification for the Great Northern War, ancient claims to Swedish territory, and recent Swedish insults, were irrelevant. The object was acquisition of a Baltic coast, a project attempted by Peter's Romanov precursors: on this point he would not compromise. His war plan had relied on Denmark countering Swedish naval power, while Russia advanced on land. Yet military defeat and economic collapse saw Denmark sue for peace within a few months.[13] Peter would have to counter the Swedish fleet that sustained their Baltic coastal empire from the Danish Narrows to the future site of St Petersburg without a coast or a ship.

Peter secured a foothold on the Baltic by military means, before building a fortress, a naval arsenal and a new capital. The importance of the projected navy was emphasised in 1706. With Swedish armies carrying all before them Peter was prepared to do anything for peace, except surrender St Petersburg. Charles XII saw no need to compromise, so the war continued.[14]

Peter's decision was neither Russian, nor logical. He built St Petersburg on a maze of low-lying flood-prone islands in the delta of the Neva River, a less than welcome similarity with Venice. The river iced up for almost a third of the year, winter days were short, and temperatures low. Thin soils supported scrubby vegetation, not successful agriculture. Above all the site was wide open to attack from the sea. It was as if Peter had deliberately chosen a site that would stretch the possibilities of contemporary urban design. Both the new metropolis and the sea-control navy that provided the rationale for his choice were extravagant, resource-hungry projects. Having located his capital Peter created a city to impress Europe: majestic masonry buildings of classical design, broad straight streets, tree-lined avenues and

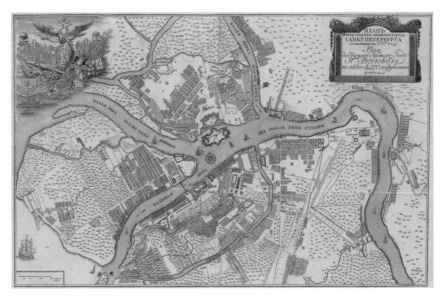

A new city on the sea: Joseph Nicolas De L'Isle's plan of St Petersburg, 1737

canals on a logical plan that placed different groups and functions in separate areas of the town.[15] Conceived as 'a kind of Dutch-style naval base and
trading centre', the canals served to reference Amsterdam and Venice, rather
than provide transport.[16] Engineers from both cities were imported to
ensure the system functioned, but the road network was perfectly capable
of handling the traffic. The Petrine canals may have proved impractical, but
they fulfilled a critical iconographic function: they made the city maritime.
Dry docks and other maritime infrastructure were built using texts in many
languages: some were translated into Russian by Peter, who also drafted
texts on architecture and shipbuilding.

Work began in 1703 in two locations: fortifications on Kotlin Island, later
Kronstadt, the critical defensive bastion that enabled the city to be built, and
the Admiralty shipyard, the founding project of the new city. Shipbuilding
was a Petrine obsession: Russia built 1,200 sea-going vessels between 1688
and 1725.[17] Peter created a naval administration to manage this output before
he acquired a Baltic coastline. The Admiralty, responsible for all aspects of
Russian naval activity, was based in a complex of buildings later known as
Main Admiralty. It included a shipyard, rope-works, fortress, church and

naval barracks, huts for workmen and residences for senior officers. It dominated the banks of the Neva, emphasising the structural and philosophical
synergy between the navy and the new capital. It was also 'the largest industrial complex in eighteenth-century Russia, one that combined the production of various industries'.[18] The combined workshop and statement of power
was ready to reveal itself to the world by 1717, when suitable engravings were
produced. Now elite Russians and foreign governments could see what the
tsar was doing. To emphasise the personal connection the artist Rostvotsev
included an imperial inspection, the tsar's flag flying on a galley. The energy,
order and output of the Admiralty attracted the notice of foreign visitors, at
least one of whom made a direct comparison with the Venetian Arsenale. It
produced galleys by the hundred, much like the Arsenale, with input from
Venetian master shipwrights. The oak used to build battleships was floated
downriver from Kazan, a two-year journey.[19]

Peter's Main Admiralty was a potent symbol of the naval revolution.
The external relief repeated the device used in 1700, Neptune handing
the trident of seapower to the tsar, who was accompanied by Minerva, the
goddess of wisdom, and a young female Russian deity, holding the club of
Hercules.[20] Peter had placed a great dockyard, an amalgam of Deptford and
the Arsenale, at the centre of a new Amsterdam, a city of canals, shipyards
and warehouses. The Admiralty was staffed by foreign engineers and
craftsmen, alongside Russian manpower raised for the 1696 Azov campaign.
Later, skilled men from civil construction were drafted into the Admiralty,
giving the navy precedence over other tasks. After Peter's death naval orders
collapsed, and in the 1730s workmen were transferred south to build vessels
on the Dniepr and the Don rivers. A decade later the workforce would be
hastily enlarged by forced labour for another war with Sweden.[21]

Peter generated a history to support the naval project by transforming his
first little boat into a 'relic', pictured in the allegorical frontispiece of the 1720
Naval Statute; the vessel was preserved, paraded and even worshipped in the
'Sermon in Praise of the Russian Fleet' delivered in St Petersburg by the
propagandist-prelate Archbishop Feofan Prokopovich in September 1720.
Engravings circulated the message that this small vessel had laid the foundations of victory over Sweden, an imperial endorsement of naval power as the
fount of national glory. In 1723 Peter marked his birthday by personally
sailing the boat down the Neva to the Admiralty, where tsar and boat were

greeted by artillery salutes. As the French ambassador observed, among all the projects designed to maintain and augment his power the tsar had 'given his most attentive care to that of his navy'. Peter's boat became the icon of Russian naval power, the ultimate emblem of the Petrine revolution. In 1872 it was paraded through Moscow by Grand Duke Constantine, the next Romanov navalist, on the bicentenary of Peter's birth, to emphasise that the navy had 'elevated Russia to Great Power status'.[22] When the Soviets rehabilitated Peter during the Second World War they placed the boat in the Leningrad Naval Museum, housed in the spectacular Bourse building on the Neva.

Peter imported Western designs and technologies to create modern fortifications for the Admiralty, a decision that had important consequences for civil design and construction. Classical architecture had been in use at Moscow in 1700, enabling Peter to celebrate success at Azov in Roman fashion. Classical design, a universal Western language, ensured that Western observers recognised Russia was a Western state. Russian nobles sent to study abroad reported favourably on the new world they encountered. Count Tolstoi, learning navigation in Venice, thought the city 'stupendous', praising its 'rich and harmonious construction'. Another Russian produced a manuscript based on Palladio's famous manual of architecture. Peter emphasised Italian style, a taste his court circle followed, to create a new language of Russian power, one that would be understood by western Europeans. His new capital would be recognisably European. In 1710 the British ambassador Charles Whitworth emphasised Peter's ambition that 'it might one day prove to be a second Amsterdam or Venice'. While the new fleet was a priority, Whitworth found the climate challenging, and judged the defences inadequate. His line about Venice may have come from Peter's confidant Prince Menshikov, who claimed the city would become a visitor attraction, where foreigners would marvel at the might and majesty of Russia.[23] The Hanoverian Resident Friedrich Weber agreed, telling British readers it was 'a Wonder of the World'.[24]

Menshikov proved prescient. In 1739 Venetian Count Francesco Algarotti came to the city to satisfy his curiosity. He was impressed by the 'magnificent canal' and the mighty ships at Kronstadt, including a massive three-decker named *Anna* in honour of the tsaritsa. Then he took the boat to St Petersburg, along the narrow channel, 'this triumphal way, this sacred way of the Neva, is not adorned with arches or temples', but low scrubby forests altogether unworthy of the location. Then, with dramatic suddenness the view changed, revealing an imperial city, full of majestic buildings. The echo of Venice was most powerful from the water. Once ashore Algarotti condemned the tsar's 'bastard' architectural conflation of Italian, French and Dutch, mocking his canals as mere decoration. The incisive Venetian quickly separated distant visual splendour from the reality of badly designed, hastily built structures.[25] Russian Baroque focused on display, yet the substance was less impressive, perhaps inevitably so, given the location and speed of construction. Peter's city, like his navy, was a monumental vanity project: both fundamentally changed the public face of Russia, but had little impact on the population beyond the city for another century and more. Peter began moving Russia to the West: the project was far from complete in 1725, 1825 or 1925. Russia rejected critical elements of Western progress associated with becoming a seapower, such as inclusive politics and an open economy, as well as a seafaring identity and the curiosity to see a world beyond national frontiers. Peter brought many Western technologies to his country – modern fortresses, warships, navigational equipment, printing presses, globes and telescopes – but he imposed them on an older reality. Seapower culture did not find a home in Petrine Russia, because the roots of that identity had not been laid in the preceding centuries. The English spent over two hundred years crafting the identity of a true seapower. Peter rammed his version down the throats of an entirely unprepared and uninterested nation in just twenty years, and was annoyed when they choked. Dressing up as a seapower was not the same as becoming one.

After his crushing defeat of Sweden at Poltava in 1709 and the plague epidemic that swept through Sweden's Baltic garrisons, Peter completed his Baltic project. In 1710 the capture of Viborg secured the land and sea flanks of St Petersburg, while seizing the Baltic provinces added well-established ports, including Riga and Reval (Tallinn) to Russia's portfolio, along with a German-speaking service nobility to lead his armed forces.

Russia's sudden emergence onto the Baltic littoral alarmed other maritime powers: 'Britain in particular insisted that Sweden must not be allowed to collapse completely, and that a balance must be maintained among the northern powers.'[26] This balance would prevent Russia from monopolising the supply of Baltic naval stores. It was maintained by sending Royal Navy battlefleets into the Baltic from 1713, to deter Russian designs on the western basin of the enclosed sea, and bolster the interests of Hanover. Russian expansionism was vulnerable to British naval might. In 1725 the Royal Navy appeared off Reval, enabling Denmark to defy Russia in a crisis over Schleswig. This demonstration of naval power persuaded the Russians to recognise the limits of their Baltic project.

In her critical survey of Peter's reign Lindsey Hughes asked the key question: 'Did Peter set much store by his Navy?' Her answers were more clear-sighted and incisive than those provided by naval analysts. The navy was expensive, but it served a higher, essentially terrestrial purpose. The primacy of territorial issues in Petrine calculations meant the most significant role of the Azov fleet was to 'keep the Turks and Tartars in check', and along with Peter's presence at Azov in 1709, may have deterred Ottoman intervention in the Great Northern War just before the battle of Poltava. A few years later Peter sacrificed the Azov fleet, as a bargaining chip, to avoid an inconvenient Turkish war. Naval power could be useful for a continental state, but seapower identity was not.

The Baltic galley fleet provided mobility, fire support and amphibious capability to help capture the strategic Finnish town of Helsingfors. Peter acknowledged Finland was a maritime theatre by appointing Admiral Feodor Apraksin to overall command. The galley battle at Hangö in 1714 led to the capture of Abö, the Finnish capital, while victory at Grengham in 1720 secured the Åland islands. These encounters, which resembled Lepanto rather than Anglo-Dutch fleet actions, were celebrated in St Petersburg. They represented a new era in Baltic geopolitics rather than serious naval prowess. The Russian sailing battlefleet did very little, beyond cover amphibious operations against weak Swedish forces. While Russia could generate galley fleets, Peter created the battlefleet by buying warships and hiring skilled manpower in the west, mostly through Holland. After 1713 he operated in a buyer's market: the end of the War of the Spanish Succession created a glut of surplus warships, officers and seamen. Ships purchased in Britain often kept their original names. Peter's line of battle included *Britannia*, *Portsmouth* and *Devonshire*, suggesting a conscious attempt to associate his fleet with the glories of the world's dominant navy. Hastily built Russian ships were short-term assets, second-hand purchases were little better. The Danish observer Georg Grund noted: 'The ships are generally in a poor state, for all of them, from the Admirals' downwards, are built only of pine and the iron on them is of poor quality. The Tsar himself admitted in 1710 that four of the older ships were not seaworthy.'

The sailing battlefleet remained far below Western standards, relying on numbers to compensate for poor quality. Even so the creation of a substantial sea-going fleet in less than a decade was impressive and, despite its manifest limitations, it met Peter's needs. It kept the Swedish sailing fleet away from his amphibious advances and offered strategic leverage in the region. Ultimately, the navy was the key to securing the seaward flanks of St Petersburg and projecting power, raiding the outskirts of Stockholm in 1720. In all cases the Russian object was territorial. No sooner had the tsar secured the central Baltic than he shifted his naval efforts to the Caspian, redeploying manpower and expertise to attack Persia. Once again Peter's warships were supporting a land offensive, focused on territorial expansion.[27]

Peter's Norwegian admiral, Cornelius Cruys, a key administrator and recruiter of foreign personnel, recognised that the end of the Great Northern War was only the beginning of the project. 'Not only all Europe but also the greater part of Asia has great respect for our fleet; therefore it is essential to maintain everything in the best order.' The fleet would enable Russia to crush regional maritime powers, as Rome had crushed Rhodes, with overwhelming, primarily military power. The purpose of the sailing battlefleet could be read in the rapid increase in battleships, especially massive three-decked First Rates, the ultimate symbol of naval power, national strength and imperial majesty. Louis XIV's *Soleil Royale*, the English *Royal Sovereign*, *Britannia* and *Victory*, colossal, gilded statements, each had more firepower than the entire Russian army. Baltic navies rarely built such ships, focusing on smaller battleships, with a shallower draft of water. The design and construction of First Rates was the ultimate test for naval architects and shipbuilders: Peter recruited men who had worked on the *Royal Sovereign*, the largest battleship afloat. He acquired British First Rate designs of 1706 and 1719, and hoped to exploit their powerful symbolism. Three of the four First Rates begun under Peter's direction were named for battle victories on land, the last for the tsar. These symbols of imperial might rarely put to sea.[28]

Russian naval development was intimately tied to the life and desires of the tsar. As Lindsey Hughes observed, 'it seems highly unlikely that the fleet, unlike the army, could have survived without the Tsar's constant attention.'[29] Peter understood this only too well. His post-war efforts to sustain the

Baltic fleet, and enhance its power, prestige and professionalism, were the desperate efforts of a man, already in the grip of a mortal illness, to perpetuate his vision of Russia's future. He needed a credible naval force to secure his wider legacy, a hard task in a country without seafaring traditions. To raise standards he insisted on sea training and annual manoeuvres, personally inspecting ships and facilities: savage punishments awaited those found wanting. He was imposing the professional culture of the Royal Navy with a 'knout' (whip). Unwilling, or even unable, to delegate the task, Peter drove the naval project until he died. The story that his death resulted from rescuing a drowning sailor may not be true, but it reflected the deeply personal nature of his naval engagement.

Peter used naval rank whenever he was afloat, and dressed in naval uniform for his second wedding in 1712, a foreign-born admiral standing as best man. 'Court life was embellished with symbols and ceremonies connected with the fleet, numerous references to Neptune in engravings and medals, and festivals honouring the fleet's "grandfather".' There are few images of St Petersburg that do not include ships. Among the best known, A. F. Zubov's 1716 panorama confines the buildings to a narrow strip in the middle ground, while the watery foreground is filled with ships. The foreground of Zubov's 1714 view of Vasil'evksy Island is dominated by Swedish ships captured at Hangö.[30] Petrine official art packed in ships to make a point, the same point, over and over again, as it tried to instil sea culture into a profoundly continental people. Peter insisted St Petersburgers attend his regattas and naval pageants in Russian-built boats and barges, of Western design. He insisted on Western boats for the same reason he demanded Western architecture for public buildings, and Western uniforms for his armies. He wanted a clean break with the past, but that agenda faltered at his death.

While Peter's navy had emerged from Russian activity on rivers, lakes and coasts, the sea had always been subordinated to the Russian focus on land and fortresses. Territorial expansion did not require Russia to become a seapower, although an amphibious capability could be useful. Between 1696 and 1721 Peter's success reflected his grasp of amphibious power, combining army and navy at the watery margins to drive his empire westward. Maritime logistics enabled the Russian army, hitherto crippled by poor roads, to use modern methods of war, especially resource-intensive sieges. The decision to create a battlefleet navy after 1721 was equally logical: Peter wanted to dominate regional powers and deter external threats. Personal engagement with the sea, ships, sailors and shipwrights enabled him to provide competent leadership for the project.

However, a sailing fleet needed resources that Russia did not have, and could not generate. Peter hired foreign shipbuilders, artisans, sailors and sea officers. Nor could he overcome the deep cultural antipathy that Russians felt for the sea by imperial diktat: of all his projects the fleet remained the most dependent on foreign expertise, requiring fresh injections from the external sources to sustain competence. Peter appointed trusted Russians to lead the service, but the attempt to create a naval cadre failed. Little wonder foreign experts were pressed to sign on for life. The British spy John Deane considered this a sign of weakness, 'prompted by the apparent unwillingness of Russians to join the navy', which he attributed to a Russian 'aversion to the sea'. Russian noble volunteers were so rare that most received a personal letter of encouragement from the tsar. The supply of lower-deck personnel was solved by military methods. 'When it came to the rank and file, sailors were conscripted, initially from the maritime provinces and rivers, where there was already knowledge of navigation, but later from other regions as well, usually by the Tsar's personal command.' Naval infantry, or Marines, were created in 1705. Naval regulations were based on translated foreign texts.[31]

To sustain his project Peter launched a powerful cultural assault on the 'Old Russian' aversion to the ocean. The past, and the parochial, had to be pushed back. He would force the sea and a navy down the throats of his subjects, without distinction, rich and poor, by diktat, demonstration and design. Like all sea-kings his ships were objects of veneration; he gave them histories and identities so that poets could sing of their glory, like the hero weapons of Homeric and Norse lore. Furthermore the navy and ships were integrated into the wider cultural remaking of Russia. ' "Naval baroque" was a vital element in Petrine culture, another phenomenon that gives the lie to the easy assumption that Peter's was a "utilitarian" reign.' Peter understood that only an organically Russian fleet, tied to the state, and the new national culture that he was shaping, would endure. Had he lived another fifteen or twenty years this might have been possible, and he might have raised a successor to follow his designs. However much the Russian people disliked the navy, and the cost, Peter demonstrated that Russia's continental expansion depended on naval support. Ultimately, the navy served narrowly military aims: it was not configured for sea control, economic warfare or personal interest. Peter did not build his navy solely to gratify his vanity. He understood the mutual relationship of sea and land power more completely than did most other statesmen of his time, as indicated by his crude but striking image: 'A potentate who has only land forces has a single arm. He who also has a fleet has two arms.'[32]

After Azov in 1696 'the value of combined land and sea operations was rarely far from Peter's mind'. He used the sea to enhance terrestrial strategy, a mirror image of armies in sea power strategy. As the Great Northern War drew to a close in 1719, devastating amphibious raids brought a defeated but defiant Sweden to the peace table. These operations relied on battlefleet sea control, which covered the galley squadrons and landing forces. A subtle, calculating strategist, Peter countered the tactical power of his enemies with mass, movement and combination.[33] He understood that, although sea power had an important role to play in Russian strategy, Russia did not need to become a seapower. Peter's Russia would be a new Roman Empire. After Poltava, a modern Zama, Russian naval power prevented Sweden from moving troops around the Baltic, leaving an outnumbered army tied down defending fortresses. Superior numbers and maritime mobility enabled Peter to grind out a result.

The limits of Russian power became obvious at the peace in 1721. Peter returned the conquered province of Finland to Sweden, even though Finnish Karelia was worryingly close to St Petersburg; Russia lacked the money and manpower to administer the country. Such fiscal weakness means the contention that Petrine Russia was intent on competing with British naval power can be dismissed as Russian propaganda, or British alarmism. After 1721 the Baltic fleet, however moribund, sustained Russian sway over Sweden and Denmark, securing the outer bastion of this inland sea. A Black Sea Fleet would take up the same roles in the later eighteenth century.

After 1721 Peter turned his attention to other opportunities across the Caspian Sea and countering the Royal Navy, but he had no intention of wasting resources on a symmetrical response. When Britain deployed battlefleets to deter further advances across the Baltic, Peter relied on forts and troops to protect St Petersburg. His fleet could impress regional powers, and perhaps move troops to secure the Danish Narrows, a strategic option that remained a Russian aim for centuries, but it was not going to take on the Royal Navy.

Great as Peter's achievement was, he could not make Russia a true seapower. Nor did he try. Every seapower box he ticked, maritime capital, naval might and sea culture, only served to highlight the problem. Continental military autocracies cannot become seapowers, only more or less mighty naval powers. Without a fundamental turn to the sea, adopting inclusive politics and a capitalist economy, such navies remain hostage to political whim, economic decline and military defeat. The mixed model adopted by the Dutch Republic and Britain only worked after political change had empowered the men of trade and money. The mercantilist state monopolies Peter used to create strategic resources and win wars were the antithesis of the political and economic base of a seapower. The ability of the contemporary United States to sustain a vast navy demonstrates the value of long-standing inclusive political institutions, a legacy of Anglo-Dutch traditions, but the modern American body politic sees the fleet in purely naval terms, much as Peter did.

The crisis of the Petrine revolution came in the unlikely, tubercular form of Tsaraevich Alexis, a weak prince swayed by the 'old' Muscovite families of his mother and his wife, an enthusiast for the old ways. Aware of these influences Peter warned his son not to oppose him, demanding his support. At Alexis's trial for treason his mistress reported him declaring that if he became tsar he would leave St Petersburg, return to Moscow, stop the wars, live in peace with the world and, critically, 'I won't launch any ships' – perhaps the most alarming words that Peter ever heard. The tsaraevich hated the central elements of Peter's project, war and Westernisation; as a potential figurehead of opposition he had to be crushed. The tsar showed himself to be as ruthless with his own family as he had been with his country, using Alexis's trial, torture and death to flush out high-ranking internal opposition. The new ways were the only ways, the ships were here to stay. For all that the naval project remained incomplete when Peter died on 28 January 1725.

Furthermore Peter had not created a blue-water sea-control force, only the seaward flank guard and logistics support for the mighty army that had extended and secured Russia's land frontiers by 1721. When Peter died Russia dominated north-eastern and central Europe, and had resumed the advance into the Caucasus, the Euxine and central Asia. Peter's famous two-armed analogy was important, and it should be understood from the perspective of the ultimate objective, the enhancement of Russian imperial control through military power: the army was his right arm, and the focus was always terrestrial. This territorially expansive empire was Roman.

For all his aggressive cultural navalism Peter's interest in the wider maritime dimension was distinctly limited. Naval might was merely one element in the state that he built to win his wars. Much of the cultural effort was a response to domestic opposition. In 1903 the historian Pavel Miliukov agued that Peter waged his wars for the fleet: in reality the fleets had been an essential tool to win those wars.[34] Peter's project had not been in vain: his navies facilitated the conquest of a continental empire, sustaining long-distance military operations. Far from spending freely on a 'pet' project, Peter carefully controlled the cost of naval power, adopting cheap solutions, exploiting Russian assets and avoiding a contest with Britain. Success brought new problems, which he had only just begun to address in 1725. His new great-power state had acquired a coast and a coastal capital city, which would have to be defended from a far more potent navy if he challenged British interests in the Baltic. Peter recognised that Russia could not generate the necessary skills and resources to meet that threat at sea.

Peter's successors effectively ignored the problem. The tortured succession to the imperial throne reversed much of the naval turn. In his brief reign Peter II, Alexis's son, abandoned both St Petersburg and the navy. By the 1760s the navy had collapsed so completely that its revival under Catherine II looked strikingly similar to the original Petrine project, equally dependant on foreign officers, shipbuilders and designs.[35]

Petrine Russia's dependence on foreign expertise has been overstated in all areas save the fleet. In most areas Peter could develop local skills, but the navy was so alien to Russian life that it had to be created and sustained by foreigners. It remained an unfinished project at his death, perhaps unfinishable, an assessment that gains strength from the vicissitudes of Russian and Soviet naval power since 1725. The Russian/Soviet state never tried to become a seapower: Peter did not change the autocratic, centralised warfare state created by Ivan IV, obsessed with territorial expansion and defensive depth. Russia had no need to become a seapower; a navy would be useful, to transport the army, secure Russia's watery flanks, and above all protect the capital.

For all the attention lavished on St Petersburg and the navy, the key to the entire Petrine project was the fortress and naval base of Kronstadt, on

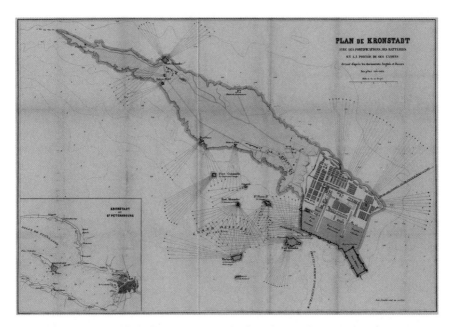

The ultimate symbol of Petrine power: the fortress complex at Kronstadt, 1853

Kotlin Island, 20 miles to the west. Work began there as Peter broke ground for his new city. Without Kronstadt, and the shallows that forced sea-going ships to sail right under the guns of his fortress, St Petersburg would have been undefendable. The island made it possible to build the city. Although Kronstadt became the greatest naval fortress on earth, the appearance of a hostile Royal Navy remained a nightmare for Russian leaders.[36] In 1733 the Russian fleet was hardly fit for sea, but Kronstadt's 700 cannon, mounted in immense bastions of Finnish granite, reflected continental anxieties about seapower, liberal culture and political inclusion.

Russia could not contest control of the Baltic in the presence of a first-class opponent in 1725, 1809 or 1854. This ongoing weakness limited Russian expansion, and obliged successive tsars to rebuild and reinforce Peter's fortress complex. The British were ready to destroy it in 1856, but Russia hastily accepted defeat. Naval might, backed by world-leading industrial and economic power, was more than a match for Peter's lumbering military empire; his command economy built on serf labour was no match for factories and steamships.[37]

While many Western analysts have argued that St Petersburg, Russia's 'window on the west', and Peter's new fleet were the twin symbols of Russian modernity, Kronstadt was the ultimate symbol of Petrine power. Peter made Kronstadt a model town, built on a grid pattern, with Western buildings and tree-lined avenues, the main square bisected by a 'Venetian' canal to reflect its central place in his project. Nor was it accidental that Peter's favourite palace, the Peterhof on the shores of the Gulf of Finland, boasted a fine view of the fortress. The Peterhof revealed much about the man. He wanted to be by the sea, surrounded by marine art, in a modest Dutch building that overlooked his primary security system. Sea views, marine art and a fine library emphasised that the Peterhof belonged to a naval tsar. Standing on high ground that fell precipitously toward the sea, it was intended to be seen from passing ships, the view dominated by massive fountains, canals and fabulous gardens, inspired by Versailles. This ceremonial flourish was the main entrance to the Petrine capital, a Russian Greenwich. The largest of the Peterhof's fountains celebrated victory over Sweden.[38] In the Great Hall a fresco of Neptune commanding the seas from a watery chariot, trident in hand, reflected the eyeline and ambition of an imperious tsar.[39]

The Peterhof demonstrated how Peter used naval culture to project Russian power onto the seas, challenge the established seapowers, and change the landlocked mentality of his subjects. After his death the seapower symbols remained, but the moving spirit had departed. The symbols endured in a continental state claiming to be a new Roman Empire; they spoke of naval might, not seapower culture. Peter's project provided a striking contrast to the development of English seapower identity between the 1430s and 1688. It took the English two centuries to ingrain the ocean into the soul of a small, insular state, a period of dynamic creativity sparked by kings and rulers, but sustained by private enterprise as the politico-economic system evolved into one that could sustain a true seapower.

Peter may have conflated seapower identity with naval might. By the time the tsar reached Amsterdam, Johan de Witt's seapower state was but a memory; Willem III ruled a heavily militarised Republic that had fought France to a standstill on land. Although Peter acquired seapower art and imagery alongside more practical items, and brandished them with the passion of an enthusiast, his revolution had more realistic, realisable objects than changing the essential nature of Russia. He exploited Western methods, in war, science, architecture and engineering, to modernise and strengthen Russia, breaking the power of the Church and the old nobility in the process. He pushed his measures to excess, the better to ensure their success: St Petersburg may have looked to the sea, but Peter's Russia did not.

Peter's revolution attempted to make Russia European, turning the focus of the unique Eurasian nation he had inherited westward. But his political models were autocratic, not inclusive. He admired Louis XIV, not William III. His greatest challenge was to reshape national culture to support a new imperial state; without that his work would be mere surface detail. The result was 'an attempt at cultural engineering rarely attempted in so short a space of time or on such a scale'.[40] He separated the Russian elite, who were obliged to acquire the new culture, from the Russian people, who were excused the modernising turn, as surely as Louis XIV's project at Versailles separated his aristocrats from their locality. Peter infused the new culture with a powerful allegorical element of classical imagery, He became, by turns, Hercules, Pygmalion, Mars, Neptune and Jupiter, as well as the successor to heroic classical empire builders, Alexander, Constantine and especially Julius Caesar. His portrait on the new rouble was classical Roman, while the medal struck to celebrate his brief command of the four Allied Fleets in 1716 featured Neptune's chariot being drawn by four sea horses, perhaps recalling Verrio's *Sea Triumph of Charles II*, an image Peter may have seen in London. The idea of assuming Neptune's mantle appealed to his vanity. Yet the Russian Baroque was not a random assembly of classical references: it used art to emphasise Petrine ambition to make Russia the new Rome. When the propagandist Feofan Prokopovich needed a suitable analogy for the victory at Poltava he turned to the Second Punic War. Poltava was the modern Zama, emphasising the continental military nature of Petrine ambition, and the secondary status of his naval project.[41]

After 1710 the assembly of native and imported art at St Petersburg, complete with powerful religious elements, provided the city with spiritual foundations as potent as those of Moscow, but far more relevant. The opening of the Admiralty shipyard in 1705 placed the city at the heart of Peter's strategic ambition. His diktat that Russian nobles use sails, not oars, to navigate the Neva, reflected a profoundly practical turn of mind. Familiarity with the tools of naval power might build support for the project and generate native officers. Compulsory regattas served the same function, imposing the new culture onto a reluctant, resistant people.[42] Peter wanted St Petersburg to be both his capital and a Russian Amsterdam, a lively, energetic sea-city. The problems posed by this agenda must have been obvious to a man familiar with the open societies of London and Amsterdam. He had no intention of sharing power with the traditional nobility, let alone of empowering non-existent native merchant princes. His sea-city would be imperial, not commercial.

At the same time Peter's taste for marine art and sea views emphasised his love of Amsterdam and, by extension, the Dutch-influenced maritime culture of London. Peter imported most of the art that decorated his walls, including portraits of himself and his wife. Townscapes, landscapes and marines were either purchased in Holland or specially commissioned. Alongside the acknowledged masters, including Rembrandt, Van Dyck and Breughel, he enjoyed lesser Dutch artists, including the detailed marine art of his erstwhile Amsterdam tutor Adam Silo (1674–1760), and the seascapes of the London-based Storck brothers, Abraham and Jacob. In truth Peter did not have the time to be fussy. In 1711 he ordered 'about four dozen pictures' of 'sea battle and seafaring vessels of various kinds, perspectives of Dutch towns and villages, with canals and boats'. He would also accept landscapes and other genres.[43] His taste in art was that of a Dutch sea captain, combining the seaman's eye for detail with an uncritical love of the subject. Charles II had the discrimination to recruit the Van de Veldes. Peter was content with second-rate alternatives. Peter's taste recalled his Dutch days, afloat and ashore, a fitting metaphor for the Petrine naval project. Seapower images were pure indulgence. Few domestic artists followed the maritime turn, because there were even fewer patrons for such work.

In a necessary part of the Petrine Revolution the regime began to create and disseminate Western-style images, promoting the Europeanisation of the state and new iconic visions – notably St Petersburg and warships – that would define it at home and abroad. Critically, Peter replaced the old Church-based education system and intellectual focus with Western bureaucratic processes, data collection and professionalism. However, he retained an old-fashioned command economy: the state controlled the printing presses, along with the texts and images that they produced.[44] Russia needed a written language to convey the wishes of the tsar and introduce his people to new systems, techniques and ideas. To escape the inevitable limitations of Church Slavonic, Russia required an accepted grammar with stable rules, and a very large number of loan words. German, French and even English were pillaged to develop a Russian vocabulary in distinct areas of activity. The first Russian grammar, published by Oxford University Press in 1696, was shaped by the tsar. Nowhere was the need for a new language more obvious than in the navy, which used Dutch as the language of command, adopted an Anglo-Dutch nautical lexicon, and depended on imported skills. Foreign words were essential because Russia had nothing suitable.[45]

Russia's 'Nautical Turn' was 'a singular achievement' that 'alone occasioned a huge lexical invasion'. Many of these loan words remain embedded in modern Russian; others fill glossaries from the sailing-ship era. These words came from Venice, Holland, France and Britain; they dealt with shipbuilding, naval ranks, ship management and shore facilities. They appear in Peter's Naval Statute of 1720, 'codifying the nautical turn'. Peter began issuing written naval instructions in 1696, for the Azov campaign, and continued updating and adding to this body of literature as the navy grew in size and experience. His obsession with rules, to impose Western systems of thought on his backward nation, reached a high point in the Naval Statute. Peter had French, Dutch Danish and British naval codes translated into Russian, printed and harmonised 'beginning with the English'. If there was no suitable English rule then a blank was to be left.[46] In 1722 Peter and his team completed the Regulation on the Administration of the Admiralty and Wharves, in which, as we have seen, he famously argued that armies constituted only a single arm, while a ruler who also possessed a navy had two arms; the analogy emphasised combined operations, the basis of Petrine success.

The 1720 Statute, a large book of 450 quarto pages, a vector for new words and ideas, was reprinted several times before the tsar's death in 1725, in Russian and English and Dutch. It remained in print essentially unaltered throughout the next century, its durability reflecting both the thoroughness of the initial exercise and the lack of interest of succeeding rulers. The frontispiece was designed by the Italian sculptor and architect C. B. Rastrelli, prominent members of the new St Petersburg cultural elite, and engraved by the Dutch artist Pieter Picart. The symbols of naval and military power, the Russian double eagle, Hebrew symbols and six lines of verse, wrap up the boy sailor tsar in his famous boat, his initial forays onto the water and his 'divinely ordained mission to create the Russian navy'. The message was reinforced in the Preface. The sense of a mission fulfilled is clear: the first big ship Peter built was the fifty-gun *Predestination*.[47] The use of religion and biblical ship references validated the new force to a deeply conservative, landlocked society.

The Statute recorded Russia's long, unsuccessful history at sea, to highlight Peter's critical role, as absolute ruler under God, in creating and commanding the new fleet. The text was written in the new Russian state language, still perfectly intelligible nearly two hundred years later, and printed in the new, simplified standard civil typeface. It was comparable with similar texts produced in the West.[48] Between 1708 and 1725 at least eighty other maritime titles were published in Russia. Many were translations, including twenty-five books on the topical issue of tactical flag signals and school textbooks for Russian students, along with trade regulations. The 'nautical turn' culminated in Semen Mordvinov's 1748 navigation manual, produced by a Petrine naval cadet who had profited from an advanced education in France. Elsewhere Russian naval education was profoundly shaped by English input: in 1698 Peter followed the advice of his hosts, taking some skilled navigation teachers to Russia. They introduced the essential Arabic numbers and advanced mathematics, opening the path for the full range of enlightenment science. Henry Farquharson spent forty-one years educating Russian naval officers, astronomers and mathematicians, translating texts and informing mapping and charting projects. He was, as Anthony Cross and James Cracraft agree, perhaps the single most influential foreigner in Petrine service. Fittingly, the Naval Academy he ran for three decades remained a stronghold of English studies in Russia throughout the Romanov era. There were striking similarities between Petrine Russian literature and that of Tudor England. Both relied on large-scale borrowing from older sea states, through translation, importing words and ideas that culminated in a truly national output. However, only one became a seapower state. The only Russian naval history written before 1720 had been a handful of celebratory sermons for Peter's naval victories, delivered by his chief propagandist Archbishop Prokopovich, who had provided the Statute with a striking sense of destiny and divinity.[49]

Peter also used engraved images to spread naval culture, commissioning views of his city, ships, charts battles and triumphs, and an atlas. This modernising art emphasised the naval base and fortress complex of Kronstadt, the home of the fleet and the outer bastion of the city. These images were meant to impress foreign governments and Russian subjects with imperial power. While their reception in the West exceeded Peter's ambitions, generating concern in Britain, the domestic maritime agenda stalled. Western artists were soon replaced by Russians, who reworked Western designs. An image of 250 ships sailing from St Petersburg to Viborg in 1710 was rendered especially powerful by the knowledge that this expedition had secured the city against attack.[50] Not only did Peter build the city, but he ensured it would be seen around Europe in images that conveyed the modernity of his vision. In the 1780s, when Russia threatened to replace France as the new Rome – the ultimate continental threat – George III, ruler of the last great seapower state, acquired a rare print of the St Petersburg Main Admiralty.[51]

Peter's great city was dominated by the maritime location: it was a port and a naval base in the Western style. Yet the city, like the navy, lost much of its allure when examined at close quarters. John Parkinson, the travelling companion to fashionable young gentlemen on the northern tour, had been overwhelmed 'by the first sight of this magnificent town, which in grandeur very far exceeds every other that I have seen', but he soon realised the facade was fragile: 'if it ever comes to be neglected it must necessarily become very forlorn and ragged, from the stucco dropping off, which will expose the shabby brickwork behind'. Parkinson's assessment of the architecture of grandeur could be applied with equal facility to Peter's grandiose naval ambitions, with which it shared many characteristics. Fifty years after Peter's death, St Petersburg achieved imperial grandeur through the scale and uniformity of Giacomo Quarenghi's work for Catherine II.[52] In the process the city lost contact with the chaotic, evolving reality of maritime cities, the commercial waterfronts of Amsterdam and London, that first attracted Peter. It became a monumental statement of terrestrial imperial grandeur, in which humdrum, decaying commercial buildings, the grubby reality of port life, were not welcome; one where the men of money were in no position to insist. The parallel with other continental attempts at imperial grandeur, from Rome and Washington DC to Brasilia and Beijing, is obvious. Such continental capitals reflect a different national vision than do thriving sea ports. This was not what Peter had in mind when he began shaping the public face of the Petrine Revolution in Russian culture.

Acutely aware of the cultural power of art, the common currency of western European regal display, Peter made it his business to replicate the great picture galleries of Versailles, London and Amsterdam. He was especially proud of the galleries at the Winter Palace and the Peterhof, which displayed numerous Venetian, Dutch and Flemish sea pictures, many of them prominently hung at Peter's favourite palace.[53] He also set up a tapestry works, inspired by the French, to create the ultimate elite art. His taste had been shaped by Amsterdam and Venice: he knew Amsterdam and recognised the connection with Venice, a city he may have visited incognito in 1698.[54] Captivated by the sea city he consumed it in pictures, prints and maps, collected on an industrial scale. He placed many on public display, to mould Russian taste. The fabled canal city of naval might, commerce and culture fuelled the tsar's dreams. Petrine Russia combined the pomp and display of Venice with more prosaic Dutch input, ship pictures, shipbuilders and merchants. The Venetians had always produced celebratory work, extraordinary spectacles of power and longevity, packed with the ships and symbols of a unique state for crowned heads and high-ranking aristocrats. Having established commercial and diplomatic links with the Republic in 1697, Peter acquired at least as many Venetian as Dutch pictures.

Russia's engagement with Venetian art survived Peter's death, although the images were consigned to storage. At her accession in 1740 his daughter Elizabeth had the pictures restored and hung in a new gallery, part of a wide-ranging celebration of Petrine progress.[55] Additional pictures were acquired through Italian residents in St Petersburg, initially as mere wall decoration, although they soon acquired cultural meaning. In 1753 Elizabeth celebrated the city's fiftieth anniversary with a series of engravings that reflected the profound impact of Venetian sensibilities on the representation of St Petersburg's prestige and power. St Petersburg became 'the Venice of the North', another image that Peter consciously created: his daughter would revive and reinforce it at a time when Russian naval power and commercial shipping were moribund. Among the most widely disseminated of these images were two panoramic views of the city from the River Neva. Although framed by mighty buildings, the Winter Palace, the Peter and Paul Fortress and Church, and the Academy of Sciences, the images are dominated by a galley, oars flourished, the imperial arms on the stern emphasising the dynastic agenda. This could be the Bacino San Marco, and the inference was intentional.[56] For all her filial piety and artistic pomp Elizabeth did little for Peter's navy; her focus was resolutely military. Russian triumphalism has remained terrestrial, and so have images of St Petersburg.

When Catherine II shifted the cultural language of St Petersburg from Venetian seapower to a modified Roman classicism, British art replaced Venetian images.[57] Richard Brompton produced a portrait of Catherine II in 1782 'with various allegorical attributes and a view of the Russian Fleet in the distance', while George Hadfield's Crimean pictures included the new naval base at Sevastopol. Sir Joshua Reynolds did not travel to Russia, but he sent Catherine a picture of the infant Hercules, linked to the child-giant Peter, an allusion to the dramatic growth of the Russian Empire. The empress greatly admired Reynolds, having his *Discourses on Art*, translated into Russian. Reynolds also worked for her favourite, Prince Potemkin.[58] When Russia resumed naval warfare on a grand scale the need for sea pictures – one of Peter's core interests – had to be met. The enterprising British marine painter Richard Paton sent four very large studies of Russian naval victories over the Turks in 1770 to St Petersburg, where Catherine put them on public display. Paton, who may have used first-hand accounts from British officers who served in those battles, received a gold medal and £1,000 for his work.[59] British marine art was the obvious tool to celebrate Russia's naval revival.

The brief, explosive irruption of Petrine seapower culture into an older Russian identity left curious legacies, their belated, distorted re-emergence reflecting the power of the great tsar's personality and the maritime iconography he so liberally scattered. A belated turn to the sea blossomed in the post-Crimean War era, as reconstruction and liberalism renewed connections with Western thought and finally brought Russia to recognise the sea and support native-born artists of the ocean. In an age of defeat and domestic upheaval, viewing Russia as a second biblical Ark, navigating the dangerous stormy seas of revolution and transformation, gained traction; it was an opportunity to reflect on the direction of travel, and the captaincy of successive tsars, on the stormy seas of modernity. Religious thought stressed the journey to insular and coastal monasteries, while the freedom of Volga boatmen offered hope to the oppressed, taking root in popular culture, while radicals endlessly reworked the shipwreck analogy to address the looming catastrophe.

Peter would have taken some comfort from contemporary attempts to escape the limits of Russia's landlocked identity, or ice-choked seas, and reach the open ocean of global commerce. The novelty of this idea can be gauged from the fact that Ivan Goncharov's naval story *Frigate Pallada*, a journey from Kronstadt to Petropavlosk, created 'a new genre of sea adventure' for an expanding Russian readership, a mere three hundred years after Ramusio, Camoens, Hakluyt and Raleigh. 'At its simplest the image of plunging out into the deep was only a reflection of the fact that Russia had at last become in the early nineteenth century a thoroughly self-conscious empire'.[60] In an age of uncertainty and pessimism seascapes represented the ultimate freedom, annihilation and even self-destruction. Russians feared the sea would overwhelm everything, ending turmoil and struggle with a biblical flood.

Nowhere was such apocalyptic thinking more potent than in low-lying, flood-prone St Petersburg, where inundation was only a stiff east wind away. The devastating flood of 22 November 1824 drowned upwards of 10,000 people, wrecked most of the fleet lying in ordinary at Kronstadt, and undermined the shore defences.[61] The great bastions of Peter, Catherine and Alexander had been overthrown by the ocean, leaving Peter's city exposed to the Royal Navy. The sea made Russia and the 'new' capital vulnerable, fear of the sea replacing older fire anxieties that dominated the Muscovite era. Peter's dream had changed Russian fears, from steppe nomads and fire to amphibious invasions and flooding. 'Fear of the sea was perhaps to be expected among an earthbound people whose discovery of the sea coincided with their traumatic discovery of the outside world.' When that outside world came to Russia's coasts in 1854 it sparked a sixty-year epoch of profound change. Amidst the chaos Russia found an artist of the ocean: the Crimean-born Romantic Ivan Aivazovsky. He represented the heroic achievements of the Black Sea Fleet under Nicholas I, and brought the ocean into national consciousness.[62]

Ultimately, seapower had the last word on tsarist ambition: warships, critical symbols of Petrine ambition, became vehicles for revolution. The battleship *Potemkin* and the cruiser *Aurora* were icons for a revolution that would abandon St Petersburg and butcher democratically minded sailors. Under the Soviets, space replaced the ocean as the field of dreams, carrying the symbolic burden of purification, deliverance and self-annihilation.[63] Yet the sea retains a quasi-mystical role in Russian thought: the recovery of Sevastopol in 2014 reflected an enduring identity with a heroic city where a million Russians had died in two great sieges.

In truth Peter exerted a profound influence on every aspect of Russian culture, save the one he really cared about – the sea. Hard as he pushed the message, the Russians were not persuaded. The explanation for this failure is economic. Peter's economic outlook had been influenced by Samuel Pufendorf's account of English trade policy, combining cloth exports with shipbuilding and naval power. Most Russian exports, grain, timber, iron and shipbuilding stores, were bulky, of low value by weight, and involved simple manufacturing processes. Improving product standards enabled Russian iron, flax and sailcloth to dominate European markets for much of the eighteenth century. While he encouraged Russian exports, Peter adopted a continental mercantilist economic model. After the Great Northern War he imposed a protectionist model, using tariffs and import substitution to protect domestic industry, and Russian capital. A levy of 37.5 per cent on imports that competed with Russian products was paired with free importation for essentials that could not be locally sourced, including precious metals, books and anti-scorbutic lemons. He wanted Russia to be the middleman in trade between Asia and Europe, pushing eastward exploration and expansion accordingly.[64]

Peter imposed a centralised, arbitrary and autocratic economic policy to sustain his expanding military state. He would not share political power with men of commerce and industry. He had no wish to create a commercial class, preferring to sell bulky low-value exports at Russian ports and collect customs dues. A society built on land and servile labour did not generate the disposable capital to create commercial wealth or incentives to trade. Without capital, legally enforceable rights to their own property, political representation and status, Russian merchants, suffering from low 'morale and self-esteem', were incapable of creating a dynamic maritime economy. Russian merchants did not get rich, or live in style, fearful that the state, or the aristocracy, would seize their property. This had a significant impact on the development of national culture.[65] Eighty years after Peter's death the travelling British cleric and commentator William Coxe ascribed Russia's backwardness to the fact that the great mass of the people remained in 'complete vassalage; nor can any effectual change be introduced in the national manners [meaning culture], until the people enjoy full security in their persons and property'. Little wonder Tsar Nicholas I banned the book.[66] Industrial development was largely driven by the demands of war: weapons, uniforms and accoutrements, gunpowder and warships were made by the state. Ironworks in the Urals grew, but lack of capital and competition left them reliant on backward methods and unskilled, servile labour. The dearth of modern roads left the domestic economy reliant on river transportation.

Peter crippled Russia by keeping most aspects of economic life under state control and retaining the serf system. Centralised control guaranteed work and maintained prices; it did not encourage competition or innovation. The economy had been geared to winning wars; after 1721 Peter set a course for mercantilist self-sufficiency, while exports would fill the state coffers. This worked in the pre-industrial era, exploiting Russian strengths, but lacked the capacity for organic development and progress. The economic base of the empire stagnated for more than a century as Russia consistently failed to generate or sustain vital technology, notably in shipbuilding, metallurgy and arms manufacture. It depended on imported goods and foreign artisans to satisfy strategic demand. The problem was especially severe in the maritime sector. Peter intended that Russian commerce should be funnelled through St Petersburg, but attempts to redirect trade from existing centres such as Archangel only served to disrupt internal patterns. The hemp business remained an Arctic phenomenon. Eventually St Petersburg became Russia's largest commercial centre, dominating imports and exports with canals linking the city to a vast economic hinterland, stretching as far as the Volga, the Urals and the Caspian.[67]

The Baltic became the focal point for Russian exports: grain, timber, flax, hemp, iron, pitch, potash, tar and furs were exchanged for cash, Western manufactures and colonial produce, including Carmarthen's tobacco. The shipping and the sailors were Dutch and British, not Russian. Russia did not follow a mercantilist maritime policy; it did not use tariff barriers or subsidies to create a merchant navy, content to leave shipping to the maritime powers. Without significant ocean-going shipping Russia could not generate the skilled manpower for an effective sailing navy. The few Russians who were free to choose a seafaring life soon realised that they were better treated on Western ships.[68] As Arcadius Kahan observed, oceanic merchant shipping, 'belongs only marginally to the economic history of Russia'. Russia never acquired a significant merchant marine, outside the coastal sector.

Lack of capital and limited skills made it uneconomic to compete, leaving Western shipping to dominate Russia's external trade. Initially, the Dutch took the largest share, but by the 1740s the British had taken over. Furthermore Kahan contended that Russian 'Navigation Acts would have been a folly, for the Russian foreign maritime trade suffered from shortcomings that were difficult to overcome: the lack of standardization of goods, the lack of quality specifications, and, most important, the relative lack of capital.' High operating costs and oppressive bureaucracy discouraged Russian merchant shipping, while trade was financed by foreign pre-payments and loans.

Western ships were better built, and cheaper, even when assembled in Amsterdam from Russian timber, while Russian seafarers lacked key skills. Russia provided the shipping where it traded with countries that had inferior shipbuilding technology, even fewer sailors and no capital. Coastal shipping continued to rely on older, native methods. Kahan's continental argument that the lack of ocean-going shipping did not hamper Russia's economic development recognises that the only reason to generate a Russian merchant marine would have been long-term economic advantage, or 'political prestige', but significantly undervalues the strategic danger that flowed from the naval weakness caused by the lack of skilled seamen. A century after Peter's death the Russian navy still relied on the same combination of raw recruits and foreign mercenaries that Peter had employed. Equally problematic was the failure to develop a significant domestic shipbuilding industry: all the relevant expertise resided in government naval facilities, largely because there was so little domestic demand.[69]

The lack of a domestic merchant shipping industry had serious strategic implications. Trade with Britain, Russia's largest customer, reflected mutual economic self-interest, not political connection. War had been a real possibility at any time after the early 1710s, and the British would target the Russian economy. Britain was happy to run a negative balance of payments with Russia, to secure critical naval stores, timber, hemp, flax, pitch, tar and pig iron. London banks did much business with Russia, while the Russia Company linked the trade with banking and consumers of Russian goods, especially the British Admiralty. In the 1720s the Royal Navy sustained a Baltic balance of power that denied Russia a monopoly in those supplies, and Britain actively sought alternative sources. The Anglo-Russian Trade Treaty of 1734 provided Britain with naval stores and other primary produce, put £25 million into the Russian economy across the rest of the eighteenth century, and helped develop Russian exports. The 1766 Treaty was less favourable to Britain, but still secured its strategic needs. Most Russian trade was carried by British ships, to Britain or third parties. In return Britain supplied luxury goods and colonial produce. When the Trade Treaty expired in 1786 the economic and strategic theorist Sir John Sinclair argued that Britain must become independent of Russian supplies, by producing the articles at home or buying them elsewhere.[70]

A new Trade Treaty of 1793 opened Black Sea trade to the British, but it was ended by Tsar Paul in 1800, and British dominance of the Russian market passed. This reflected Russia's growing economic weight, and the strategic pressures created by reliance on Baltic grain, timber and naval stores between 1807 and 1812. After 1815, British economic and imperial policies reduced this dependency. Foreign Secretary Lord Castlereagh saw Canada as an alternative to the Baltic, adjusting duties to promote Canadian forestry.[71]

The slow but significant reduction of Britain's advantage in the eighteenth-century Russian market reflected a relationship in decline. When Russia used military power to defeat Sweden and Turkey and close regional markets, Britain recognised that wherever the Russian Empire extended it would block British competition with high tariff barriers. However, British trade remained critical to the socio-economic structure of Russia: the abrupt closure of that trade in 1801 led to the death of Tsar Paul. A decade later the devastating consequences of joining Napoleon's 'Continental System' persuaded his son to risk war with France. While Russia remained a military great power these events demonstrated that Russia depended on British purchasing power to keep the domestic economy liquid and fund the imperial ambitions of the tsarist state. British policymakers read the links between autarkic economics, naval power and the reconstruction of Kronstadt that marked the regime of Nicholas I – even if the Turkish Question dominated the headlines – and they generated the necessary response. British statesmen and strategists knew that Russia remained as vulnerable to naval power in the Baltic as it had been in 1703, developing naval and economic strategies to maximise their power, part of Britain's traditional strategy of limited maritime economic war. In 1855 Britain defeated Russia with a trade embargo that cut the supply of capital, leaving Russia bankrupt.[72] Sea power strategies of blocking exports and threatening to bombard St Petersburg decided the 'Crimean' war.

British manufacturers provided critical services in the eighteenth century, owning rope-yards in the city and saw mills at Kronstadt. The British entrepreneur William Gomm provided a very British assessment of Russia's 'failure to convert its own resources into a major merchant marine and navy and thus transform the country into a significant sea power'.[73] Russia ignored the sea, and made no attempt to generate the maritime base for a seapower state. Gomm's observations were part of a sustained analysis, emphasising just how closely the British were watching Russia's navy, empire and capital city. When Russia emerged as a Eurasian military great power, one with considerable diplomatic influence, British statesmen recognised Peter's continental mercantilist economy would restrict their access to internal markets, control exports and cut out middlemen. Peter was well aware that Baltic naval stores were critical to the British seapower state: he had seen them flooding into Amsterdam and London. He also understood their value to the Bourbon powers, exploiting the diplomatic power of naval stores by establishing consuls at Cadiz and other ports where Russian produce was traded.[74] While they affected to be impressed by Peter's armada, they knew it was greatly inferior to the Royal Navy. Whereas Russia had created a powerful army-support service, Britain possessed a blue-water sea-control battlefleet and the cruisers to protect a dynamic maritime economy, something Russia did not possess.

If the survival of Peter's naval project suggests his work had a permanent character, the endlessly cyclical, frequently catastrophic history of Russia at sea tells a different story. The fleet was an alien import, imposed on a determinedly continental people who had little exposure to, and no interest in, the ocean. Just as Peter had to force Russians to take to the sea, only the diktat of later regimes could keep them there. When the pressure was lifted, by war, bankruptcy, or imperial disinterest, the service slumped backwards into a shambolic, unseaworthy ruin.[75] After Peter's death Russia retained just enough naval power to overawe faltering and distracted Baltic rivals.[76] It did not aspire to any more until Catherine II's wars with the Ottomans and Sweden, when Britain provided a refresher course in navy-building. The fleet remained pre-eminently a defensive force, committed to the security of St Petersburg and the Baltic provinces.[77]

This should not be read as a criticism. Russia needed enough naval power to dominate the Baltic. After 1721, with Sweden defeated and browbeaten, there was little to fear, not least because Denmark aided Russia in keeping Sweden down. The cost of the navy had been hard to justify after the peace of 1721, and only the tsar's will sustained naval expansion. Later Russian regimes emphasised core security interests, land defence and south-ward expansion. They lacked the ambition and the resources to compete with the Royal Navy, relying on the fortress at Kronstadt to keep the Royal Navy away from St Petersburg. Peter II reduced the threat by moving the capital back to Moscow. By the late 1720s the fleet lay at Kronstadt, largely unrigged, wholly neglected and without crews. Most of the fleet had decayed beyond economic repair, while the essential human capital Peter had worked so hard to create, Russian seamen to man his great symbols of national might, had dispersed, drifting back to the shore, or shipping out on the Western merchant ships. The imported leadership had effectively disap-peared by the 1740s, leaving the service moribund.[78] The last functional elements of the Petrine naval legacy were the forts that provided security and the core infrastructure, around which a new force could be built.

St Petersburg opened Russia to European imports, be they goods, men, money or ideas. It was the key to sustaining the modernising drive, and while it remained the capital the state was committed to Europe, despite the high security costs it imposed. Post-Soviet Russia addressed the Romanov legacy by erecting a garish monumental statue of Peter, by Zurab Tsereteli, in the Moskva River in 1997, celebrating the Russian navy's tercentenary. A monstrous Peter appears as the helmsman of the state. Quite what the average twenty-first-century Muscovite is expected to make of the nautical turn is unclear, or how the statue reflected the naval ambitions of Leningrad-born President Putin. St Petersburg never replaced Moscow in the hearts and minds of the great mass of the Russian people: the cultural power of the Third Rome survived the tsar's flirtation with other ideologies, including the ocean. Images of the sea, ships, battles and charts, together with Admiralty buildings, dockyards, warships and sea forts, remained foreign imports, created or inspired by foreign craftsmen, and drawing on foreign models. Instead it was the vehicles for this process, the newly standardised and more businesslike Russian language and script that the tsar employed, and the translation of Western scientific, military and naval texts into that language, which left the most durable mark on the nation, ensuring that old Muscovites made their case in the new Petrine language.[79]

While continental analysts were impressed by the Petrine naval revolution, a phenomenon they only dimly understood, counting his ships rather than assessing their combat effectiveness, British and Venetian commentators saw through the facade. They understood the tsar had no intention of reshaping Russia into a seapower state, and that St Petersburg could be read in very different ways, ways that emphasised the defences at Kronstadt, rather than the fleet. They knew Peter's project was Roman, with powerful echoes of Louis XIV's drive for universal monarchy and imperial status.

British assessments exposed critical points of distinction between Peter's project and their own seapower state. Peter's fleet was markedly inferior to the Royal Navy, but it posed a serious geo-strategic challenge as the seaward arm of a massive army, one that appeared intent on swallowing up whole kingdoms and controlling their trade. As Russian troops drove into northern Germany, where Britain's new Hanoverian king was a major player, they threatened to close the Baltic to British commerce, touching a raw nerve in the ultimate seapower state.

Peter's growing power forced the English to assess his ambitions. In 1705 the newly installed ambassador to St Petersburg observed 'how great a lover the Czar is of shipping', advising his government to allow the tsar to recruit English shipwrights, whom he preferred to all others. English shipwrights and officers were ideally placed to report on Russian naval prospects.[80] In 1725 John Deane, a captain in Peter's Baltic fleet, emphasised the tsar's central role in the creation of the navy, the riverine and coastal agenda, and the long-term project to build a suitable navy for the new empire. Russia dominated the Baltic, and its ships were equipped with locally sourced masts, yards, sails, anchors and cable. However, they were only formidable if 'well-manned'.[81] Significantly, the total tonnage of Russia's fleet was little larger than that of Sweden, or even Denmark, but Russia had far more battleships.[82] The balance between battleships and cruisers reflected Peter's desire to control the Baltic and the fact that he had no interest in other naval tasks such as trade defence, fishery protection and colonial patrols outside the enclosed sea. A battlefleet could secure Russia's strategic interests, providing diplomatic leverage and security for the new littoral provinces and especially St Petersburg. With British and Dutch merchant ships carrying Russia's exports, at the purchaser's risk, insured in London or Amsterdam, he did not need to worry about the defence of trade. The maritime powers prevented Sweden from damaging

Russian exports. Deane also reflected on the inherent weaknesses of the project: Peter's commitment, energy and above all single-mindedness were irreplaceable. Only Peter could have achieved so much, yet his navy never reached the core of Russian identity. His death marked the high-water mark of Russian naval power.

Ultimately, Russia never developed the political method, economic policy and cultural identity required to be a seapower, something that was, and still remains, a conscious choice. Powerful autocratic centralising tendencies, and the overwhelming importance of continental territory in an empire that expanded on foot, made the sea marginal – even for a uniquely sea-minded tsar. Furthermore, as Deane observed, 'The disciplinary regime was arbitrary and violent, Russian junior officers treated warrant officers very badly.' Despite letting men of all ranks volunteer to serve in the English and Dutch fleets in the late war, the tsar had very few seamen: 'For the Russians in general have an aversion to the sea.'[83] Deane saw a broken-spirited people, rendered listless by despotic power. Poor diet made them prone to scurvy, while religious fasting left them too weak to work. Once at sea Deane found his men willing enough. But Peter's despotic command left officers and crew paralysed by 'fear, ignorance and confusion', as likely to blow up their own ship through panic or incompetence as do any damage to the enemy. Deane expected Russian naval progress would falter. The tsar had built many ships, 'yet his seamen, properly so called, are not more numerous, within these last four years. And the vast charge he is yearly at to discipline his men, and to keep up his fleet to its present height, while little or no service is done him in return of such expense, must inevitably exhaust his treasures and render him less formidable.' Everything depended on the upcoming Persian War: a reverse there would 'ruin many, if not most of his great undertakings'. The shortage of seamen, their limited skills and the poor sea-keeping of many ships restricted the navy to operations 'not far from the Tsar's own coasts'.[84] While the Russians liked to assume the Roman mantle, they lacked the efficiency, ruthlessness and, perhaps critically, the professionalism that had made the Romans formidable at sea.

Deane's paper secured him the post of consul-general at Kronstadt, but he was promptly expelled as a spy.[85] He would not be the last naval officer dispatched on diplomatic service to observe the activities of a potential naval rival. The central role of Kronsatdt and St Petersburg in the development of

Russian naval power and maritime trade ensured that British commercial agents, an essential element in booming trade relations, were ideally placed to provide intelligence. The naval engineer Samuel Bentham arrived in 1780, at the end of a mission to spy on the navies and naval facilities of north-western Europe, under the cover of scientific enquiry, for the Board of Admiralty. Bentham found many of the Russian ships 'were not in very good condition'. Catherine II had begun a naval project on the Black Sea consciously reminiscent of Peter's work in the Baltic, but that did not mean Russia had become a seapower. As the British ambassador to St Petersburg, Sir Charles Whitworth, stressed in 1791, Russia remained profoundly continental, and military. The tsarina and Prince Potemkin looked to secure trade in the Amur River basin, but Russia had 'no notion of drawing advantage from another country by any means other than conquest'.[86]

When Admiral Sir Cyprian Bridge, a former head of naval intelligence, prepared John Deane's account for publication in 1899, he connected it with contemporary British concerns about a rising Russian navy. Bridge's analysis of the Great Northern War was incisive: Sweden, a maritime state, had overstretched itself in continental wars; when Peter realised this he attacked their under-resourced fleet, while pinning down the Swedish army in Poland and the Ukraine. Having secured control of the Baltic he dictated the course of the war, rolling up the isolated parts of Sweden's empire.[87] Peter out-thought Charles XII, who risked everything on a military campaign. Had Charles used his fleet and army to recapture St Petersburg he could have secured command of the Baltic at low cost. Bridge concluded by warning the British against over-extension on the continent.

Peter never attempted to turn Russia into a seapower. This self-declared Roman Emperor focused on terrestrial extension and absolute power. The oceanic foundations he laid were narrowly naval, not maritime, lacking the merchants and capitalists to drive the economy, the merchant ships and sailors to move Russian exports, and an inclusive political system to sustain the enterprise. Peter's command economy, centralised state and retention of abso-lute power were incompatible with maritime enterprise and seapower iden-tity, as he must have known from his residence in Holland and England. While it is possible Peter did not recognise the deeper cultural roots of seapower on his first journey to the West, he returned to Holland and France twenty years later well aware of the synergy between merchants, popular assemblies, trade and power. In 1717 he chose to bring home the tools of French autocratic monarchy: Louis XIV's tapestry works, the Academy of Sciences and the official *Gazette* were essential assets for autocratic rule, while the Peterhof and its flamboyant gardens were designed by a French architect from Versailles, and the French Academy advised on the inscription for a massive equestrian statue modelled on those erected for the Sun King.[88] Peter wanted to be Louis XIV, the new Caesar, not William III, the modern Hannibal. He built a great navy to support the army that secured his fundamentally terrestrial aims. His economic views were mercantilist rather than capitalist, as befits a state rich in raw materials and unskilled labour, but desperately short of cash and credit.[89] He left commercial shipping to true seapowers.

The Russian fleet, like that of the Sun King, was a useful asset, not a core capability. When Peter forced his people to sea, compelling a servile, land-locked peasantry to serve afloat, he rediscovered an old truth. Sailors, unlike soldiers and labourers, cannot be dragooned into action or controlled by fear. To be professional they must be free men, not galley slaves chained to their oars: without freedom there will be no navy, for navies are defined by people, not ships. In the absence of a pre-existing organic maritime culture Peter tried to generate a sea-going population, but failed. He may have built a maritime window on the West, but could hardly bring his people to look through it, far less to sail on the seas that connected it to the world. Fifty years after his death Catherine II had to reconstitute the fleet with a major draft of foreign expertise to deal with second-rank Ottoman and Swedish navies, demonstrating that navies created by the will of an autocrat cannot be guaranteed to exist beyond their lifetime. Despite victories over second- and third-rate opponents, and the occasional dispatch of a major fleet beyond the Baltic, the British were never in any doubt that Russia was not a naval power of the first rank, or that this reality reflected fundamental weaknesses. The problem was not ships, or admirals, it was a matter of seamen and culture. As Admiral Sir George Collier observed, Russia 'can never become a great Maritime Power'.[90] Even at the height of the Cold War the Soviet fleet, the most impressive naval force ever operated by a Russian Empire, remained a fundamentally defensive asset, little different in concept to the Petrine service. Fleet Admiral Sergei Gorshkov, architect of the fleet, emphasised defensive military functions within the wider strategic effort. The fleet existed to block the impact of sea-based forces on Russian terrestrial interests. He recognised the absolute primacy of continental concerns. His Red Fleet went out to sea to hunt down Polaris submarines and 'protect our motherland', not to contest sea control. The occasional forays of Russian fleets, to Tsushima, or to Syria, may catch the headlines, but the underlying rationale has not changed.[91]

Like other continental military hegemons Petrine Russia used naval force for terrestrial missions, relying on fortresses and armies to meet the challenge of British seapower. Ultimately, the erection of ever more powerful forts at Kronstadt reflected the Russian navy's core role as a strategic defence. Russian battlefleets were used cautiously, usually in defensive roles, often sacrificed to save bases or territory. The classic Russian naval operations in major conflicts are Sevastopol in 1854–5, Port Arthur in 1904–5 and Sevastopol in 1942–3. Although all ended in defeat, the heroic defence of those naval bases was celebrated. Russians understood the reality of their naval project. In the first decade of the nineteenth century a massive stock exchange was erected on the St Petersburg waterfront. Outside stood a pair of rostral columns, based on the Roman originals of Caio Duilio, pillars adorned with the beaks of captured galleys, marking the destruction of seapower states. By a stroke of fate the building became the Naval Museum that chronicled Russia's resistance to seapower.

The short, ineffective existence of the St Petersburg Bourse emphasised the reality that Russia, in its various forms, has never been, and will never become, a seapower. A vast land empire, focused on Moscow, Russia combined mystic religious dreams of a third Roman universal monarchy with the bitter legacy of Mongol occupation and endless western invasions. Those experiences emphasised the primacy of security and stability, defensible borders, strong fortresses and buffer zones. Peter did not attempt to change that reality. He used naval power with great skill to enhance his military campaigns, and built a Western city on the sea to link his country with the science, technology and machinery he needed to develop the country. Yet the enduring emblem of his reign is neither St Petersburg nor the navy, but the great fortress at Kronstadt, the defensive bastion that made it possible to build them. Peter's genius lay in choosing what to borrow, what to copy and what to ignore. He chose the military absolutism of Louis XIV and Imperial Rome, despite a deeply personal fascination with the maritime; Russian culture still bears his unique imprint.

CHAPTER 8

England
THE LAST SEAPOWER

The failure of Peter the Great's explosive reorientation of Russian culture to include the ocean emphasised the reality that seapower states cannot be constructed overnight. The English/British seapower state was created over a period of two hundred years.[1] In the 1430s Englishmen debated exchanging the continental ambitions of the Hundred Years War for a seapower model, although such arguments were premature.[2] Not only were England's commercial horizons limited, but insularity conveyed no strategic benefit. Medieval ships could not command the northern seas, and without ship-killing weapons they had little ability to prevent an invasion. Mediterranean galleys proved unequal to the rough, changeable Channel, while cumbersome sailing ships lacked firepower. Unless naval forces could secure the island and control trade, seapower identity was neither realistic nor useful. Furthermore, English kings had no intention of sharing power with the merchants who might support the maintenance of a powerful fleet. Despite these barriers the maritime culture of Burgundian Flanders began to influence English policy. King Edward IV was profoundly impressed by Flemish marine art, but his turbulent career emphasised the inability of

Importing seapower: William III landing at Torbay in 1688, by J. M. W. Turner

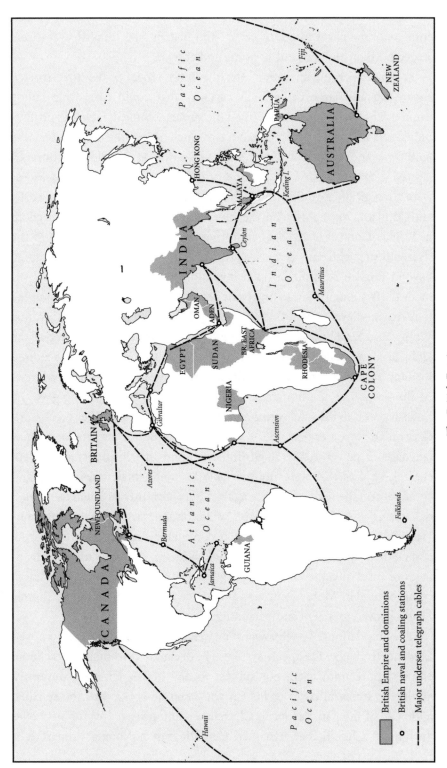

The British Empire

contemporary naval forces to secure the British Isles. English wars were waged both on and for land, at home and abroad.

Seapower became an option after the development of the three-masted square rig and large carvel-built carracks that could carry ship-killing cannon. These warships transformed the strategic context. Edward's posthumous son-in-law Henry VII built two such ships, the *Regent* and the *Sovereign*, and erected artillery forts to command invasion anchorages, layered defences against a repetition of his own invasion. These measures were strategically significant, but they did not change a culture shaped by faith, land and royal power. Furthermore England was not the only kingdom in Britain. Control of the seas could not prevent Scottish invasions in the sixteenth or eighteenth centuries. To the west much of Ireland remained beyond English control, an open invitation to hostile powers. Henry VII made the first small effort to find trade beyond Europe. Henry VIII attempted to revive medieval England's ambitions in Europe, but his advisers, Cardinal Wolsey and Sir Thomas More, recognised that the scale and power of the Holy Roman Empire, and a French nation state that had just acquired Brittany, meant the kingdom could not generate the necessary resources. At the same time the humanist turn and movable-type printing gave the English access to the intellectual and cultural riches of seapower precursors. Greek texts were a critical vector, while Flemish marine art provided a new language of power. Acute Englishmen realised that insularity gave them choices, choices that were not available to continental states. If England could rely on the sea for security against European threats it had the option of focusing on distant lands. Security and economics were closely connected. Habsburg control of Antwerp, which dominated English exports of wool and cloth, shaped More's *Utopia*, a book suffused with the cultural advantages of insularity, the Greek language and three-masted ships.[3] Although compromised by More's continued adherence to a universal Roman Church, *Utopia* proved prescient and persuasive.

The foundations of a seapower state were laid when Henry VIII removed England from the European system. He declared his kingdom to be an empire entire unto itself, not subject to any higher temporal authority, adding an imperial cover to his Crown. Then he broke with the spiritual authority of the pan-European Church, assuming supreme authority over an English Church that remained Catholic, but no longer Roman. It is unclear how far Henry recognised the connection between his actions and those of Venice. To secure his new-made state from foreign invasion Henry developed a standing Royal Navy with heavy-gun armed capital units, led by the *Henry Grace à Dieu*, the first iconic warship in English history, along with coastal forts and an art in which bronze artillery connected ships, forts and royal authority. Henry's naval display was reinforced by crafting a triumphal approach to London, which was first used to impress Charles V in 1522. Starting at the twin forts of Tilbury and Gravesend the processional route passed the royal dockyards at Woolwich and Deptford, Greenwich Palace and the Tower of London, before ending at Whitehall.[4]

Henrician seapower was funded by the dissolution of the monasteries, which filled the royal coffers and released timber, stone and bronze for national defence projects. It was delivered by lawyers and merchants, who became key stakeholders in the new system, a new aristocracy that stood to lose everything in a return to the old faith, and old relationships with Europe. In 1545/6 Henry's fleet defeated a French invasion attempt, and the mythic power of the Mediterranean galley, taking control of the English Channel. Once sea power strategy could secure England against larger states, insularity could be celebrated. The language Henry used to redefine his kingdom as an imperial seapower shaped contemporary culture. Nowhere was the impact of seapower more potent than in the evolution of Elizabethan language. Not only did Shakespeare reuse Henry VIII's words about England being an empire entire unto itself, but he and his peers shaped a seapower-inflected language packed with maritime references that ranged far beyond obvious ideas of power and glory to shipwreck and celestial navigation.[5] The striking impact of sailors on late Tudor culture reflected the anxious days of the Armada, the promise of gold that lured Raleigh to Guiana, and the sense of an oceanic future that inspired *The Tempest*.

The nature of the threat that faced the English state had become clear when Charles V combined the Crown of Spain with that of the Holy Roman Empire. During his reign Spain constructed a suitably imperial identity, as the new Rome, a message that helped justify the conquest of an American empire, while unifying Charles's disparate territories through faith and power.[6] David Lupher has shown that this identity weakened after Charles's abdication ended the direct connection between Spain and the empire, but it remained a powerful theme in Spanish imperialism, emphasising terres-trial military might, and downplaying the critical role of the ocean. Under Charles V, Habsburg Spain assumed it had a destiny to rule, as the modern Roman Empire, bridging the Mediterranean to annihilate an imperial rival. This ideology informed the conquest of Tunis, the art that celebrated power, and the project to invade England. Like many another continental empire Spain linked greatness with constant wars of aggression, like the ancient empires of the classical world.[7]

Spanish efforts reached a suitably Roman consequence in 1535, when Charles V launched a massive amphibious operation to capture the north African corsair city of Tunis from the Muslims. With over 350 ships and a large field army the emperor's pan-European force was larger than the armada his son would send fifty years later: it was large enough to attempt the conquest of England. Not only did Charles see his enterprise in a suit-ably Roman mould, with himself as the new Scipio Africanus, but he was struck by the proximity of Tunis to the ruins of Carthage. His campaign was 'the embodiment of the memory and glory of ancient Rome'.[8] Images of ancient Carthage decorated the Royal Palace at Granada, while Charles commissioned a cycle of twelve tapestries to commemorate the dynastic glory of the expedition a decade later, designed by the artist who accompa-nied the army, aided by poets and historians.[9] These images of glory estab-lished a model of classically inspired overseas conquest that endured. They became a totem of Habsburg imperium, initially displayed in Brussels, and then at the Alcazar in Madrid. A second set belonged to Charles's sister the Dowager Queen of Portugal, who left them to her son. King Sebastian attempted his own Tunis campaign, with catastrophic consequences. When Philip II presided over the Portuguese Cortes in 1581 he displayed this set of the Tunis tapestries. While the Habsburgs hoarded their tapestries the English used the superb set commissioned by Lord Howard of Effingham, who had seen the Tunis set, to celebrate his victory over the Armada to line the walls of the House of Lords. They became the backdrop to every debate about war, power and policy until 1834, when the building was destroyed by fire. These Anglo-Flemish masterpieces had long been the ultimate visual representation of English seapower.

The Roman analogy remained potent through Philip II's long war with England and his conflicts with the Ottoman Empire, another claimant to the legacy of Rome. In 1586 Bernardino de Escalante, cleric and inquisitor, launched the project to conquer England. He had spent fourteen months in the kingdom, in the service of his royal master, Philip II, and he would have been familiar with the Tunis tapestries and Livy's text. In 1591, despite the failure of the first armada, Escalante called for another, consciously comparing the struggle between Spain and England to the Punic conflict. He knew enough Roman history to realise that the failure of Regulus' expedition had been followed by the success of Scipio's. Spain was the new Rome and 'only a direct attack on England would stop Elizabeth and her subjects from supporting the Dutch, ravaging the Indies and attacking Spanish ports and ships'.[10] The rising power and wealth of Spain, which provided military power for the Counter-Reformation, made it necessary to develop the Navy Royal of Elizabeth's reign into a technologically advanced sea-control fleet, relying on gunnery and seamanship. This fleet defeated the Spanish amphibious task force that entered the Channel in the summer of 1588, a campaign that became the foundation myth of the English state, combining divine judgement, superior skill and a national hero neither royal nor aristocratic. Francis Drake and his vehement Protestant faith emphasised England's divergence from Catholic Europe, and showed the English a world beyond the seas, wide open for commerce. What Drake did at sea Richard Hakluyt and Walter Raleigh reinforced from the library, shaping a history and mythology of seapower that consciously connected English success with precursor states, incorporating the classical seapower agenda of Thucydides.[11] While Victorian authors delighted in connecting the Elizabethans with their own global pre-eminence, they did not realise the conscious creation of the Tudor seapower identity or the contingent nature of its ultimate success. A century of turmoil and trouble separated the Armada from the Dutch invasion of 1688 and the final emergence of an English seapower state, a century in which nothing was certain.

Between the Reformation and 1604 the English state found few occasions on which to express its cultural identity to visiting monarchs. However, Queen Elizabeth made three processions to St Paul's Cathedral in the City of London to celebrate a defining naval victory. Consciously based on Roman triumphs Elizabeth paraded captured trophies and standards into the temple. After the restoration of peace in 1604 the Danish King Christian IV visited London with a fleet of great ships. King James's brother-in-law also employed Dutch artists to represent seapower. Suitably inspired, James, a highly ceremonial monarch, created a new icon of national power, the great ship *Prince Royal*.[12] The new ship rejected the lessons of the Spanish War, which had emphasised fast, agile ships, to focus on size and firepower. Charles I pushed the model to its limits with the astonishing *Sovereign of the Seas*, a gilded masterpiece of Caroline allegory and art, myth and magic, wrapped around the world's most powerful fighting ship.

Lacking the financial strength to sustain the naval power required to secure the kingdom, the Tudor state relied on private enterprise to reinforce the war fleet. However, Elizabeth and her Stuart successors were unwilling to share power with the rising economic powerhouse that became the City of London, and without that concession the City was not prepared to supply the monarch with funds for the navy. Consequently, England acquired ships, the art and architecture of seapower, a maritime national hero and a suitable foundation myth, but it lacked the political structures and economic means essential to sustain a seapower identity. Seventeenth-century political turmoil was a question of identity, choosing between, on the one hand, absolutist monarchy, obsessed with religious orthodoxy, landed wealth and stability, and, on the other, an egalitarian oligarchy led by commercial wealth and overseas trade, willing to use sea power strategy to become a great power in defiance of the limitations of location and population. Initial attempts to establish a new identity foundered on the rocks of royal absolutism. The legal argument of John Selden's *Mare Clausum*, that the kings of England had ruled the adjacent seas for six hundred years, was represented by Charles I's great ship *Sovereign of the Seas*, built with deeply divisive taxes.[13] Without the support of Parliament, which had been alarmed by this statement of absolutist royal grandeur, Charles could not develop the new identity, or secure the seas.

It fell to an oligarchic republic to test the English seapower model, using a second windfall of landed wealth, from sequestered royal and royalist property, to build the largest battlefleet in Europe. Taking command of the Channel this fleet forced the leading maritime trading nation, the Dutch Republic, to surrender some trade. The regicide Republic broke the spell of royal absolutism, demonstrating how to mobilise the state's latent power to improve security and enhance economic development. In 1650, as Julian Corbett observed, the Commonwealth fleet made England into a significant power in the Mediterranean. It crushed the last Royalist forces at sea, disciplined the Barbary corsairs, and browbeat Spain and Portugal into complying with English demands:

> Henceforward the national navy was to be a regular force of Government ships, built and maintained for war alone ... For the first time the protection of the mercantile marine came to be regarded almost as the chief end for which the regular navy existed, and the whole of naval strategy underwent a profound modification in English thought ...
>
> We forget that so soon as the mercantile marine became a recognised burden on the navy, the main lines of commerce became also the main lines of naval strategy, and the crossing of the trade routes its focal points. This, although strategists, for the purposes of commending their views to the public and Treasury, naturally write in terms of commerce, we must never forget that what they were really aiming at was the command of the sea by the domination of the great trade routes and the acquisition of focal points as naval stations.[14]

There would be no going back: henceforth the City of London would expect naval protection, whoever sat on the throne. The navy served the City, and the City provided the necessary funds.

The new strategic focus on commerce and sea control was represented by a new iconic ship, one that spoke of military might and a ruthless determination to dominate. Cromwell followed Henry VIII and Charles I, using the *Naseby* to represent personal ambition, and a new, distinctly different state. Where Charles I deployed the Saxon King Edgar commanding seven kings as the figurehead of his great ship, the *Naseby* featured Cromwell, the armoured horseman, trampling seven foes.

The Commonwealth secured command of the seas by building a navy focused on battles fought using big ships and linear tactics to maximise firepower, and creating a professional officer corps. These developments enhanced the strategic power of navies; they became suitable symbols for an aspiring great power. At his Restoration in 1660 Charles II recognised the new identity had taken root among his subjects, and spent his reign balancing personal ambitions for an autocratic Catholic state against the economic opportunities and security benefits of seapower. These identities were fundamentally irreconcilable, as Louis XIV and Peter the Great would discover. Unwilling to share power with Parliament, Charles could not mobilise the resources to sustain the navy. His flagship, Cromwell's *Naseby*, hastily renamed *Royal Charles*, symbolised a transient state, as yet unsure of its identity. In 1667 Johan de Witt's seapower fleet captured the *Royal Charles*, highlighting the political impasse that had left the English fleet unmanned, and exposing the Restoration regime's failure to create political consensus around seapower. Charles possessed a potent battlefleet, but Parliament did not trust him with the money to use it.

The logic of seapower was impossible to ignore, as the Duke of Buckingham observed in the build-up the Third Anglo-Dutch War:

> The undoubted interest of England is Trade, since it is that only which can make us either Rich or Safe, for without a powerful Navy, we shall be Prey to our Neighbours, and without Trade we could neither have Sea-Men nor Ships.[15]

The king hoped his navy could seize enough trade from the Dutch to make him independent of Parliament, but the Dutch fleet proved strong enough to outlast him for a second time in 1672–4.

Unable to break the political impasse Charles turned his attention to the language of seapower. Familiar with the royal naval art of his predecessors, and contemporary cultural trends in the Dutch Republic and France, Charles promoted himself as Neptune, sovereign of the seas, alongside his cousin Louis XIV, the self-proclaimed Jupiter and Roman Emperor. Charles moved the centre of seapower culture across the North Sea, and began work on a new Palace at Greenwich, the ceremonial entrance to London, because he required 'an auditorium for diplomatic entries'.[16] When de Witt's 'True Freedom' Republic collapsed in April 1672, Charles invited Dutch seafarers, merchants and skilled artisans to come to England. The two Willem van de Veldes responded. Charles paid them each a retainer of £100 a year: the Elder would draw his ships, the Younger would paint them. James, Duke of York, the Lord High Admiral, provided a further £50 each. Any pictures would be paid for separately. Charles also provided a studio in the Queen's House, part of the evolving Greenwich Palace complex. Such patronage greatly exceeded anything the Dutchmen had obtained in their native land, even in the great days of Dutch seapower, commerce and empire. In return they transformed the king's fleet into totems of power and glory as England evolved into a seapower state. England acquired naval power and cultural leadership in parallel, inextricably intertwined through the iconic power of 'Great Ships'.

Royal and elite patronage would be essential to the creation of English marine art; unlike the United Provinces there were few private buyers among the middling sort. Lisa Jardine has described the English 'plundering' the cultural riches of the Republic, but such comments miss the deeper import of conscious emulation. The English did far more than obtain artefacts; marine art was part of the transfer of seapower.

Willem van de Velde the Elder became the English official war artist, sailing around the battles off the Schooneveld in 1673, just as he had with the Dutch fleet the year before. Realising that a 'sovereign of the seas' needed great art, Charles recalled Willem before the last major battle, taking him on a royal visit to the fleet. This resulted in a majestic statement of royal dominion from his son's easel. Willem the Elder also created tapestry designs of naval battles for James, Duke of York.[17] Willem the Younger developed a new iconography for the English, replacing the calm scenes of shipping favoured by the Dutch with the ship in a storm, and the stern and quarter view of flagships. The English preference for ships weathering the storm may have reflected troubled times, while the stern and quarter, 'the most imposing and distinctive view of a man of war', emphasised royal power, naval prowess and the prominent place of senior officers in the lexicon of national glory.[18] Willem treated England's great warships as specific and iconic, reflecting English naval symbolism dating back to *The Embarkation of Henry VIII at Dover* of 1539. Initially, these images promoted royal agendas, but after 1688 they represented the nation, as the king ceded control of the Royal Navy to the City of London. Royal patronage prompted the leading men of Restoration England to hire the Van de Veldes to decorate their homes, adopting the new language of seapower.

Early versions of the 'new' images were installed at Ham House, the residence of the Duke of Lauderdale, a key royal adviser, in 1673.[19] Remmelt Daalder's contention that the royal brothers valued the Van de Veldes' work 'for its more workaday aspects, namely the ability to produce accurate depictions of ships and events at sea', underestimates royal ambition and the impact of images that conveyed the seapower message to English audiences. They shaped an English taste that still endures.

Not that Charles was content with one language of power. Having made peace with the Dutch in 1674 he soothed the disappointment of an inconclusive conflict with a fabulous Baroque allegory by Antonio Verrio. *The Sea Triumph of Charles II* represents the king riding in Neptune's chariot, pursued by Victory, the motto 'Sovereign of the Seas under heaven' bolstered by an imperial crown. Stuart claims to maritime sovereignty had been central to the outbreak of the two Dutch wars. Having made Charles the aquatic equal of Louis XIV, Verrio decorated the state apartments of Windsor Castle.[20] The *Sea Triumph*, which used the artistic language of Louis XIV's court, formed a striking contrast to the sober images of the Van de Veldes, but the combination transformed the cultural history of seapower.

Charles's bid to be Sovereign of the Seas did not impress Parliament, which refused to hand him unfettered access to the nation's resources. Restoration England was a rich country, and a weak state. Stuart seapower identity emphasised royal magnificence, rather than commercial expansion. James II discovered that the English would not follow him back into the Roman Church or the European absolutist system that it helped to sustain, agendas incompatible with a true seapower identity. At James II's fall the iconic vessels that linked the Crown to the fleet, along with Britannia, a maritime warrior princess, trident in hand, the Pallas Athena of English seapower, came to embody the nation. James's contribution to the construction of an English seapower identity was to break the deadlock that had paralysed the process for decades. The prospect of a Catholic dynasty forced the country to choose between absolutism and oligarchy. The landed elite and the City of London handed the crown to the half-Stuart Dutch Stadholder and his Protestant Stuart wife, in return for a share of political power. The commercial classes were committed to seapower. Recognising London as another, larger, Amsterdam, William III compromised. He needed English money and resources to resist Louis XIV's universal monarchy, while both seapower cities feared Louis's mercantilist economic policies. Within half a decade the Revolution Settlement had created a Constitutional Monarchy, State Bank and National Debt, enabling England to become a true seapower by releasing deep reserves of fiscal power and national determination that had remained beyond the reach of William's absolutist uncles. The initial tranche of debt rebuilt the battlefleet after a heavy defeat at Beachy Head in 1690 left England vulnerable to invasion by James II and his French allies.

At Beachy Head, Louis XIV's navy repeated the triumph of Caio Duilio, shattering Anglo-Dutch naval power and securing sea control. Had they understood sea power the French might have won the war. By occupying the western approaches to the English Channel the French could have crushed Anglo-Dutch trade, using privateers screened by the battlefleet, forcing the allies to fight, or submit. Instead the French wasted time preparing an invasion to overthrow the English state. Suitably alarmed, the English mobilised their fiscal power and rebuilt the battlefleet before Louis could assemble an army. Having defeated the French battlefleet at Barfleur-La Hougue in 1692, the Royal Navy was rapidly reconfigured from a top-heavy battlefleet into a fully rounded sea-control force, with a major increase in trade defence vessels, and a rapidly acquired focus on escorting convoys.[21] It had become the navy of a seapower state, a point the House of Commons emphasised when it voted through the Convoys and Cruisers Act of 1708, which enshrined trade defence in law. The navy served the City of London, not the Crown. In return the City funded William's European wars, support that it exploited to develop extra-European trade, and crush the commercial threat of a revived Antwerp. None of William's successors would contest the new order.

Investing in the national debt committed the City of London and the landed elite to the Revolution Settlement: a restored Catholic monarch would not repay the money. With aristocracy and capital committed to the new order, support for the exiled Stuarts was restricted to the landless and penniless. Despite internal opposition and external enemies, seapower Britain would flourish for 250 years, years in which the nature and identity of the state was constantly debated, melding past and present into a continuum of seapower ideas and agendas.

England became a seapower by adopting a republican model, turning their kings into hereditary figureheads, to hide the dominion of the City of London over landed interests. To be a true seapower England had to link the men of money with the ultimate instrument of power: when the navy of Charles II and James II became the City of London's navy, the City opened its coffers. The new political model released unprecedented resources, which were used to sustain suitably maritime strategies. Although the first monarch of the new system, the Dutch Stadholder, facilitated the process, thereafter the new system did not require royal leadership. This was essential, for, as

Johan de Witt had observed, hereditary systems often fail to produce suitable leaders. While the English adopted the oligarchic political structure of a seapower state, they retained a regal figurehead, and preserved the status of the landed aristocracy. Although indebted to the Dutch for much of their new political model the English created a structure that enabled the capitalists to share power with manufacturing and an open aristocracy.[22] The open aristocracy enabled capitalists to convert commercial profit into elite landed status.

When the revived Anglo-Dutch fleet defeated the French at Barfleur, they pursued the scattered remnants of the Sun King's fleet into the shallow bays of northern Normandy. At Cherbourg and La Hougue they burnt several great ships, including Louis's iconic flagship, *Soleil Royal*. Both Van de Velde the Younger and Abraham van Diest captured the moment when Louis XIV's naval ambitions went up in smoke, along with his hopes of a universal monarchy.[23] This powerful statement of seapower triumphant formed a striking contrast to the Carthaginian destruction that Louis had expected to impose on the defeated seapowers.

In two great wars between 1688 and 1713 England became 'the sea power, without any second'.[24] Seapower broke Louis XIV's Roman ambitions, enhanced English trade and extended the maritime empire. William and the English ministers who took control after his death in 1702 transferred sea power from an Anglo-Dutch consortium to a British preserve as the Republic faded. Having become a seapower by shifting power from the king, Parliament's first peacetime act in 1697 was to demobilise William's army, in case it became a tool of royal autocracy. English security, unlike that of the Dutch, depended on a battlefleet, not armies and fortresses.[25] This decision ensured England dominated the sea when war resumed in 1702, while military mobilisation was dominated by mercenaries, professional formations hired for war. This approach was popular with politicians who opposed Crown power, and echoed the choices of other seapowers. The British were still raising mercenary formations for service in the Crimean War one hundred and fifty years later. Parliament decided that Britain's contribution to alliance warfare would be naval and economic, not military. Even in the existential conflicts between 1793 and 1815 Britain did not conscript soldiers, other than for home defence, or attempt to raise a continental army. Instead it steadily increased taxation to sustain the costly strategic instruments of a classic seapower state, the oceanic sea-control battlefleet and the cruisers that secured British trade.[26] The choice was a fundamental part of being a seapower. William understood the commercial imperatives and strategic logic of seapower. In the brief period of peace between 1697 and 1702 he worked tirelessly to secure commercial advantages for his states, deploying fleets to the Baltic and developing Partition Treaties that secured colonial territory and commercial advantages for both countries by permitting a Bourbon to be King of Spain. War broke out because Louis underestimated the determination of the seapowers to secure trade and maintain the Franco-Belgian border.[27]

Despite using the navy as a deterrent William III did not need his uncle's artistic propaganda: the 'Glorious Revolution' had enshrined seapower at the core of the new political system. His primary concern was to resist French hegemony on land. William and Mary transformed Charles II's incomplete Palace at Greenwich into a Hospital for decayed seafarers, and cancelled the Van de Veldes' retainer. Verrio, a Catholic, was obliged to resign. However, the new iconography had already taken hold, the artists found other patrons: not only did 'it became all the rage to commission ship portraits', but Verrio returned to royal service.[28] Seapower identity had taken root in England, exemplified in Willem van de Velde the Younger's commanding *Royal Sovereign* of 1704.

Early in the new century the artistic languages of seapower were melded on the ceiling of the Painted Hall at Sir Christopher Wren's Naval Hospital at Greenwich, transforming Charles's self-aggrandising palace into a statement of national consequence. Designed for maximum impact the opening broadside of a new English seapower identity was located at the ceremonial gateway to London. The Hospital provided British seapower with a cultural core, largely borrowed or stolen, while the Painted Hall celebrated the fleets that secured the trident of the oceans, the scientists who would help retain it occupying the margins of an image centred on the triumph of William III and Queen Mary, the success of the 1688 Revolution and the defeat of Louis XIV's Catholic absolutism. The list of donors revealed how royal patronage, wealthy City men and the estates of attainted Jacobites funded a Baroque palace to house elderly and injured seamen, men who had fought and suffered to transform the Stuart boast of sovereignty at sea into a Hanoverian reality. King, state and wealth were united in a single gesture of munificence that placed the sea at the heart of British identity, celebrating the defeat of continental imperialism, Jacobite absolutism and Bourbon mercantilist economics.[29] Because marine art followed the realities of power the artist had to be English. Sir Francis Thornhill, was chosen for his nationality as well as his talent.

As the ceremonial entrance to London, an artistic embodiment of a dynamic seapower culture and a popular tourist attraction, the Painted Hall required a guide book. Thornhill's *An Explanation of the Painting in the Royal-Hospital at Greenwich* of 1726 explained the allegorical display in French and English.[30] Although the fabulous Hall was rarely used for dining, William III's birthday was an annual fixture.

On his journey from Hanover to London, George I was taken ashore at Greenwich, where the as yet incomplete Painted Hall provided a masterclass in English exceptionalism. Accommodating decayed men of the sea in the nation's finest Baroque palace emphasised that Britain was a seapower, not a continental state, and the navy ranked far higher than the army.[31] Having made their submission to seapower the Hanoverian dynasty would be painted onto the west wall.[32] George ruled an enlarged state, including Scotland and Ireland. These new parts of the United Kingdom were never wholly convinced by the seapower vision. The Lowland majority in Scotland found opportunities and profit in the 1707 Act of Union; Jacobite Highlanders did not, and like many in Ireland remained problematic. Predominantly Catholic communities resisted English identities based on Protestantism and seapower, retaining links to Rome and a Catholic distaste for the oceans. The impact of seapower identity beyond the lands of the Tudor monarchy, England and Wales, was uneven at best. The Royal Navy remained resolutely English long after 1707, as Earl St Vincent's disdain for Scots officers a century later suggests.

The new state, and the seapower values of oligarchic government that reflected land and capital, generated the same hatred and fear among continental autocracies as older seapowers. By 1713 Britain had become a European great power, fleets working from recently acquired bases at Gibraltar and Minorca commanded the western Mediterranean, while others restrained Russian ambitions in the Baltic. Naval power promoted economic expansion, balanced continental rivalries and distracted imperial opponents. The British would devote much effort to European politics, as the Venetians had in previous centuries: in both cases the object was a stable, balanced state system in which the powers' unique status would be secure and their trade could prosper.

Despite the Hanoverian monarchs being significant players in the politics of Germany, as Electors of the Holy Roman Empire, key stakeholders in the British seapower state, including the City of London, rejected any attempt to make Europe the primary policy focus. Taking their intellectual lead from Henry St John, Lord Bolingbroke, the 'Patriot' opposition to George II and Robert Walpole stressed that seapower and empire were the 'British' future, not the entangling, exposed 'Beggarly Electorate'. For Bolingbroke, an avid classicist, Thucydides was the ideal tutor for statesmen and generals.[33] In *The Idea of the Patriot King* of 1738 he demanded a national renewal through the example of a heroic monarch, with Queen Elizabeth an obvious model. The tools of greatness were 'fleets covering the ocean, bringing home wealth by the returns of industry, carrying assistance or terror abroad by the direction of wisdom, and asserting triumphantly the right and honour of Britain, as far as waters roll and winds can waft them'.

As Isaac Krammick observed, 'the strains of "Rule Britannia" seem to arise from these lines', because both texts were written for the 'Patriot' opposition that gathered around Frederick, Prince of Wales.[34] 'Rule Britannia', the unofficial national anthem, was written for the 'Patriots', and celebrated naval glory in the Caribbean. The sentiments, especially the powerful seapower themes, were nothing new for the author, poet and playwright James Thompson. In 1727 the arrest of British seafarers in the Caribbean by Spanish coastguards prompted the poem 'Britannia', a hymn to seapower:

> This is your glory; this is your wisdom: this
> The native power for which you were design'd
> By fate, when fate designed the firmest state,
> That e'er was seated on the subject sea.[35]

It was no coincidence that Thompson penned these lines as a new German king took the British throne. They were an overt reminder that the seapower identity that had been read to his father at Greenwich remained the national agenda. In 1730 Thompson added classical references in *Sophonisba*, a Carthaginian tragedy, combining seapower and history to shape an evolving identity.[36] Carthage had become common currency in British and French debates. Not only did 'Rule Britannia' celebrate naval-imperial glory, but it made the City of London central to national identity.[37]

After 1713 English intellectuals linked their new-found consequence with older seapowers, but they were unwilling to explore the deeper meaning of their condition. This task fell to a Frenchman. Startled by the defeat of Louis XIV's proto-Roman ambitions at the battle of Blenheim in 1704, Charles de Secondat, Baron Montesquieu, sought a philosophical explanation for the failure of Bourbon imperium through the contrasting classical exemplars of contemporary policy. Having moved to London to study the English system, Montesquieu consumed Bolingbroke's polemical works as they appeared. These urged a seapower policy, driven by trade and reliant on naval might, to balance Europe, not engage in it, sustaining the theme through classical analogies.[38]

Montesquieu considered Britain the modern Carthage, a commercial republic, combining a great navy with a political system controlled by the merchant class, enabling the state to access deep economic resources to sustain long wars, and an empowered citizen class. These strengths had enabled England to defeat the new Roman universal monarchy.[39]

Montesquieu described Britain as a republic without a hint of irony. He understood how the British state functioned, and how it had been transformed from a marginal actor into a great power between 1688 and 1714, to the great disadvantage of absolutist France. Only a 'republic' could sustain the necessary long-term focus on maritime commerce and naval might. That Montesquieu chose Carthage as his model revealed the underlying reality of French ambition and his reading of Livy. A century and a half later, the American naval officer and strategist Captain Alfred Thayer Mahan produced a theoretical model of sea power that had six bases. It was nothing more than a gloss on the French analysis of Bolingbroke.[40] Mahan proved especially popular in Victorian Britain because he echoed established British literary classics, and endorsed current strategic thinking.

Montesquieu's analysis exercised a profound influence on French thinking about culture, strategy and seapower. The French dehumanised Britain as a Punic 'other' because it was a seapower 'corrupted' by the culture of commerce and the perfidious politics of a 'nation of shopkeepers'. It must be 'destroyed'. There was nothing original in the post-1790 republican tirade, or the use of this language by other continental empires. For all their insulting

intent French commentaries, a perversion of Montesquieu's rational analysis, proved singularly ineffective. The British proudly owned their Punic
progenitors; this time pan-European continental empires would go down in
flames. Although the British were the new Carthaginians, eighteenth-century
British aristocrats identified with the Roman republican elite, landed men
who shared political power, and ensured schools and universities taught
their sons the classic virtues of honour, integrity and courage. They had
themselves portrayed as Roman senators, to stress the virtue that justified
their opposition to corrupt ministers and kings who tried to assume more
power. Like Roman senators they opposed universal rights and populist
democracy – because they would weaken the state, and remove their privileges. Yet behind their togas and temples they knew Britain was not Rome,
subtly modifying the arguments to incorporate, rather than reject, the men
of trade and the sea, men with whom they shared political power, into whose
families they were content to marry. In Georgian Britain land, money and
trade combined to tame the cultural threat of populist politics: these men
believed the oligarchic compromise could not be destroyed without wrecking
the British state. Hannibal would have understood.

European powers consistently overestimated Britain's willingness to
compromise seapower to secure Hanover. After 1760, when George III
assumed the throne, German links faded: George never left southern England.
He was an English king, with a taste for sea pictures, seagoing and science. His
'empire' was British, not Holy or Roman, and he appointed an official marine
artist. These choices proved critical to the development of national culture.[41]
They were severely tested by the American War of Independence, when what
was quickly becoming a Roman Empire of land and people rose in revolt. The
British seapower state learnt a hard lesson: the imperial glory of 1763 had
disguised the underlying reality of profound weakness. Britain lacked the
political cohesion and military might to suppress the rising or retain the
territory. In the face of French, Spanish and Dutch hostility Britain abandoned the American Colonies and concentrated on retaining the sugar
islands of the Caribbean, India and the strategic fortress of Gibraltar. Once
that had been achieved, peace was secured by the economic exhaustion of
France and Spain. The empire that emerged after 1783 was significantly less
'continental than its short-lived precursor'.[42] In the cycle of wars that ravaged
Europe between 1793 and 1815 the British focused on command of the sea,

the key to security and economic advantage for insular states, while working with allies to restrict French expansion, whenever that was possible. They fought on alone for long periods, waiting for economic attrition and the impact of French occupation to bring other powers back into the conflict. Eventually, Napoleon's pan-European empire was overthrown and the British went home. They had no desire to become a continental power.

Following, if not quite understanding, Montesquieu, French politicians thought it an insult to call the British 'Carthaginians'. Napoleon added the 'nation of shopkeepers' line, perhaps unaware that all seapower states were 'nations of shopkeepers'. Montesquieu's argument would resonate on both sides of the Channel down to Napoleon's abdication, an event anticipated by George Canning, MP for the great seaport of Liverpool and future prime minister, on 10 January 1814. Canning connected his constituents with the Carthaginians:

> I say, we have reason to rejoice, that, throughout this more than Punick war, in which it has so often been the pride of our enemy to represent herself as the Rome and England as the Carthage of modern times, (with, at least, this colour for the comparison, that the utter destruction of the modern Carthage has uniformly been proclaimed to be indispensable to the greatness of her rival,) – we have, I say, reason to rejoice, that, unlike our assigned prototype, we have not been diverted by internal dissension from the vigorous support of a vital struggle; that we have not suffered distress nor clamour to distract our counsels, or to check the exertion of our arms.[43]

His emphasis on the existential nature of French war aims was significant.[44] France had long been the 'other' that shaped British identity, but after 1713 it had not aspired to 'universal monarchy', as it had under Louis XIV. The Revolution and empire revived that threat, melding it with radical social agendas that heightened British anxiety, and reinforced cohesion across classes and regions. Canning's speech celebrated that cohesion, using classical learning and an acute ear for the temper of public opinion to highlight the role the great port city had played in the anticipated victory. That Canning 'usually preferred to point in a direction to which public opinion was already inclined' gave his words a peculiar significance.[45]

Not that the analogy was restricted to French insults. Under the Hanoverians the Circular Harbour had been rebuilt. The Royal Dockyards were reconstructed in majestic, classical form, vast edifices of brick and stone, recorded as art and model to inform the king and ensure such costly projects became part of the deterrent. A classical Admiralty building on Whitehall, the nerve centre of the seapower state, represented the political will to act, while British naval art captured each new round of victory.[46] Between 1793 and 1814 J. M. W. Turner developed an artistic language to represent the role of British seapower in opposing Napoleonic military imperialism, evolving a seapower drawn from the Van de Veldes.[47] Turner reworked Willem van de Velde the Younger's great ship, the *Royal Sovereign* of 1704, into a national icon for a new age. His triptych of HMS *Victory* and mighty *Trafalgar* two decades later represented challenge and response, triumph against all odds, security based on naval might, and the high cost of that success – anticipating Byron's celebration of Nelson as 'Britannia's God of War'. Furthermore he joined Canning in celebrating Britain's 'Carthaginian' victory, expanding the language of Claude Lorrain. In 1843 a young John Ruskin emphasised what it meant to be a seapower by referring to Turner's great picture of 1815, *Dido building Carthage, or, the Dawn of the Carthaginian Empire*:

> The principal object in the foreground ... is a group of children sailing toy boats. The exquisite choice of this incident, as expressive of the ruling passion which was to be the source of future greatness, in prefer-ence to the tumult of busy stonemasons or arming soldiers, is quite as appreciable when it is told as when it is seen – it has nothing to do with the technicalities of painting; a scratch of the pen would have conveyed the idea and spoken to the intellect as much as the elaborate realizations of colour. Such a thought as this is something far above all art; it is epic poetry of the highest order.

Ruskin contrasted such profundity with Claude Lorrain's *Seaport with the Embarkation of the Queen of Sheba*, the image that had inspired Turner.[48] While Turner wished his artistic talent to be judged alongside Claude, he had a very different sense of purpose to his French precursor.[49] Claude evinced no interest in seapower as culture and identity, because his patrons did not see the sea. Turner transformed the Mediterranean harbour at sunrise into a celebration of Britain's role in the defeat of Napoleon, the latest enemy of seapower. As British seapower identity evolved into an industrial age the childish toys of 1815 became the dynamic steamboat of *The Fighting Temeraire*, the harbinger of future glories.

Turner spent fifty years painting seapower, engaging with the classical canon as he developed the distinctive vision that culminated in the *Temeraire*. Not only did that picture catch British seapower on the cusp of transition from wooden walls to industrial power, but it remains the ultimate English picture. Nor was Turner the only Englishman to see the connection. In 1845 diplomatic disputes with France, coinciding with the development of steam-powered warships, sparked an invasion panic. General Sir George Murray, Master General of the Ordnance, responsible for national defence, advised his old friend the Duke of Wellington, Commander in Chief of the Army, that the French:

> conceiving themselves to be <u>Romans</u> of modern date, will at all times cherish the idea, that to attack us in our own country will prove, as in the case of the Carthaginians, the most efficient mode of crushing that ascendancy, so mortifying to them, that this country has so long enjoyed.[50]

Although such existential anxieties prompted an invasion panic, they soon subsided. There would be no modern Zama. British confidence was restored by naval mobilisation and new totems, Nelson's Column and Trafalgar Square, the capstone of the seapower project, were completed. Nelson's death in the moment of victory and elaborate state funeral established him as the war god of the British state, deified by the City of London, whose interests he had served so well. With Nelson's old comrade in arms, Prince William Henry, on the throne between 1830 and 1837 as William IV, the synergy of state, monarchy and fleet was complete. British royalty would serve at sea with distinction long into the twentieth century. The future King George VI fought at the battle of Jutland, completing the synergy of monarchy and seapower begun in 1714.

Turner's admiration of science, industry and technology, highlighted in the *Temeraire*, changed the language of seapower identity. In 1856, five years after his powerful assessment of seapower, an older John Ruskin, critic, poet and philosopher, put the wooden warship at the centre of seapower culture in a hymn to the collective efforts of a maritime society:

> Take it all in all, a Ship of the Line is the most honourable thing that man, as a gregarious animal, has ever produced. By himself, un-helped, he can do better things than ships of the line; he can make poems and pictures, and other such concentrations of what is best in him. But as a being living in flocks, and hammering out, with alternate strokes and mutual agreement, what is necessary for him in those flocks, to get or produce, the ship of the line is his first work. Into that he has put as much of his human patience, common sense, forethought, experimental philosophy, self-control, habits of order and obedience, thoroughly wrought handwork, defiance of brute elements, careless courage, careful patriotism, and calm expectation of the judgement of God, as can well be put into a space of 300 feet long by 80 broad. And I am thankful to have lived in an age when I could see this thing so done.[51]

For this achievement, and this alone, he considered his own century was worthy of reverence. Ruskin believed the evolution of the ship, from primitive raft to modern steamer, bore witness to something innate and wonderful in the human spirit. There is little reason to doubt that Pericles, Hannibal, Enrico Dandolo and Johan de Witt had anticipated those sentiments.

Yet Ruskin was already out of date. By 1856 the language of power was shifting to iron and steam, and soon the wooden warship would be but a memory. Where older seapowers had operated in eras of relative technological stability, nineteenth-century Britain needed a new language of seapower that embraced industrial progress. It replaced *Henry Grace à Dieu*, *Sovereign of the Seas* and *Victory* with iron and steel leviathans, exemplified by *Warrior*, two *Dreadnoughts* and the 'Mighty *Hood*', ships that expressed naval power, industrial pre-eminence and national purpose as carefully designed statements in iron and steel. *Warrior* combined styling cues from the old wooden fleet with a sinister black-paint scheme to emphasise scale and power. The ironclad *Dreadnought* of the 1870s, a floating fortress of iron, focused on four heavy guns and two slab-sided funnels that embodied mechanical power. Lord Fisher's epochal *Dreadnought* of 1906 reused those funnels to connect two otherwise very different ships.[52] *Dreadnought* became an Edwardian style icon, and sparked a major arms race. The carefully contrived elegance of HMS *Hood*, achieved through the careful spacing of funnels, superstructure, turrets and masts, was allied to unprecedented length, and spoke of speed and power. In all cases the most important function of the 'great' ships was deterrence.[53] They combined power and history, their old names laden with meaning and myth, catalogues of battle honours and architecture every inch as contrived as terrestrial structures. This was a theatre of power that Charles I had understood.

Turner did not live to see the new order at sea, but they were the direct descendants of the tiny steamboat that towed the *Temeraire*, a name reused for a dreadnought battleship, in a fleet that paid homage to Nelson's navy and other heroic vessels dating back to 1588. These choices were conscious, forcing the rising navy of Imperial Germany to confront the Royal Navy's history. Their impact was obvious: in June 1916 Kaiser Wilhelm II blustered that 'the magic of Trafalgar in broken'. He was wrong. Twenty-five years later the catastrophic destruction of HMS *Hood*, on Empire Day 1941, appeared to herald the end of British seapower, but *Bismarck* was hunted down and sunk a few days later.

British seapower endured because it combined the strategic advantages of insularity with territorial and resource growth, bringing Scotland and, to an extent, Ireland into a state that combined economic dynamism with an expanding population. The territorial empires created on either side of the American Revolution reflected a drift from naval and commercial ports into the hinterland, as settlers sought land, and imperial rivals tried to overturn Britain's advantages. Sir Penderel Moon claimed, 'The English owed their dominion in India to the French; for it was the French example and French rivalry that drew them unwittingly along the path of conquest.'[54] Expansion in North America down to 1776 added significantly to British strategic reach, shipping and manpower, much as the Dominions did in the first half of the twentieth century. Colonies, money and industry ensured Britain was never dwarfed by the European great powers, even those with far larger populations, in large part because the Europeans never pooled their resources to attack the eccentric seapower state. Even between 1779 and 1782 the new League of Cambrai was limited to three long-standing imperial rivals, France, Spain and the Dutch Republic. The rest of Europe was more concerned with local terrestrial issues. Steadily increasing imperial resources, men, money, industry and materiel solved the age-old seapower problem of relative scale. Empire enabled Britain to match the strategic power of larger states such as France, and even the great terrestrial empires.

Between 1688 and 1945 Britain worked within a multi-polar state system to prevent the creation of successive universal monarchies in Europe, sustaining anti-hegemonic coalitions with money and naval might, which compensated for military weakness. Having no ambition to become a European territorial power, beyond a handful of offshore naval bases, Britain consistently upheld the status quo against radical change, a position that attracted allies with similar ambitions. Autocratic and authoritarian European powers could not combine forces to destroy Britain, nor control the spread of seapower's insidious tools, commerce, ideology and politics, because their rivalries were far deeper than any antipathy they had for the offshore islanders. Europe could only become a serious threat if it were controlled by a single hegemonic power. Even Napoleon failed that test. A far greater threat came from a state that pushed political inclusion beyond the British compromise, to levelling democracy. British political elites had always understood the dangers of democracy; most had been educated in the classics, and knew both Plato and Thucydides rather better than they did the history of their own country. The extension of the franchise beginning in 1832 was a slow, drawn-out process, because the legislators knew that every concession diluted the ability of the state to focus on power, profit and identity.

Ultimately, the British seapower state would be destroyed by the United States of America, a rival that stood outside the European state system, and indeed the world order, until the dawn of the twentieth century. Furthermore America wrecked British power while acting as an ally, not an overt enemy, much as Britain had reduced the Dutch between 1689 and 1713. Anglo-American relations since 1782 have often been read in the uplifting terms that Churchill used in his *History of the English Speaking Peoples*, the growth of a shared identity, based on language, law, inclusive politics and enterprise, the sheer scale of the new Republic leading to an inevitable, peaceful transfer of leadership from the tiny island kingdom on the margins of Europe to a far mightier state across the Atlantic, a process speeded up by the immense cost of waging two global wars against Germany. Such rosy hindsight misrepresents fundamental cultural differences, the divergent character and ambition that drove the worldviews of a seapower empire and a continental military state. The two countries were and remain profoundly different. At heart that difference was a question of self-shaped culture and identity.

While both have been great strategic naval powers – the contemporary United States Navy may be the most dominant navy in world history – their aims were strikingly divergent. In 1890 Alfred Thayer Mahan recognised US sea power as the product of strategic and policy choices open to any state with a coast, money and manpower. The United States demonstrated no interest in becoming a seapower state at any time after Andrew Jackson became president.[55]

Cultural difference lay at the heart of the American Revolution, which reshaped British as well as American identity. The British learnt an old seapower lesson: the difficulty in retaining control over settler elites with divergent political and economic agendas focused on the land. They returned to sea control and commerce, moving into the Asia-Pacific region. When new colonies of settlement demanded self-government it was conceded; in return, the imperial garrisons that accounted for almost the entire cost of imperial government were removed. With no troops to pay there was no need for a Stamp Act, nor any power to impose one. The United States moved in the other direction. Although Americans shared British anxieties about standing armies, they needed them to clear the land of Native Americans and deal with servile uprisings.[56] The army was always America's senior service. Many Americans dreamt of ruling a continent; few saw their future on the ocean. After 1800 the Democratic-Republican Party looked inland, modelling itself on an idealised Republican Rome and an imagined Republican France, oblivious to the totalitarian militaristic projects of their illiberal idols. These republicans ensured that the United States would be a continental power, with defence structures dominated by the army and, since 1947, an air force. America adopted continental intellectual and cultural models from France, and after 1871 Imperial Germany. These links can be traced in the methods and training of the US army, the structure of American universities, and the nature of American industry. The American way of war is essentially a resource-heavy version of the German model: firepower, superior technology, big logistics, detailed planning and 'decisive' battle. The purpose of this military is unclear. Self-sufficient in food, fuel and 99 per cent of raw materials, the United States is the world's largest market, intimately connected to the resources and markets of Canada and Mexico. It has no obvious need for external trade or a large army. The sea is literally peripheral: it cannot embody or represent the nation, however much it may appeal to coast dwellers. For nearly half its existence the United States managed with minimal levels of naval power, and came close to abolishing the fleet more than once. After independence the navy was sold, after the Civil War it was left to rot, and in the late 1940s the army and the air force almost destroyed it.[57]

When the United States was created British statesmen were concerned that a country dominated by ports and oceanic trade might become a seapower rival. In 1794 America created a navy for the classic seapower mission of protecting national shipping against pirates, a mission that remained significant during the next fifty years, as no sea-control battlefleet emerged. Instead America lost sight of the sea. During the Wars of the French Revolution and Empire, American merchants made their fortunes carrying goods to France through a British blockade. When Britain seized US blockade-breakers the Democratic-Republican administrations of Jefferson and Madison banned overseas commerce to preserve peace. They were looking elsewhere for an American future. In 1803 Jefferson acquired a vast tract of North America from Napoleon, the 'Louisiana Purchase', transforming the nation from a maritime trading state based around prosperous Atlantic port cities into a continental power, with aspirations to reach the Pacific. Jefferson detested the ship-owners and merchants of the north-east and by 1812 ships and the sea were a minor issue when the United States invaded Canada and Spanish Florida. Both attacks failed, leaving the Madison administration, which had ignored the navy, to rely on privateering, the strategic choice of weak naval powers. The Royal Navy defeated the threat with convoys, patrols, blockades and coastal offensives, before promoting slave and Native American resistance in the Southern States. After the downfall of Napoleon the British captured and burned Washington DC, teaching America that sea power was a terrible weapon in the hands of skilled men. The US-born British naval officer Edward Brenton served with distinction in the War of 1812, reminding the Americans that they had achieved none of their war aims, and that furthermore:

Great Britain has it in her power, while she commands the seas, to convulse the continent of America, by exciting and assisting her discontented subjects. Had twenty thousand men been sent from England, as was originally intended, the rising of the slaves in Virginia would have been most probably fatal to the Southern States.[58]

While the War of 1812 ended with a status quo ante peace, Britain prevented any discussion of the tools of sea power, economic blockade and the right to impress sailors at the Treaty of Ghent and the Congress of Vienna of 1815. Consequently, British naval power dominated US strategic thinking for the next eighty years, focusing defence spending on American Kronstadts.[59]

In 1815 a bankrupt and humiliated Republican administration turned to the press to win a war it had so manifestly lost. In the process it replaced British cultural links with a forceful new identity, one that addressed the boundless opportunities and deep scars of their country, including slavery, the future of Native Americans and levelling democracy. The British recognised the strident triumphalist tone, the constant drumbeat of aggression, and the overt menace of democratic politics. The new self-contained continental culture turned away from the sea, as it had little need for oceans.[60] Although Turner's Carthaginian pictures inspired Thomas Cole's five-part 'The Course of Empire' in the 1830s, which read a similar lesson to a New York audience, Cole subtly shifted the focus from sea to land.[61] The aggressive pursuit of a continental agenda as 'Manifest Destiny' reflected a US cultural identity forged in the disasters of 1812. The Continental United States, another Roman Republic bent on continental hegemony, backed by an explosive growth in manpower, money and industry, demonstrated an alarming propensity for attacking its neighbours. From 1846 to 1848 a large section of the continent, stretching from Arizona to California, was wrenched out of Mexico. Little wonder Latin and South American states feared their mighty neighbour.[62] US national heroes were military, several becoming president, while the country's literature and art moved inland, a shift emphasised by the new capital city, the first artificial city in the new nation, strategically placed at the end of a marginal navigation. Yet post-1815 bravado masked a deep-rooted identity crisis, one that was only resolved when the Civil War (1861–5) imposed northern culture on the south and west. That the Union was preserved by force emphasised the most important reality of the rapidly expanding nation: its greatest enemy was not foreign aggression but internal discord. In the homogenisation of identity the ocean, already a minor theme in the north-east, effectively disappeared, along with the navy and the ocean-going merchant marine.[63] America still used naval power for diplomacy and the promotion of trade, most famously in 1852 when Commodore Perry 'opened' Japan, but it did so in a maritime world dominated by the Royal Navy, in an era dominated by internal concerns.

After 1815 the frontier controlled the shaping of American culture and identity. In 1898 Frederick Jackson Turner observed: 'The existence of an area of free land, its continuous recession, and the advance of American settlement westward explains American development.' Jackson's frontier had the same impact on American culture as the Mediterranean had on the Greeks.[64] The open frontier and the lure of free land explain why the United States diverged from the maritime culture of the early English/British settlers. The immigrants who left the coast for the frontier were Scots/Irish and German, not English: the frontier made them Americans. The ocean gave way to frontier violence and overland exploration, Captain Cook to Lewis and Clark. Once the frontier closed, in cultural terms, the US began looking abroad for an empire.[65] In 1906, Mahan, a prominent exponent of US imperialism, the obvious rationale for a large new navy, planned a book examining 'the influence of territorial and commercial expansion on American history', taking Turner's thesis to sea and across the Pacific. Expansion would replace sea power as the driving element. The project remained inchoate in 1913. Only a few sketches remain. Mahan found the weight of evidence daunting, and the field already occupied.[66] He may have recognised that any such work would highlight US continental exceptionalism and the irrelevance of seapower as culture and identity to its future development.

Having helped overthrow Napoleon's continental imperialism, Britain displayed classic seapower sensibilities. British statesmen took no territory in continental Europe. Having secured the tools of seapower, Britain employed its influence to shape a stable, peaceful, balanced European state system, to prevent a renewed hegemonic thrust by France, or Russia, and open the continent for British commerce. The only territories Britain retained were offshore island bases, Malta, Corfu, Heligoland and Mauritius; the latter, once linked to Cape Town, controlled the trade between Europe and Asia. Britain had no desire to extend its occupation into the interior of Africa. Instead it compelled Algiers to end the enslavement of European sailors, and crushed the Atlantic slave trade. Britain exploited technology, money and power to create the first globalised economy. It knocked down trade barriers, by force or by finance, pioneered new forms of capital movement, invented and laid the first global communications network, the submarine telegraph cable, and used it to build new markets. Britain created a world economy to sustain the seapower fleet that made it a great power.

After 1815 the only threat to Britain's global dominance came from an alliance between France, the only European great power with an oceanic navy, and either Russia or the United States, continental states with significant fleets. This was why British ministers had excluded the Americans from the Vienna peace process. The British statesman Lord Palmerston recognised the threat posed by America's latent power, expansive aims and levelling democracy.[67] Well aware that election slogans such as 'Manifest Destiny' were primarily directed at domestic audiences, Palmerston, who had served in government during the War of 1812, carefully monitored American expansionism, blocking attempts to filibuster Cuba from Spanish rule. The fortress and port of Havana, which commanded the Caribbean, could not be allowed to fall into American hands.

Despite mutual suspicions, and strikingly divergent aims, Britain and the United States kept the peace because the Americans feared British sea power, and the British had no desire to acquire any more continental territory. Both political leaderships were more concerned to trade than fight. Securing limited aims through deterrence was classic seapower behaviour. Between 1815 and 1861 Britain and America had many disputes, but:

> statesmen on both sides always managed to avoid war. The issues were never so serious that good sense, clear diplomatic signalling and timely concession could not avert a conflict that would have profited neither side. Having secured Canada and kept the Spanish in Cuba, Britain was unlikely to fight over the remaining points, not because it could not, but because to do so would weaken its ability to support more significant interests in Europe.[68]

However, Britain was changing. Victory over Napoleon was followed by economic distress, political demands for reform, and pressure to increase the electorate. The old political system privileged aristocratic interests and commercial wealth, largely excluding the middle and working classes. It provided ample opportunities for men of wealth and rank to advance through the political ranks. Public schools ensured the sons of commercial wealth were assimilated into a quasi-aristocratic elite governing oligarchy. The open elite enabled the British system to evolve, adapting to new forms of wealth and power, while avoiding the explosive resentment created by rigid hierarchies and closed elites. It was not democratic. While British statesmen studied ancient Athens, and used ancient Greek in their speeches, to exclude the lower orders, they had no interest in adopting Athenian democracy. The legislators assembled at Westminster were the political nation.[69] The 'Great Reform Act' of 1832, which enfranchised a wealthy middle class, was driven by the anxiety of the Whig party, out of office for half a century, to secure partisan advantage. In government for most of the next two decades the Whigs captured the levers of power, and used Reform to keep them. However, widening the franchise and removing safe seats, long used by rising statesmen, forced politicians to focus on domestic issues. Later extensions of the franchise continued to dilute the critical role of seapower identity in British public life and political support for the navy. By 1884 a growing sense that the political nation had forgotten the critical importance of naval power to the seapower state prompted a spectacular new approach. Alarmist newspaper agitation, discretely backed by the navy, launched four decades of high-profile campaigning that kept naval power at the top of the political agenda. This campaign, backed by the City of London, created populist navalism for a more democratic age.[70] It became increasingly difficult to sustain as twentieth-century reforms moved inexorably towards universal adult suffrage.

The seapower vision shared by eighteenth-century statesmen, and the political class they represented, did not survive into the twentieth century, when a greatly expanded electorate focused on economic well-being and the welfare state. Ancient Athens had used democracy to generate and sustain seapower, but modern democracy, as Mahan feared, proved ill-suited to sustain seapower identity and sea-power navies. In 1890 he observed that 'Popular governments are not generally favourable to military expenditure, however necessary, and there are signs that England tends to drop behind.'[71] Mahan's words reflected his distaste for the excesses of US democracy, a distaste shared by British statesmen and opinion-formers who had seen the reality for themselves. The current state of 'Western' fleets, outside the United States, supports Mahan's assessment that democracy has little space for seapower.

During the American Civil War, the Federal Government came close to starting a war with Britain. The USS *San Jacinto* seized passengers from the British mail steamer *Trent*, in violation of international law. Britain mobilised a fleet to attack New York, and banned the export of Indian saltpetre, a vital ingredient of gunpowder. President Lincoln promptly gave way. The crisis was typical of Anglo-American relations in the period; the British usually conceded minor points, but were quick to sustain their vital interests, including international law.[72]

After the end of the Civil War in 1865, British observers recognised US power was based on military and industrial mobilisation, rather than naval capability. The evisceration of the United States Navy was even more significant. As the United States focused on closing the internal frontier, harnessing domestic resources and developing industrial power, the navy slipped out of sight, reduced to a moribund collection of obsolete wooden gunboats, attempting to uphold US interests against local powers such as Chile, which had more powerful fleets.[73] Mahan commanded one of these craft.

As they grappled with the political consequences of US military power, including the dispute over the *Alabama* claims, the British returned to the old debate about the rise and fall of empires. They began using the concept of seapower in a recognisably modern form in the 1840s, examining older seapower states such as Athens and Venice, hoping to avoid an imperial 'fall' of the type so eloquently addressed by Edward Gibbon in the era of the American Revolution.[74] The debate was widened to include the newly enfranchised, schoolchildren and colonial populations. New 'Victorian Myths of the Sea' emerged, projecting a simplified past onto the present, as a guide to current and future policy.[75] The notion that Trafalgar had stopped a French invasion, the single most impressive myth, ensured the battle was worshipped rather than examined.[76] Once again a Frenchman provided critical insight. Alexis de Tocqueville, a worthy successor to Montesquieu, had many friends among the British Liberal elite. In 1835

Democracy in America predicted that Russia and America would dominate the next century. Pairing the autocratic monolith of the east with the rising republic of the west as the powers of the past and future implied Britain dominated the present.[77] *Democracy* would influence Liberal thinking for decades.[78]

Among those to reflect on de Tocqueville's prediction, John Robert Seeley, Regius Professor of History at Cambridge, traced the origins of the empire to the Tudors.[79] By demolishing 'the purely popular, romantic and fantastic views of the subject which prevail', he tried to 'bring out clearly the exact questions which need to be investigated'. Seeley made a significant contribution to seapower theory, observing that Britain's advantage over France as an imperial power reflected an island state's ability to focus on the sea and avoid costly European commitments.[80] In *The Expansion of England* of 1883, Seeley, like de Tocqueville, contrasted Britain, a seapower, with Russia and America, 'enormous political aggregations', by which he meant empires, created by 'modern inventions which diminish the difficulties created by time and space'.[81] Both were continuous land powers, but 'Between them, equally vast, but not as continuous, with the ocean flowing through it in every direction, lies, like a world-Venice, with the sea for streets, Greater Britain.'

While seapower had important political and cultural consequences, they could be fleeting. For all their brilliance Athens and Venice had been crushed by larger land powers. Seeley argued that only a 'Greater Britain' could compete with the emerging superpowers. He warned that a serious commitment to Europe would constitute a critical danger to the empire, while 'sooner or later we must lose India because sooner or later some war in Europe will force us to withdraw our English troops'.[82]

Expansion sold 80,000 copies in two years, inspiring politicians, journalists and empire-builders from Lord Roseberry and Joseph Chamberlain to W. T. Stead, Alfred Milner, Cecil Rhodes and Mahan.[83] Seeley's multi-disciplinary problem-solving methodology foreshadowed modern approaches. He used seapower sparingly, subtly and with powerful effect. British readers who applauded Mahan's *The Influence of Sea Power upon History* in 1890 had been predisposed to the message by Seeley.[84]

Seeley's 'Greater Britain' of closer political and economic linkage between the various dominions, colonies and dependencies of the empire was a delusion. Imposing Roman imperium on a chaotic scatter of islands, ports and hinterlands that stretched across the globe was at once impossible, as 1776 had demonstrated, and irrelevant. Down to the mid-1870s British statesmen saw empire as a burden to be shared, and then shed: they would civilise, stabilise and democratise before handing the costly task of government and defence to settlers or locals. If colonies of settlement were the first to acquire self-government, the others were only waiting to reach the necessary political maturity. This was a wise decision. In the wars of the twentieth century aid willingly provided by Canada, Australia, New Zealand, South Africa and the colonies transformed British strategic power. The Dominions shared values and heritage: they did not need to be compelled to provide support. Maritime empires have always operated looser federal structures than land empires, colonies such as Carthage and North America evolving into separate states. In both cases the transfer of political power to local authorities created a desire for autonomy in key issues such as taxes and trade, empowering lawyers and merchants to run cities and provinces. Attempts to impose Roman-style central control on the diffuse commercially minded British Empire prompted revolts. After 1782 the British avoided antagonising local sensibilities. Britain was a new Carthage, not a new Rome. It lacked the manpower, resources and continuous land mass to be Roman. That identity was seized by the Americans. The British were happy to use the cultural language of Roman imperial might to sustain their self-image, notably with Nelson's Column and the architecture of Imperial Whitehall, but their deepest concern was to prevent the emergence of a new Roman Empire.

Even the exponents of a minimalist British Empire recognised there were some things that had to remain under central control. Sea power was, and remains, indivisible: it must be centrally directed, and delivered by an integrated force. To that end Britain recognised that a few key points must remain imperial, including Bermuda, Halifax, Gibraltar, Malta, Mauritius, Aden, Cape Town, Trincomalee, Singapore and Hong Kong. Suitably fortified, with excellent communication links, dry docks and naval facilities, they enabled a seapower empire to function effectively around land empires.

Joseph Chamberlain's attempt to create a version of Seeley's cohesive empire, based on a preference for imperial tariffs and closer political union, was a non-starter. The British economy was capitalist, using income from overseas investments, many outside the formal empire, to fund imports, while the City of London dominated the world economy. Britain remained a quasi-city-state, with London a global Venice or Amsterdam. Manufacturing industry was only a second string in the national economy. Chamberlain's Birmingham could not replace the City of London as the dominant economic interest. Halford Mackinder's powerful polemic of 1904, 'The Geographical Pivot of History', attempted to frighten the country to change its culture from seapower to continental empire.[85] His friend Julian Corbett developed a far more sophisticated approach, a 'Sea Commonwealth' of independent nations bound by the shared reliance on command of the sea for security and prosperity. Corbett's thinking reflected Britain's distinctive seapower culture, which could evolve to sustain sea power after direct rule had become impossible. After the American Revolution, Britain granted local self-government to colonies of settlement in Australia, Canada, New Zealand and South Africa in a 'Commonwealth' sustained by mutual interest based on economic ties and sea control, rather than military force.[86] Those ideas evolved after 1945 as Britain ceased to be a great power, sustaining much of the cultural and strategic connectivity that Corbett had sought.

The critical point was that Britain had to make clear choices, as all the other seapower great powers had, between morphing into a second-rate version of a 'Roman' contiguous terrestrial empire of land and people, or striving for an expanding maritime empire of ports, sea routes and commerce. The first was a normative aspiration, emphasising the terrestrial nature of human societies, culture and identity, the second a conscious choice to be different, based on political and strategic logic. After 1782 Britain was careful to avoid making too great a commitment to an expanding territorial empire, India aside. The rapid concession of local self-government in Canada and Australasia avoided settler unrest, and weakened the leverage that seizing these territories might exert over the metropole. Furthermore the defence of almost the entire imperial portfolio was based on sea power strategy. India was secured by command of the sea, and the ability to project power into the Baltic against Russia.[87] Canada would be held by attacking US commerce and coastal cities.[88] French pressure against British colonies, or more likely British floating commerce, would be countered by the seizure of French colonies, the destruction of French commerce, and an aggressive blockade of the French coast. All three would be limited wars of economic endurance. Britain had no desire to destroy any rival, only to be left alone to draw profits and dividends from the global economy.[89] The eastern arc of empire, from Aden to Hong Kong, depended on Indian troops and resources, and even then lacked the disposable military manpower to consider a serious conflict on land. The Second Boer War, 1899–1902, exposed those limits, much as Syracuse had those of Athens. It was no accident that attempts to overhaul the army after 1902 were overtaken by an alliance with Japan and ententes with France and Russia. These agreements enabled Britain to focus on the most serious short-term problem of the Edwardian era, the hegemonic ambitions of Imperial Germany. Germany, like previous proto-hegemonic powers in Europe, rapidly discovered that Britain would pay a high price to block that ambition. Temporary connections with France and Russia, the two greatest threats to the empire between 1815 and 1904, and allies since 1892, was a price the British would pay to keep the Germans off the Scheldt Estuary, but, like the redistribution of the Royal Navy back to European waters, these links did not reflect anything permanent. It was not, as some feared, like the recall of the Roman Legions, nor did it presage the end of empire. British thinkers were already at work on a more open imperial structure, with political power moving to the Dominions. Ireland remained a problem, but even that was on the verge of settlement when a European war broke out – forcing Britain to face the economic and diplomatic problems of waging global war for the first time in a century.

Between 1890 and 1914 the British state created a level of popular navalism unimagined since Pericles' day, and did so in competition with the rising naval might of Imperial Germany.[90] British seapower was mobilised to deter, not fight, the ambitions of the latest great power to seek continental hegemony.[91] Parallels with the Napoleonic Empire were obvious, and alarming, not least the massive naval build-up designed to keep Britain out of Europe while Germany took control and laid the foundations for the next stage of the project. *Weltmacht*, world power, could only be achieved over the ruins of the Royal Navy. The larger the British fleet, the less likely it was that Germany would attack. The striking development of seapower as public entertainment after 1890 reflected the need to keep an ever-expanding electorate engaged with the message, despite the competing attractions of tax cuts, old-age pensions and welfare provision. The cost of seapower rose exponentially as the Victorian epoch ended, calling into question the validity of the project, and encouraging efforts to obtain support from the empire and Dominions. Yet Britain also faced another threat, the power and ambition of the United States. Where Germany threatened to become the hegemonic power in Europe, the United States had already become the hegemon of the Americas.

During the late nineteenth century Britain and the United States developed in very different ways, although shared economic interests always outweighed political differences. They had no obvious reason to fight, but they were increasingly at odds over commerce and influence. To this end the United States finally rebuilt the navy in the 1890s.[92] The 'New' American navy was 'Roman', serving the interests of a continental great power. Like the Roman navy it was built to win battles and project military power, in contrast to the 'Old' navy mission of securing trade.[93] Over the next fifty years the proto-Roman Republic in the west used the battlefleet navy and economic pressure to challenge Britain, the 'Carthaginian' seapower. The United States Navy approached the Royal Navy in size and fighting power, by focusing on the 'decisive battle' concept of continental military powers. This approach was reinforced by Congress, which regularly trimmed smaller units from the budget. The 'New' navy never became a seapower navy, because the sea had long ceased to be central to America as an economy, a state or a culture, and it lacked the necessary capacity for trade defence.

Instead the US navy was used to throw Spain out of Cuba in 1898, securing control of the Caribbean. Britain reduced regional naval deployments, leaving the US to police the area. This was typical: as long as British shipping was secure the state was happy to cut costs and shift resources to meet other challenges. At the same time the US acquired an empire in Asia, occupying the Philippines. Here the Royal Navy made sure the United States rather than Germany inherited the old Spanish Empire. Having annexed Hawaii, the US stretched across the Pacific to Asia, taking an increasingly interventionist role, to the consternation of China and Japan. In effect Britain and the US began to pool strategic sea power; the British carried the main burden in Europe, covering the US against potential challenges from Germany and Russia. In return the US secured the Western Hemisphere and took an increasing role in Asia. Mahan argued this partnership was essential to US interests.

This sense of a shared future led Mahan to ignore the instructions issued to the American delegation at the First Hague Peace Conference of 1897, which sustained the old US position of reducing or ending the strategic significance of sea power. Mahan anticipated the US would need these tools in the twentieth century, as an ally of Britain against the rising land power of Germany. The United States needed to work with Britain, even if it did not share British seapower culture.[94]

In August 1914 Britain entered the First World War to remove German forces from Belgium, the obvious base for an invasion, and prevent Germany dominating the continent. Both were critical to sustaining Britain's global position, but they were not existential. Britain had survived Napoleon's conquest of Europe, and his naval threat from the Scheldt. Initially, British strategy, building on two centuries of hard-won experience, focused on sea control and business as usual, to sustain another long war of economic attrition. Seapower, supply and funding would be the primary tools: any military commitment to Europe would be strictly limited. Yet the statesmen of 1914 allowed that commitment to drift from limited to unlimited, adding an unprecedented burden to an already strained war economy, while calling on ever larger supplies of Dominion and Colonial manpower. Between 1914 and 1918 European coalitions and imperial support enabled Britain to play a leading role in blocking Wilhelmine hegemony. But the seapower state paid a heavy price for that success, opening a flank to a very different rival.

The decision to conscript men into a mass continental army in 1916, in the hope that it might secure victory in Europe, shattered the British seapower state.[95] The long-standing link between global power and the domestic base was sundered, to sustain a European war of choice. In 1797, 1803 and 1807 Britain had faced the same choice, and consistently upheld the seapower model, sea power strategy, economic warfare and global security. After the 1916 decision, a new Sicilian Expedition, the British seapower state would never be the same again. Britain remembers the Great War above all others because it was the first time it had acted as a military great power, while the unprecedented human cost of the conflict destroyed Edwardian self-confidence. The Somme and Passchendaele changed Britain: mass military participation and unprecedented losses turned an army that few Britons cared to think about into a national institution that challenged the primacy of the Royal Navy. While this pleased British generals and French politicians, it destroyed a great power. The parallel between the Dutch war effort of 1688–1713 and that of Britain between 1917 and 1945 is striking. In both cases over-mighty allies used money and resources to force the smaller partner off the great-power standard. Both powers reached their end economically by fighting on land: they won the war, but lost the future. The major difference was that Britain handed sea power to the United States, which was not a seapower state.

To fund the military effort British overseas investments were sold off, loans taken out in New York, and hard-won overseas markets sacrificed. Taking on continental military roles had always damaged seapower states. One such war was bad enough, but fighting two within thirty years left Britain unable to maintain great-power status. By 1945 it lacked the money, bases and resources to command the sea. Just as the Dutch had lost their grip on the oceans to the insular British, the Americans exploited the strategic depth provided by two great oceans to watch events in Europe, and wait. In both World Wars US policymakers treated Britain as a strategic and economic rival to be defeated, even if it chose to do so with fiscal tools.

In 1914 the United States decided to remain neutral, and continued trading with Britain, France and Germany. While President Woodrow Wilson's administration thought German militarism posed a serious threat to US interests, it was equally determined to end Britain's dominance of global trade and the overwhelmingly powerful navy that dominated the oceans. Those tools threatened US commercial expansion, a reality demonstrated when British economic warfare blocked American exports to Imperial Germany. To ensure this never happened again, to make the world safe for American capitalism, Wilson set out to cripple British strategic power. The end of the seapower state would be a by-product of that decision.

America declared war on Germany in April 1917, when Germany attempted to provoke Mexico into recovering territory the United States had seized in the 1840s. US belligerence reinforced British economic warfare, while the threat of American troops helped bring the conflict to an end in late 1918. With Germany defeated, Wilson saw the peace process as an opportunity to attack the British position, using the massive naval construction programmes of 1916 and 1918 to force Britain to renounce the claim to search neutral shipping and blockade hostile powers. The biggest ships in these programmes, six battlecruisers, were named *Lexington*, *Saratoga, Ranger, Constitution, United States* and *Constellation*, two being American military victories over Britain, three being ships that captured British vessels, and one as the first American warship to capture a comparable ship from a major power, in this case France.[96] These names were not accidental: they reflected Wilson's agenda, and those of his successors. America maximised naval power to leverage Britain, threatening to contest sea control in a costly arms race. This overt hostility continued throughout the interwar era, as every single American aircraft carrier ordered before 1942 used a name from the same anti-British lexicon. This choice was culturally significant: carriers were the only warships that did not have pedestrian, terrestrial names controlled by Congress.

Wilson brought his agenda to Europe in 1919, sparking an Anglo-American 'Naval Battle of Paris', souring relations at the Paris Peace Conference. Having broken German 'militarism', Wilson was determined to end British 'navalism', a crude stereotype created in Berlin, largely from Napoleonic rhetoric, to distract the US from the reality that Germany had started the war and committed war crimes, including the abuse of civilian populations in occupied Belgium and sinking merchant ships without warning. Wilson wanted to remove all obstacles to the triumph of American capital and an export edition of American democracy.[97] He relied on naval construction and crude economic leverage. In 1914 Britain had massive investments in America; by 1919 the economic balance had been reversed. The US profited from remaining neutral; Britain was indebted to it for war materiel and loans raised in New York to support Russia and France. Wilson thought Britain would not risk a naval arms race, a logical assumption for a continental statesman. He was wrong: Britain did not consider seapower a matter of logical calculation. Prime Minister Lloyd George called Wilson's bluff, observing that a British prime minister who signed away the right to blockade would be out of office in a matter of hours. Wilson blinked first, accepting British accession to his 'League of Nations' project as a face-saving line of retreat. The words he used came from a memo written for the Admiralty by the seapower theorist Sir Julian Corbett. Corbett argued that once Wilson's League had been established the issue of Maritime Belligerent Rights would become moot. Although Wilson would deny the British had any influence on this thinking, such claims can be dismissed.[98] Britain preserved its sea power status, and its seapower identity for another two decades.

The possibility of a major naval arms race, which would also involve Japan, was avoided by the Washington Treaty of 1922. The Treaty fixed world naval power at levels that suited the Americans, rather than the British. These were low levels that reflected the reluctance of Congress to provide funds.[99] The US neither needed nor wanted a global sea-control navy, but it was most anxious that Britain should not have one. By cutting the scale of British naval strength the Washington process reduced the strategic weight and diplomatic impact of naval force in world politics between 1922 and 1941. This weakness was obvious to a seapower relying on global trade. At follow-on limitation conferences in Geneva and London in 1927 and 1930, Britain argued for more cruisers to defend that trade. The Americans ignored the argument, because they had no desire to spend money on ships to defend non-existent shipping. US cruisers were built to fight in fleet battles; Britain relied on them to control sea lanes. For the United States a 'Navy Second to None' was both a political mantra for domestic consumption and a diplomatic tool to leverage Britain. In the late 1930s the US began to build up the navy as part of the 'New Deal' economic package to reduce domestic unemployment. The choice reflected Franklin D. Roosevelt's personal interest. Having been assistant navy secretary in Wilson's administration, he would complete Wilson's project to break the last seapower state.

While the two countries avoided open conflict in this period their divisions, largely a reflection of profound differences of culture, interest and perception, gravely weakened the democracies when Fascists, Communists and Imperial Japan attacked their neighbours. The United States only acknowledged the depth of the problem after the Fall of France in June 1940. It responded by lending just enough money, munitions and machinery to keep Britain in the war, while stripping away vital economic and strategic assets, to ensure it could not recover.[100] Ideological concerns about British imperialism, dating back to Thomas Jefferson, blinded Americans to far graver dangers. Roosevelt failed to grasp the strategic threat posed by Soviet Russia. The US was finally brought into the conflict by the Japanese attack on Pearl Harbor in December 1941. By that time the Royal Navy had waged global war for thirty months, securing critical sea lanes.[101] Once at war the United States Navy created a 'military-industrial complex' and long-term procurement programmes that would be politically difficult to shut down.[102]

By 1945 the United States Navy had outgrown the Royal Navy, winning the Pacific Naval War single-handed. Yet naval victory was always a limited measure, too limited for a deeply continental American nation. The US looked to complete the victory in both theatres with overwhelming military power. When the Romans fought Carthage victory at sea was only a precursor to decisive military action and 'unconditional' surrender. In 1944 a vast US army landed in Europe and, in combination with the Soviet army, utterly defeated Germany. The army planned a similar invasion of Japan, only to be overtaken by a new, more 'total' method of waging war. The United States Army Air Force had failed to defeat Japan by conventional strategic bombardment, but the atom bomb turned land-based aviation into a decisive weapon. What Rome achieved with a siege in the Third Punic War, America achieved with atomic bombs. The ongoing debate about whether these weapons were 'necessary' exposes the fundamental strategic dichotomy between the continental military concept of 'total' war and seapower concepts of 'limited' war. It did not matter that a naval blockade might have forced Japan to surrender: the United States had to win by a knock-out blow, using overwhelming land-based power. Victory by sea power required patience and compromise, qualities that the democratic United States was culturally ill-equipped to deliver. Overwhelming power encouraged absolute approaches, notably Roosevelt's politically motivated 'unconditional surrender' mantra, which ensured the conflict became one of annihilation. Most wars end in negotiation, but Roosevelt's America, like Ancient Rome and Napoleonic France, preferred the simplicity of dictating terms to dead states.

This underlying reality became obvious once the war ended. In 1947 the American Army Air Force became a free-standing service, committed to the modern concept of total war through strategic bombardment with nuclear weapons. Then it combined with the army, its parent organisation, to wipe out the navy as a fighting force. This may have been a response to the navy's massive wartime construction programme. The air force would take over all aviation, while the army secured the marine corps.[103] In the absence of a major naval rival America could not find a strategic concept to justify the navy: the defence of sea lanes and trade did not count. The anti-naval programme, pushed through by the new Department of Defense, was well on the way to success by 1950. The outbreak of the Korean War in June 1950, which remained 'limited', and largely maritime, saved the navy and the marine corps just as the Cold War gave the US an enemy to prepare against. The emerging Soviet fleet prompted an unprecedented peacetime naval build-up, one that the US has sustained to this day, dominating the oceans ever since, wielding more naval power than every other navy combined.

After 1945 Britain ceased to be the strategic sea power. This was inevitable: US wartime policy ensured Britain ended the war absolutely bankrupt, and rapidly lost control of the imperial system that sustained and justified an oceanic navy. At the same time the British stopped telling themselves the time-honoured seapower stories, the powerful base of solid fact and the serried ranks of mythic constructions, that had shaped and then sustained seapower culture and identity since the Tudors. Rather than discuss the reality of what had happened between 1939 and 1945, British commentators fell back on allegorical readings of wartime disasters, using the sinking of HMS *Prince of Wales* and the capture of the Singapore naval base as emblems of weakness and failure. Such losses were the common currency of armed conflict. The loss of the battleship *Royal George* and the fortress of Minorca in 1782 were equally calamitous events, with equally limited strategic impact. Most analysts recognise that the Royal Navy performed exceptionally well between 1939 and 1945. Britain had not been defeated in war: it had succumbed to an overwhelming economic assault on the strategic sinews of seapower, sinews shaped in the 1690s. American loans of money and materiel had come with carefully contrived strings. British decisionmakers accepted the US would be the dominant naval power because without money they could not compete, and without an empire they would lack the necessary rationale. Furthermore, the US, rather than threatening Britain's survival, could secure the sea lanes for British trade. Britain used its last diplomatic credit and resource to draw the Americans into a binding commitment to defend western Europe against a looming Soviet threat, setting up NATO in 1948. This ensured that the trident of sea power passed, if only nominally, to a Western democratic consortium that could guarantee their security, rather than a distant, potentially isolationist continental superpower that might not.

Not that the lesson was fully understood. In 1956 an Anglo-French attempt to recover control of the Suez Canal, which they jointly owned, from the new nationalist Egyptian government, was blocked by US economic pressure. Only fifty years before the United States had unilaterally created a new country to build the other great trans-Isthmian Canal. Suez ended any lingering illusion that Britain might retain a fragment of the global power it had exercised a decade earlier. British decisionmakers hastily abandoned 'East of Suez' commitments and cut naval procurement. There was no point having a navy if the Americans prevented it being used to secure British national interests.

After 1956 Western sea power was reduced to the collective effort of medium-sized sea states, led by the wholly continental agendas of the United States. Despite Suez, Britain retained a significant place in the US-led consortium, because the two powers agreed that the Soviet Union threatened their interests. The Royal Navy focused on classic sea power missions, trade defence and oceanic security, leaving the United States to focus on naval-battle and power projection, the 'military' missions of a continental navy. In the early 1970s a decaying, crumbling post-Imperial Britain abandoned its history and the profound ties of culture and family that linked Britons of many heritages across the Commonwealth to join the European Economic Community, a continental protectionist collective with very different economic and political concerns.

As the British economy recovered the fault lines in the relationship with Europe deepened. Britain wanted to be free to operate in the world and retain its unique institutions, while Europe pressed it to integrate. Parallels with the use of a tariff zone to create Germany in the nineteenth century are hard to avoid. Britain rejected the Euro currency, the passport-free internal travel zone and finally the integrationist political project that defines the contemporary European Union. Beneath the froth of Brexit lay some striking cultural differences that can be traced back to Henry VIII's rejection of European domination, secular as well as spiritual, the defeat of the Spanish Armada and the creation of a global empire. Britain remains different because the carefully crafted seapower identity has survived attempts to postulate an alternative European identity, one in which the Hundred Years War matters more than the legacies of an oceanic empire such as the Commonwealth and the presence of millions of people of imperial or post-imperial heritage in modern Britain, its major role in world trade, London's Trafalgar Square and the Falklands conflict of 1982.

Britain, like Venice and Holland, managed the process of decline. Once these states lost their empires they were too weak to sustain the dominant navies that made them great powers. Athens and Carthage only differed in the nature of the defeat leading to the loss of empire. The transfer of naval hegemony to the US was relatively painless because, although the two states took fundamentally different views of the world ocean, their ideological synergy ensured they did not pose an existential threat to each other. Bankrupt Britain abandoned naval hegemony without a struggle because it passed to a power that would use it in ways that were generally, although not always specifically, acceptable. With that the last seapower great power left the international stage. Henceforth the world would belong to super-powers, vast continent-sized states, self-sufficient military empires that look to land, air and space power. In the Cold War the sea occupied a marginal strategic role, a 'flank' to be secured and a supply line to be protected. While contemporary America possesses a vast military navy, it thinks and acts like a land power. Britain does not. This critical distinction helps explain how relations between the two powers evolved over the past two centuries, years in which Britain accepted the inevitability of relative decline, following a path marked out by older seapowers, while shifting the burden of global power to the United States. The final transfer of power occurred midway through a century dominated by three global conflicts, conflicts in which existential threats from Germany and then the Soviet Union aligned British and US interests. These threats were continental, not maritime. In such conflicts against potential hegemonic powers Britain needed continental alliance partners to carry the military burden. The United States would be the last such ally.

However, naval power still mattered at the margins. In 1982 US support provided a critical edge for Britain in the Falklands conflict. When European 'allies' refused to supply artillery rounds, the US stepped in, providing air-to-air missiles, diplomatic cover and much more. In return the British agreed not to beat the Argentines too badly. In 1991 only the Royal Navy operated with the Americans at the fighting end of the First Gulf War, a sure sign of deep, long-term links and cross-training. The end of the Cold War shifted the global balance back towards the sea with a boom in global trade, which has made control of sea communications as important today as it has ever been. Modern Britain enjoys most of the benefits of being a seapower without the cost of maintaining a large navy; but the continued existence of the United States Navy should not be taken for granted. Recent trends in US naval deployment have made it essential to take up the slack in the European theatre, just as Britain's role in Europe has undergone a profound change. Britain did not build two big aircraft carriers in anticipation of Brexit, but these behemoths will represent a state that has recovered something of its seapower heritage by stepping away from a continentally focused organisation. Just how useful they will be in helping post-Brexit Britain renew the global connections of an independent sea state remains to be seen.

CHAPTER 9

Seapower Today

Although there are no more seapower great powers, the old contest between sea states and continental hegemons has continued into the twenty-first century. The Western liberal world, largely shaped by the political, economic and intellectual legacy of seapower states, has retained strategic sea power since 1945, under a US umbrella. This has enabled sea states, and other global economic actors, to function as seapowers, at relatively low cost and with little strategic risk. Contemporary sea states, states with the sea at the heart of their identity and economy, include Japan, the Netherlands, Denmark, Britain, Norway and Singapore, and they are not alone. Such states are disproportionately engaged in international oceanic trade, maritime identities occupy prominent places in their culture, and they will be the first to respond when the peaceful use of the sea is threatened. How far their democratic electorates are prepared to accept the economic costs and human risks of that status remains uncertain. That they will need to do so is obvious, but many of the dangers that threaten them are beyond the reach of conventional naval forces. Throughout the period since 1945 Western seapower has faced the sustained hostility of hegemonic continental

Incinerating seapower: a US atom bomb test at Bikini Atoll, 1946 empires, the Soviet Union and latterly the People's Republic of China, states that have been anxious to prevent their subjects obtaining the same progressive, inclusive political systems as in the West.

Any challenge to Western strategic sea control, by the Soviet Union, Russia or China, has existed in the minds of alarmists who confuse numbers with capability and boasting with delivery. The Soviet fleet was built to defend a Russian Empire from attacks by Western amphibious forces, carrier aviation and by the 1960s Polaris missiles. It was not built to challenge Western sea control. After 1989 the Soviet Navy collapsed because it was irrelevant to the survival of Russia: any resurgence in recent years reflects the views of a Leningrad-born president rather than reality. Contemporary Russia has no more desire to be a seapower that it did in Peter the Great's day, it still relies on command economics and a form of absolute rule. In 2014 President Putin seized the Crimea, recovering the naval base at Sevastopol, a potent symbol of national heroism. In the process he seriously damaged the prospects of a Russian naval revival. The choice was perfectly logical, if we accept that Russia has never been a seapower, and that the sea has never been vital to core Russian security concerns. Putin's choice had consequences. In response two French-built helicopter carriers were embargoed and sold to Egypt. In 2017 Putin abandoned his projected aircraft carriers: the only Soviet shipyard that could build carriers is in the Ukraine, along with the factory that makes marine gas turbines. Modern Russian warships use the same lexicon of heroic nationalist names as their tsarist precursors, a connection that emphasises the recurrent circular reality of Russian attempts to sustain a great navy, an endless cycle of creation, defeat, disintegration and recreation.

The economic sanctions, in essence updated maritime economic warfare, imposed on Russia after the seizure of the Crimea and support for 'separatists' in Eastern Ukraine have worked. Assisted by the halving of global oil prices they pushed Russia into recession, leading Putin to lash out at world trade with a series of counterproductive autarkic measures. It remains to be seen how long Russia can endure the cost, and how far seapower can exploit values such as democratic accountability, which have been potent weapons in the arsenal of seapower since the battle of Salamis.

Russia, China and the United States are far too big, and far too powerful, to rely on seapower, a decidedly eccentric identity of limited strategic weight. While the United States began life as a sea state, operating in the Atlantic economy, acquiring a continent by conquest and purchase changed that identity. Modern American views of the sea are strategic, rather than cultural. After the Cold War the United States Navy, recalling what happened in 1948, needed a new naval 'threat' to avoid evisceration. An expanding Chinese fleet, strikingly similar to the old Soviet force in technology and strategy, has generated considerable alarm, and helped sustain the navy's budget. This is necessary because the United States has no obvious need for oceanic security, nor much interest in global shipping. It is no more a seapower state than China. Neither meets the criteria Alfred Thayer Mahan used to define sea power back in 1890. They are vast, essentially continuous land powers/empires with extraordinary domestic resource bases in almost all areas. The exploitation of domestic shale gas reserves may emphasise this point, by encouraging increasingly autarkic economic policies. Both states have vast domestic gas reserves, which would make them effectively self-sufficient in hydrocarbons. While it seems likely that both will maintain or even grow their navies, they will do so for diplomatic and strategic purposes. Neither sees the defence of oceanic trade as a core mission.

China, like Russia, has no ambition to contest sea control beyond its own rather generously defined littoral. Chinese ships and rhetoric serve internal agendas, while Chinese attitudes to the sea remain profoundly negative, as they have been for millennia. China will never become a seapower as long as it remains a vast land empire, containing many subject peoples, where the key to the Mandate of Heaven is to feed the people and maintain domestic order. The sea is so unimportant, or so dangerous, that China does not have a navy. Instead there are three separate forces, revealingly described as the People's Liberation Army's Navy (PLAN), which operate independently of one another. The late nineteenth-century Qing Empire used the same method of enhancing political control – with catastrophic operational consequences.

The Chinese state has maintained domestic political legitimacy by creating a high-growth economy based on manufacturing for export. The aim is to keep the population content through rising living standards, while withholding democratic accountability and political inclusion. In the eighteenth century Chinese imperial governments, equally focused on internal stability, were wiser. They restricted trade to a single port, Quangdo, which was as far from Beijing as possible, prevented contact between Westerners and the local populace, and stopped trade altogether when necessary. Today decades of export-led growth, fuelled by state borrowing, have kept the masses employed and political dissent under control, but rising wages and structural inefficiency have reduced China's competitive edge, and the state has not generated enough high-value manufacturing to compensate. Without the dynamic of a free market Chinese industry remains unresponsive and outmoded: states have never been the best managers of economic activity. Exports are falling, while the economy is carrying mountains of debt from the associated housing boom. Labour disputes are rising, and there is no democratic outlet for popular discontent. The Chinese leadership must be aware that only a liberalised market, upheld by the rule of law and democratic accountability, can generate the type of sustainable growth that China needs. However, they also realise that, as Mikhail Gorbachev discovered, once those doors have been opened they cannot be shut, and the one-party state will be among the first victims. The 'Western' liberal capitalist economic model, created by seapower states, seems likely to outlast continental totalitarian alternatives. The looming crisis, more existential than economic, suggests that China remains a vast empire, dominated by domestic concerns, one where maritime economic activity has always been marginal. China cannot carry on as it is, and cannot change without risking the entire imperial structure. Both economic failure and democratic reform risk breaking the monolith. The navy of the People's Liberation Army would be among the first casualties: it only exists to support the internal political agenda. Any state where the navy is merely a seagoing appendage of the army is self-evidently neither a seapower nor interested in oceanic dominion.

Although China has a long coast, and an equally long history of maritime activity, it has far longer land borders. Historically, these were shared with unstable and aggressive neighbours. While the Chinese state was humiliated by sea-based invasions in the nineteenth century, it was never overthrown by them. Overland invaders achieved this feat on many occasions. In the past two decades Chinese maritime history has become a contested space, as state propaganda and sensational Western texts compete to rewrite reality, fuelling a debate about China's maritime intentions conducted with strikingly cavalier attitudes to Thucydides' concept of seapower. Both Chinese and American commentators frequently use seapower to describe states with large navies.

For decades the argument has been made that Imperial China was interested in the oceans and the world beyond, based on the astonishing 'Treasure Fleet' voyages of Zheng-He. Quite how these short-lived imperial ventures could signal a profound national engagement is never made clear. Fortunately, academic scholarship has overturned the illusion. The Chinese Imperial Archives provide ample evidence that, far from being the Chinese Columbus beloved of sensational literature and Communist Party propaganda, Zheng-He and his fleets were sent to crush expatriate Chinese maritime traders with lethal force, to protect the 'tribute' system and the diplomatic relationship with foreign states that it sustained. There was no 'lost opportunity': Zheng-he's mission had a profoundly negative purpose. His master, the Yongle Emperor, also moved the capital to Beijing, to be close to the prime security threat and policy focus, namely nomad armies north of the Great Wall. The 'treasure fleets' were cancelled because costs exceeded returns. Chinese maritime activity in the late imperial era was rational, coherent and restricted. A vast continental empire, more concerned with internal stability than external relations, China feared foreign trade would promote instability, by introducing foreign ideas, both secular and spiritual, and spreading personal wealth to merchants, socially destabilising actors who occupied the lowest strata of the Confucian social system. Then as now China was drawn to trade by domestic need: in the eighteenth century it needed to import food; in the twenty-first century it needs to import wealth to lift the people out of poverty. In both cases the object was to sustain the regime's domestic authority, not to engage with the wider world.[1]

At the heart of this assessment lies a critical reality. Continental hegemons have never feared the strategic impact of naval power; they fear seapower as the vector for the cornucopia of liberal, progressive and inclusive ideas that created seapower states. Plato recommended cities be moved 8 miles inland, to protect citizens from this malaise. In 150 BC Rome demanded that Carthage be demolished and rebuilt 8 miles inland. The senators had no reason to fear Carthage; it had neither ships nor soldiers: instead they were terrified of levelling democracy, spread by sea. Today dangerous ideas are more easily spread by the internet, the latest advanced communication system pioneered by seapower states. The Chinese government's response, censorship and control, illustrates what it fears, and why it will never be a seapower. Blocking access is a very old idea, one that accepts the argument has been lost.

The dramatic collapse of the Shanghai stock market in August 2015 reinforced the point. A command economy directed by a One Party State is wholly incompatible with a capital market, a classic seapower system that depends on the rule of law and democratic accountability. The stock market was either an act of criminal folly or a fraud, designed to ruin the newly prosperous middle classes before they demanded political change. The current Chinese defence build-up is primarily aimed at domestic audiences, who are constantly reminded that the Party will make China a superpower, if it is left in sole charge of the state. The people are warned against Western liberal agendas, with a rhetoric that owes as much to Plato and Confucius as Lenin and Mao. The 19th Party Congress of October 2017 finally admitted that Xi Jinping would become president for life, a political shift that had begun five years earlier. As he follows Louis Napoleon Bonaparte's course to imperial status, Xi will sustain the naval build-up, because external threats remain critical to the regime's self-justification.

The central question this raises is whether China will become an expansive, aggressive Roman Empire or a satiated Chinese Empire. While the answer may appear obvious, it has important implications. The Chinese navy is a significant element in a programme that seeks to reduce the risk of economic and political instability, the key to the continuing dominance of the Communist Party and its quasi-Imperial leader, posed by the divergent cultural, economic and political ideas vectored through seapower. China has no interest in sea control beyond a degree of the strategic depth, including a secure bastion area for ballistic missile submarines. It prefers terrestrial possessions, artificial islands, railroads, pipelines and canals to oceanic activity. China's strategic and political cultures are best understood through the lens of the 'Great Wall' and the 'Great Firewall', barriers that are the antithesis of seapower identity.

To sustain the export of manufactured goods, to sustain economic growth, deliver rising living standards within a rigid one-party state and control the spread of information, the Chinese leadership has devised a 'New Silk Road'. This state-funded project would link China to Europe by rail to offload industrial over-production while controlling the spread of ideas. By contrast maritime connections have a long history of spreading unwelcome ideas, and are easily interdicted in war. In a replay of the famous geopolitical debate between Alfred T. Mahan and Halford Mackinder the Chinese are backing the 'Heartland' model of rail links, despite Mahan's crushing sentence that 'as a highway, a railroad competes in vain with a river – the greater speed cannot compensate for the smaller carriage'.[2] This analysis remains valid. A 'Silk Road' would constrict and channel trade, enabling China to control how the route was used, including banning internet access, control all movement and demand tribute, like the old empire. It would be a catastrophe for global trade, reducing the states that fell under Chinese dominion to the status of tribute-bearing subjects.

By contrast, despite alarmist rhetoric from some American commentators, the PLAN does not threaten Western sea control. The ships are numerous but not advanced. A second-hand, forty-year-old ex-Soviet carrier, laid down in the Ukraine at the height of the Cold War, cannot be compared with US carriers. It may be used to inform future carrier development, or remain a cheap status symbol. Rather than seeking sea control the Chinese regime wants to make the sea irrelevant to its security needs, to conquer the sea on the land, a classic continental response to seapower. The Romans wiped out every other navy in the Mediterranean, by conquering the countries that owned them, seapowers and land powers alike, and incorporating them into the empire. This was the ultimate negative form of sea control. The Chinese island chain programme has turned offshore reefs and shoals, to which China has no legal claim, into defensive bastions, to exclude rival navies from the area where Chinese ballistic missile submarines are stationed and from which US carrier aviation could strike. The synergy with Soviet thinking is obvious.

The ultimate seapower irony in the contest between the United States and China for maritime dominion in East Asia is that neither has any claim to be a seapower, however large their navies might be. Their rivalry is conducted in terms that reflect that salient fact. Both address continentalised seas through which claims and counter-claims are based on ridiculous lines drawn on charts of the deep ocean, as if the high seas could be turned into provinces. In this exercise the Chinese have been more inventive, stretching logic and cartography into new forms, while US responses cite the United Nations Convention on the Law of the Sea of 1982, an International

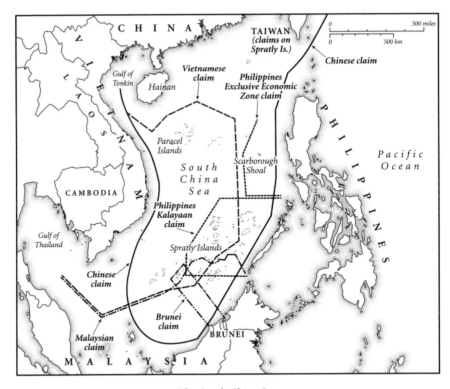

The South China Sea

Agreement that Washington has signally failed to sign. The end result of this contest, consciously or otherwise, will be the completion of the ultimate continental agenda: annihilating the ability of sea states to resist land-based hegemons. The continentalisation of maritime space would replace freedom, choice and progress with the unending monotony of universal continental monocultures. Across time seapower had been the choice of smaller, maritime states that reject this option. Eliminating the ungoverned oceanic space which enabled that choice would pave the way for a global state, leaving seapower identity to tertiary operators, superpower clients. Yet whichever great continental power became the universal monarchy there would soon be maritime barbarians hammering at their sea gates.

Chinese and Russian responses to the challenge of seapower culture echo those of older continental hegemons: censorship, command economies, denial strategies and the continentalisation of maritime space with legal restraints, physical barriers, land-based weapons and strategy. While China has found new tools for this mission, notably in the extension of territorial jurisdiction far out to sea, using international legislation to restrict the free use of the sea, it contains powerful echoes of Catherine II's 'Armed Neutrality' of 1780, which her son revived in 1801, and successive Russian attempts to close the Baltic to British warships. Trans-national threats, including terrorism, piracy, weapons of mass destruction, hydrocarbons, people smuggling and over-fishing are frequently cited to justify the reduction in free movement on the high seas. With access to the resources and markets of Africa becoming increasingly important China appears to be developing power-projection capabilities to exploit opportunities or forestall competitors. It is unlikely that China plans to wage war at sea in the classic symmetrical sense; its assets are configured to enhance land-based control. The PLAN is, after all, the Army's Navy.

The Chinese project may succeed, because fault lines between sea and land identity are emerging in the Western collective. Donald Trump's populist protectionism conveys a hemispheric isolationist message, while the United Kingdom's decision to leave the continental protectionist European Union moves in the opposite direction. The British decision reflected many agendas, but deep within lay a residual seapower culture, a sense that 1588 and Trafalgar were critical landmarks in the construction of a national identity that reflects a long engagement with seapower, one where Turner's tiny steam boat remains a portentous emblem. The European Union, an unaccountable protectionist system that has impoverished and infantilised most member states, to the advantage of German industry, in order to integrate old, culturally diverse nations into a homogenised monolith, is in danger of becoming a *Zollverein* for the twenty-first century. On its current trajectory Europe will become an empire, not a nation, closer to Russia and China than the liberal democratic nation states that are the legacy of seapower. The problems facing contemporary seapower can be read in the refugee/migrant crisis in the Mediterranean. European politicians have failed to agree policy, leaving defence and constabulary forces without a clear mission. European navies could control the relevant sea passages, as they did off Somalia, but they cannot be tasked until there is consensus on the desired outcome. The resultant political tensions within the EU emphasise the inability of continental collectives to grasp oceanic issues.

This is not a criticism of Chinese, Russian, European or American decision-making. These vast states cannot be seapowers, they necessarily prioritise the land. Any criticism is directed at those who attempt to create the illusion that such states could be seapowers. A few years ago an eminent Chinese academic asked me when China would become the next great seapower. Having pointed out that his model of a 'seapower' was the United States, the contemporary naval hegemon, I suggested China might take over that position, at vast expense in blood and treasure, in fifty years, but it, like the United States, would never be a seapower. When continental powers suffer military defeat or economic collapse they cut their navies before their armies or air forces. It is unlikely China will be any different. The only questions are how bad the economic downturn will be, and how much internal unrest will follow. The Chinese Empire would survive without a navy, but not without an army.

China is important because the greatest challenge facing contemporary sea states is the creeping continentalisation of maritime space, restrictions on the right to use the seas. The extension of territorial waters and Exclusive Economic Zones in the United Nations Convention on the Law of the Sea provided a legal framework to challenge the age-old right of innocent passage by shrinking the 'high seas'. China has used such territorial claims, along with the seizure of islands and shoals from weak neighbours and the creation of artificial islands, to sustain wholly unfounded claims to exclusive maritime dominion. Soon the Western Pacific Basin[3] will be covered by land-based defences deployed to deny maritime access. Continental strategies have always attempted to reduce the threat from the sea, using coastal forts, mines and restrictive treaties. Chinese policy has provoked hostility in regional states, and encouraged the United States Navy and other fleets to assert the right of innocent passage as part of a continuing commitment to the global economy. Sea states must act together to ensure the seas remain open for trade, as well as for diplomacy and war: without ocean access their political and economic model will fail, along with their values. Japan is taking the lead in responding to the Chinese challenge, adopting a strikingly maritime strategic posture for its Self Defence Forces, while extending their reach and capabilities. One such initiative seeks to counter possible Chinese attempts to seize choke points and other key territory, using a rapidly expanding amphibious capability.[4] It may be assumed that the United States is both cognisant of and content with these developments.

The future of seapower depends on the coherence of the Western liberal consortium. While the United States continues to provide high-end warfighting capability, the strategic component of Western sea control is secure, enabling sea states to flourish and protect the global common. This situation should not be taken for granted: the United States is not a seapower, and has shown signs of reverting to the isolationism of the 1920s. However, American superpower status depends on the ability to operate globally, without reliance on host nation support, making the navy the key enabler. In an uncertain era it is important that the sea states of the 'West' fill capability gaps left by American reductions, both to support the system and to protect the interests that it upholds.

The existence of sea states and the vitality of the global economy are intimately connected. They always have been. Trade makes controlling maritime communications worth fighting for and economic warfare, in one form or another, a useful strategic tool, a critical reason why medium-sized powers have chosen that identity. The link between maritime trade, capital formation and modern Western democratic tax-raising bureaucratic powers does not need to be restated. Nor, I suspect, does the role of maritime actors, states and non-state actors, in the creation of an ever wider globalised economy, linked by advanced communications, and secure, legally enforceable means of exchange. Sea states still rely on external resources, food, raw materials, funds and fuel to sustain their economies. Continental superpowers are largely sustained by internal resources, their autarkic agendas and command economies designed to serve internal purposes, and they show limited interest in international exchange. Currently, the continental United States provides the naval power, and the strategic deterrent, that shields the 'West' from a variety of hostile actors, but it should not assumed that such generosity is open-ended, or free. The largely autarkic United States expects its allies to provide support, and retains the right to withdraw into isolation. The only other superpower, Communist China, has rejected key elements of seapower culture – democracy, the rule of law and the inclusion of capitalists in the political system – because it has the autocratic domestic agenda of a hegemonic continental empire. The occasional maritime headline cannot disguise that reality. If China were to replace the United States as oceanic hegemon it would shatter the global economy and the seapower model that sustains it. The global economic consequences would be catastrophic.

While the liberal-democratic capitalist system remains dominant on the oceans it retains the option of employing sea power strategy, which has changed very little since Thucydides, to influence rivals. Sea power strategy begins with diplomacy, deterrence and constabulary functions – which include economic sanctions, followed by economic warfare and projecting power from the sea. Sea states will continue to build and operate navies to protect their vital national interests, and as part of the US-led Western liberal collective. Economic sanctions remain a powerful tool, and the threat they pose explains why Russia and China still talk of war and conquest as part of the 'bread and circuses' of totalitarian politics. While sea states do not choose war, because it is bad for business, they may find that, like their seapower precursors, they do not have the option. The right of innocent passage through continentalised maritime space must be upheld, jointly and collectively – lest the oceans that Mahan described as 'the great common' are lost. This is a mission the West should undertake as a collective act, linked to commercial activity, not a military threat.

CONCLUSION

Although the last seapower great power faded away in the 1940s the cultural legacy of seapower states remains fundamentally important in the contemporary world where 'Western' states, liberal, inclusive polities, engage with the world by sea, for trade, culture and security. Not only are these states a 'work of art', as Burckhardt observed, but their identities reflect choices made by the seapower states that shaped the development of Western liberal ideology. A seapower, the ancient Greek *thalassokratia*, was a state that consciously chose to create and sustain a fundamental engagement between nation and ocean, from political inclusion to the rule of law, across the entire spectrum of national life, in order to achieve great power status. It was a cultural choice, not a question of naval power.[1] The choice was facilitated by inclusive politics, a democracy or an oligarchic republic. These states depended on maritime trade for essential imports, including food, and represented their choice in art, architecture, ships and words. Once created this artificial identity had to be sustained by constant repetition, slowly wired into the identity of the state, and yet constantly adjusted to meet new realities. In Venice the message was hastily modified after Lepanto

Celebrating seapower heroes: the Nelson Column at Great Yarmouth as the Republic moved from a Papal-Habsburg alliance to one with France, and by extension the Ottomans. Similarly, Trafalgar was developed to replace the English victory over the Armada with a British triumph, one that included Scotland and Ireland in the new identity. When the message began to fade the test of a seapower was the ability of key economic interest groups, the 'City of London' and its precursors, to mobilise the necessary political support to sustain the project.

The enemies of seapower, from Ancient Mesopotamian empires to contemporary China, have been continental imperial hegemons, dominated by military power, absolute rule, terrestrial imperialism and command economies. They fear the inclusive, progressive ideologies of seapower, using armed force, on land and sea, to destroy the cultural challenge. The Punic Wars, as Sir Walter Raleigh realised, remain the ultimate conflict between these divergent cultures: Rome annihilated Carthaginian culture because it represented a profound challenge to the Roman political system. Louis XIV had similarly stark intentions when he invaded the Dutch Republic in 1672, while Napoleon, the ultimate modern universal monarch, was quick to deploy 'Carthaginian' as a term of abuse, annihilating the fleet and culture of Venice in 1797, and planning to do the same to Britain. Imperial Germany revived French insults that derided Britain as a commercially driven 'Carthaginian' sea power predestined to lose the next Punic conflict. When the First World War broke out this rhetoric became hysterical, unintentionally revealing Imperial Germany's 'Roman' ambitions to be a continental hegemon. Once again sea power ensured the new Romans failed.[2] Modern continental hegemons remain undemocratic, impose centralised economies, abuse the legal process and shape cultural identities around military might and the domination of conquered peoples. The Soviet Union, the latest of these imperial edifices to fail, was destroyed by the extraordinary effort required to keep progressive politics and economics at bay. It will not be the last.

Distinguishing sea power as a strategy that can be exercised by any state with a navy from seapower, the cultural core of a relatively weak state that makes the maritime dimension central to its identity, and seeks to achieve asymmetric influence thereby, reminds us of the importance of cultural divergence in the creation of national identity, even in such crowded spaces as 'Britain' and 'Europe'. Seapower states depended on sea communications for security and prosperity. They created commercial empires, varying from the Delian League to modern multinational corporations, to sustain costly fleets, and emerged from polities that combined commercial wealth, much of it linked to sea trade, with hereditary and landed power. They privileged naval over military forces, and restricted their terrestrial footprint to strategic bases and economic entrepôts. They had maritime capital cities and maritime heroes, made the sea central to their culture, and retained the innate curiosity that propelled exploration and discovery. These characteristics distinguished the Athenian model of empire from the Persian, Carthaginian from Roman, British from Russian. Continental powers extended by land, securing territory by military conquest. Being relatively weak, seapowers were obliged to look elsewhere; they pursued trade rather than conquest, acquiring strategic islands and enclaves rather than provinces. When seapower states forgot this reality, and most did, they were forcibly reminded of their weakness. These states chose seapower because they lacked the scale and weight to be continental great powers.

There are no more seapower great powers, but such states shaped the Western liberal world, and left a potent progressive legacy to their successors, modern sea states that emphasise political inclusion, the rule of law, free-market economics, overseas trade, cultural identities suffused with salt water, from literature and art to national heroes and monuments, oceanic capital cities and an overriding curiosity, a willingness to travel, to learn and to exchange ideas. Most open societies pay lip service to an Athenian political legacy, but few understand the critical connection between seapower and inclusive politics. Plato's aversion to the maritime dimension has warped the argument. Modern sea states need to recognise the seapower heritage of liberal progressive politics, outward-facing economies and global engagement the better to recognise what separates them from continental military powers.

Not only is the fault line between Roman and Carthaginian worldviews as resonant today as it was in Hannibal's time, but the distinction to be drawn between the political structures, economies, cultural output and created identities of seapower states and continental states provides important insights for many fields of enquiry. The best way to understand the strikingly different ideas about sea power strategy advanced by Alfred Thayer Mahan and Sir Julian Corbett between 1890 and 1911 is to recognise that Corbett lived in a seapower state at its zenith, where naval might was the dominant strategic instrument, and the sea a central element of national identity, and that Mahan did not. J. M. W. Turner's work was dominated by the reality that he lived and worked in a seapower state, his formative years shaped by an existential twenty-year-long struggle with Republican and Imperial France, one which French leaders categorised as a rerun of the Punic Wars. Turner responded by reimagining Carthage as a seapower exemplar, emphasising the role of seapower culture and sea power strategy in the defeat of Napoleon. His art influenced an open-ended search for pattern and meaning in the decline of older seapower states that shaped British intellectual life down to 1945. Both artist and debate resonate through time and space as unique contributions to our ability to synthesise past, present and future.

The five states at the heart of this study created unique seapower identities in order to achieve great-power status, because they lacked the scale and human resources to resist conventional continental great powers. All were relatively weak, effectively dependant on seaborne commerce for economic prosperity and food. Losing sea control would expose them to utter ruin. They became naval powers to address this vulnerability and, having created a suitable fleet, evolved into seapower states to maximise their relative advantage. England turned to the sea because it faced a rising threat from hegemonic European powers, both secular and spiritual. This negative choice, driven by weakness, worked for so long as larger states were unable or unwilling to sustain the costly programmes required to defeat the Royal Navy. Athens and Carthage, the first seapower great powers, were annihilated when their fleets were defeated, and then subsumed into universal monarchies that hated and feared seapower. Having studied the history of their precursors, Venice, the Dutch Republic and Britain managed their decline with more skill.

The strategy of seapower states emphasised limited war, using alliances to prevent the emergence of a 'universal monarchy'. As continental land powers morphed into military superpowers, seapower states were unable to compete. Carthage was annihilated because there was only one superpower, but the last three seapowers were able to choose to act as sea states within relatively balanced security structures that they could influence, but not dominate. Britain was able to delay this choice by combining insularity and wealth with the manpower and resources of a global empire, advantages that enabled a small island off the north coast of Europe to remain a great power until 1945. In the end economic ruin, the loss of empire and the atomic bomb brought the British seapower state to an end, enabling the economic and industrial power of the United States to separate sea power strategy from seapower identity.

Seapower states created empires of trade, using the sea to connect ports and naval bases, the nodal points of maritime economics and strategy, while avoiding over-extension on land. In some regions successive seapower empires overlapped. Corfu would be a naval base for Athens, Venice and Britain, while Cape Town, the key to European trade with Asia, was located by the Portuguese, developed by the Dutch and taken by the British. When seapowers created land empires, as the British did in India, they were eccentric to the seapower concept, and often run as commercial concerns. These land empires, however successful, created cultural confusion, prompted the hostility of continental powers, the misapplication of strategic resources and an overestimation of military might.

Seapower flowed from inclusive political systems, oligarchic republics where the men of commerce and capital shared power with landed aristocracies and constitutionally constrained rulers. Political inclusion enabled the state to mobilise resources for the maintenance of costly navies in peace and war. Seapower navies focused on trade defence, backed by a deterrent battlefleet. Continental great-power navies lacked any connection with merchant shipping or trade, focusing on 'decisive' fleet battle and power projection. Seapower states had maritime heroes, culture, ceremonies and art; maritime words were prominent in their languages, they engaged with wider worlds and tried to understand distant countries.

Seapower states favoured limited war, naval strength, professional armies and alliances to uphold the status quo. They tended to be clear-sighted about the benefits of war, often emphasizing commercial interest. Their strategic preferences were frequently compromised by the need to operate with allies that followed continental agendas. In the Napoleonic era Britain relied on economic warfare, peripheral operations and extensive economic support to allies, rather than mass armies. In the twentieth century it would be bankrupted and broken by the human and economic costs of waging two total wars as a continental great power, deploying mass conscript armies alongside a dominant navy. Modern Britain operates as a medium power within alliance systems that are dominated by continental concerns. This may explain why British politicians followed the United

States into futile continental conflicts, notably in Afghanistan, a country where British interests are remarkable only by their absence.

Seapower identity still matters, even though it has become a collective Western possession rather than the sole preserve of individual states. However, it lacks the single-minded focus and clarity of exposition that can be traced in the seapower great powers. The problem has been exacerbated by the separation of seapower identity from sea power strategy. For sixty years Western sea states have relied on the United States Navy for oceanic security. No longer responsible for their own maritime security, they have failed to sustain or promote maritime identities, a national focus on the ocean or the naval forces needed to protect their own interests at sea. This failure matters because maritime identities have always been constructed. They require constant refreshment: the modern concept of 'sea-blindness' reflects the failure of states and governments to sustain that identity. While the connection between overseas trade, resource dependency and naval budgets used to be synergistic, the modern world takes the free use of the seas for granted, and assumes shipping services are wholly detached from national policy. In this case the extension of democracy has, as Mahan anticipated, weakened the link between states and the sea, enabling continental powers to compete.

Smaller sea states such as ancient Rhodes, early modern Genoa, and post-seapower Venice, have existed throughout history: sea-centred polities operating as commercial centres, naval contractors and bankers in multi-polar political systems. They shared much of the culture of seapower, without the scale or ambition to achieve great-power status. Today such states remain heavily engaged with the sea, as a percentage of national economic output, through dependence on overseas resources, with relatively high proportions of the workforce engaged in shipping, offshore economic interests, oil and gas, fishing, and wind farms, shipyards, docks, ports, international finance and other maritime economic activity. This engagement is not capable of accurate calculation, because it includes such intangibles as culture, identity, history and mythology. However judged, it is not primarily a military calculation. Sea states have proliferated since 1945 because, with a few notable exceptions, the ability to use the oceans freely for commercial purposes has not been in doubt. Sea states do not control the oceans; the shipping that delivers food, fuel and raw materials is effectively unguarded, often beyond the control of nation states. Many sea states rely on a combination of international law and shared interest, rather than naval force, to ensure shipping moves without hindrance from other nations, or non-state actors. Indeed most contemporary naval peacetime missions are concerned with terrestrial issues, from anti-ballistic missile defences to countering piracy, the narcotics trade, arms smuggling and people trafficking. Since 1945 the defence of maritime trade has only rarely been an issue, with the Tanker War of the late 1980s and Somali piracy the high points of Western activity.

Sea control has been exercised by Western liberal states, singly or jointly, since the sixteenth century. This situation is unlikely to change. North Korea, Al-Qaeda and ISIS may share a profound aversion to the liberal-democratic world order, but they lack the capacity to challenge it at sea. That capacity was, as Peter the Great recognised, both costly and hard to acquire. Instead Al-Qaeda attacked the World Trade Center, a powerful symbol of the commerce that spreads the ideology of democracy, personal liberty, political accountability, the rule of law and freedom of choice. The oceans have always been the vector for radical and dangerous ideas. Plato and Confucius wanted to move away from the sea, but the direction of human progress has consistently been in the other direction, towards the ocean and inclusion, away from the inward-facing stasis of totalitarian politics.

Seapower still matters because the great fault lines of global politics consistently return to the contrasting nature of land and sea states. Contemporary tensions between the 'West', the liberal, democratic trading nations of the world, and their opponents – including Russia, China, North Korea and fundamentalist Islam – reflect deep cultural differences between continental systems of authoritarian rule, ideological conformity, command economies, closed borders and deep-rooted anxieties about the ocean as a vector for destabilising ideas that can be traced back to ancient philosophers and the seapower state legacy of inclusive politics, open, outward-looking societies, the rule of law, personal liberty and economic opportunity. That tension, between stasis and progress, closed minds and open seas, is the single greatest dynamic in human history. It remains as important today as it was when Ruskin penned his immortal lines, even if we cannot recapture his absolute conviction. Seapower remains a constructed identity, one that evolves across time and space. Recognising the continuities of this process enables us to understand how we, whoever we are, arrived at the present. The future has always belonged to seapower, but that identity remains a question of choice.

Cultural Seapowers
A CONCEPTUAL AIDE-MÉMOIRE

- They are consciously created 'works of art', following Burckhardt's argument.
- The process is national, centrally directed and reflects the shared ambitions of an oligarchic elite combining commerce and capital with land and social rank.
- They emphasise maritime commerce and revenues drawn from commerce in the economic and fiscal life of the state.
- They have oligarchic/progressive politics, and are culturally advanced and outward-looking.
- They give the commercial classes a significant share in political power.
- They prioritise naval over military power.
- They enact legislation to create, secure or improve the maritime and naval resource base – be it ships, seamen, raw materials or trade routes.
- They are active in suppressing piracy – which is both a hindrance to trade and the cause of higher insurance rates.
- They depend on core trade routes, for which they are prepared to fight.
- They use naval power to protect trade, convoying merchant shipping.

- They are open to trade with other nations – but use economic measures to crush dangerous rivals.
- They secure a limited portfolio of overseas bases, either as imperial outposts or through alliances, which provide critical logistics and strategic facilities for naval forces. These are heavily fortified, especially against attack from the land.
- In war they employ limited strategies based on economic blockade – because they lack the military power to deliver a knockout blow.
- In war they employ mercenaries or rely on allies, waging war on land with money, not men.
- They can only operate effectively in a strategic context where several land powers exist, because:
  - seapowers are defeated by drawing them into large-scale existential land wars; and
  - they are ultimately unable to resist truly hegemonic continental powers.

GLOSSARY

Continental or military power: a political unit, state or empire, focused on land- and army-based strategies. This includes land-based aviation.

Democracy: a political system based on a mass franchise. Classical Athens used this system, with voting restricted to adult male citizens, to create the seapower state. The franchise was widened to include rowers, to sustain popular support for the naval war effort, to the consternation of Plato and Thucydides. Modern democracies, with far broader franchises, have been less enthusiastic about seapower and navies, as Mahan anticipated.

Great power: a state in the highest rank of the pre-1945 world order, on the basis of a combination of military might, manpower, wealth and resource; seapowers have always achieved this status through a combination of assets different from land-based powers, emphasising money and naval might.

Identity: the constructed self-image of an individual, group or nation. In this book the reference is national. Identity is neither imposed, nor organic, it is a constantly contested construction, reflecting the interaction between past and present, differing agendas and intentions. Maritime or seapower identity is unusual in that it does not relate to family, tribe, faith or land. It is therefore especially difficult to create and sustain. Seapower identities have been created by political action and public works, including statues and palaces, shipsheds and dockyards, naval demonstrations and festivals, subsidised artistic and literary output, as well as self-interest, the sheer scale of seafaring activity, overwhelming threats and carefully crafted public-relations exercises. Pericles understood the process, so did Henry VIII, Johan de Witt, Peter the Great and Admiral Lord Fisher. They knew it was an uphill task, because terrestrial identity has always been the 'normal' setting.

Maritime empire: the overseas empire of a continental state.

Maritime power: a state with a strong economy based on the sea, and often an effective navy focused on the defence of seagoing commerce.

Naval power: the possession of a large, potentially dominant naval force. This concept is often linked to a focus on naval battle and the search for 'decisive' victory as the precursor to continental warfare.

Oligarchy: a political system dominated by relatively small elite groups, in which different interest groups negotiate power through political debate. The oligarchic republics that controlled seapowers and sea states necessarily combined landed and commercial wealth under a constitutional head of state, a doge or a king.

Republic: a political system where power is shared. This definition, as Montesquieu stressed, includes constitutional monarchies, such as England/Britain after 1688.

Sea control: the exercise of sea power, exerting control over the surface of the sea to ensure that it can be used to invade a hostile state, or destroy its floating trade, while denying those options to an enemy.

Seapower: an identity consciously created by medium-sized powers attempting to exploit the asymmetric strategic and economic advantages of maritime power, to enable them to act as great powers. Key indicators of this aspiration include the development of oligarchic/republican political models that empower the commercial elite, focusing on naval forces rather than land forces, developing a culture suffused with the sea, and distinctively divergent from land-based models. It is a constructed identity, requiring endless repetition and reassertion. While these ideas, policies and agendas were relatively simple, exemplary precursors were often employed to deflect criticism of radical change and, in decline, to offer insight into future trends

Sea power: the strategic advantage gained by dominating the oceans with superior naval force. The basic definition was set out by Alfred T. Mahan in 1890. It can be held by any state or coalition with the requisite resources and political will.

Sea state: a state dominated by the sea, as the basis of economic activity, security and culture, but not capable of becoming, or aspiring to be, a great power, for want of scale, resource or political will. Unlike seapower this identity tends to reflect underlying realities rather than conscious construction, although it has often been carefully developed. The last three seapower great powers evolved into sea states when they lost the ability to compete with contemporary great powers or super-powers. Contemporary sea states include Britain, Denmark, the Dutch Republic, Singapore and Japan, all of which are disproportionately engaged in maritime economic and strategic activity, including banking, insurance and finance, have their capital cities on the ocean or sea, have liberal inclusive politics and take an active role in the security of the oceanic shipping.

Superpower: after 1945 the United States and the Soviet Union, imperial states that possessed exponentially superior resources than 'great powers', which they combined with the leadership of large coalitions of similar states. They dominated a bipolar world order. After the implosion of the Soviet Union the United States remained the sole superpower. Currently the People's Republic of China aspires to that status, but lacks both the strategic reach and a constellation of allies necessary to achieve it.

Universal monarchy: an imperial power seeking to dominate a large part of the relevant political world. Xerxes claimed it, Alexander the Great achieved it, if only briefly, Rome attempted it, and these examples inspired the projects of continental rulers from Charlemagne to Hitler. Seapowers invariably opposed this political model, whether political or spiritual, as incompatible with their existence and their political and economic freedom.

NOTES

Preface

1. J. Ruskin, *The Stones of Venice*, Vol. I: *The Foundations*, London: Smith, Elder, 1851, p. 1; A. D. Lambert, '"Now is come a Darker Day": Britain, Venice and the Meaning of Sea Power', in M. Taylor, ed., *The Victorian Empire and Britain's Maritime World 1837–1901: The Sea and Global History*, London: Palgrave Macmillan, 2013, pp. 19–42.
2. For the use of new technology to improve his ability to record and analyse the 'Stones' see K. Jacobsen and J. Jacobsen, *Carrying off the Palaces: John Ruskin's Lost Daguerreotypes*, London: Quaritch, 2015.
3. Turner's obsession with the cultural significance of Holland, Carthage and Venice was informed by his overarching impulse to shape a British maritime identity during the wars of the French Revolution and Empire, and to sustain that identity through the long years of peace that followed. F. G. H. Bachrach, *Turner's Holland*, London: Tate Publishing, 1994.
4. Ruskin, *Stones of Venice*, Vol. I, p. 2.

Introduction

1. J. Ruskin, *The Stones of Venice*, Vol. I: *The Foundations*. London: Smith, Elder, 1851, pp. 6 and 11.
2. George Grote (1794–1871), among the most widely read historians of the age, devoted his creative life to a monumental *History of Greece* published in twelve volumes between 1846 and 1856. G. Grote, *History of Greece*, Vol. 5, London, 1849, pp. 69–70. See Frederic Lane's *Venice: A Maritime Republic*, Baltimore, MD: Johns Hopkins University Press, 1973, p. 180, for another study of a seapower that emphasises the critical point that a seapower identity is created by human agency, not inexorable 'laws'.

3. J. Burckhardt, *The Civilisation of Italy in the Renaissance*. First published in 1860, this was a book that quickly became a widely sought-after possession, appearing in many languages.

4. A. T. Mahan, *The Influence of Sea Power upon History 1660–1783*, Boston, MA: Little, Brown, 1890, chapter 1, pp. 25–89, contains the core of Mahan's seapower argument.

5. For Ruskin's discussion of seapower identity in Carthage see his first book, *Modern Painters*, Vol. I, London: Smith, Elder, 1843. The Library Edition of Ruskin's works, edited by E. T. Cook and Alexander Wedderburn (1902–12), places this text in volume III. See pp. 112–13.

6. J. Ruskin, *The Stones of Venice*, Vol. II: *The Sea Stories*, London: Smith Elder, 1853, p. 141; R. Hewison, *Ruskin's Venice*, New Haven, CT, and London: Yale University Press, 2000, p. 38.

7. J. Ruskin, *Praeterita*, Oxford: Oxford University Press, 1978, p. 197. Ruskin used the edition produced by Thomas Arnold in 1835. Arnold's role in perpetuating the Roman indictments of Carthage and Hannibal will be addressed in chapter 3. His son Matthew pondered the nature of British identity and the possibility of decline; S. Collini, *Matthew Arnold*, Oxford: Oxford University Press, 1988, p. 74, anxious that Britain was 'declining into a sort of greater Holland'. On Victorian obsessions with Ancient Greece see: R. Jenkyns, *The Victorians and Ancient Greece*, Oxford: Basil Blackwell, 1980; F. M. Turner, *The Greek Heritage in Victorian Britain*, New Haven, CT, and London: Yale University Press, 1981.

8. Mahan was astonished by the seapower writings of Raleigh and Bacon, which he belatedly discovered after the publication of his key text in 1890.

9. Mahan to Roy Marston (his English publisher), 19 February 1897: R. Seager and D. D. Macguire, *Letters and Papers of Alfred Thayer Mahan*, 3 vols., Annapolis, MD: USNIP, 1975, vol. II, pp. 493–4.

10. This book is not intended to be exhaustive. It focuses on the connected worlds of classical and modern Europe, which were linked by a culture that was transmitted and shared, along with Eurasian and Asian states that were influenced by European thinking. For a global history of sea states see L. Paine, *The Sea and Civilisation: A Maritime History of the World*, London: Atlantic Books, 2013. The index has no entries for seapower or sea power.

11. C. G. Reynolds, '"Thalassocracy" as a Historical Force', in *History and the Sea: Essays on Maritime Strategies*, Columbia, SC: University of South Carolina Press, 1989, pp. 20–65, is a good example. The paper was delivered in 1977.

12. C. E. Behrman, *Victorian Myths of the Sea*, Athens, OH: Ohio University Press, 1977, is the classic assessment of the complex interrelationship between fact and fable in the construction of seapower identity.

13. The brain-enhancing qualities of Omega 3 are well known.

14. C. G. Starr, *The Influence of Sea Power on Ancient History*, Oxford: Oxford University Press, 1989, p. 4.

15. Mahan, *The Influence of Sea Power*, pp. iv–v, 13–21. Theodor Mommsen's *Roman History*, a three-volume study of the Republic published in 1854–6, was suffused with German nationalism; G. P. Gooch, *History and Historians of the Nineteenth Century*, London: Longman, 1913, p. 458.

16. Mahan was inspired by the strategic ideas of Antoine-Henri Jomini, analyst of Napoleon's wars.

17. The Venetian scholar/publisher Aldus Manutius produced the first Greek texts of Herodotus, Thucydides and Xenophon between 1500 and 1510. M. Lowry, *The World of Aldus Manutius*, Oxford: Basil Blackwell, 1979, pp. 144, 300. The Herodotus and Thucydides texts appeared in 1502. Tudor England supplemented these resources with navigational expertise and voyage literature from Spain and Portugal, and charts and seapower imagery from the Low Countries.

18. W. H. Sherman, *John Dee: The Politics of Reading and Writing in the English Renaissance*, Amherst, MA: University of Massachusetts Press, 1995, pp. 126, 152–3.

19. J. A. MacGillivray, *Minotaur: Sir Arthur Evans and the Archaeology of the Minoan Myth*, London: Jonathan Cape, 2000, p. 85.

20. Pericles' sea power arguments may also refer back to the experience of the First Peloponnesian War, in the 450s. L. Rawlings, *The Ancient Greeks at War*, Manchester: Manchester University Press, 2007, pp. 105–6; R. Meiggs, *The Athenian Empire*, Oxford: Oxford University Press, 1972, p. 173, fn 3.

21. J. S. Corbett, *Some Principles of Maritime Strategy*, London: Longman, 1911. Corbett's text, especially p. 14, explained the strategic options open to a seapower great power like Britain when facing continental military rivals.

22. Paine, *The Sea and Civilisation*, provides a comprehensive overview.

Chapter 1

1. The parallel with Imperial and Communist China is obvious.

2. F. Braudel, *The Mediterranean in the Ancient World*, London: Allen Lane, 2001, pp. 17, 73–4, 82.

3. Ibid., pp. 90–1, 95–6, 121.

4. Another parallel with Imperial China.

5. D. Fabre, *Seafaring in Ancient Egypt*, London: Periplus, 2005, demonstrates the profound aversion of the priestly class to the ocean.

6. C. Broodbank, *The Making of the Middle Sea: A History of the Mediterranean from the Beginning to the Emergence of the Classical World*, London: Thames & Hudson, 2013, pp. 464, 401.

7. Ibid., p. 69; P. Horden and N. Purcell, *The Corrupting Sea: A Study of Mediterranean History*, Oxford: Basil Blackwell, 2000, pp. 347–50.

8. Broodbank, *The Making of the Middle Sea*, p. 367.

9. Horden and Purcell, *The Corrupting Sea*, pp. 348 and 347–50; B. Cunliffe, *Europe between Oceans: Themes and Variations 9000 BC–AD 1000*, New Haven, CT, and London: Yale University Press, 2008, pp. 179–82; Broodbank, *The Making of the Middle Sea*, pp. 336, 377–89, 394–5, 415.

10. Horden and Purcell, *The Corrupting Sea*, pp. 5 and 11. Or, as Mahan observed: 'As a highway, a railroad competes in vain with a river – the greater speed cannot compensate for the smaller carriage.' A. T. Mahan, *The Problem of Asia*, Boston, MA: Little, Brown, 1900, p. 38.

11. The phrase is Plato's.

12. Horden and Purcell, *The Corrupting Sea*, p. 5.

13. Ibid., pp. 342, 438.

14. Ibid., p. 11. Those 'routes' were described in the *Odyssey*.

15. Cunliffe, *Europe between Oceans*, pp. 188, 199–200.

16. Broodbank, *The Making of the Middle Sea*, pp. 352–7, quote at p. 357.

17. Braudel, *The Mediterranean in the Ancient World*, pp. 135–8

18. Cunliffe, *Europe between Oceans*, pp. 187–96.

19. Broodbank, *The Making of the Middle Sea*, pp. 381–8, 410–11.

20. Braudel, *The Mediterranean in the Ancient World*, pp. 149–50.

21. G. Markoe, *The Phoenicians*, London: British Museum Press, 2000, pp. 15–21.

22. Broodbank, *The Making of the Middle Sea*, p. 450.

23. Ibid., pp. 462–7. Those countries that block the free exchange of ideas.

24. Markoe, *The Phoenicians*, p. 11.

25. Braudel, *The Mediterranean in the Ancient World*, pp. 208–9.

26. Markoe, *The Phoenicians*, pp. 22–37, as did the Venetians, the Dutch and the British.

27. Ezekiel 27.

28. Braudel, *The Mediterranean in the Ancient World*, pp. 214–15.

29. Cyprus and Crete were used by Tyre, Athens, Venice and Britain.

30. Broodbank, *The Making of the Middle Sea*, pp. 494–503.

31. Cunliffe, *Europe between Oceans*, pp. 236–53.
32. Markoe, *The Phoenicians*, p. 98.
33. Cunliffe, *Europe between Oceans*, pp. 289–91.
34. Markoe, *The Phoenicians*, pp. 182–8. The Tyrians were trading with the Moroccan Atlantic port of Essouira by 650 BC.
35. Cunliffe, *Europe between Oceans*, p. 285.
36. Ibid., pp. 298–9.
37. Ibid., pp. 270–98; Horden and Purcell, *The Corrupting Sea*, Map p. 127.
38. R. Carpenter, *Beyond the Pillars of Hercules: The Classical World Seen through the Eyes of its Discoverers*, London: Tandem Books, 1963, pp. 143–4.
39. Markoe, *The Phoenicians*, pp. 87, 68.
40. Broodbank, *The Making of the Middle Sea*, p. 484.
41. Markoe, *The Phoenicians*, pp. 199–201, 164.
42. Broodbank, *The Making of the Middle Sea*, pp. 357, 445, 485–6.
43. J. Naish, *Seamarks: Their History and Development*, London: Stanford Maritime, 1985, pp. 15–24.
44. Broodbank, *The Making of the Middle Sea*, p. 488; Horden and Purcell, *The Corrupting Sea*, pp. 115–22.
45. Broodbank, *The Making of the Middle Sea*, pp. 492, 496.
46. Ibid., p. 505; Horden and Purcell, *The Corrupting Sea*, p. 116.
47. Broodbank, *The Making of the Middle Sea*, pp. 508–9.
48. F. C. Lane, *Profits from Power: Readings in Protection Rent and Violence-Controlling Enterprises*, Albany, NY: State University of New York Press, 1979, pp. 3, 10.
49. Centuries later the Romans developed Delos to control Rhodes in the same manner.
50. H. T. Wallinga, 'The Ancestry of the Trireme', in J. Morison, ed., *The Age of the Galley: Mediterranean Oared Vessels since Pre-Classical Times*, London: Conway Press, 1995, pp. 36–48, reproduced at p. 43. The relief image shows penteconters with rams and without.
51. Broodbank, *The Making of the Middle Sea*, pp. 525–35.
52. Ibid., p. 537.
53. Ibid., pp. 536–7.
54. Ibid., pp. 520–1. Tyrants were oligarchs who broke the power of their peer group in order to retain political power. The suffetes were frequently referred to as 'Kings' but this is anachronistic.
55. Broodbank, *The Making of the Middle Sea*, pp. 542–3.
56. D. Blackman and B. Rankov, eds, *Shipsheds of the Ancient Mediterranean*, Cambridge: Cambridge University Press, 2013; for Samos see pp. 210–13.
57. Broodbank, *The Making of the Middle Sea*, p. 547.
58. Ibid., p. 561.
59. Ibid., p. 569.
60. Ibid., p. 581.
61. Cunliffe, *Europe between Oceans*, pp. 317–18.
62. Broodbank, *The Making of the Middle Sea*, pp. 583–4.
63. Ibid., pp. 603, 607.
64. Ibid., p. 603.
65. Ibid., p. 606.

Chapter 2

1. See Arnaldo Momigliano's essential essay, 'Sea-Power in Greek Thought', in *Secondo contributo alla storia degli studi classici*, Rome: Storia e Letteratura, 1966, pp. 57–68.
2. Wallinga, 'The Ancestry of the Trireme', at pp. 7–12, supports Thucydides' analysis; Braudel, *The Mediterranean in the Ancient World*, emphasises the Phoenician contribution.
3. Parallels with English sea power myths before and after 1588 are clear and compelling.

4. J. Gould, *Herodotus*, London: Weidenfeld & Nicolson, 1989, H.3.4 and H.3.122.2.

5. H. T. Wallinga, *Ships and Sea-Power before the Great Persian War*, Leiden: Brill, 1993, pp. 99–101.

6. E. Foster, *Thucydides, Pericles, and Periclean Imperialism*, Cambridge: Cambridge University Press, 2013, p. 15 fn. 9, for a sample of such opinions. Foster agues that Thucydides was a critic of Athenian imperialism, and of Pericles' intransigent, materialistic imperial vision.

7. L. Rawlings, *The Ancient Greeks at War*, Manchester: Manchester University Press, 2007, pp. 105–6; R. Meiggs, *The Athenian Empire*, Oxford: Oxford University Press, 1972, p. 247, citing Thucydides, T.II.69.

8. Foster, *Thucydides, Pericles*, pp. 15–27.

9. Rawlings, *The Ancient Greeks at War*, p. 106.

10. V. Gabrielsen, *Financing the Athenian Fleet: Public Taxation and Social Relations*, Baltimore, MD: Johns Hopkins University Press, 1994, pp. 19–26.

11. Wallinga, *Ships and Sea-Power*, pp.117–19, the quote is from Herodotus.

12. Ibid., p. 126.

13. H.5.66, H.5.78. I have used the 1858 translation by George Rawlinson throughout, unless otherwise specified. Gould, *Herodotus*, p. 15.

14. H.5.91 and H.6.21.

15. Wallinga, *Ships and Sea-Power*, pp. 130–7.

16. Gabrielsen, *Financing the Athenian Fleet*, p. 32.

17. It is significant that among the many major continental powers to build great navies the only one that has been able to sustain this level of effort across long decades of relative peace is the United States. The USA is an example of a democratic political model largely derived from British liberal traditions, created to maximise the political and economic resource base for sea power in the 'Glorious Revolution' of 1688, to resist the universal-monarchy ambition of Bourbon France.

18. Gould, *Herodotus*, pp. 70–9, renders Xerxes' ambition 'impious and wicked', while Rawlinson opted for 'unholy and presumptuous': H.7.8.3 and H.8.109.3.

19. Wallinga, *Ships and Sea-Power*, p. 161.

20. H.8.86.

21. Wallinga, *Ships and Sea-Power*, pp. 161–4.

22. In Rex Warner's edition 'became a people of sailors'; the Landmark has 'became a naval people'. T.1.18, T.1.93.

23. H.7.96, H.7.128, and H.8.121. Royal Navy trophies on display at the United States Naval Academy, Annapolis, serve the same function.

24. H.9.9 and H.8.142.

25. H.9.120 and Gould, *Herodotus*, p. 86.

26. Gould, *Herodotus*, pp. 102–5.

27. The date of his death in unknown, but internal evidence suggests it was between 430 and 400 BC. Reference to the great calamities that befell the Greeks from the 'contentions among their own chief men respecting the supreme power' (H.6.98) demonstrates a late date for the completion of the standard text.

28. H.7.162.1, Gould, *Herodotus*, p. 118; P. A. Stadler, 'Thucydides as a "Reader" of Herodotus', in E. Foster and D. Lateiner, eds., *Thucydides and Herodotus*, Oxford: Oxford University Press, 2012, pp. 39–63, at p. 43 for dates.

29. H.9.73; T.1.102.

30. H.8.112 and Gould, *Herodotus*, p. 117.

31. T.1.90 and W. Blösel, 'Thucydides on Themistocles: A Herodotean Narrator?', in Foster and Lateiner, eds., *Thucydides and Herodotus*, pp. 216–36, at pp. 220–33.

32. Meiggs, *The Athenian Empire*, pp. 156–7; T.1.93.

33. Meiggs, *The Athenian Empire*, pp. 75–7.

34. Ibid., pp. 62, 70–1.

35. Ibid., pp. 75–6, 86 and 205–7.

36. Ibid., pp. 69, 242, 247, 252.
37. Ibid., pp. 259–60.
38. Ibid., p. 254.
39. Ibid., pp. 86–90.
40. T.1.102; Meiggs, *The Athenian Empire*, pp. 89–94.
41. Meiggs, *The Athenian Empire*, pp. 217–33. Parallels with the role of the British Privy Council in the jurisdiction of the empire are obvious. British courts sustained the colonial status of new settlements. After 1776 classically educated British statesmen knew better than to demand tribute from colonies, and were doubly anxious about revolts.
42. *Pseudo Xenophon*, 2.11–12.
43. P. Zagorin, *Thucydides*, Princeton, NJ: Princeton University Press, 2005, p. 70.
44. Meiggs, *The Athenian Empire*, pp. 104–5.
45. Ibid., pp. 184–5, 116, 123, 125, 173.
46. M. Taylor, *Thucydides, Pericles, and the Idea of Athens in the Peloponnesian War*, Cambridge: Cambridge University Press, 2010, pp. 24–6.
47. Meiggs, *The Athenian Empire*, pp. 156–7.
48. Athenian devotion to tradition was a prominent feature of their culture, despite the radical shift from land to sea.
49. Pausanias, *Description of Greece*, 1.28.2; Meiggs, *The Athenian Empire*, pp. 94–5.
50. D. Blackman and B. Rankov, eds., *Shipsheds of the Ancient Mediterranean*, Cambridge: Cambridge University Press, 2013, pp. 525–34.
51. Meiggs, *The Athenian Empire*, pp. 256, 265.
52. Ibid., pp. 199, 203–4. Thucydides disagreed, preferring deeper causes.
53. Ibid., pp. 272–5.
54. Ibid., pp. 91, 201, 204, 272–5.
55. Taylor, *Thucydides, Pericles*, pp. 30 and 33.
56. T.1.142.6–7.
57. T.1.143.4.
58. Meiggs, *The Athenian Empire*, pp. 217 and 266, citing the Old Oligarch.
59. Ibid., p. 343.
60. Ibid., pp. 344–7.
61. Taylor, *Thucydides, Pericles*, pp. 41–3, 68–75.
62. Rawlings, *The Ancient Greeks at War*, pp. 109–11.
63. Meiggs, *The Athenian Empire*, p. 258.
64. Churchill's 1915 Dardanelles attack reflected a similar overestimation of the impact of seapower.
65. E. Robinson, *Democracy beyond Athens: Popular Government in the Greek Classical Age*, Cambridge: Cambridge University Press, 2011, pp. 230–1.
66. Robinson, *Democracy beyond Athens*, pp. 236 and fn. 79; V. Gabrielsen, *The Naval Aristocracy of Hellenistic Rhodes*, Aarhus: Aarhus University Press, 1997. This has been the case in all seapower states.
67. Wallinga, *Ships and Sea-Power*, 1993, pp. 101–2.
68. Ibid., pp. 43–84 and T.1.143.1.
69. Gabrielsen, *Financing the Athenian Fleet*, pp. 36–9, 144, 173–5, 219–26.
70. Ibid., pp. 180–217.
71. Foster, *Thucydides, Pericles*, p. 218.
72. See Meiggs, *The Athenian Empire*, pp. 372–4, on the removal of successful generals.
73. Wallinga, *Ships and Sea-Power*, pp. 71–2. George Gooch's characterisation of Meyer (1855–1930) in *History and Historians of the Nineteenth Century*, London, 1913, pp. 483–4, amplifies the anti-democratic, imperialist assumptions that drove his history of Greece. He argued that the Macedonian military imperialism of Philip II was the solution to the Greek problem.
74. M. Reinhold, 'Classical Scholarship, Modern Anti-Semitism and the Zionist Project: The Historian Eduard Meyer in Palestine', *Bryn Mawr Classical Review* (May 2005).

75. Useful parallels can be drawn with the creation of British seapower between 1690 and 1714.
76. The assumption that Thucydides endorsed and supported Pericles and his strategy cannot be sustained.
77. Taylor, *Thucydides, Pericles*, pp. 1–3, quote pp. 3, 8 and 108.
78. Ibid., pp. 79–90.
79. T.6.24.3 and Taylor, *Thucydides, Pericles*, pp. 121 and 148.
80. Meiggs, *The Athenian Empire*, pp. 306–19.
81. T.7.21.3 and Taylor, *Thucydides, Pericles*, pp. 178, 167–8.
82. Taylor, *Thucydides, Pericles*, p. 198, citing A. W. Gomme, *A Historical Commentary on Thucydides: Volume One*, Oxford: Oxford University Press, 1958. 1945, 1.107.4.
83. T.1.107–8.
84. Taylor, *Thucydides, Pericles*, pp. 272–3, 277.
85. By contrast the endless cycle of construction and collapse that marks the history of the Russian Navy reflects the failure of cultural engagement.
86. Rawlings, *The Ancient Greeks at War*, p. 120.
87. J. S. Morrison, *The Athenian Trireme: The History and Reconstruction of an Ancient Greek Warship*, Cambridge: Cambridge University Press, 1995, pp. 52–4, and Gabrielsen in ibid., p. 240.
88. R. Osborne, ed. and trans. *The Old Oligarch: Pseudo-Xenophon's Constitution of the Athenians* (Lactor), Cambridge: Cambridge University Press, 2004, p. 17, 1.2.
89. See Taylor, *Thucydides, Pericles* for the latest discussion of this critique.
90. Rawlings, *The Ancient Greeks at War*, pp. 110–11.
91. Plato, *Laws*, iv, 35–42, 705, 949, 952.
92. Aristotle, *Politics*, vii, 4, 1327 11.
93. V. Gabrielsen, 'Rhodes and the Ptolemaic Kingdom: The Commercial Infrastructure', in K. Buraselis, M. Stefanou and D. T. Thompson, *The Ptolemies, the Sea and the Nile: Studies in Waterborne Power*, Cambridge: Cambridge University Press, 2013, pp. 66–81.
94. Cicero, *De Republica*, ii, 4.7; Livy v 54. 4; Polybius vi, 52.
95. Appian, *Pun* 86–9.

Chapter 3

1. M. M. Fantar, *Carthage: The Punic City*, Tunis: Alif, 1998, p. 31.
2. G. C. Picard and C. Picard, *The Life and Death of Carthage*, London: Sidgwick and Jackson 1968, pp. 1–5, 15.
3. Ibid., p. 43.
4. Fantar, *Carthage*, plan 1, for an excellent graphic of the site, as an arrow-headed peninsula, with massive walls across the neck of the arrowhead, securing both the city and a significant agricultural area. See also p. 41.
5. Ibid., pp. 38–40.
6. Picard and Picard, *The Life and Death of Carthage*, pp. 61–6.
7. Fantar, *Carthage*, pp. 50–7.
8. Ibid., pp. 88–90; Markoe, *The Phoenicians*, London: British Museum Press, 2000, pp. 87–92
9. G. Markoe, *The Phoenicians*, pp. 105–7; Fantar, *Carthage*, p. 100.
10. Carthage has produced more Egyptian artefacts than any other site in the western Mediterranean. R. Docter, R. Boussoffara, and P. ter Keurs, eds., *Carthage: Fact and Myth*, Leiden: Sidestone Press, 2015. pp. 58–9.
11. C. Broodbank, *The Making of the Middle Sea: A History of the Mediterranean from the Beginning to the Emergence of the Classical World*, London: Thames and Hudson, 2013, p. 582.

12. F. Braudel, *The Mediterranean in the Ancient World*, London: Allen Lane, 2001, pp. 221–2.

13. The synergy with Venetian, Dutch and British models is absolute. Markoe, *The Phoenicians*, pp. 69–86.

14. R. Miles, *Carthage Must Be Destroyed: The Rise and Fall of an Ancient Civilisation*, London: Allen Lane, 2010, pp. 115–21. Miles demolishes the old Syracusan legend that Carthage had allied with Persia against the 'Greeks'. This self-serving propaganda was designed to improve the standing of the Syracusan tyrant in the Greek-speaking world, providing the basis for subsequent Roman propaganda.

15. Picard and Picard, *The Life and Death of Carthage*, pp. 78–80, 86; Miles, *Carthage Must Be Destroyed*, p. 122.

16. Miles, *Carthage Must Be Destroyed*, p. 137; Picard and Picard, *The Life and Death of Carthage*, p. 171.

17. Fantar, *Carthage*, pp. 58–63.

18. Broodbank, *The Making of the Middle Sea*, p. 579.

19. Markoe, *The Phoenicians*, pp. 102–3 and 67.

20. M. Pitassi, *The Navies of Rome*, Woodbridge: Boydell and Brewer, 2009, pp. 1, 8, 18.

21. A. Goldsworthy, *The Fall of Carthage: The Punic Wars, 265–146 BC*, London: Cassell, 2000, p. 69.

22. W. V. Harris, *War and Imperialism in Republican Rome 327–70 BC*, Oxford: Clarendon Press, 1979, p. 183.

23. Ibid., p. 184.

24. Pitassi, *The Navies of Rome*, pp. 32–44, 47, 92.

25. Goldsworthy, *The Fall of Carthage*, p. 72.

26. Pitassi, *The Navies of Rome*, p. 88; F. F. Armesto, *Civilisations*, London: Macmillan, 2000, p. 437.

27. Harris, *War and Imperialism*, pp. 185.

28. Ibid., p. 187.

29. W. M. Murray, *The Age of the Titans: The Rise and Fall of the Great Hellenistic Navies*, Oxford: Oxford University Press, 2012, pp. 12–30.

30. For the naval battles see Goldsworthy, *The Fall of Carthage*, and the older standard W. L. Rodgers, *Naval Wars under Oars*, Annapolis, MD: Naval Institute Press, 1940.

31. Picard and Picard, *The Life and Death of Carthage*, pp. 195–201.

32. The mercenary war fascinated Sir Walter Raleigh, who, as an Elizabethan Englishman, found it both relevant and alarming: see W. Raleigh, *History of the World*, London, 1614, bk V, ch. 2.

33. Picard and Picard, *The Life and Death of Carthage*, pp. 205–13; Harris, *War and Imperialism*, pp. 190–4.

34. Fantar, *Carthage*, p. 67.

35. Harris, *War and Imperialism*, pp. 200–2.

36. J. Guilmartin, *Gunpowder and Galleys: Changing Technology and Warfare at Sea in the Sixteenth Century*, Cambridge: Cambridge University Press, 1974.

37. Picard and Picard, *The Life and Death of Carthage*, pp. 215–54.

38. Pitassi, *The Navies of Rome*, pp. 90–4.

39. Picard and Picard, *The Life and Death of Carthage*, pp. 256–63; Harris, *War and Imperialism*, pp. 138–9.

40. Livy, *The Histories*, trans. E. S. Shuckburgh, London: Macmillan, 1889, bk XIV, 30.43

41. The revival of British navalism in the 1890s was propelled by such fears.

42. Picard and Picard, *The Life and Death of Carthage*, pp. 274–7.

43. O. Spengler, *The Decline of the West*, Vol. II, London: Allen and Unwin, 1926, pp. 422 and 191.

44. Although originally reliant on a natural anchorage and suitable beaches for hauling out galleys, Carthage had constructed harbours by the sixth century BC: Fantar, *Carthage*, pp. 41–5.

45. Ibid., pp. 87–8.

46. H. Gerding, 'Carthage', in D. Blackman and B. Rankov, eds., *Shipsheds of the Ancient Mediterranean*, Cambridge: Cambridge University Press, 2013, pp. 307–19 at p. 307.

47. D. Blackman and B. Rankov, 'Conclusions: Not Just Ship Garages', in idem, *Shipsheds of the Ancient Mediterranean*, pp. 255 and 259.

48. Gerding, 'Carthage', p. 315.

49. B. Rankov, 'Roman Shipsheds', in Blackman and Rankov, eds., *Shipsheds of the Ancient Mediterranean*, pp. 30–54.

50. Harris, *War and Imperialism*, pp. 233–4.

51. Ibid., pp. 240–4, 252–4.

52. Miles, *Carthage Must Be Destroyed*, p. 336.

53. Picard and Picard, *The Life and Death of Carthage*, pp. 288–9.

54. A. J. Toynbee, *Hannibal's Legacy: The Hannibalic War's Effects on Roman Life*, London: Oxford University Press, 1965.

55. Picard and Picard, *The Life and Death of Carthage*, pp. 287–8.

56. Harris, *War and Imperialism*, pp. 237–9. For the eight-mile issue see p. 239 fn. 4.

57. Plato *The Laws*, 704b–5b.

58. Harris, *War and Imperialism*, p. 240.

59. Picard and Picard, *The Life and Death of Carthage*, pp. 290–1.

60. P. Horden, and N. Purcell, 'The Mediterranean and "the new Thalassology"', in *American Historical Review* (June 2006), pp. 722–40.

61. Spengler, *The Decline of the West*, Vol. II, p. 422.

62. Fantar, *Carthage*, p. 96. The Barcids considered Melquart and Hercules to be the same deity.

63. R. Waterfield, *Taken at the Flood: The Roman Conquest of Greece*, Oxford: Oxford University Press, 2014, p. 75.

64. Picard and Picard, *The Life and Death of Carthage*, pp. 287–8.

65. Spengler, *The Decline of the West*, vol. I, p. 36.

66. Pitassi, *The Navies of Rome*, pp. 144–56.

67. I. Samotta, 'Herodotus and Thucydides in Roman Republican Historiography', in E. Foster and D. Lateiner, eds., *Thucydides and Herodotus*, Oxford: Oxford University Press, 2012, pp. 345–73.

Chapter 4

1. The influence of St Augustine's deeply negative assessment of the ocean and seafaring remained potent in Catholic nations.

2. J. Bryce, *The Holy Roman Empire*, London: Macmillan, 1901, pp. 172 and 188.

3. The canal-side houses of Amsterdam provide a similar study in legally driven architecture.

4. C. Diehl, 'The Economic Decline of Byzantium', in C. Cipolla, ed., *The Economic Decline of Empires*, London: Methuen, 1970, pp. 92–102, provides a concise assessment.

5. D. Howard, 'Venice and the Mamluks', in S. Carboni, ed., *Venice and the Islamic World 828–1797*, New Haven, CT, and London: Yale University Press, 2007, p. 76.

6. P. F. Brown, *Venice and Antiquity*, New Haven, CT, and London: Yale University Press, 1996.

7. M. Georgopoulou, *Venice's Mediterranean Colonies: Architecture and Urbanism*, Cambridge: Cambridge University Press, 2001, p. 2.

8. For Saladin's support of this trade see B. Lewis, 'The Arabs in Eclipse', in Cipolla, ed., *The Economic Decline of Empires*, p. 109.

9. M. Fusaro, *Political Economies of Empire in the Early Mediterranean: The Decline of Venice and the Rise of England 1450–1700*, Cambridge: Cambridge University Press, 2015, pp. 176–7.

10. F. C. Lane, *Venice: A Maritime Republic*, Baltimore, MD: Johns Hopkins University Press, 1973, p. 23. Lane's work remains the most persuasive analysis of the subject, the result of a lifetime's study of the city and the experience of writing about sea power and strategy during the Second World War.

11. T. A. Kirk, *Genoa and the Sea: Policy and Power in an Early Modern Maritime Republic, 1559–1684*, Baltimore, MD: Johns Hopkins University Press, 2005, pp. 128 and 135.
12. Lane, *Venice*, p. 27. Lane is clearly using Mahan's definition, not that of Thucydides.
13. Ibid., p. 43.
14. S. Carboni, 'Moments of Vision: Venice and the Islamic World, 828–1797', in Carboni, ed., *Venice and the Islamic World*, pp. 10–35 at pp. 13–15.
15. Howard, 'Venice and the Mamluks', in Carboni, ed., *Venice and the Islamic World*, pp. 73–88 at pp. 73–6.
16. Carboni, ed., *Venice and the Islamic World*, p. 22.
17. Lane, *Venice*, p. 170.
18. F. Moro, *Venice at War: The Great Battles of the Serenissima*, Venice: Studio LT2, 2007, p. 91.
19. E. Concina, *A History of Venetian Architecture*, Cambridge: Cambridge University Press, 1998, p. 81.
20. Ibid., p. 114.
21. Ibid., pp. 120–2; D. Savoy, *Venice from the Water*, New Haven, CT, and London: Yale University Press, 2012, touched on the Arsenale at p. 56 without examining this critical statement of Venetian power.
22. The Naval Museum close by the Arsenale reflects these concerns, alongside the Venetian veneration of naval trophies.
23. Concina, *A History of Venetian Architecture*, pp. 220–1; R. Chrivi, F. Gay, M. Crovato and G. Zanelli, *L'Arsenale dei Veniziani*, Venice: Filippi, 1983, p. 28.
24. Concina, *A History of Venetian Architecture*, p. 118.
25. Brown, *Venice and Antiquity*, pp. 108–9.
26. Fusaro, *Political Economies of Empire*, p. 86.
27. Georgopoulou, *Venice's Mediterranean Colonies*, pp. 3–19, 45–73.
28. For a succinct statement of the continental argument see Moro, *Venice at War*. The battles studied are largely on land. Moro argues the Venetians fought for independence, then for trade, and then for empire. After 1720, with the Republic unable to wage war against major powers, the elite feared social change and became repressive.
29. Lane, *Venice*, p. 235.
30. Ibid., p. 237.
31. Concina, *A History of Venetian Architecture*, p. 171.
32. Lane, *Venice*, p. 242; Brown, *Venice and Antiquity*, p. 146.
33. The strategic significance of this location, and the enclosed bay, is indicated by the number of major naval and amphibious battles fought in the area between the fourth century BC and 1941.
34. This section is largely based on F. C. Lane, 'Naval Actions and Fleet Organization, 1499–1502', in J. R. Hale, ed., *Renaissance Venice*, London: Faber, 1973, pp. 146–73.
35. J. F. Guilmartin, *Gunpowder and Galleys: Changing Technology and Warfare at Sea in the Sixteenth Century*, Cambridge: Cambridge University Press, pp. 76, 96, 102–4.
36. Ferdinand Columbus owned a copy, as did the Habsburg Emperor Rudolf II; the latter, now in the British Library, is the only surviving example: M. P. McDonald, *Ferdinand Columbus: Renaissance Collector*, London: British Museum Press, 2004, pp. 104–5.
37. Moro, *Venice at War*, pp. 175–8.
38. I. Fenlon, *The Ceremonial City: History, Memory and Myth in Renaissance Venice*, New Haven, CT, and London: Yale University Press, pp. 326–7.
39. F. Gilbert, 'Venice in the Crisis of the League of Cambrai', in Hale, *Renaissance Venice*, pp. 274–92, quote p. 292.
40. Lane, *Venice*, 1973, p. 213.
41. Ibid., 1973, pp. 357, 375, 383. Lane is a better guide to Carpaccio's shipping than Brown; P. F. Brown, *Venetian Narrative Painting in the Age of Carpaccio*, New Haven, CT, and London: Yale University Press, 1988.
42. Ibid., pp. 9–10. Brown mistakes sailing ships for galleys.

43. Ibid., 1996, pp. 148–64.
44. J. Schulz, 'Jacopo de' Barbari's View of Venice: Map Making, City Views, and Moralized Geography before the Year 1500', *The Art Bulletin*, vol. 60, no. 3 (1978), pp. 425–74; Fenlon, *The Ceremonial* City, p. 90.
45. Brown, *Venetian Narrative Painting*, pp. 9–15, 79–83, 132, 137, 182, 240.
46. Ibid., p. 145.
47. M. Lowry, *The World of Aldus Manutius*, Oxford: Basil Blackwell, 1979, p. 144.
48. 'Aldus Manutius and his Greek Collaborators'. Exhibition at the Marciana Library, October 2016.
49. Brown, *Venice and Antiquity*, pp. 226 and 268.
50. Concina, *A History of Venetian Architecture*, pp. 176, 183–4.
51. Fenlon, *The Ceremonial City*, pp. 134 and 307; see pp. 1–2 for Pompeo Battoni's picture *The Triumph of Venice* of 1732, dominated by the two Roman gods, created for Marco Foscarini, the last Official Historian of the Republic and ambassador to the Papal Curia.
52. Lane, *Venice*, p. 223; D. Howard, *The Architectural History of Venice*, New Haven, CT, and London: Yale University Press, 1980, pp. 3–13.
53. Savoy, *Venice from the Water*, pp. 104–5 and 109.
54. Ibid., pp. 9 and 46–9; italics in the original.
55. Ibid., p. 82.
56. Ibid., pp. 41–2.
57. M. Strachan, *The Life and Adventures of Thomas Coryate*, London: Oxford University Press, 1962; J. Naish, *Seamarks: Their History and Development*, London: Stanford Maritime, 1985, pp. 25–6.
58. D. Howard and H. McBurney, eds., *The Image of Venice: Fialetti's View and Sir Henry Wotton*, New Haven, CT, and London: Yale University Press, 2014.
59. Fusaro, *Political Economies of Empire*, pp. 176–7.
60. Brown, *Venice and Antiquity*, makes extensive use of Livy at pp. 277–81, but, like Lane, *Venice*, does not address Carthage.
61. G. B. Parks, 'Ramusio's Literary History', in *Studies in Philology*, vol. 52, no. 2 (1955), pp. 127–48.
62. Lane, *Venice*, p. 307.
63. Fusaro, *Political Economies of Empire*, pp. 36, 43–4, 52–5.
64. Fenlon, *The Ceremonial City*, p. 168.
65. Guilmartin, *Gunpowder and Galleys*, pp. 209–31, has an excellent discussion of these issues.
66. The commanding presence of Andrea Vicentino's massive picture of the battle (painted 1596–1605) in the Doge's Palace reflected both a recent fire that had created the space and the overwhelming psychological importance of the event. The armoured image of the Venetian commander Sebastiano Venier, who became Doge in 1577, standing proudly on his lantern galley, dominates the image. Fenlon, *The Ceremonial City*, pp. 172–5.
67. Ibid., pp. 188–91.
68. Guilmartin, *Gunpowder and Galleys*, pp. 235–68, quote at p. 264.
69. Brown, *Venice and Antiquity*, pp. 282–4.
70. Fenlon, *The Ceremonial City*, pp. 194–210.
71. Ibid., p. 219; Concina, pp. 219–21.
72. Fenlon, *The Ceremonial City*, pp. 313–14, 325–6, 331. Other public spaces were used to celebrate Lepanto, especially churches, but the Ducal Palace was the cult centre.
73. P. Burke, *Venice and Amsterdam: A Study of Seventeenth-Century Elites*, London: Polity Press, 1994, p. 127.
74. Fusaro, *Political Economies of Empire*, p. 73.
75. Ibid., pp. 17, 20–3.
76. Lane, *Venice*, p. 321, citing F. Braudel, *The Mediterranean in the Age of Philip II*, London: Collins, 1973.

77. Fusaro, *Political Economies of Empire*, pp. 176–8.

78. Ibid., pp. 174–5.

79. Ibid., pp. 188–90.

80. Ibid., pp. 158–9, 199.

81. D. Ormrod, *The Rise of Commercial Empires: England and the Netherlands in the Age of Mercantilism*, Cambridge: Cambridge University Press, 2003, pp. 32–3, cited in Fusaro, *Political Economies of Empire*, p. 201, see also p. 355.

82. J. Addison, *Remarks on Several Parts of Italy, in the Years 1701, 1702, 1703*, London, 1705, cited in Burke, *Venice and Amsterdam*, p. 99, see also pp. 56–7, 133–8.

83. Addison, *Remarks*, cited in G. Bull, *Venice, the Most Triumphant City*, London: Folio Society, 1981, pp. 99–102, 116.

84. Lane, *Venice*, p. 452.

85. Burke, *Venice and Amsterdam*, pp. 104–6.

86. Lane, *Venice*, p. 417.

87. Fusaro, *Political Economies of Empire*, pp. 303, 351.

88. Lane, *Venice*, p. 425.

89. The exhibits included drawings of a Venetian ship of the line carried out of the Lagoon on flotation devices known as 'camels', a technology borrowed from the Dutch. One of these engravings was published by Lane, *Venice*, p. 413. Compare with J. Bender, *Dutch Warships in the Age of Sail, 1600–1714: Design, Construction, Careers and Fates*, Barnsley: Seaforth Publishing, 2104, p. 289, which records the first use of this system in 1690, to lift a three-decked ship across the Pampus shoal at Amsterdam.

90. Fusaro, *Political Economies of Empire*, p. 357.

91. R. Winfield and S. S. Roberts, *French Warships in the Age of Sail: Design Construction and Fates 1786–1861*, Barnsley: Seaforth Publishing, 2015, pp. 96–7. Nine seventy-four gun ships were built at Venice, and for Napoleon's Italian navy none carried Venetian names. See also L. Sondhaus, 'Napoleon's Shipbuilding Program at Venice and the Struggle for Naval Mastery in the Adriatic, 1806–1814', *Journal of Military History*, vol. 53 (1989), pp. 349–62.

92. G. P. Gooch, *History and Historians of the Nineteenth Century*, London: Longman, 1913, pp. 82, 160–1.

93. Fusaro, *Political Economies of Empire*, p. 22.

94. A. D. Lambert, '"Now is Come a Darker Day": Britain, Venice and the Meaning of Seapower', in M. Taylor, ed., *The Victorian Empire and Britain's Maritime World, 1837–1901: The Sea and Global History*, London: Palgrave Macmillan, 2013, pp. 19–42.

95. Fenlon, *The Ceremonial City*, pp. 134 and 307.

96. Fusaro, *Political Economies of Empire*, pp. 1, 8–10. Lambert, '"Now is Come a Darker Day"', p. 38.

Chapter 5

1. The motto on the reverse of the medal celebrating the inauguration of the new Amsterdam Town Hall in 1655. K. K. Fremantle, *The Baroque Town Hall of Amsterdam*, Utrecht: Haentjens Dekker and Gumbert, 1959, p. 169.

2. L. Sicking, *Neptune and the Netherlands: State, Economy, and War at Sea in the Renaissance*, Leiden: Brill, 2004, and J. D. Tracy, 'Herring Wars: The Habsburg Netherlands and the Struggle for Control of the North Sea ca. 1520–1560', *The Sixteenth Century Journal*, vol. 24 no. 2 (1993), pp. 249–72 at pp. 254–6.

3. Tracy, 'Herring Wars', pp. 261–4.

4. In an echo of Thomas More's *Utopia*, Pieter de la Court raised the idea of separating the maritime provinces from the rest with a huge moat in his 1662 text *The Interest of Holland*. His book was published in London in 1746: http://oll.libertyfund.org/titles/court-the-true-interest-and-political-maxims-of-the-republic-of-holland.

5. P. Brandon, *War, Capital, and the Dutch State (1588–1795)*, Leiden: Brill, 2015, pp. 20–1, 34.

6. G. E. Halkos and N. C. Kyriazis, 'A Naval Revolution and Institutional Change: The Case of the United Provinces', in *European Journal of Law and Economics*, vol. 19 (2005), pp. 41–68, 58.

7. Tracy, 'Herring Wars', p. 272. It is hard to understand what is meant by the reference to 'Dutch naval supremacy in the early seventeenth century' on this page. Before 1650 the Dutch had nothing to match the capital ships of England, Sweden or Denmark.

8. Ibid, p. 60.

9. I. J. van Loo, 'For Freedom and Fortune: The Rise of Dutch Privateering in the First Half of the Dutch Revolt, 1568–1609', in M. van der Hoeven, ed., *Exercise of Arms: Warfare in the Netherlands (1568–1648)*, Leiden: Brill, 1998, pp. 173–96 at pp. 185 and 191; P. C. Allen, *Philip III and the Pax Hispanica, 1598–1621: The Failure of Grand Strategy*, New Haven and London: Yale University Press, pp. 42, 142–3.

10. Brandon, *War, Capital, and the Dutch State*, p. 114.

11. This term, along with 'New Navy' and 'Second Rate Navy', were introduced by Jaap Bruijn.

12. Brandon, *War, Capital, and the Dutch State*, pp. 58–61.

13. A. P. van Vliet, 'Foundation, Organization and Effects of the Dutch Navy (1568–1648)', in van der Hoeven, ed., *Exercise of Arms*, pp. 153–72 at pp. 156–7; Brandon, *War, Capital, and the Dutch State*, pp. 63–4, 83, and see Annex 1, pp. 323–85, for a full list of all those who served on the Admiralty boards.

14. J. R. Bruijn, *The Dutch Navy of the Seventeenth and Eighteenth Centuries*, St. John's, Newfoundland: IMEHA, 2015, first edn, 1992, pp. 3–7; Brandon, *War, Capital, and the Dutch State*, p. 60.

15. J. Glete, *War and the State in Early Modern Europe: Spain, the Dutch Republic and Sweden as Fiscal-Military States, 1500–1660*, London: Routledge, 2002, pp. 162–70.

16. Van Vliet, 'Foundation, Organization and Effects of the Dutch Navy', pp. 158–61.

17. J. D. Davies, 'British Perceptions of Michiel de Ruyter and the Anglo-Dutch Wars', in J. R. Bruijn, R. P. van Reine and R. van Hövell tot Westerflier, *De Ruyter: Dutch Admiral*, Rotterdam: Karwansaray, 2011 pp. 122–39, for the pioneering anonymous 1677 English biography of the admiral.

18. Van Loo, 'For Freedom and Fortune', pp. 184–5.

19. Ibid., p. 191; Bruijn, *The Dutch Navy of the Seventeenth and Eighteenth Centuries*, pp. 13–21; Brandon, *War, Capital, and the Dutch State*, p. 101.

20. Halkos and Kyriazis, 'A Naval Revolution and Institutional Change', p. 57.

21. Bruijn, *The Dutch Navy of the Seventeenth and Eighteenth Centuries*, pp. 22–4.

22. C.-E. Levillain, 'William III's Military and Political Career in Neo-Roman Context, 1672–1702', *The Historical Journal*, vol. 48 (2005) pp. 321–50 at p. 325.

23. Fremantle, *The Baroque Town Hall of Amsterdam*, p. 27.

24. M. Bulut, 'The Role of the Ottoman and Dutch in the Commercial Integration between the Levant and Atlantic in the Seventeenth Century', *Journal of the Economic and Social History of the Orient*, vol. 45 (2002), pp. 197–230 at p. 216.

25. J. I. Israel, *The Dutch Republic: Its Rise, Greatness and Fall, 1477–1806*, Oxford: Oxford University Press, 1995, pp. 610–12, 700–2.

26. C. Lawrence, 'Hendrick de Keyser's Heemskerck Monument: The Origins of the Cult and Iconography of Dutch Naval Heroes', in *Simiolus: Netherlands Quarterly for the History of Art*, vol. 21, no. 4 (1992), pp. 265–95 at p. 272, and S. Schama, *The Embarrassment of Riches: An Interpretation of Dutch Culture in the Golden Age*, London: Collins, 1987, p. 248.

27. Israel, *The Dutch Republic*, pp. 401–2. The battle took place on 25 April 1607.

28. Lawrence, 'Hendrick de Keyser's Heemskerck Monument', pp. 275–83.

29. Ibid., pp. 266 and 291; K. Skovgaard-Petersen, *Historiography at the Court of Christian IV: 1588–1648*, Copenhagen: Museum Tusculanum Press, 2002, discusses Pontanus's Danish career, without reference to the Amsterdam History.

30. Halkos and Kyriazis, 'A Naval Revolution and Institutional Change', p. 59.

31. M. de Jong, 'Dutch Public Finance During the Eighty Years War: The Case of the Province of Zeeland, 1585–1648', in van der Hoeven, ed., *Exercise of Arms*, pp. 133–52 at p. 151.

32. Halkos and Kyriazis, 'A Naval Revolution and Institutional Change', p. 63.
33. Older historiography portrayed the Republic as a weak state, lacking the strong central-ised authority to mobilise resources for war. This critique was created in the post-1815 Kingdom, to normalise the experience of an unusual state and deprecate the success of bourgeois government. Glete, *War and the State in Early Modern Europe*, pp. 140–2.
34. Ibid., pp. 147 and 150.
35. H. L. Zwitzer, 'The Eighty Years War', in van der Hoeven, ed., *Exercise of Arms*, pp. 33–56 at pp. 24 and 33 for Polybius, Vegetius and Tacitus; Glete, *War and the State in Early Modern Europe*, pp. 141, 156–62. The relative absence of such references from modern discussions of strategy, policy and naval affairs undervalues the powerful impact of Athenian, Venetian and Genoese models on Dutch thinking about war and the state.
36. Schama, *The Embarrassment of Riches*, pp. 241–6.
37. Glete, *War and the State in Early Modern Europe*, pp. 171–2.
38. Levillain, 'William III's Military and Political Career', pp. 331–2.
39. J. I. Israel, *The Dutch Republic*, p. 720.
40. H. H. Rowen, *John de Witt Grand Pensionary of Holland, 1625–1672*, Princeton, NJ: Princeton University Press, 1978; Brandon, *War, Capital, and the Dutch State*, pp. 74–5, 118–19.
41. Rowen, *John de Witt*, pp. 56, 62, 67.
42. Quote from a Dutch pamphlet of 1653: Rowen, *John de Witt*, pp. 65 and 71.
43. Brandon, *War, Capital, and the Dutch State*, pp. 87 and 91.
44. Schama, *The Embarrassment of Riches*, pp. 117 and 224; P. Burke, *Venice and Amsterdam: A Study of Seventeenth-Century Elites*, London: Polity Press, 1994, p. 49. Rowen, *John de Witt*, pp. 80–1, 95, 98.
45. Van Vliet, 'Foundation, Organization and Effects of the Dutch Navy', pp. 162–3.
46. Bruijn, *The Dutch Navy of the Seventeenth and Eighteenth Centuries*, pp. 48, 59–61; Levillian, 'William III's Military and Political Career', p. 333 fn. 65.
47. Israel, *The Dutch Republic*, pp. 679–80.
48. G. Clark, ed., *Sir William Temple's Observations Upon the United Provinces of the Netherlands*, Oxford: Clarendon Press, 1972, p. 128. First published in 1673, read by contemporaries and later writers, p. 131.
49. 'Holland's economy was vulnerable during naval hostilities, and public unrest could easily erupt – as it did in 1653 and later, in 1665 and 1672.' Bruijn, *The Dutch Navy of the Seventeenth and Eighteenth Centuries*, pp. 56 and 65; Israel, *The Dutch Republic*, p. 720.
50. Rowen *John de Witt*, pp. 71–9; B. Capp, *Cromwell's Navy: The Fleet and the English Revolution 1648–1660*. Oxford: Oxford University Press, 1990, pp. 6–9.
51. G. Rommelse and R. Downing, 'The Fleet as an Ideological Pillar of Dutch Radical Republicanism, 1650–1672', in *The International Journal of Maritime History*, vol. 27, no. 3 (2015), pp. 387–410.
52. Glete, *War and the State in Early Modern Europe*, p. 170.
53. Bruijn, *The Dutch Navy of the Seventeenth and Eighteenth Centuries*, pp. 66–71.
54. Brandon, *War, Capital, and the Dutch State*, p. 119. The reference comes from Brandt's 1687 *Life of de Ruyter* at p. 100.
55. Schama, *The Embarrassment of Riches*, pp. 252–4. The celebration of English/British dockyards and infrastructure served the same function: see George III's decision to commission models and paintings of his dockyards.
56. Rommelse and Downing, 'The Fleet as an Ideological Pillar of Dutch Radical Republicanism, 1650–1672', pp. 391–2, 395, 397. A century later Britain took the same view of Barbary predation, well aware that the shipping of the newly independent United States lacked national protection. G. Rommelse, 'Een Hollandse maritieme identiteit als ideologische bouwsteen van de Ware Vrijheid', in *Holland Historisch Tijdschrift*, vol. 48 (2016), pp. 133–41; Brandon, *War, Capital, and the Dutch State*, pp. 49–50.
57. Van Vliet, 'Foundation, Organization and Effects of the Dutch Navy', p. 172.

58. Schama, *The Embarrassment of Riches*, pp. 249–51.
59. Brandon, *War, Capital, and the Dutch State*, p. 93.
60. Schama, *The Embarrassment of Riches*, pp. 67, 75–8, 115.
61. Burke, *Venice and Amsterdam*, pp. 43–51.
62. R. W. Unger, *Dutch Shipbuilding before 1800*, Amsterdam: Van Gorcum, 1978, p. 42. Witsen's 1671 book, the first Dutch text, reached a second edition in 1690. The Dutch had no tradition of building to plans, which was why Peter the Great abandoned Amsterdam for Deptford, where he learnt how to build ships using a transferable system suitable for his backward country.
63. Rowen, *John de Witt*, p. 11.
64. Burke, *Venice and Amsterdam*, pp. 93–100; Schama, *The Embarrassment of Riches*, pp. 492–3, 618–19, for a sample list of seventeenth-century elite book owning.
65. G. Rommelse, 'National Flags as Essential Elements of Dutch Naval Ideology, 1600–1800', forthcoming. I wish to thank Dr Rommelse for sharing this paper with me.
66. Burke does not mention the art of the sea, commercial or naval, in either Venice or Amsterdam, a significant oversight in a study of elite values and taste in seapower states.
67. H. J. Horn, *Jan Cornelisz Vermeyen: Painter of Charles V and his Conquest of Tunis*, New York: Davaco Publishers, 1989. These tapestries were created in Brussels.
68. R. Daalder, *Van de Velde and Son: Marine Painters*, Leiden: Primavera Press, 2016, pp. 50–3.
69. Israel, *The Dutch Republic*, pp. 557–8; M. Russell, *Visions of the Sea: Hendrick C. Vroom and the Origin of Dutch Marine Painting*, Leiden: Brill, 1983.
70. Schama, *The Embarrassment of Riches*, pp. 246–9 and p. 638 fn. 45.
71. R. Strong, *Henry Prince of Wales and England's Lost Renaissance*, London: Thames and Hudson, 1986, p. 189, plates 97–8. Henry also received a storm at sea by Vroom, shaping English taste.
72. Justin Dee quoted in Sarah Gristwood, 'A Tapestry of England's Past', *History Today*, vol. 60, no. 9 (2010): http://www.historytoday.com/sarah-gristwood/tapestry-england%E2%80% 99s-past#sthash.fI4ziuXb.dpuf.
73. T. Campbell, *Threads of Splendour: Tapestry of the Baroque*, New Haven, CT, and London: Yale University Press, 2007, p. 111, a passage based on a German text of 1613. The tapestries having served their purpose, James moved them to the Tower of London.
74. The 1613 image is on the cover of N. A. M. Rodger, *The Safeguard of the Sea: A Naval History of Britain, Vol. I: 649–1649*, London: HarperCollins, 1997, plate 54. Most ship illustrations in this book were created by Low Countries artists.
75. Israel, *The Dutch Republic*, p. 559.
76. Daalder, *Van de Velde and Son*, pp. 1–127, for the Dutch career of the two Willem Van de Veldes.
77. See Bruijn, *The Dutch Navy of the Seventeenth and Eighteenth Centuries*, p. 103, for admirals with art collections.
78. For example, the 1665 print reproduced in Schama, *The Embarrassment of Riches*, pp. 302–3.
79. Daalder, *Van de Velde and Son*, pp. 166–9.
80. M. S. Robinson, *The Paintings of the Willem van de Veldes*, no. 264, London: Sotheby's and the National Maritime Museum, 1990, pp. 299–301, and 'The Battle of the Texel' of 1687, which was painted for Tromp, no. 315, pp. 188–93; J. Bender, with an introduction by J. D. D. Davies, *Dutch Warships in the Age of Sail, 1600–1714: Design, Construction, Careers and Fates*, Barnsley: Seaforth Publishing, 2104, p. 252.
81. Fremantle, *The Baroque Town Hall of Amsterdam*, p. 55.
82. Ibid., pp. 30–5.
83. Ibid., pp. 88–91.
84. Ibid., pp. 134–40; see J. Burckhardt, *Recollections of Rubens*, London: Phaidon, 1951, pp. 16–17.

85. Fremantle, *The Baroque Town Hall of Amsterdam*, p. 25 and ch. 4; Schama, *The Embarrassment of Riches*, pp. 224–5.

86. Fremantle *The Baroque Town Hall of Amsterdam*, pp. 39–41, 43, 48–50, 58, 67.

87. Ibid., pp. 21, 36–7.

88. Ibid., pp. 28–9, 42, 55, 190, quotes at pp. 29 and 55.

89. Ibid., pp. 8, 38–9, 55, 172. By the time King Louis Bonaparte turned the building into a royal palace everything Amsterdam had hoped to render permanent had crashed in ruins, the 'True Freedom' Republic that inaugurated the building long since displaced by a continental Stadholderate.

90. Israel, *The Dutch Republic*, p. 869.

91. Brandon, *War, Capital, and the Dutch State*, p. 93.

92. Bruijn, *The Dutch Navy of the Seventeenth and Eighteenth Centuries*, p. 126. The naval magazine remains the repository of the nation's seafaring glory, the museum of Dutch maritime history. It still dominates the eastern sightlines of the harbour.

93. Israel, *The Dutch Republic*, pp. 749–50.

94. Rowen, *John de Witt*, pp. 176 and 189.

95. Rommelse and Downing, 'The Fleet as an Ideological Pillar of Dutch Radical Republicanism, 1650–1672', p. 398.

96. Clark, ed., *Sir William Temple's Observations*. James Boswell read the text before visiting the Republic a century later. E. A. Pottle, *Boswell in Holland, 1763–1764*. London: Heinemann, 1952, pp. 280–1.

97. Schama, *The Embarrassment of Riches*, pp. 284–5; Clark, ed., *Sir William Temple's Observations*, p. 129.

98. Clark, ed., *Sir William Temple's Observations*, pp. 100, 116–26.

99. Israel, *The Dutch Republic*, p. 780.

100. Ibid., pp. 776–85.

101. Quoted in D. Onnenkink, 'The Ideological Context of the Dutch War (1672)', in D. Onnenkink and G. Rommelse, eds., *Ideology and Foreign Policy in Early Modern Europe (1650–1750)*, Farnham: Ashgate Press, p. 133.

102. Schama, *The Embarrassment of Riches*, pp. 260 and 271.

103. S. T. Bindoff, *The Scheldt Question to 1839*, London: Allen and Unwin, 1945, pp. 116, 126, 131; P. Sonnino, 'Colbert', *European Studies Review* (January 1983), pp. 1–11.

104. F. S. Gaastra, *The Dutch East India Company: Expansion and Decline*, Zutphen: Walberg Pers, 2003. The English edition of *Geschiedenis van de VoC*, p. 20.

105. C. Boxer, *The Dutch Seaborne Empire*, London: Collins, 1965, p. 24.

106. Clark, ed., *Sir William Temple's Observations*, pp. 60, 163, 117.

107. Burke, *Venice and Amsterdam*, pp. 46–7.

108. Brandon, *War, Capital, and the Dutch State*, pp. 94–8, 100–1, 109.

109. Gaastra, *The Dutch East India Company*, pp. 37–65.

110. Rommelse and Downing, 'The Fleet as an Ideological Pillar of Dutch Radical Republicanism, 1650–1672', p. 401; the claim in Hugo Grotius, *The Freedom of the Seas or The Right which Belongs to the Dutch to Take Part in the East Indian Trade*, New York: Oxford University Press, 1916, that countries had the right to sail the seas without appropriation by any country, countering Spanish, Portuguese and English claims to sovereignty of the seas, was, in turn, countered by John Selden's defence of English claims, *Mare Clausum*.

111. Gaastra, *The Dutch East India Company*, pp. 60 and 81.

112. Ibid., pp. 132 and 148.

113. J. A. de Moor, '"A Very Unpleasant Relationship": Trade and Strategy in the Eastern Seas: Anglo-Dutch Relations in the Nineteenth Century from a Colonial Perspective', in G. J. A. Raven and N. A. M. Rodger, eds., *Navies and Armies: The Anglo-Dutch Relationship in War and Peace 1688–1988*, Edinburgh: John Donald, 1990, pp. 49–69.

114. Gaastra, *The Dutch East India Company*, pp. 166, 171–2.

115. Ibid., pp. 23–31, 171.

116. Ibid., pp. 56 passim and p. 164.
117. H. W. Richmond, *The Navy in India, 1763–1783*, London: Ernest Benn, 1931, pp, 251–73; Gaastra, *The Dutch East India Company*, pp. 166–710; C. N. Parkinson, *War in the Eastern Seas, 1793–1815*, London: Allen and Unwin, 1954, pp. 78–81.
118. Rowen, *John de Witt*, pp. 596 and 633.
119. Ibid., p. 781; S. B. Baxter, *William III and the Defense of European Liberty 1650–1702*, New York: Harcourt, Brace, 1966, pp. 46–7.
120. Rowen, *John de Witt*, pp. 611 and 633.
121. Daalder, *Van de Velde and Son*, p. 134; Schama, *The Embarrassment of Riches*, pp. 271–3; Rommelse and Downing, 'The Fleet as an Ideological Pillar of Dutch Radical Republicanism, 1650–1672', pp. 406–7. For the politics of such acts see R. Bevan, *The Destruction of Memory: Architecture at War*, London: Reaktion Books, 2016.
122. Baxter, *William III and the Defense of European Liberty 1650*–1702, p. 83.
123. Israel, *The Dutch Republic*, pp. 878–83.
124. Daalder, *Van de Velde and Son*, pp. 129–88, for the Van de Veldes' years in England.
125. Israel, *The Dutch Republic*, pp. 883–8, seriously underrates the artistic achievement of the English period.
126. Clark, ed., *Sir William Temple's Observations*, p. 49.
127. De Witt preferred the supple, calculating Charles to his Catholic brother: Rowen, *John de Witt*, pp. 678–91, 732, 781–2.
128. Ibid., pp. 711 and 730.
129. Ibid., pp. 744, 748, 752, 813, 819,
130. Ibid., pp. 688, 759, 770, 778, 815; P. Burke, *The Fabrication of Louis XIV*, New Haven, CT, and London, 1992, p. 76.
131. Schama, *The Embarrassment of Riches*, pp. 28–31; for the print see pp. 280–3.
132. Bruijn, *The Dutch Navy of the Seventeenth and Eighteenth Centuries*, pp. 75–7.
133. Temple, who had the highest regard for Johan de Witt, lamented his fate: Clark, ed., *Sir William Temple's Observations*, p. 95.
134. Rowen, *John de Witt*, pp. 839, 847, 859; Levillian, 'William III's Military and Political Career', p. 327.
135. Levillian, 'William III's Military and Political Career', pp. 333 and 336; Burke, *The Fabrication of Louis XIV*, p. 109.
136. Rowen, *John de Witt*, p. 852; Onnekink, 'The Ideological Context of the Dutch War', pp. 131–44.
137. Brandon, *War, Capital, and the Dutch State*, p. 316.
138. Israel, *The Dutch Republic*, pp. 618–19, 630; Brandon, *War, Capital, and the Dutch State*, pp. 120–1.
139. Glete, *War and the State in Early Modern Europe*, p. 171.
140. However, the restricted draught ensured they were armed with nothing heavier than 24 pounders, while comparable English and French ships used full cannon of 40 to 42 pounds: Bender, *Dutch Warships in the Age of Sail*, pp. 273–311.
141. Baxter, *William III and the Defense of European Liberty 1650–1702*, p. 258.
142. E. S. van Eyck van Heslinga, 'A Competitive Ally: The Delicate Balance of Naval Alliance and Maritime Competition between Great Britain and the Dutch Republic 1674–1795', in Raven and Rodger, eds., *Navies and Armies*, pp. 1–11 at p. 10.
143. Israel, *The Dutch Republic*, pp. 985–6, 972–5.
144. Brandon, *War, Capital, and the Dutch State*, pp. 84–5, 124–9, 133–8.
145. Bruijn, *The Dutch Navy of the Seventeenth and Eighteenth Centuries*, pp. 85–8; Daalder, *Van de Velde and Son*, pp. 130–49.
146. Glete, *War and the State in Early Modern Europe*, p. 171.
147. J. Addison, *The Present State of the War and the Necessity of an Augmentation*, London, 1707; Schama, *The Embarrassment of Riches*, pp. 286–7.
148. Bruijn, *The Dutch Navy of the Seventeenth and Eighteenth Centuries*, pp. 93–111.
149. Burke, *Venice and Amsterdam*, pp. 129–35, 138–9.
150. Brandon, *War, Capital, and the Dutch State*, p. 311.

151. Baxter, *William III and the Defense of European Liberty 1650–1702*, p. 398.

152. Burke, *Venice and Amsterdam*, pp. 125–39.

153. Schama, *The Embarrassment of Riches*, pp. 284–6.

154. For the falling away of the Dutch economy see Israel, *The Dutch Republic*, pp. 998–1,005.

Chapter 6

1. R. M. Berthold, *Rhodes in the Hellenistic Age*, Ithaca, NY: Cornell University Press, 1984, remains the standard account and is followed in this chapter, unless otherwise stated. See pp. 21–2.

2. Ibid., pp. 42–58.

3. J. Naish, *Seamarks: Their History and Development*, London: Stanford Maritime, 1985, pp. 15–24.

4. Polybius 30.5.6–8 cited in Berthold, *Rhodes in the Hellenistic Age*, p. 233.

5. Berthold, *Rhodes in the Hellenistic Age*, p. 146.

6. Ibid., p. 166.

7. Ibid., p. 199.

8. T. A. Kirk, *Genoa and the Sea: Policy and Power in an Early Modern Maritime Republic, 1559–1684*, Baltimore, MD: Johns Hopkins University Press, 2005, p. 141.

9. M. Salonia, *Genoa's Freedom: Entrepreneurship, Republicanism and the Spanish Atlantic*, Lanham, MD: Lexington Books, 2017.

10. S. A. Epstein, *Genoa and the Genoese: 958–1528*, Chapel Hill, NC: University of North Carolina, 1996, pp. 266–71, 276–9.

11. Ibid., p. 272, citing E. Ashtor, *The Levant Trade in the later Middle Ages*, Princeton, NJ: Princeton University Press, 1983, pp. 32–3.

12. Epstein, *Genoa and the Genoese*, pp. 274–5, 280–1.

13. Kirk, *Genoa and the Sea*, pp. 3–15.

14. Salonia, *Genoa's Freedom*, pp. 92–7, 125.

15. J. H. Parry, *The Spanish Seaborne Empire*, London: Hutchinson, 1966, pp. 39 and 43.

16. J. Burckhardt, *The Civilisation of Italy in the Renaissance*, London: Penguin, 1990, p. 73. Burckhardt acknowledged that this situation changed after Andrea Doria's assumption of power.

17. Epstein, *Genoa and the Genoese*, pp. 296–7; Kirk, *Genoa and the Sea*, p. 101.

18. Epstein, *Genoa and the Genoese*, p. 314.

19. Salonia, *Genoa's Freedom*, p. 122.

20. Epstein, *Genoa and the Genoese*, pp. 315–18, 329–30.

21. Cited in Salonia, *Genoa's Freedom*, pp. 139 and 141.

22. L. Stagno, *Palazzo del Principe: The Villa of Andrea Doria*, Genoa: Sagep, 2005, pp. 1–54.

23. Salonia, *Genoa's Freedom*, p. 25: Kirk, *Genoa and the Sea*, pp. x–xi.

24. Kirk, *Genoa and the Sea*, pp. 100–1, 202.

25. Ibid., p. xii.

26. C. Cipolla, 'The Economic Decline of Italy', in C. Cipolla, ed., *The Economic Decline of Empires*, London: Methuen, 1970, pp. 196–215 at p. 215.

27. Kirk, *Genoa and the Sea*, p. x.

28. P. Burke, *The Fabrication of Louis XIV*, New Haven, CT, and London: Yale University Press, 1992, pp. 97–101, 162; S. B. Baxter, *William III and the Defense of European Liberty 1650–1702*, New York: Harcourt, Brace, 1966, p. 212; Kirk, *Genoa and the Sea*, p. 202.

29. Burke, *The Fabrication of Louis XIV*, p. 162. The meaning of these gestures is best understood through Jacob Burckhardt's assessment that the Revocation of the Edict of Nantes was a political measure to impose unity on the state. As editor Gottfried Dietz observed Burckhardt identified Louis's France as 'the first perfected example of a modern state which exercised supreme coercive power on nearly all branches of culture', citing Burckhardt's argument that Louis's state was a 'pseudo-organism existing by and for itself'. J. Burckhardt, *Reflections on History*, Indianapolis, IN: Liberty Classics, 1979, pp. 17 and 136.

30. P. Russell, *Prince Henry 'the Navigator'*, New Haven, CT, and London: Yale University Press, 2000. Russell emphasizes the medieval, chivalric crusading aspects of Henry's life, demolishing much of the 'navigator' mythology, including the legend of his navigation school at Sagres, at pp. 6–7. For Ceuta see p. 70.
31. Ng Chin-keong, *Boundaries and Beyond: China's Maritime Southeast in Late Imperial Times*, Singapore: National University of Singapore Press, 2016, p. 18.
32. R. Mathee, 'The Portuguese in the Persian Gulf: An Overview', in J. R. Marcris and S. Kelly, eds., *Imperial Crossroads: The Great Powers and the Persian Gulf*, Annapolis, MD: USNIP, 2012, p. 7.
33. Kirk, *Genoa and the Sea*, pp. 12, 14, 46.
34. E. Sanceau, *The Reign of the Fortunate King 1495–1521*, New York: Archon Books, 1969.
35. P. Pereira, *Torre de Belém*, London: Scala, 2005, pp. 17–22, explores the purpose and meaning of this emblematic building, which combined ropes, knots and navigational instruments with powerful Christian symbols, at a high-profile location, as the outer defence of Lisbon.
36. J. V. Vivens, 'The Decline of Spain in the Seventeenth Century', in C. Cipolla, ed., *The Economic Decline of Empires*, London: Methuen, 1970, pp. 8 and 128.
37. C. R. Boxer, *Four Centuries of Portuguese Expansion, 1415–1825*, Berkeley, CA: University of California Press, 1969, p. 89.
38. Ibid., p. 10.
39. L. Th. Lehmann, 'The Polyeric Quest: Renaissance and Baroque Theories about Ancient Men of War', PhD thesis, Rotterdam, 1995, pp. 59–60.
40. F. Oliviera, *Arte de Guerra do Mar: Estrategia e Guerra naval no Tempo dos Descombrimentos*, Lisbon: Edições 70 Lda, for a facsimile and a modern setting of the text. Introduction by A. S. Ribeiro,
41. Boxer, *Four Centuries of Portuguese Expansion*, pp. 47–8.
42. Ibid., pp. 49–53.
43. The classic study of Portugal's client relationship with the British is in A. D. Francis, *The Methuens and Portugal, 1691–1708*, Cambridge: Cambridge University Press, 1966, p. 268.
44. Boxer, *Four Centuries of Portuguese Expansion*, pp. 65–8.
45. Ibid., pp. 81–2, 87–8.
46. Ibid., p. 54.

Chapter 7

1. In the case of Russia and China the need of the post-1950 United States navy for a suitable naval threat has sustained impressive research efforts directed at the naval development of first the Soviet Union and then China. While these have enhanced our ability to understand these organisations, and their assets, they consistently misread their intentions, conflating Mahanian sea power with Venetian seapower. While China has had a long engagement with the sea, discussions of a Chinese 'seapower' future, both domestic and occidental, have been driven by contemporary concerns, rather than historical scholarship. For an example of serious historical research on the subject see: Ng Chin-keong, *Boundaries and Beyond: China's Maritime Southeast in Late Imperial Times*, Singapore: National University of Singapore Press, 2016.
2. J. H. Billington, *The Icon and the Axe: An Interpretative History of Russian Culture*, New York: Random House, 1970, p. 113.
3. The work of Jan Glete, especially *Navies and Nations*, is critical to understanding this European phenomenon, and its link to democratic politics, commercial expansion and national culture.
4. L. Hughes, *Russia in the Age of Peter the Great*, New Haven, CT, and London: Yale University Press, 1998, p. 25.
5. S. Willis, *Admiral Benbow: The Life and Times of a Naval Legend*, London: Quercus, 2010, pp. 236–46, 256.

6. J. Cracraft, *The Petrine Revolution in Russian Culture*, Cambridge, MA: Belknap Press/ Harvard University Press, 2004, pp. 45–52; S. B. Baxter, *William III and the Defense of European Liberty 1650*-1702, New York: Harcourt, Brace, 1966, p. 363.

7. Cracraft, *The Petrine Revolution in Russian Culture*, p. 54. The armour was entirely in keeping with the naval vision. At that time English naval heroes like Benbow were portrayed in armour. Willis, *Admiral Benbow*, p. 253.

8. Cracraft, *The Petrine Revolution in Russian Culture*.

9. Ibid., frontispiece.

10. For an incisive assessment of the role of naval power in Petrine strategy see W. C. Fuller, *Strategy and Power in Russia 1600–1914*, New York: Free Press, 1992, pp. 69–71.

11. Hughes, *Russia in the Age of Peter the Great*, pp. 3, 17–18.

12. Ibid., pp. 27–8, 49, 82.

13. Ibid., p. 29.

14. Ibid., pp. 31–2; C. A. G. Bridge, ed., 'Introduction' to *History of the Russian Fleet during the Reign of Peter the* Great, London: Navy Records Society, 1899, pp. xxi–xxii.

15. J. Cracraft, *The Petrine Revolution in Architecture*, Chicago, IL: University of Chicago Press, 1988, pp. 150, 173, 179, 181. The site floods on average once a year.

16. Billington, *The Icon and the Axe*, pp. 181–3.

17. Cracraft, *The Petrine Revolution in Architecture*, pp. 119–21.

18. A. Kahan, *The Plow, the Hammer and the Knout: An Economic History of Eighteenth-Century Russia*, Chicago, IL: University of Chicago Press, 1985, pp. 87–8.

19. Cracraft, *The Petrine Revolution in Architecture*, pp. 208, 217, 220, 232.

20. Ibid., pp. 87–8; K. Zinovieff and J. Hughes, *Guide to St. Petersburg*, Woodbridge: Boydell & Brewer, 2003, pp. 67–86.

21. Kahan, *The Plow, the Hammer and the Knout*, pp. 86–8.

22. Cracraft, *The Petrine Revolution in Russian Culture*, pp. 90–1.

23. Ibid., pp. 132–8, 151–3, 155, 196. The remark was made in 1710.

24. A. Cross, *By the Banks of the Neva: Chapters from the Lives and Careers of the British in Eighteenth-Century Russia*, Cambridge: Cambridge University Press 1999, p. 333, citing F. C. Weber, *The Present State of Russia: Volume 1*, London, 1723, p. 4.

25. Cracraft, *The Petrine Revolution in Architecture*, pp. 228–9; J. Tredrea and E. Sozaev, *Russian Warships in the Age of Sail, 1696–1860: Design, Construction, and Fates*, Barnsley: Seaforth, 2010, p. 115, for this ship, and the short lives of all contemporary Russian warships.

26. Hughes, *Russia in the Age of Peter the Great*, pp. 41–2.

27. Ibid., pp. 83–6.

28. Tredrea and Sozaev, *Russian Warships in the Age of Sail*, pp. 110–11. While the Tsar worked on the design the constructors were English.

29. Hughes, *Russia in the Age of Peter the Great*, p. 87.

30. Ibid., pp. 82, 87–8, plate 19; G. Kaganov, 'As in the Ship of Peter', *Slavic Review*, no. 50 (1991), pp. 754–67.

31. Bridge, ed., *History of the Russian Fleet*, pp. 84–9, 102–5; Hughes, *Russia in the Age of Peter the Great*, pp. 83–5.

32. Hughes, *Russia in the Age of Peter the Great*, p. 89.

33. Fuller, *Strategy and Power in* Russia, pp. 69–71.

34. Hughes, *Russia in the Age of Peter the Great*, p. 466. Miliukov's argument appears to reflect the contemporary Russian naval build-up.

35. Russia built eight copies of HMS *Victory*: Tredrea and Sozaev, *Russian Warships in the Age of Sail*, pp. 151–5.

36. Cracraft, *The Petrine Revolution in Architecture*, pp. 208–9, 227.

37. A. D. Lambert, *The Crimean War: British Grand Strategy against Russia, 1853–1856*, Farnham: Ashgate, 2011.

38. Zinovieff and Hughes, *Guide to St. Petersburg*, pp. 382–90.

39. Cracraft, *The Petrine Revolution in Architecture*, p. 197.

40. Hughes, *Russia in the Age of Peter the Great*, p. 203.
41. Ibid., p. 207.
42. Ibid., pp. 212–16, 265.
43. Ibid., p. 237.
44. Cracraft, *The Petrine Revolution in Russian Culture*, pp. 12–16, 254–5.
45. Ibid., pp. 3, 35, 39.
46. Hughes, *Russia in the Age of Peter the Great*, p. 85; Cracraft, *The Petrine Revolution in Russian Culture*, pp. 50, 57, 61, citing Peter's instructions of April 1718.
47. Cracraft, *The Petrine Revolution in Russian Culture*, pp. 63–4.
48. Ibid., pp. 69–70.
49. Ibid., pp. 79–87, 210–19.
50. Hughes, *Russia in the Age of Peter the Great*, p. 231.
51. L. Salmina-Haskell, *Panoramic Views of St Petersburg from 1716 to 1835*, Oxford: Ashmolean, 1993, unpaginated.
52. Cross, *By the Banks of the Neva*, pp. 279–80, 297.
53. Cracraft, *The Petrine Revolution in Architecture*, pp. 189–90. Peter acquired some Van de Veldes, without appreciating their power.
54. The Tsar had planned a state visit as part of his European tour, and may have visited during a stay in Vienna, with his confidante Prince Menshikov, who also became a patron of Venetian art. S. Androsov, 'Peter the Great's St. Petersburg: Between Amsterdam and Venice', in S. Androsov, I. Artemieva, I. Boele and J. Rudge, *Venezia! Art of the 18th Century*, London: Lund Humphries, 2005, pp. 38–66.
55. I. Artemieva, 'Russia and Venetian Artists in the Eighteenth Century', in Androsov et al., *Venezia!*, pp. 67–93.
56. Cracraft, *The Petrine Revolution in Architecture*, pp. 224–5. Engraving by E. Vinogradov, drawn by M. I. Makhaev. Salmina-Haskell, *Panoromic Views of St Petersburg*, at images 9 and 10 and entries for Makhaev. Both authors ignore the centrality of the ships.
57. Artemieva, 'Russia and Venetian Artists in the Eighteenth Century', pp. 90–2.
58. Cross, *By the Banks of the Neva*, pp. 310, 315 and 322–3. N. Penny, *Reynolds*, London: The Royal Academy, 1986, pp. 35–6, 51, 312–3, 349 and 151.
59. Cross, *By the Banks of the Neva*, pp. 322–3, and A. Cross, 'Richard Paton and the Battle of Chesme', *Study Group on Eighteenth-Century Russia Newsletter*, no. 14 (1986), pp. 31–7. The medal is in the British Museum.
60. Billington, *The Icon and the Axe*, pp. 361–5.
61. Tredrea and Sozaev, *Russian Warships in the Age of Sail*, p. 216. Almost all the warships had to be broken up.
62. Billington, *The Icon and the Axe*, pp. 370–3. Both the number and scale of Aivazovsky's pictures are truly heroic – *The Storm*, for instance, emphasising human frailty amidst the vastness of the sea, and *The Ninth Wave* addressing the final flood in the Book of Revelation. Recently, auction prices for his aggressively nationalistic images have rocketed, as Russian oligarchs compete for trophies of the old regime.
63. Billington, *The Icon and the Axe*, p. 482.
64. Hughes, *Russia in the Age of Peter the Great*, pp. 145–8; R. H. Fisher, *Bering's Voyages*, London: Hurst, 1977, pp. 156–9.
65. Kahan, *The Plow, the Hammer and the Knout*, p. 167: Hughes, *Russia in the Age of Peter the Great*, p. 149.
66. Cross, *By the Banks of the Neva*, p. 352, from W. Coxe, *Travels into Poland, Russia, Sweden and Denmark*, 5th edn, London, 1802, vol. III, pp. 193, 135, 131, 158.
67. Hughes, *Russia in the Age of Peter the Great*, pp. 150–5: Kahan, *The Plow, the Hammer and the Knout*, pp. 136, 247–9.
68. Bridge, ed., *History of the Russian Fleet*, p. 109.
69. Kahan, *The Plow, the Hammer and the Knout*, pp. 285–6, 295–8.
70. Ibid., pp. 197–203; Cross, *By the Banks of the Neva*, pp. 355–6.

71. Cross, *By the Banks of the Neva*, pp. 47–9: J. Davey, *The Transformation of British Naval Strategy: Seapower and Supply in Northern Europe, 1808–1812,* Woodbridge: Boydell Press, 2012, ch. 1; A. D. Lambert, *The Challenge: Britain Against America in the Naval War of 1812,* London: Faber, 2012, p. 388, for Canadian timber and naval stores; A. D. Lambert, *The Last Sailing Battlefleet, 1815–1850,* London: Conway, 1991, pp. 108–24, for timber policy.

72. Kaha, *The Plow, the Hammer and the Knout*, p. 166.

73. Cross, *By the Banks of the Neva*, pp. 68, 73–8, citing Kaplan, 'Russia's Impact on the Industrial Revolution in Great Britain', in *Forschungen zur Osteuropaischen Geschichten,* vol. XXIX, Berlin, 1981, p. 9.

74. Hughes, *Russia in the Age of Peter the Great*, p. 56.

75. Cracraft, *The Petrine Revolution in Russian Culture,* p. 94, citing M. S. Anderson, *War and Society in Europe of the Old Regime, 1618–1789,* London: Fontana, 1988, pp. 94, 96, 99.

76. Tredrea and Sozaev, *Russian Warships in the Age of Sail,* pp. 115–17, for the retention of unseaworthy battleships after Peter's death. See W. Sharp, *Life of Admiral Sir William Symonds,* London: Longmans, 1856, pp. 238–51.

77. Cracraft, *The Petrine Revolution in Russian Culture,* pp. 94–5, citing J. Glete, *Navies and Nations: Warships, Navies and State Building in Europe and America, 1500–1860,* Stockholm: Almqvist and Wisksell, 1993, pp. 196–7, and his essay in J. Black, ed., *War in the Early Modern World,* New Haven, CT, and London: Yale University Press, 1999, pp. 44–6, which stressed Peter's cautious use of his battlefleet, in stark contrast to his highly aggressive use of littoral assets in combination with the army in Finland.

78. Cross, *By the Banks of the Neva*, pp. 176–7.

79. Cracraft, *The Petrine Revolution in Russian Culture,* pp. 301–9.

80. Ibid., pp. 54–6

81. Bridge, ed., *History of the Russian Fleet*, p. 114. The autograph continuing the narrative to 1725 is in PRO SP XCI 9, ff107 and confirmed Deane's authorship. D. Bonner-Smith, *Mariner's Mirror,* vol. XX (1934), pp. 373–6. Bonner-Smith was then the Admiralty Librarian.

82. Glete, *Navies and Nations*, Table 22/24, pp. 235–6.

83. The report was clearly intended as an intelligence brief.

84. Bridge, ed., *History of the Russian Fleet,* pp. 103–4, 116, 126–7.

85. Cross, *By the Banks of the Neva*, pp. 50–3. See D. K. Reading, *The Anglo-Russian Commercial Treaty of 1734,* New Haven, CT, and London: Yale University Press, 1938, pp. 96–7.

86. R. Morriss, *Science, Utility and Maritime Power: Samuel Bentham in Russia, 1779–1791,* Farnham: Ashgate, 2015, pp. 51–2, 59, 219–21.

87. Bridge, 'Introduction', *History of the Russian Fleet*, p. xxii.

88. P. Burke, *The Fabrication of Louis XIV,* New Haven, CT, and London: Yale University Press, 1992, p. 172; Cracraft, *The Petrine Revolution in Architecture*, pp. 158, 185.

89. Cracraft, *The Petrine Revolution in Architecture*, p. 18.

90. Cross, *By the Banks of the Neva*, p. 222. Cross cites a 1775 report, based on Charles Knowles' papers. The term 'maritime' has a specific meaning, addressing the total engagement of the state with the sea.

91. S. G. Gorshkov, *The Sea Power of the State,* Annapolis, MD: USNIP, 1979, pp. 135, 178–9, 189, 217, 253, 281 (quote). I am indebted to Captain Chris O'Flaherty RN, the 2017 Hudson Fellow at the University of Oxford, for a fruitful discussion of Gorshkov's thinking.

Chapter 8

1. This process will be the subject of a full-length study, and can only be sketched here. G. O'Hara, *Britain and the Sea since 1600,* Basingstoke: Palgrave Macmillan, 2010, and J. Scott, *When the Waves Ruled Britannia: Geography and Political Identities 1500–1800,* Oxford: Oxford University Press, 2011, offer significant, distinctive correctives to the Eurocentric terrestrial approaches that have dominated British writing about war, policy and identity for the last fifty years.

2. G. F. Warner, ed., *The Libelle of Englyshe Polycye*. London: Oxford University Press, 1926, p. xvi.
3. A. D. Lambert, *Crusoe's Island*, London: Faber, 2016, pp. 8–11.
4. S. Thurley, 'The Vanishing Architecture of the River Thames', in S. Doran and R. Blyth, eds., *Royal River: Power, Pageantry and the Thames*, Greenwich: Royal Museums, 2012, pp. 20–5 at p. 20. For the architectural monumentality of the royal dockyards see: J. G. Coad, *The Royal Dockyards 1690–1850*, Aldershot: Scolar Press, 1989, and D. Evans, *Building the Steam Navy: Dockyards, Technology and the Creation of the Victorian Battlefleet, 1830–1906*, London: Conway, 2004.
5. A. F. Falconer, *Shakespeare and the Sea*, London: Constable, 1964, p. 2; *Cymbeline* 3.1.13; see also A. F. Falconer, *A Glossary of Shakespeare's Sea and Naval Terms including Gunnery*, London: Constable, 1965. The author, Alexander Falconer, was a naval officer who became a Professor of English.
6. D. A. Lupher, *Romans in a New World: Classical Models in Sixteenth-Century Spanish America*, Ann Arbor, MI: University of Michigan Press, 2003, pp. 176 and 186.
7. J. Sureda, *The Golden Age of Spain*, New York: Vendome Press, 2008, p. 148.
8. During Charles's reign as king and Holy Roman Emperor the Spanish developed an ideology in which they were the new Romans. This constructed identity helped justify imperial conquests in the Americas and north Africa. The two theatres were connected: Hernán Cortés, conqueror of the Aztec Empire, ended his military career in north Africa. While the Roman analogy became less of a commonplace under Philip II, it remained potent through the long war with England.
9. Sureda, *The Golden Age of Spain*, pp. 43–9; H. J. Horn, *Jan Cornelisz Vermeyen: Painter of Charles V and his Conquest of Tunis*, New York: Davaco Publishers, 1989.
10. G. Parker, *The Grand Strategy of Philip II*, New Haven, CT, and London: Yale University Press, 1998, pp. 27 and 275.
11. Hakluyt modelled his work on Ramusio's text, while Raleigh exploited Thucydides, which was familiar to the Greek-reading elite of Elizabethan England, from the queen and her chief ministers to the imperial magus John Dee through Aldine editions.
12. M. Bellamy, *Christian IV and his Navy: A Political, and Administrative History of the Danish Navy, 1596–1648*, Leiden: Brill, 2006, pp. 37 and 156. Plate 4, Isaac Isaacs' *Allegory of the Sound* of 1623 provides an obvious model of later English classical seapower motifs. See also R. Strong, *Henry, Prince of Wales and England's Lost Renaissance*, London: Thames and Hudson, 1986, pp. 57–9, plates 11–14.
13. A. R. Young, *His Majesty's Royal Ship: A Critical Edition of Thomas Heywood's 'A True Description of his Majesties Royall Ship'*, New York: AMS Press, 1990. Young did not mention Thucydides or Pericles.
14. J. S. Corbett, *England in the Mediterranean: A Study of the Rise and Influence of British Power within the Straits, 1603–1713*, vol. 1, London: Longman and Co., 1904, pp. 196–7.
15. George Villiers, 2nd Duke of Buckingham, *A Letter to Sir Thomas Osborn*, London, 1672, p. 11.
16. S. Thurley, 'The Vanishing Architecture of the River Thames', in Doran and Blyth, eds., *Royal River*, pp. 20–5 at p. 25.
17. *King Charles II visiting the fleet in the Thames Estuary, 5 June 1672*. R. Daalder, *Van de Velde and Son: Marine Painters*, Leiden: Primavera Press, 2016, p. 145, picture at p. 154.
18. Sir Richard Edgecumbe: ibid., p. 163. See the extensive commissions for Van de Velde the Younger from Admiral Sir Edward Russell, and for Peter Monamy from Admiral Sir George Byng for this trend.
19. Daalder, *Van de Velde and Son*, pp. 142–3.
20. The Neapolitan Antonio Verrio exploited the rich allegorical classicism of the Baroque to emphasise the international standing of the monarchy. C. Brett, 'Antonio Verrio (*c.* 1636–1707): His career and surviving work', *The British Art Journal*, vol. 10, no. 3

(Winter/Spring 2009–10), pp. 4–17. Charles never paid for the *Sea Triumph*: James II did, in 1688.

21. P. Crowhurst, *The Defence of British Trade 1689–1815*, Folkestone: Dawson, 1977, ch. 2: 'The Organisation of Convoys and their Departure', pp. 43–80.

22. P. Brandon, *War, Capital, and the Dutch State (1588–1795)*, Leiden: Brill, 2015, p. 35.

23. Van de Velde the Younger worked for Admiral Sir Edward Russell, later Lord Orford, commander of the allied fleet, and a leading man in the Revolution of 1688, painting his flagship, the victory at la Hougue and other testaments to Russell's glory. Five pictures remain at the family home: Daalder, *Van de Velde and Son*, pp. 170–5.

24. Mahan, *The Influence of Sea Power upon History*, p. 225.

25. C. E. Levillian, 'William III's Military and Political Career in Neo-Roman Context, 1672–1702', *The Historical Journal*, vol. 48 (2005), pp. 337–9.

26. P. O'Brien, 'Fiscal Exceptionalism: Great Britain and its European rivals from Civil War to triumph at Trafalgar and Waterloo', in D. Winch and P. O'Brien, eds., Oxford: Oxford University Press, 2002, p. 250; J. Brewer, *The Sinews of Power: War, Money, and the English state, 1688–1783*, Cambridge, MA: Harvard University Press, p. 90.

27. S. B. Baxter, *William III and the Defense of European Liberty 1650–1702*, New York: Harcourt, Brace, 1966, pp. 367–88.

28. Verrio's 'Heaven Room' at Burghley for the Earl of Exeter is his masterpiece. J. Musson, 'Laughing with the Gods: The Heaven Room at Burghley', *Country Life* (5 July 2017), pp. 80–4; Daalder, *Van de Velde and Son*, p. 166.

29. B. Ford, ed., *The Cambridge Cultural History of Britain: Seventeenth-Century Britain*, Cambridge: Cambridge University Press, 1989. Neither Verrio and his picture feature, nor are the Van de Veldes mentioned. S. Thurley, *Hampton Court: A Social and Architectural History*, New Haven, CT, and London: Yale University Press, 2003, pp. 199–200, 213 and 419 for a portrait of Prince George of Denmark, closely based on Verrio's work for Charles II. P. Burke, *The Fabrication of Louis XIV*, New Haven, CT, and London: Yale University Press, 1992.

30. J. Bold, *Greenwich: An Architectural History of the Royal Hospital for Seamen and the Queen's House*, New Haven, CT, and London: Yale University Press, 2000, pp. 95–104 and 145.

31. English marine artist Channel Islander Peter Monamy captured George's arrival: F. B. Cockett, *Peter Monamy 1681–1749 and his Circle*, Woodbridge: Antique Collectors Club, 2000, pp. 52–3, 55.

32. Bold, *Greenwich*, pp. 132–72.

33. Lord Bolingbroke, *Letters on the Use and Study of History*, Letter V.

34. I. Krammick, *Bolingbroke and his Circle: The Politics of Nostalgia in the Age of Walpole*, Cambridge, MA: Harvard University Press, 1968, pp. 34–6.

35. B. Simms, *Three Victories and a Defeat: The Rise and Fall of the First British Empire, 1714–1783*, London: Penguin, 2007, pp. 204–7. Simms's argument that Europe was critical to Britain's rise as an imperial power is well made, but compounds an essentially negative agenda in Europe with a strikingly positive approach to the world beyond, undervaluing the influence of the City of London, the East India Company and other commercial interests on national policy.

36. Sophonisba was given in marriage to an elderly Numidian king at the final crisis of the Second Punic War. R. Miles, *Carthage Must Be Destroyed: The Rise and Fall of an Ancient Civilisation*, London: Allen Lane, 2010, p. 309.

37. D. Armitage, *The Ideological Origins of the British Empire*, Cambridge: Cambridge University Press, 2000, p. 173. Lord Louis Mountbatten had 'Rule Britannia' played when the Japanese surrendered Singapore in 1945. A. Jackson, *The British Empire and the Second World War*, London: Continuum, 2008, p. 459.

38. Krammick, *Bolingbroke and his Circle*, pp. 148–9; H. T. Dickinson, *Bolingbroke*, London: Constable, 1970, pp. 305–6.

39. P. Rahe, *Montesquieu and the Logic of Liberty: War, Religion, Commerce, Climate, Terrain, Technology, Uneasiness of Mind, the Spirit of Political Vigilance, and the Foundations of*

the Modern Republic, New Haven, CT, and London: Yale University Press, 2009, pp. 3–61, esp. p. 59. Raleigh was the first to make the connection in *History of the World* (1614), Book II, where he observed: 'The importance of sea-power in the wars of the Romans and Carthaginians is shown from the struggle between England and Spain.'

40. Mahan, *The Influence of Sea Power upon History*, pp. 25–89. Mahan was also indebted to nineteenth-century French theorists, notably Xavier Raymond.

41. Simms, *Three Victories and a Defeat*, pp. 469–73; J. Marsden, ed., *The Wisdom of George III*, London: Royal Household, 2004; A. Russett, *Dominic Serres R.A. 1719–1793*, Woodbridge: Antique Collector's Club, 2001.

42. S. Conway, *The War of American Independence, 1775–1783*, London: Longman, 1995; V. T. Harlow, *The Founding of the Second British Empire 1763–1793, Vol. II: New Continents and Changing Values*, London: Longmans, 1964.

43. Canning Speech at Liverpool, 10 January 1814: G. Canning, *Speeches of the Right Hon. George Canning delivered on Public Occasions in Liverpool*, Liverpool: Thomas Kaye, 1835, p. 106, full speech at pp. 81–112.

44. L. Colley, *Britons: Forging the Nation 1707–1837*, New Haven, CT, and London: Yale University Press, 1992, stresses the central role of war and overseas commerce in the creation of British national identity, and the role this identity played in sustaining the total war effort against Revolutionary and Napoleonic France between 1793 and 1815, a war largely waged from the sea. M. Lincoln, *Representing the Royal Navy: British Sea Power 1750–1815*, Aldershot: Ashgate, 2003, examines the contested interpretations of the navy in the Georgian age, and emphasises the central role of the organisation in national life. A. D. Lambert, *Nelson: Britannia's God of War*, London: Faber and Faber, 2004, examines the construction of the British national hero, a sea power totem. T. Jenks, *Naval Engagements: Patriotism, Cultural Politics, and the Royal Navy 1793–1815*, Oxford: Oxford University Press, 2006, develops Colley's approach in specific naval contexts.

45. R. Muir, *Wellington: Waterloo and the Fortunes of Peace, 1814–1852*, New Haven, CT, and London: Yale University Press, 2015, p. 106.

46. For British marine art after Van de Velde see E. Hughes, ed., *Spreading Canvas: Eighteenth-Century British Marine Painting*, New Haven, CT, and London: Yale University Press, 2016.

47. F. G. H. Bachrach, *Turner's Holland*, London: Tate Gallery, 1994. Tromp was a favourite subject.

48. J. Ruskin, *Modern Painters: Vol. I*, London: Smith, Elder, 1843. In Cook and Wedderburn's 'Library Edition' this text is in vol. III at pp. 112–13. The Claude already hung in London's National Gallery. For a very similar modern reading see E. Shanes, *Young Mr Turner: J. M. W. Turner, A Life in Art. The First Forty Years, 1775–1815*, New Haven, CT, and London: Yale University Press, 2016, pp. 454–6.

49. Turner left this picture to the National Gallery, to be hung opposite the Claude. They remain as he instructed.

50. Murray to Wellington, 19 September 1845: WND 2/132/82. Wellington Papers, Hartley Library, University of Southampton.

51. J. Ruskin, *Harbours of England*, London: Smith, Elder, 1856, p. 25. The text introduced a series of British harbour views, engraved from paintings by Turner.

52. For a discussion of the iconic ship see A. D. Lambert, 'The Power of a Name: Tradition, Technology and Transformation', in R. J. Blyth, A. Lambert and J. Rüger, eds., *The Dreadnought and the Edwardian Age*, Farnham: Ashgate, 2011, pp. 19–28.

53. J. Rüger, *The Great Naval Game: Britain and Germany in the Age of Empire*, Cambridge: Cambridge University Press, 2007.

54. Sir P. Moon, *The British Conquest and Dominion of India*, London: Duckworth, 1989, p. 11.

55. A. Roland, W. J. Bolster and A. Keyssar, *The Way of the Ship: America's Maritime History Re-envisioned, 1600–2000*, Hoboken, NJ: John Wiley and Sons Inc., 2008, dates the end of the United States' maritime phase to 1817.

56. R. H. Kohn, *Eagle and Sword: The Beginnings of the Military Establishment in America*, New York: Free Press, 1975.

57. P. E. Pedisich, *Congress Buys a Navy: Economics, and the Rise of American Naval Power, 1881–1921*, Annapolis, MD: USNIP, 2016; J. Barlow, *The Revolt of the Admirals: The Fight for Naval Aviation 1945–1950*, Annapolis, MD: USNIP, 1994.

58. E. P. Brenton, *The Naval History of Great Britain*, London: Henry Colburn, 1825, vol. 5, pp. 199–205, and A. D. Lambert, 'Winning without Fighting: British Grand Strategy and its Application to the United States, 1815–1865', in B. Lee and K. Walling, eds., *Strategic Logic and Political Rationality: Essays in Honour of Michael J. Handel*, Newport, RI: United States Naval War College, 2003, pp. 164–95.

59. Lambert, 'Winning without Fighting', p. 176.

60. A. D. Lambert, 'Creating Cultural Difference: The Military, Political and Cultural Legacies of the War of 1812', in A. Forrest, K. Hagemann and M. Rowe, eds., *War, Demobilization and Memory: The Legacy of War in the Era of Atlantic Revolutions*, London: Palgrave Macmillan, 2016, pp. 303–19.

61. W. H. Truettner and A. Wallach, eds., *Thomas Cole: Landscape into History*, New Haven, CT, and London: Yale University Press, 1994. The link with Turner's 'Carthaginian Pictures' was explicit. And the motto came from Lord Byron's 'Childe Harold', pp. 91–2.

62. D. Loveman, *No Higher Law: American Foreign Policy and the Western Hemisphere since 1776*, Chapel Hill, NC: University of North Carolina Press, 2010, pp. 100–14.

63. Roland, et al., *The Way of the Ship*.

64. F. J. Turner, 'The Significance of the Frontier in American History', in J. M. Faragher, ed., *Rereading Frederick Jackson Turner*, New Haven, CT, and London: Yale University Press, 1998, pp. 30–60, at pp. 33, 43 and 59. It was hardly surprising that a man named for President Andrew Jackson, the arch-exponent of continental expansion, should develop this argument.

65. Faragher, ed., 'Introduction', *Rereading Frederick Jackson Turner*, p. 10.

66. Mahan to Jameson, 21 July 1913: R. Seager and D. D. Macguire, *Letters and Papers of Alfred Thayer Mahan*, 3 vols., Annapolis, MD: USNIP, 1975, Vol. 3, pp. 504–5; Seager, *Alfred Thayer Mahan*, p. 596. Mahan and Turner knew each other: ibid., pp. 438–9, and Seager and Macguirem, Vol. 3, pp. 240 and 244. Turner lectured at the United States Naval War College, the home of Mahan's sea power thesis from 1903. R. A. Billington, *Frederick Jackson Turner: Historian, Scholar, Teacher*, New York: Oxford University Press, 1973, p. 486.

67. Henry John Temple, Second Viscount Palmerston (1784–1865), served in government from 1805 to 1828, and as Foreign Secretary 1830–41, 1846–51, and Prime Minister 1855–65.

68. Lambert, 'Winning without Fighting, p. 177.

69. D. Ahn, 'From "jealous emulation" to "cautious politics": British Foreign Policy and Public Discourse in the Mirror of Ancient Athens (ca. 1730–ca. 1750)', in D. Onenkink and G. Rommelse, eds., *Ideology and Foreign Policy in Early Modern Euorpe (1650–1750)*, Farnham: Ashgate Press, 2011, pp. 93–130.

70. This approach was widely copied, notably in Germany and the United States.

71. Mahan, *The Influence of Sea Power upon History*, p. 67.

72. John Thaddeus Delane to William Howard Russell, 11 November 1861, in *History of 'The Times'*, Vol. II, London: Times Newspapers, 1939, p. 373. George Bancroft, who had been the US ambassador in London from 1846 to 1848, and well known to Palmerston and Delane, produced history that promoted the myth of US victory in the War of 1812 which, by encouraging educated Americans to hold unrealistic opinions about the outcome of another war, contributed to Anglo-American antagonism.

73. Loveman, *No Higher Law*, pp. 140–9.

74. E. Gibbon, *The Decline and Fall of the Roman Empire*. A book written during the American Revolutionary War with the explicit intention of providing a model of imperial decline for the education of contemporary British statesmen. R. Porter, *Gibbon*, London: Weidenfeld & Nicolson, 1988.

75. C. E. Behrman, *Victorian Myths of the Sea*, Athens, OH: Ohio University Press, 1977, pp. 91–109.

76. A. D. Lambert, 'The Magic of Trafalgar: The Nineteenth-Century Legacy', in D. Cannadine, ed., *Trafalgar in History: A Battle and its Aftermath*, London: Palgrave, 2006, pp. 155–74.

77. H. Brogan, *Alexis de Tocqueville: A Life*, New Haven, CT, and London: Yale University Press, 2006, p. 274.

78. A. de Tocqueville, *Democracy in America*, published in an English translation by the Whig intellectual Henry Reeve in 1835.

79. M. Bentley, *Modernizing England's Past: English Historiography in the Age of Modernism 1870–1970*, Cambridge: Cambridge University Press, 2005, pp. 70–5, for the late Victorian imperial context of Seeley's work. J. Burrow, *A Liberal Descent*, Cambridge: Cambridge University Press, 1981, pp. 231–50.

80. D. Wormell, *Sir John Seeley and the Uses of History*, Cambridge: Cambridge University Press, 1980, pp. 41–2; J. R. Seeley, *The Expansion of England*, London: Macmillan, 1883, pp. 1, 43, 89–97.

81. Steamboats, railways and the electric telegraph.

82. J. R. Seeley, *The Expansion of England*, London: Macmillan, 1883, pp. 288, 291–2, 300–1.

83. Wormell, *Sir John Seeley and the Uses of History*, pp. 129, 154–6, 179–80.

84. Seager, *Alfred Thayer Mahan*, pp. 68, 205, 430, 642. Mahan read Seeley's *Eccce Homo*, a study of Christ, in the 1870s, crediting him, among others, with inspiring his seapower thesis. The Russophobia of Mahan's *The Problem of Asia* (1900) was inspired by Seeley.

85. H. J. Mackinder, 'The Geographical Pivot of History', *The Geographical Journal*, vol. XXIII (1904).

86. J. S. Corbett, 'The Sea Commonwealth', in A. P. Newton, ed., *The Sea Commonwealth and other Essays*, London: J. M. Dent and Sons, 1919, pp. 1–10.

87. A. D. Lambert, ' "This Is All We Want": Great Britain and the Baltic Approaches 1815–1914', in J. Sevaldsen, ed., *Britain and Denmark: Political, Economic and Cultural Relations in the 19th and 20th Centuries*, Copenhagen: Tusculanum Press, 2003, pp. 147–69.

88. Lambert, 'Winning without Fighting'.

89. A. D. Lambert, 'Wirtschaftliche Macht, technologischer Vorsprung und Imperiale Stärke: GrossBritannien als einzigartige globale Macht: 1860 bis 1890', in M. Epkenhans and G. P. Gross, *Das Militär und der Aufbruch der Moderne 1860 bis 1890*, Munich: Oldenbourg, 2003.

90. For competitiveness in the imperial theatre of naval display see Rüger, *The Great Naval Game*.

91. J. G. C. Röhl, *The Kaiser and his Court: Wilhelm II and the Government of Germany*, Cambridge: Cambridge University Press, 1994, pp. 162–89, esp. pp. 174–6 for Germany's hegemonic ambitions.

92. The first diplomatic use of the 'New Navy' was to pressure Brazil into economic concessions. S. C. Topik, *Trade and Gunboats: The United States and Brazil in the Age of Empire*, Stanford, CA: Stanford University Press, 1997.

93. M. R. Shulman, *Navalism and the Emergence of American Naval Power: 1882–1893*, Annapolis, MD: USNIP, 1993.

94. A. Anderson, unpublished PhD Thesis; L. M. Gelber, *The Rise of Anglo-American Friendship, 1898–1906*, Oxford: Oxford University Press, 1938, pp. 134–5.

95. D. French, *British Strategy and War Aims: 1914–1916*, London: Unwin Hyman, 1986, pp. 103–12.

96. US legislation directed that large cruisers be named for states.

97. W. J. Reissner, *The Black Book: Woodrow Wilson's Secret Plans for Peace*, Lanham, MD: Lexington Books, 2012.

98. A. Link, ed., *Woodrow Wilson Papers: Volume 55*, Princeton, NJ: Princeton University Press, 1982, pp. 160–2.

99. Pedisch, *Congress Buys a Navy*.

100. D. Todman, *Britain's War: Into Battle 1937–1941*, New York: Oxford University Press, 2016, a trenchant counterblast to the rose-tinted Churchillian version.
101. A. Boyd, *The Royal Navy in Eastern Waters: Linchpin of Victory 1935–1942*, Barnsley: Seaforth, 2017, for a thorough demolition of the old mythology of decline, as far as it relates to the Royal Navy.
102. J. R. Davidson, *The Unsinkable Fleet: The Politics of U.S. Navy Expansion in World War II*, Annapolis, MD: USNIP, 1996.
103. Barlow, *The Revolt of the Admirals*, 1994.

Chapter 9

1. Ng Chin-keong, *Boundaries and Beyond: China's Maritime Southeast in Late Imperial Times*, Singapore: National University of Singapore Press, 2016.
2. A. T. Mahan, *The Problem of Asia*, Boston: Little, Brown, 1900, p. 38. Corbett concurred in 'The Capture of Private Property at Sea', *The Nineteenth Century* (June 1907), reprinted in A. T. Mahan, ed., *Some Neglected Aspects of War*, Boston: Little, Brown, 1907.
3. This is also, misleadingly, referred to as the 'South China Sea'.
4. A. Patalano, 'Japan as a Maritime Power: Deterrence, Diplomacy and Maritime Security', in M. M. McCarthy, ed., *The Handbook of Japanese Foreign Policy*, London: Routledge, 2018, pp. 155–72. I am indebted to Dr Patalano for an advance copy of his important paper.

Conclusion

1. The *Oxford English Dictionary* ignores the issue of identity. It states that Seapower is: 1. 'A nation or state having international power or influence on sea.' 2. 'The strength and efficiency of a nation (or of nations generally) for maritime warfare.'
2. M. Stibbe, *German Anglophobia and the Great War, 1914–1918*, Cambridge: Cambridge University Press, 2001, pp. 33, 64, 67, 70–1.

BIBLIOGRAPHY

Addison, J. *The Present State of the War and the Necessity of an Augmentation*. London, 1707.

Ahn, D. 'From "jealous emulation" to "cautious politics": British Foreign Policy and Public Discourse in the Mirror of Ancient Athens (ca. 1730–ca. 1750)', in D. Onenkink and G. Rommelse, eds., *Ideology and Foreign Policy in Early Modern Europe (1650–1750)*. Farnham: Ashgate Press, 2011, pp. 93–130.

Allen, P. C. *Philip III and the Pax Hispanica, 1598–1621: The Failure of Grand Strategy*. New Haven and London: Yale University Press, 2000.

Anderson, M. S. *War and Society in Europe of the Old Regime, 1618–1789*. London: Fontana, 1988.

Androsov, S. 'Peter the Great's St. Petersburg: Between Amsterdam and Venice', in Androsov et al., eds., *Venezia!*, pp. 38–66.

Androsov, S., Artemieva, I., Boele, I. and Rudge, J., eds. *Venezia! Art of the 18th Century*. London: Lund Humphries, 2005.

Armesto, F. F. *Civilisations*. London: Macmillan, 2000.

Armitage, D. *The Ideological Origins of the British Empire*, Cambridge: Cambridge University Press, 2000.

Artemieva, I. 'Russia and Venetian Artists in the Eighteenth Century', in Androsov et al., eds., *Venezia!*, pp. 67–93.

Bachrach, F. G. H. *Turner's Holland*. London: Tate Publishing, 1994.

Barlow, J. *The Revolt of the Admirals: The Fight for Naval Aviation 1945–1950*. Annapolis, MD: USNIP, 1994.

Baxter, S. B. *William III and the Defense of European Liberty 1650–1702*. New York: Harcourt, Brace, 1966.

Behrman, C. E. *Victorian Myths of the Sea*. Athens, OH: Ohio University Press, 1977.

Bellamy, M. *Christian IV and his Navy: A Political and Administrative History of the Danish Navy, 1596–1648*. Leiden: Brill, 2006.

Bender, J., with an introduction by Davies, J. D. D. *Dutch Warships in the Age of Sail, 1600–1714: Design, Construction, Careers and Fates.* Barnsley: Seaforth Publishing, 2014.

Bentley, M. *Modernizing England's Past: English Historiography in the Age of Modernism 1870–1970.* Cambridge: Cambridge University Press, 2005.

Berthold, R. M. *Rhodes in the Hellenistic Age.* Ithaca, NY: Cornell University Press, 1984.

Bevan, R. *The Destruction of Memory: Architecture at War.* London: Reaktion Books, 2016.

Billington, J. H. *The Icon and the Axe: An Interpretative History of Russian Culture.* New York: Random House, 1970.

Billington, R. A. *Frederick Jackson Turner: Historian, Scholar, Teacher.* New York: Oxford University Press, 1973.

Bindoff, S. T. *The Scheldt Question to 1839.* London: Allen and Unwin, 1945.

Black, J., ed. *War in the Early Modern World.* London: Routledge, 1999.

Blackman, D. and Rankov, B., eds. *Shipsheds of the Ancient Mediterranean.* Cambridge: Cambridge University Press, 2013.

Blösel, W. 'Thucydides on Themistocles: A Herodotean Narrator?', in Foster and Lateiner, eds., *Thucydides and Herodotus,* pp. 216–36.

Bold, J. *Greenwich: An Architectural History of the Royal Hospital for Seamen and the Queen's House.* New Haven, CT, and London: Yale University Press, 2000.

Bolingbroke, Lord. *Letters on the Use and Study of History.* London, 1779.

Bonner Smith, D. 'Note', *The Mariner's Mirror,* vol. XX (1934), pp. 373–6.

Boxer, C. *The Dutch Seaborne Empire.* London: Collins, 1965.

Boxer, C. R. *Four Centuries of Portuguese Expansion, 1415–1825.* Berkeley, CA: University of California Press, 1969.

Boyd, A. *The Royal Navy in Eastern Waters: Linchpin of Victory 1935–1942.* Barnsley: Seaforth Publishing, 2017.

Brandon, P. *War, Capital, and the Dutch State (1588–1795).* Leiden: Brill, 2015.

Braudel, F. *The Mediterranean in the Age of Philip II.* London: Collins, 1973.

Braudel, F. *The Mediterranean in the Ancient World,* London: Allen Lane, 2001.

Brenton, E. P. *The Naval History of Great Britain.* London: Henry Colburn, 1825.

Brett, C. 'Antonio Verrio (*c.* 1636–1707): His Career and Surviving Work', *The British Art Journal,* vol. 10, no. 3 (Winter/Spring 2009–10), pp. 4–17.

Brewer, J. *The Sinews of Power: War, Money, and the English State, 1688–1783.* Cambridge, MA: Harvard University Press, 1988.

Bridge, C. A. G., ed. *History of the Russian Fleet during the Reign of Peter the Great.* London: Navy Records Society, 1899.

Brogan, H. *Alexis de Tocqueville: A Life.* New Haven, CT, and London: Yale University Press, 2006.

Broodbank, C. *The Making of the Middle Sea: A History of the Mediterranean from the Beginning to the Emergence of the Classical World.* London: Thames and Hudson, 2013.

Brown, P. F. *Venetian Narrative Painting in the Age of Carpaccio.* New Haven, CT, and London: Yale University Press, 1988.

Brown, P. F. *Venice and Antiquity.* New Haven, CT, and London: Yale University Press, 1996.

Bruijn, J. R. *The Dutch Navy of the Seventeenth and Eighteenth Centuries.* St John's, Newfoundland: IMEHA, 2015 (1992).

Bryce, J. *The Holy Roman Empire.* London: Macmillan, 1901.

Bull, G. *Venice, the Most Triumphant City.* London: Folio Society, 1981.

Bulut, M. 'The Role of the Ottoman and Dutch in the Commercial Integration between the Levant and Atlantic in the Seventeenth Century', *Journal of the Economic and Social History of the Orient,* vol. 45 (2002), pp. 197–230.

Burckhardt, J. *The Civilisation of Italy in the Renaissance.* London: Penguin, 1990 (1860).

Burckhardt, J. *Recollections of Rubens.* London: Phaidon, 1951.

Burckhardt, J. *Reflections on History.* Indianapolis, IN: Liberty Classics, 1979.

Burke, P. *The Fabrication of Louis XIV*. New Haven, CT, and London: Yale University Press, 1992.

Burke, P. *Venice and Amsterdam: A Study of Seventeenth-Century Elites*. London: Polity Press, 1994.

Burrow, J. *A Liberal Descent*. Cambridge: Cambridge University Press, 1981.

Campbell, T. *Threads of Splendour: Tapestry of the Baroque*. New Haven, CT, and London: Yale University Press, 2007.

Canning, G. *Speeches of the Right Hon. George Canning delivered on Public Occasions in Liverpool*. Liverpool: Thomas Kaye, 1835.

Capp, B. *Cromwell's Navy: The Fleet and the English Revolution 1648–1660*. Oxford: Oxford University Press, 1990.

Carboni, S. 'Moments of Vision: Venice and the Islamic World, 828–1797', in Carboni, ed., *Venice and the Islamic World, 828–1797* pp. 10–35.

Carboni, S., ed. *Venice and the Islamic World 828–1797*. New Haven, CT, and London: Yale University Press, 2007.

Carpenter, R. *Beyond the Pillars of Hercules: The Classical World Seen through the Eyes of its Discoverers*. London: Tandem Books, 1963.

Chrivi, R., Gay, F., Crovato, M. and Zanelli, G. *L'Arsenale dei Veniziani*. Venice: Filippi, 1983.

Cipolla, C. 'The Economic Decline of Italy', in Cipolla, ed., *The Economic Decline of Empires*, pp. 196–215.

Cipolla, C. *The Economic Decline of Empires*. London: Methuen, 1970.

Clark, G., ed. *Sir William Temple's Observations Upon the United Provinces of the Netherlands*. Oxford: Clarendon Press, 1972.

Coad, J. G. *The Royal Dockyards 1690–1850*. Aldershot: Scolar Press, 1989.

Cockett, F. B. *Peter Monamy 1681–1749 and his Circle*. Woodbridge: Antique Collectors Club, 2000.

Colley, L. *Britons: Forging the Nation 1707–1837*. New Haven, CT, and London: Yale University Press, 1992.

Collini, S. *Matthew Arnold*. Oxford: Oxford University Press, 1988.

Concina, E. *A History of Venetian Architecture*. Cambridge: Cambridge University Press, 1998.

Conway, S. *The War of American Independence, 1775–1783*. London: Longman, 1995.

Corbett, J. S. 'The Capture of Private Property at Sea', *The Nineteenth Century* (June 1907), reprinted in A. T. Mahan, ed., *Some Neglected Aspects of War*. Boston, MA: Little Brown, 1907.

Corbett, J. S. *England in the Mediterranean: A Study of the Rise and Influence of British Power within the Straits, 1603–1713*. London: Longman and Co., 1904.

Corbett, J. S. 'The Sea Commonwealth', in A. P. Newton, ed., *The Sea Commonwealth and other Essays*. London: J. M. Dent and Sons, 1919, pp. 1–10.

Corbett, J. S. *Some Principles of Maritime Strategy*. London: Longman, 1911.

Cracraft, J. *The Petrine Revolution in Architecture*. Chicago, IL: University of Chicago Press, 1988.

Cracraft, J. *The Petrine Revolution in Russian Culture*. Cambridge, MA: Belknap Press/Harvard University Press, 2004.

Cross, A. *By the Banks of the Neva: Chapters from the Lives and Careers of the British in Eighteenth-Century Russia*. Cambridge: Cambridge University Press, 1999.

Cross, A. 'Richard Paton and the Battle of Chesme', *Study Group on Eighteenth-Century Russia Newsletter*, no. 14 (1986), pp. 31–7.

Crowhurst, P. *The Defence of British Trade 1689–1815*. Folkestone: Dawson, 1977.

Cunliffe, B. *Europe between Oceans: Themes and Variations 9000 BC–AD 1000*. New Haven, CT, and London: Yale University Press, 2008.

Daalder, R. *Van de Velde and Son: Marine Painters*. Leiden: Primavera Press, 2016.

Davey, J. *The Transformation of British Naval Strategy: Seapower and Supply in Northern Europe, 1808–1812*. Woodbridge: Boydell Press, 2012.

Davidson, J. R. *The Unsinkable Fleet: The Politics of U.S. Navy Expansion in World War II*. Annapolis, MD: USNIP, 1996.

Davies, J. D. 'British Perceptions of Michiel de Ruyter and the Anglo-Dutch Wars', in J. R. Bruijn, R. P. van Reine and R. van Hövell tot Westerflier, eds., *De Ruyter: Dutch Admiral*. Rotterdam: Karwansaray, 2011, pp. 122–39.

de Jong, M. 'Dutch Public Finance During the Eighty Years War: The Case of the Province of Zeeland, 1585–1648', in van der Hoeven, ed., *Exercise of Arms*, pp. 133–52.

de Moor, J. A. '"A Very Unpleasant Relationship": Trade and Strategy in the Eastern Seas: Anglo-Dutch Relations in the Nineteenth Century from a Colonial Perspective', in Raven and Rodger, eds., *Navies and Armies*.

de Tocqueville, A. *Democracy in America*. English trans. by H. Reeve. London, 1835.

Dickinson, H. T. *Bolingbroke*. London: Constable, 1970.

Diehl, C. 'The Economic Decline of Byzantium', in C. Cipolla, ed., *The Economic Decline of Empires*. London: Methuen, 1970.

Docter, R., Boussoffara, R. and ter Keurs, P., eds. *Carthage: Fact and Myth*. Leiden: Sidestone Press, 2015.

Doran, S. and Blyth, R., eds. *Royal River: Power, Pageantry and the Thames*. Greenwich: Royal Museums, 2012.

Epstein, S. A. *Genoa and the Genoese: 958–1528*. Chapel Hill, NC: University of North Carolina, 1996.

Evans, D. *Building the Steam Navy: Dockyards, Technology and the Creation of the Victorian Battlefleet, 1830–1906*. London: Conway, 2004.

Fabre, D. *Seafaring in Ancient Egypt*. London: Periplus, 2005.

Falconer, A. F. *A Glossary of Shakespeare's Sea and Naval Terms including Gunnery*. London: Constable, 1965.

Falconer, A. F. *Shakespeare and the Sea*. London: Constable, 1964.

Fantar, M. H. *Carthage: The Punic City*. Tunis: Alif, 1998.

Faragher, J. M., ed. *Rereading Frederick Jackson Turner*. New Haven, CT, and London: Yale University Press, 1998.

Fenlon, I. *The Ceremonial City: History, Memory and Myth in Renaissance Venice*. New Haven, CT, and London: Yale University Press, 2007.

Fisher, R. H. *Bering's Voyages*. London: Hurst, 1977.

Ford, B., ed. *The Cambridge Cultural History of Britain: Seventeenth-Century Britain*. Cambridge: Cambridge University Press, 1989.

Foster, E. *Thucydides, Pericles, and Periclean Imperialism*. Cambridge: Cambridge University Press, 2013.

Foster, E. and Lateiner, D., eds. *Thucydides and Herodotus*. Oxford: Oxford University Press, 2012.

Francis, A. D. *The Methuens and Portugal, 1691–1708*. Cambridge: Cambridge University Press, 1966.

Fremantle, K. K. *The Baroque Town Hall of Amsterdam*. Utrecht: Haentjens Dekker and Gumbert, 1959.

French, D. *British Strategy and War Aims: 1914–1916*. London: Unwin Hyman, 1986.

Fuller, W. C. *Strategy and Power in Russia 1600–1914*. New York: Free Press, 1992.

Fusaro, M. *Political Economies of Empire in the Early Mediterranean: The Decline of Venice and the Rise of England 1450–1700*. Cambridge: Cambridge University Press, 2015.

Gaastra, F. S. *The Dutch East India Company: Expansion and Decline*. Zutphen: Walberg Pers, 2003.

Gabrielsen, V. *Financing the Athenian Fleet: Public Taxation and Social Relations*. Baltimore, MD: Johns Hopkins University Press, 1994.

Gabrielsen, V. *The Naval Aristocracy of Hellenistic Rhodes*. Aarhus: Aarhus University Press, 1997.

Gabrielsen, V. 'Rhodes and the Ptolemaic Kingdom: The Commercial Infrastructure', in K. Buraselis, M. Stefanou and D. T. Thompson, *The Ptolemies, the Sea and the Nile: Studies in Waterborne Power*. Cambridge: Cambridge University Press, 2013.

Gelber, L. M. *The Rise of Anglo-American Friendship, 1898–1906*. Oxford: Oxford University Press, 1938.

Georgopoulou, M. *Venice's Mediterranean Colonies: Architecture and Urbanism*. Cambridge: Cambridge University Press, 2001.

Gerding, H. 'Carthage', in Blackman and Rankov, eds., *Shipsheds of the Ancient Mediterranean*, pp. 307–19.

Gilbert, F. 'Venice in the Crisis of the League of Cambrai', in Hale, ed., *Renaissance Venice*, pp. 274–92.

Glete, J. *Navies and Nations: Warships, Navies and State Building in Europe and America, 1500–1860*. Stockholm: Almqvist and Wisksell, 1993.

Glete, J. *War and the State in Early Modern Europe: Spain, the Dutch Republic and Sweden as Fiscal-Military States, 1500–1660*. London: Routledge, 2002.

Goldsworthy, A. *The Fall of Carthage: The Punic Wars, 265–146 BC*. London: Cassell, 2000, p. 69.

Gomme, A. W. *A Historical Commentary on Thucydides: Volume One*. Oxford: Oxford University Press, 1958.

Gooch, G. P. *History and Historians of the Nineteenth Century*. London: Longman, 1913.

Gould, J. *Herodotus*. London: Weidenfeld & Nicolson, 1989, pp. 102–5.

Gorshkov, S. G. *The Sea Power of the State*. Annapolis, MD: USNIP, 1979.

Gristwood, S. 'A Tapestry of England's Past', *History Today*, vol. 60, no. 9 (2010).

Grote, G. *History of Greece*, 12 vols, London, 1849.

Grotius, H. *The Freedom of the Seas or The Right which Belongs to the Dutch to Take Part in the East Indian Trade*. New York: Oxford University Press, 1916.

Guilmartin, J. *Gunpowder and Galleys: Changing Technology and Warfare at Sea in the Sixteenth Century*. Cambridge: Cambridge University Press, 1974.

Hale, J. R., ed. *Renaissance Venice*. London: Faber, 1973.

Halkos, G. E. and Kyriazis, N. C. 'A Naval Revolution and Institutional Change: The Case of the United Provinces', in *European Journal of Law and Economics*, vol. 19 (2005), pp. 41–68.

Harlow, V. T. *The Founding of the Second British Empire 1763–1793, Vol. II: New Continents and Changing Values*. London: Longmans, 1964.

Harris, W. V. *War and Imperialism in Republican Rome 327–70 BC*. Oxford: Clarendon Press, 1979.

Hewison, R. *Ruskin's Venice*. New Haven, CT, and London: Yale University Press, 2000.

History of 'The Times', vol. II. London: Times Newspapers, 1939.

Horden, P. and Purcell, N. *The Corrupting Sea: A Study of Mediterranean History*. Oxford: Basil Blackwell, 2000.

Horden, P. and Purcell, N. 'The Mediterranean and "the new Thalassology"', in *American Historical Review* (June 2006), pp. 722–40.

Horn, H. J. *Jan Cornelisz Vermeyen: Painter of Charles V and his Conquest of Tunis*. New York: Davaco Publishers, 1989.

Howard, D. *The Architectural History of Venice*. New Haven, CT, and London: Yale University Press, 1980.

Howard, D. 'Venice and the Mamluks', in Carboni, ed., *Venice and the Islamic World 828–1797*, pp. 72–89.

Howard, D. and McBurney, H., eds. *The Image of Venice: Fialetti's View and Sir Henry Wotton*. New Haven, CT, and London: Yale University Press, 2014.

Hughes, E., ed. *Spreading Canvas: Eighteenth-Century British Marine Painting*. New Haven, CT, and London: Yale University Press, 2016.

Hughes, L. *Russia in the Age of Peter the Great*. New Haven, CT, and London: Yale University Press, 1998.

Israel, J. I. *The Dutch Republic: Its Rise, Greatness and Fall, 1477–1806*. Oxford: Oxford University Press, 1995.

Jackson, A. *The British Empire and the Second World War*. London: Continuum, 2008.

Jacobsen, K. and Jacobsen, J. *Carrying off the Palaces: John Ruskin's Lost Daguerreotypes*. London: Quaritch, 2015.

Jenks, T. *Naval Engagements: Patriotism, Cultural Politics, and the Royal Navy 1793–1815*. Oxford: Oxford University Press, 2006.

Jenkyns, R. *The Victorians and Ancient Greece*. Oxford: Basil Blackwell, 1980.

Kaganov, G. 'As in the Ship of Peter', *Slavic Review*, vol. 50 (1991), pp. 754–67.

Kahan, A. *The Plow, the Hammer and the Knout: An Economic History of Eighteenth-Century Russia*. Chicago, IL: University of Chicago Press, 1985.

Kirk, T. A. *Genoa and the Sea: Policy and Power in an Early Modern Maritime Republic, 1559–1684*. Baltimore, MD: Johns Hopkins University Press, 2005.

Kohn, R. H. *Eagle and Sword: The Beginnings of the Military Establishment in America*. New York: Free Press, 1975.

Krammick, I. *Bolingbroke and his Circle: The Politics of Nostalgia in the Age of Walpole*. Cambridge, MA: Harvard University Press, 1968.

Lambert, A. D. *The Challenge: Britain Against America in the Naval War of 1812*. London: Faber, 2012.

Lambert, A. D. 'Creating Cultural Difference: The Military, Political and Cultural Legacies of the War of 1812', in A. Forrest, K. Hagemann and M. Rowe, eds., *War, Demobilization and Memory: The Legacy of War in the Era of Atlantic Revolutions*. London: Palgrave Macmillan, 2016.

Lambert, A. D. *The Crimean War: British Grand Strategy against Russia, 1853–1856*. Farnham: Ashgate, 2011.

Lambert, A. D. *Crusoe's Island*. London: Faber, 2016.

Lambert, A. D. *The Last Sailing Battlefleet, 1815–1850*. London: Conway, 1991.

Lambert, A. D. 'The Magic of Trafalgar: The Nineteenth-Century Legacy', in D. Cannadine, ed., *Trafalgar in History: A Battle and its Aftermath*. London: Palgrave, 2006, pp. 155–74.

Lambert, A. D. *Nelson: Britannia's God of War*. London: Faber and Faber, 2004.

Lambert, A. D. ' "Now is come a Darker Day": Britain, Venice and the Meaning of Sea Power', in M. Taylor, ed., *The Victorian Empire and Britain's Maritime World 1837–1901: The Sea and Global History*. London: Palgrave Macmillan, 2013, pp. 19–42.

Lambert, A. D. 'The Power of a Name: Tradition, Technology and Transformation', in R. J. Blyth, A. Lambert and J. Rüger, eds., *The Dreadnought and the Edwardian Age*. Farnham: Ashgate, 2011.

Lambert, A. D. ' "This Is All We Want": Great Britain and the Baltic Approaches 1815–1914', in J. Sevaldsen, ed., *Britain and Denmark: Political, Economic and Cultural Relations in the 19th and 20th Centuries*. Copenhagen: Tusculanum Press, 2003, pp. 147–69.

Lambert, A. D. 'Winning without Fighting: British Grand Strategy and its Application to the United States, 1815–1865', in B. Lee and K. Walling, eds., *Strategic Logic and Political Rationality: Essays in Honour of Michael J. Handel*. Newport, RI: United States Naval War College, 2003.

Lambert, A. D. 'Wirtschaftliche Macht, technologischer Vorsprung und Imperiale Stärke: Gross Britannien als einzigartige globale Macht: 1860 bis 1890', in M. Epkenhans and G. P. Gross, *Das Militär und der Aufbruch die Moderne 1860 bis 1890*. Munich: Oldenbourg, 2003.

Lane, F. C. 'Naval Actions and Fleet Organization, 1499–1502', in J. R. Hale, ed., *Renaissance Venice*. London: Faber, 1973, pp. 146–73.

Lane, F. C. *Profits from Power: Readings in Protection Rent and Violence-Controlling Enterprises*. Albany, NY: State University of New York Press, 1979.

Lane, F. C. *Venice: A Maritime Republic*. Baltimore, MD: Johns Hopkins University Press, 1973.

Lawrence, C. 'Hendrick de Keyser's Heemskerck Monument: The Origins of the Cult and Iconography of Dutch Naval Heroes', in *Simiolus: Netherlands Quarterly for the History of Art*, vol. 21, no. 4 (1992), pp. 265–95.

Lehmann, L. Th. 'The Polyeric Quest: Renaissance and Baroque Theories about Ancient Men of War'. PhD thesis, Rotterdam, 1995.

Levillain, C.-E. 'William III's Military and Political Career in Neo-Roman Context, 1672–1702', *The Historical Journal*, vol. 48 (2005), pp. 321–50.

Lewis, B. 'The Arabs in Eclipse', in Cipolla, ed., *The Economic Decline of Empires*, pp. 102–20.

Lincoln, M. *Representing the Royal Navy: British Sea Power 1750–1815*. Aldershot: Ashgate, 2003.

Link, A., ed. *Woodrow Wilson Papers: Volume 55*. Princeton, NJ: Princeton University Press, 1982.

Livy, *The Histories*, trans. E. S. Shuckburgh. London: Macmillan, 1889.

Loveman, D. *No Higher Law: American Foreign Policy and the Western Hemisphere since 1776*. Chapel Hill, NC: University of North Carolina Press, 2010.

Lowry, M. *The World of Aldus Manutius*. Oxford: Basil Blackwell, 1979.

Lupher, D. A. *Romans in a New World: Classical Models in Sixteenth-Century Spanish America*. Ann Arbor, MI: University of Michigan Press, 2003.

McDonald, M. P. *Ferdinand Columbus: Renaissance Collector*. London: British Museum Press, 2004.

MacGillivray, J. A. *Minotaur: Sir Arthur Evans and the Archaeology of the Minoan Myth*. London: Jonathan Cape, 2000.

Mackinder, H. J. 'The Geographical Pivot of History', *The Geographical Journal*, vol. 23 (1904).

Mahan, A. T. *The Influence of Sea Power upon History 1660–1783*. Boston, MA: Little, Brown, 1890.

Mahan, A. T. *The Problem of Asia*. Boston, MA: Little, Brown, 1900.

Mahan, A. T., ed. *Some Neglected Aspects of War*. Boston, MA: Little, Brown, 1907.

Markoe, G. *The Phoenicians*. London: British Museum Press, 2000.

Marsden, J., ed. *The Wisdom of George III*. London: Royal Household, 2004.

Mathee, R. 'The Portuguese in the Persian Gulf: An Overview', in J. R. Marcris and S. Kelly, eds., *Imperial Crossroads: The Great Powers and the Persian Gulf*. Annapolis, MD: USNIP, 2012.

Meiggs, R. *The Athenian Empire*. Oxford: Oxford University Press, 1972.

Miles, R. *Carthage Must Be Destroyed: The Rise and Fall of an Ancient Civilisation*. London: Allen Lane, 2010.

Momigliano, A. 'Sea-Power in Greek Thought', in *Secondo contributo alla storia degli studi classici*. Rome: Storia e Letteratura, 1966, pp. 57–68.

Moon, Sir P. *The British Conquest and Dominion of India*. London: Duckworth, 1989.

Moro, F. *Venice at War: The Great Battles of the Serenissima*. Venice: Studio LT2, 2007.

Morrison, J. S. *The Athenian Trireme: The History and Reconstruction of an Ancient Greek Warship*. Cambridge: Cambridge University Press, 1995.

Morriss, R. *Science, Utility and Maritime Power: Samuel Bentham in Russia, 1779–1791*. Farnham: Ashgate Press, 2015.

Muir, R. *Wellington: Waterloo and the Fortunes of Peace, 1814–1852*. New Haven, CT, and London: Yale University Press, 2015.

Murray, W. M. *The Age of the Titans: The Rise and Fall of the Great Hellenistic Navies*. Oxford: Oxford University Press, 2012.

Musson, J. 'Laughing with the Gods: The Heaven Room at Burghley', *Country Life* (5 July 2017), pp. 80–4.

Naish, J. *Seamarks: Their History and Development*. London: Stanford Maritime, 1985.

Ng Chin-keong, *Boundaries and Beyond: China's Maritime Southeast in Late Imperial Times*. Singapore: National University of Singapore Press, 2016.

O'Brien, P. K. 'Fiscal Exceptionalism: Great Britain and its European Rivals from Civil War to Triumph at Trafalgar and Waterloo', in D. Winch and P. K. O'Brien, eds., *The Political Economy of British Historical Experience, 1688–1914*. Oxford: Oxford University Press, 2002, pp. 245–65.

O'Hara, G. *Britain and the Sea since 1600*. Basingstoke: Palgrave Macmillan, 2010.

Oliviera, F. *Arte de Guerra do Mar: Estrategia e Guerra naval no Tempo dos Descobrimentos*. Lisbon: Edições 70 Lda, 2008.

Onnekink, D. 'The Ideological Context of the Dutch War (1672)', in D. Onnenink and G. Rommelse, eds., *Ideology and Foreign Policy in Early Modern Europe (1650–1750)*. Farnham: Ashgate Press, pp. 131–44.

Ormrod, D. *The Rise of Commercial Empires: England and the Netherlands in the Age of Mercantilism*. Cambridge: Cambridge University Press, 2003.

Osborne, R., ed. and trans. *The Old Oligarch: Pseudo-Xenophon's Constitution of the Athenians* (Lactor). Cambridge: Cambridge University Press, 2004.

Paine, L. *The Sea and Civilisation: A Maritime History of the World*. London: Atlantic Books, 2013.

Parker, G. *The Grand Strategy of Philip II*. New Haven, CT, and London: Yale University Press, 1998.

Parkinson, C. N. *War in the Eastern Seas, 1793–1815*. London: Allen and Unwin, 1954.

Parks, G. B. 'Ramusio's Literary History', in *Studies in Philology*, vol. 52, no. 2 (1955), pp. 127–48.

Parry, J. H. *The Spanish Seaborne Empire*. London: Hutchinson, 1966.

Patalano, A. 'Japan as a Maritime Power: Deterrence, Diplomacy and Maritime Security', in M. M. McCarthy, ed., *The Handbook of Japanese Foreign Policy*. London: Routledge, 2018.

Pedisich, P. E. *Congress Buys a Navy: Economics, and the Rise of American Naval Power, 1881–1921*. Annapolis, MD: USNIP, 2016.

Penny, N. *Reynolds*. London: The Royal Academy, 1986.

Pereira, P. *Torre de Belém*. London: Scala, 2005.

Picard, G. C. and Picard, C. *The Life and Death of Carthage*. London: Sidgwick and Jackson, 1968.

Pitassi, M. *The Navies of Rome*. Woodbridge: Boydell and Brewer, 2009.

Porter, R. *Gibbon*. London: Weidenfeld & Nicolson, 1988.

Pottle, E. A. *Boswell in Holland, 1763–1764*. London: Heinemann, 1952.

Rahe, P. *Montesquieu and the Logic of Liberty: War, Religion, Commerce, Climate, Terrain, Technology, Uneasiness of Mind, the Spirit of Political Vigilance, and the Foundations of the Modern Republic*. New Haven, CT, and London: Yale University Press, 2009.

Raleigh, W. *History of the World*. London, 1614.

Rankov, B. 'Roman Shipsheds', in Blackman and Rankov, eds., *Shipsheds of the Ancient Mediterranean*, pp. 30–54.

Raven, G. J. A. and Rodger, N. A. M., eds. *Navies and Armies: The Anglo-Dutch Relationship in War and Peace 1688–1988*. Edinburgh: John Donald, 1990.

Rawlings L. *The Ancient Greeks at War*. Manchester: Manchester University Press, 2007.

Reading, D. K. *The Anglo-Russian Commercial Treaty of 1734*. New Haven, CT, and London: Yale University Press, 1938.

Reinhold, M. 'Classical Scholarship, Modern Anti-Semitism and the Zionist Project: The Historian Eduard Meyer in Palestine', *Bryn Mawr Classical Review* (May 2005).

Reissner, W. J. *The Black Book: Woodrow Wilson's Secret Plans for Peace*. Lanham, MD: Lexington Books, 2012.

Reynolds, C. G. '"Thalassocracy" as a Historical Force', in *History and the Sea: Essays on Maritime Strategies*. Columbia, SC: University of South Carolina Press, 1989.

Richmond, H. W. *The Navy in India, 1763–1783*. London: Ernest Benn, 1931.

Robinson, E. *Democracy beyond Athens: Popular Government in the Greek Classical Age*. Cambridge: Cambridge University Press, 2011.

Robinson, M. S. *The Paintings of the Willem van de Veldes*. London: Sotheby's and the National Maritime Museum, 1990.

Rodger, N. A. M. *The Safeguard of the Sea: A Naval History of Britain. Volume One: 649–1649*. London: HarperCollins, 1997.

Rodgers, W. L. *Naval Wars under Oars*. Annapolis, MD: Naval Institute Press, 1940.

Röhl, J. G. C. *The Kaiser and his Court: Wilhelm II and the Government of Germany*. Cambridge: Cambridge University Press, 1994.

Roland, A., Bolster, W. J. and Keyssar, A. *The Way of the Ship: America's Maritime History Re-Envisioned, 1600–2000*. Hoboken, NJ: John Wiley and Sons Inc., 2008.

Rommelse, G. 'Een Hollandse maritieme identiteit als ideologische bouwsteen van de Ware Vrijheid', in *Holland Historisch Tijdschrift*, vol. 48 (2016), pp. 133–41.

Rommelse, G. 'National Flags as Essential Elements of Dutch Naval Ideology, 1600–1800', forthcoming.

Rommelse, G. and Downing, R. 'The Fleet as an Ideological Pillar of Dutch Radical Republicanism, 1650–1672', in *The International Journal of Maritime History*, vol. 27, no. 3 (2015).

Rowen, H. H. *John de Witt Grand Pensionary of Holland, 1625–1672*. Princeton, NJ: Princeton University Press, 1978.

Rüger, J. *The Great Naval Game: Britain and Germany in the Age of Empire*. Cambridge: Cambridge University Press, 2007.

Ruskin, J. *Harbours of England*. London: Smith, Elder, 1856.

Ruskin, J. *Modern Painters: Vol. I*. London: Smith, Elder, 1843.

Ruskin, J. *Praeterita*. Oxford: Oxford University Press, 1978.

Ruskin, J. *The Stones of Venice Vol. I: The Foundations*. London: Smith, Elder, 1851.

Ruskin, J. *The Stones of Venice Vol. II: The Sea Stories*. London: Smith, Elder, 1853.

Russell, M. *Visions of the Sea: Hendrick C. Vroom and the Origin of Dutch Marine Painting*. Leiden: Brill, 1983.

Russell, P. *Prince Henry 'the Navigator'*. New Haven, CT, and London: Yale University Press, 2000.

Russett, A. *Dominic Serres R.A. 1719–1793*. Woodbridge: Antique Collector's Club, 2001.

Salmina-Haskell, L. *Panoramic Views of St Petersburg from 1716 to 1835*. Oxford: Ashmolean, 1993.

Salonia, M. *Genoa's Freedom: Entrepreneurship, Republicanism and the Spanish Atlantic*. Lanham, MD: Lexington Books, 2017.

Samotta, I. 'Herodotus and Thucydides in Roman Republican Historiography', in Foster and Lateiner, eds., *Thucydides and Herodotus*, pp. 345–73.

Sanceau, E. *The Reign of the Fortunate King 1495–1521*. New York: Archon Books, 1969.

Savoy, D. *Venice from the Water*. New Haven, CT, and London: Yale University Press, 2012.

Schama, S. *The Embarrassment of Riches: An Interpretation of Dutch Culture in the Golden Age*. London: Collins, 1987.

Schulz, J. 'Jacopo de' Barbari's View of Venice: Map Making, City Views, and Moralized Geography before the Year 1500', *The Art Bulletin*, vol. 60, no. 3 (1978), pp. 425–74.

Scott, J. *When the Waves Ruled Britannia: Geography and Political Identities 1500–1800*. Oxford: Oxford University Press, 2011.

Seager, R. *Alfred Thayer Mahan: The Man and his Letters*. Annapolis, MD: USNIP, 1977.

Seager, R. and Macguire, D. D. *Letters and Papers of Alfred Thayer Mahan*, 3 vols. Annapolis, MD: USNIP, 1975.

Seeley, J. R. *The Expansion of England*. London: Macmillan, 1883.

Shanes. E. *Young Mr Turner: J. M. W. Turner, A Life in Art. The First Forty Years, 1775–1815*. New Haven, CT, and London: Yale University Press, 2016.

Sharp, W. *Life of Admiral Sir William Symonds*. London: Longmans, 1856.

Sherman, W. H. *John Dee: The Politics of Reading and Writing in the English Renaissance*. Amherst, MA: University of Massachusetts Press, 1995.

Shulman, M. R. *Navalism and the Emergence of American Naval Power: 1882–1893*. Annapolis, MD: USNIP, 1993.

Sicking, L. *Neptune and the Netherlands: State, Economy, and War at Sea in the Renaissance*. Leiden: Brill, 2004.

Simms, B. *Three Victories and a Defeat: The Rise and Fall of the First British Empire, 1714–1783*. London: Penguin, 2007.

Skovgaard-Petersen, K. *Historiography at the Court of Christian IV: 1588–1648*. Copenhagen: Museum Tusculanum Press, 2002.

Sondhaus, L. 'Napoleon's Shipbuilding Program at Venice and the Struggle for Naval Mastery in the Adriatic, 1806–1814', *Journal of Military History*, vol. 53 (1989), pp. 349–62.

Sonnino, P. 'Colbert', *European Studies Review* (January 1983), pp. 1–11.

Spengler, O. *The Decline of the West*, 2 vols. London: Allen and Unwin, 1926.

Stadler, P. A. 'Thucydides as a "Reader" of Herodotus', in Foster and Lateiner, eds., *Thucydides and Herodotus*, pp. 39–63.

Stagno, L. *Palazzo del Principe: The Villa of Andrea Doria*. Genoa: Sagep, 2005.

Starr, C. G. *The Influence of Sea Power on Ancient History*. Oxford: Oxford University Press, 1989.

Stibbe, M. *German Anglophobia and the Great War, 1914–1918*. Cambridge: Cambridge University Press, 2001.

Strachan, M. *The Life and Adventures of Thomas Coryate*. London: Oxford University Press, 1962.

Strong, R. *Henry, Prince of Wales and England's Lost Renaissance*. London: Thames and Hudson, 1986.

Sureda, J. *The Golden Age of Spain*. New York: Vendome Press, 2008.

Taylor, M. *Thucydides, Pericles, and the Idea of Athens in the Peloponnesian War*. Cambridge: Cambridge University Press, 2010.

Thurley, S. *Hampton Court: A Social and Architectural History*. New Haven, CT, and London: Yale University Press, 2003.

Thurley, S. 'The Vanishing Architecture of the River Thames', in Doran and Blyth, eds., *Royal River*, pp. 20–5.

Todman, D. *Britain's War: Into Battle 1937–1941*. New York: Oxford University Press, 2016.

Topik, S. C. *Trade and Gunboats: The United States and Brazil in the Age of Empire*. Stanford, CA: Stanford University Press, 1997.

Toynbee, A. J. *Hannibal's Legacy: The Hannibalic War's Effects on Roman Life*. London: Oxford University Press, 1965.

Tracy, J. D. 'Herring Wars: The Habsburg Netherlands and the Struggle for Control of the North Sea ca. 1520–1560', *The Sixteenth Century Journal*, vol. 24, no. 2 (1993), pp. 249–72.

Tredrea, J. and Sozaev, E. *Russian Warships in the Age of Sail, 1696–1860: Design, Construction, and Fates*. Barnsley: Seaforth Publishing, 2010.

Truettner, W. H. and Wallach, A., eds. *Thomas Cole: Landscape into History*. New Haven, CT, and London: Yale University Press, 1994.

Turner, F. J. 'The Significance of the Frontier in American History', in Faragher, ed., *Rereading Frederick Jackson Turner*, pp. 30–60.

Turner, F. M. *The Greek Heritage in Victorian Britain*. New Haven, CT, and London: Yale University Press, 1981.

Unger, R. W. *Dutch Shipbuilding before 1800*. Amsterdam: Van Gorcum, 1978.

van der Hoeven, M., ed. *Exercise of Arms: Warfare in the Netherlands (1568–1648)*. Leiden: Brill, 1998.

van Eyck van Heslinga, E. S. 'A Competitive Ally: The Delicate Balance of Naval Alliance and Maritime Competition between Great Britain and the Dutch Republic 1674–1795', in Raven and Rodger, eds., *Navies and Armies*, pp. 1–11.

van Loo, I. J. 'For Freedom and Fortune: The Rise of Dutch Privateering in the First Half of the Dutch Revolt, 1568–1609', in van der Hoeven, ed., *Exercise of Arms*, pp. 173–96.

van Vliet, A. P. 'Foundation, Organization and Effects of the Dutch Navy (1568–1648)', in van der Hoeven, ed., *Exercise of Arms*, pp. 153–72.

Villiers, G., 2nd Duke of Buckingham. *A Letter to Sir Thomas Osborn*. London, 1672.

Vivens, J. V. 'The Decline of Spain in the Seventeenth Century', in C. Cipolla, ed., *The Economic Decline of Empires*. London: Methuen, 1970.

Wallinga, H. T. 'The Ancestry of the Trireme', in J. Morison, ed., *The Age of the Galley: Mediterranean Oared Vessels since Pre-Classical Times*. London: Conway Press, 1995.

Wallinga, H. T. *Ships and Sea-Power before the Great Persian War*. Leiden: Brill, 1993.

Walsh, R., ed. *Select Speeches of George Canning*. Philadelphia, PA: Key and Biddle, 1842.

Warner, G. F., ed. *The Libelle of Englyshe Polycye*. London: Oxford University Press, 1926.

Waterfield, R. *Taken at the Flood: The Roman Conquest of Greece*. Oxford: Oxford University Press, 2014.

Willis, S. *Admiral Benbow: The Life and Times of a Naval Legend*. London: Quercus, 2010.

Winfield, R. and Roberts, S. S. *French Warships in the Age of Sail: Design Construction and Fates 1786–1861*. Barnsley: Seaforth Publishing, 2015.

Wormell, D. *Sir John Seeley and the Uses of History*. Cambridge: Cambridge University Press, 1980.

Young, A. R. *His Majesty's Royal Ship: A Critical Edition of Thomas Heywood's 'A True Description of his Majesties Royall Ship'*. New York: AMS Press, 1990.

Zagorin, P. *Thucydides*. Princeton, NJ: Princeton University Press, 2005.

Zinovieff, K. and Hughes, J. *Guide to St. Petersburg*. Woodbridge: Boydell and Brewer, 2003.

Zwitzer, H. L. 'The Eighty Years War', in van der Hoeven, ed., *Exercise of Arms*, pp. 33–56.

INDEX

Detailed coverage of a subject is indicated in **bold**. Locators for illustrations are entered in *italics*.